Concept and Judgment in Brentano's Logic Lectures

Studien zur Österreichischen Philosophie

Gegründet von

Rudolf Haller †

Herausgegeben von

Mauro Antonelli

BAND 48

The titles published in this series are listed at *brill.com/soph*

Concept and Judgment in Brentano's Logic Lectures

Analysis and Materials

By

Robin D. Rollinger

BRILL

RODOPI

LEIDEN | BOSTON

The Library of Congress Cataloging-in-Publication Data is available online at http://catalog.loc.gov
LC record available at http://lccn.loc.gov/2020041633

Typeface for the Latin, Greek, and Cyrillic scripts: "Brill". See and download: brill.com/brill-typeface.

ISSN 0167-4102
ISBN 978-90-04-44302-0 (hardback)
ISBN 978-90-04-44303-7 (e-book)

Copyright 2021 by Robin D. Rollinger. Published by Koninklijke Brill NV, Leiden, The Netherlands.
Koninklijke Brill NV incorporates the imprints Brill, Brill Hes & De Graaf, Brill Nijhoff, Brill Rodopi, Brill Sense, Hotei Publishing, mentis Verlag, Verlag Ferdinand Schöningh and Wilhelm Fink Verlag.
Koninklijke Brill NV reserves the right to protect this publication against unauthorized use. Requests for re-use and/or translations must be addressed to Koninklijke Brill NV via brill.com or copyright.com.

This book is printed on acid-free paper and produced in a sustainable manner.

Contents

Preface VII

Analysis

Introduction 3

1 The Neo-Scholastic Background 25
  1. The Tasks of Logic 26
  2. Concept 28
  3. Judgment 32
  4. Syllogism 33
  5. Concluding Remarks 36

2 Definition and Value of Logic 37
  1. The Relevant Manuscripts 37
  2. Logic as the Art of Judging 38
  3. Logic, Psychology, and Philosophy 45
  4. The Value of Logic 52
  5. Psychologism 56
  6. Language 61
  7. Dialectic 72
  8. Concluding Remarks 75

3 Concept 77
  1. Presentations and Names 78
  2. Distinctions among Concepts 83
  3. Distinctions among Modes of Presentation 96
  4. Distinctions among Names 99
  5. Relations among Presentations 101
  6. Definition 102
  7. Concluding Remarks 105

4 Judgment 106
  1. Critique of Kant's Table 107
  2. Complexity and Simplicity 109
  3. Form 112

4	Form and Matter	114
5	Intensity	118
6	Motive	118
7	Modality	120
8	Expression of Judgments	124
9	Relations between Judgments	125
10	Evidence	128
11	Syllogism	132
12	Concluding Remarks	136

Materials

Preparatory Note to Materials   141

5   Franz Hillebrand, *Die elementare Logik und die in ihr nötigen Reformen nach den Vorlesungen des Dr. Franz Brentano* (Wintersemester 1884/85, Wien)   144

6   Franz Hillebrand, *Elementary Logic and the Reforms Necessary in It according to the Lectures of Dr. Franz Brentano* (Winter Semester 1884/85, Vienna)   217

7   Franz Hillebrand, *The New Theories of Categorical Inferences* (1891)   282

Bibliography   375
Index   386

Preface

The first part of the present volume is an analysis of Franz Brentano's lectures on logic, primarily on the basis of the notes contained under the signature EL 80 (among his manuscripts as these are preserved in the Houghton Library at Harvard University). Brentano repeatedly used and revised these notes, at first in Würzburg (as early as 1870) and then in Vienna (probably as late as 1877 or later), though they were superceded by another, very different set of notes on logic (EL 72), some of which he used for the winter semester 1878/79, but with considerable revisions and additions for 1884/85 and for an (unannounced) continuation into the summer semester 1885. While EL 80 provides us with an alternative term-logic of his own making, the latter notes are much more remote from what we ordinarily call "logic" in either traditional or contemporary terminology. The former include such staples of logic as a treatment of both deductive and inductive inference. (Brentano's views on induction and the closely related theory of probability are topics that would better receive treatment in a separate study and are accordingly not subjected to analysis in the present volume.)

The second part of the present volume includes a German edition and English translation of notes that Franz Hillebrand took from Brentano's lectures on logic in 1884/85, though not from the summer semester 1885. I shall give further details regarding Hillebrand's notes below. Belonging also to the second part of the present volume is an English translation of Hillebrand's *Die neuen Theorien der kategorischen Schlüsse*, in which he elaborates on Brentano's syllogistic logic in connection with the theory of judgment, as he also defends this logic against contemporaneous rivals regarding the same issues. This short work by Hillebrand involves elaborations on some points that are not made focal in the first part of the present volume and vice-versa.

The analysis in the first part is a documented study and accordingly contains extensive quotations from archival materials. In this way I intend to correct some of the free-wheeling interpretations of Brentano's philosophy that have come before the public in recent decades. Whenever I quote from unpublished manuscripts, I provide the German text as well (in italics when the quotation is short, but not the lengthy quotations in the main text, as the publisher finds italics in that case undesirable). In the second part, however, italics are used in brackets to indicate the editor/translator's comments.

Further details concerning the themes and motives of this treatment of Brentano's logic are provided in the Introduction.

The colleagues who have played a role in one way or another in the creation of this volume are far too numerous to be listed here. Nevertheless, a few of them should not go unmentioned. I thank Johannes Brandl who played an important role in prompting me to construct a preliminary edition of EL 80 (https://gams.uni-graz/context:bag-nachlass), which has been funded by *Österreichische Fond für wissenschaftliche Forschung* (FWF) (project: P 19157-G08). Thomas Binder is also to be thanked for providing me with digital facsimiles of manuscripts from the Brentano Archives and also for transcribing much of EL 80 for the preliminary edition. (In spite of its imperfections, many of which are due to my own oversights and are yet to be corrected, this transcription has helped various researchers to find their way into Brentano's thought and can still prove to be a basis for a proper edition of the relevant manuscript.) Finally, I thank Mauro Antonelli, the editor of *Studien zur Österreichischen Philosophie*, for bearing with me throughout the preparation of the present volume, which is an outcome of the project "From Logical Objectivism to Reism: Bolzano and the School of Brentano" P401 15–18149S (Czech Science Foundation), realized at the Institute of Philosophy of the Czech Academy of Sciences.

Robin D. Rollinger
October 2020, Prague

Analysis

Introduction

Philosophy without logic is for many a contemporary philosopher altogether unthinkable. Such a thing could only belong to the same family as a round square or an unextended body. Yet, there have been times in the history of philosophy in which logic was little more than an object of contempt.[1] This was particularly the case in early modern philosophy, even to the point where such contempt finds expression in the canon. David Hume's *Treatise of Human Nature*, for instance, has become practically a must-read for students of philosophy. It has had this status in the English speaking world for a very long time and has also been translated into numerous languages. It is a text not only for seminars all over the world, but also the focus of extensive secondary literature. Although Hume's *Treatise* is hardly ever concerned with logic, we find the following statement in that work:

> Our scholastic head-pieces and *logicians* shew no such superiority above the mere vulgar in their reason and ability, as to give us any inclination to imitate them in delivering a long system of rules and precepts to direct our judgment, in philosophy.[2]

Though one might expect an advocacy for philosophy without logic from an irrationalist or mystic, Hume is hardly one of those. He is surely among the soberest thinkers. According to Bertrand Russell, "in Hume ... the scientific impulse reigns quite unchecked."[3] Indeed, some of the most passionate lovers of logic[4] (of whom there are at present many) have sung high praises for Hume.

---

[1] For a generous selection of references regarding the philosophical rejection of logic, see Evra 2008, 80 ff.

[2] Hume [1739] 1978, 175. Emphasis mine. Although it is true that Hume thinks that he can offer certain rules for thinking that can replace logic, these are not subject to any kind of formalization. Logic, as it is understood in this volume, must at least to *some* degree and in *some* of its parts be formalizable.

[3] Russell 1918, 1.

[4] Generally speaking, empiricism and positivism were for quite a long time tendencies that reflected Hume's attitude towards logic, whereas thinkers of a more rationalist and mathematical character engaged in logical pursuits. A very important turning point occurred in the Vienna Circle during the 1920s when its members acknowledged both Hume and "logistic" as inspirations. The very terms for their movement, namely "logical empiricism" and "logical positivism", were a novel combination of words. Of course the logic that inspired them was not the scholastic or neo-scholastic logic (the "school-logic" or "old logic," as it is called in the seventh chapter of the present volume) to which Hume had been reacting,

© ROBIN D. ROLLINGER, 2021 | DOI:10.1163/9789004443037_002

With regard to his stance on logic, however, he has had little influence in recent times. For more than a century, logic has been subject to cultivatation and expansion beyond the wildest dreams of our predecessors. Not only has logic become expansive, but it has also become remarkably diversified.[5] "Logic is an old subject," Willard van Orman Quine once quipped, "and since 1879 it has been a great one."[6] Thus we see two extremes in the history of philosophy regarding logic. Some have seen this discipline as negligible, while others have regarded it as an immense and ever-expanding field of research. Hume is a prime example of the former, while Quine is one of the latter.[7]

We can, however, discern a perspective that lies in between these two extremes of No Logic and Great Logic. From this perspective, logic is a tool that is of considerable value in application to other domains of philosophy such as metaphysics and ethics, perhaps even in other sciences and daily life, but hardly deserving of the attention that it gets nowadays from logical specialists. Logic in this sense is a modest endeavor. In the present volume I shall concern myself with a logic of this kind, which we may deem Modest Logic as lying in between No Logic and Great Logic. Yet, we should not expect a modest philosophy to go with Modest Logic any more than we expect such modesty from Hume's No Logic. We shall accordingly contextualize Brentano's logic in his philosophical orientation in order to show its significance from his perspective, at least insofar as this is possible in a volume of this size and scope.

It is not my intention here to make a contribution to the history of logic. In the attempt to determine an individual philosopher's approach to this discipline we always confront a fundamental question, namely "whether one wants to concentrate on what the author himself understood by 'logic' or what is considered as a genuinely logical issue from our contemporary point of view."[8] Leaving aside the assumption that there is one single contemporary point of view, the contemporarian approach may be well justified in the treatment of a

---

but rather the symbolic logic of Leibniz, Peano, Frege, Schröder, Russell, Whitehead, and Wittgenstein. Nonetheless, their praise of a highly artificial calculus stands in vivid contrast with the older empiricism and positivism.

5 Haack 1978, vii: "The variety of this growth is as impressive as its scale." This author attributes the growth of logic to Frege 1879. See the following footnote on this point.

6 Quine 1950/59, vii. Here a reference is made to Frege 1879. Perhaps Quine underestimated the movement of algebraic logic which started prior to that work, although this issue lies beyond the scope of the present discussion.

7 Quine in fact did lecture on Hume. See Pakaluk 1989. This illustrates the above-made point that lovers of logic make an exception for Hume, one of the outstanding haters of logic.

8 Lenzen 2004, 1.

philosophical orientation in logic that is already quite familiar. The alternative approach, however, seems to be more appropriate for considering the logical work of someone such as Franz Brentano, whose views on most philosophical topics still are hardly familiar to many. We must first familiarize ourselves with his views before we grind them through state-of-the-art machinery and dispense with whatever does not appeal to our taste. From contemporary points of view, scholars will regard Brentano's logic as, at best, one of the many attempts to reform this discipline, whereas it is of much greater importance within the context of his more wide-ranging philosophical efforts which merit our attention.[9] In the present work I shall accordingly discuss Franz Brentano's logic on his own terms.[10] As this volume is not an attempt to contribute to the history of logic as such, it is not a critique of Brentano's logic or his wider philosophy either. It is rather an elaboration on this logic, which could be the foundation for such a critique from a contemporary perspective. At present there is still hardly enough known about Brentano's philosophy to justify subjecting it to extensive critical assessments, though this is hardly to assert that it is immune to criticisms on isolated points.

Before we enter into the content of Brentano's logic, it will be helpful to provide some context. This introduction deals with the relevant context with

9   In recent overviews of Brentano's philosophy, there is unfortunately seldom any place for a discussion of his logic. See, for instance, Albertazzi 2006, Textor 2017, Kriegel 2017, and Kriegel 2018, most of which have merits in various respects, except that they lack attention to Brentano's logic as such. Jacquette 2004, however, has the merit of containing a contribution that is concerned with this matter, though strictly in accordance with the interests of contemporary logicians. We may in any case regard the contributor's assessment of Brentano as "not a giant, but ... no pygmy either" Simons 2004, 46 as accurate. There is, after all, hardly anything else a logician can be who pursues the path between the two extremes of philosophy without logic (e.g. in the case of Hume) and extremely logical philosophy (e.g. in the case of Quine). We find a similar assessment in Scholz 1961, 48: "His [Brentano's] interpretation of the elementary 'forms' of Aristotelian logic ('All S are P,' etc.) and the reformation of the Aristotelian syllogism deduced therefrom, constitute in the judgment of those who are well oriented in modern exact logic the most interesting corrections upon Aristotelian logic, many eccentricities in detail notwithstanding. So far as we can humanly judge, the adjustment in Aristotelian logic is of enduring character. It is, however, the only portion of Brentano's *Logik* about which this can be asserted." Such assessments, however, arise from a consideration of the *Logik* from a contemporary standpoint rather than Brentano's own.
10   The fact that Brentano was hardly a logician by contemporary standards need not distract us. There is considerable interest in Kant's views on logic, as these have been made available in Kant 1992, although one concedes without further ado that "Kant is not a major contributor to the development of formal logic" (Young 1992: xvi).

regard to his own philosophical career,[11] whereas the first chapter will expand on the historical – more specifically, neo-scholastic – background of Brentano's logic.

As a student Brentano was interested in both mathematics and philosophy. Although he chose the latter as his major study, he subsequently continued to keep informed about advances in the former domain.[12] In his philosophical studies he attended the Universities of Munich, Berlin, and Münster and finally received his doctorate *in absentia* in Tübingen. Among the prominent professors whose lectures he attended were Ernst von Lassaulx (Munich), Adolf Trendelenburg (Berlin),[13] and Franz Jakob Clemens (Münster).[14] Not only was he quite familiar with scholasticism through Clemens, but under the influence of Trendelenburg he also became well acquainted with the philosophy of

---

11   Most of the biographical data about Brentano is taken here from Kraus 1919.
12   See Ierna 2012.
13   Trendelenburg indeed published a work that bore the title *Logische Untersuchungen*, which might well indicate that his views on logic would be highly relevant to the present study. In Brentano's lectures on metaphysics he moreover rejects the Trendelenburgian position "The law of non-contradiction holds only for being, not for motion which is prior to being [*Das Gesetz des Widerspruchs gilt nur für das Sein, nicht für die Bewegung, die früher ist als das Sein*]" (M 96/31784). (See Trendelenburg 1862, vol. I, 187, regarding the point under consideration.) Against such a position, Brentano argues, "A restriction of the validity of the law of non-contradiction is unacceptable and inconceivable. If he [Trendelenburg] clearly kept in mind what the law of non-contradiction says, namely that the same thing cannot at the same time be true and false (for this in fact means 'to be' and 'not to be', but not a reality at rest), it could have never entered his mind that it has no application to motion. If this were really so, it would have to be possible for the moved to be at the same time not moved, which even Trendelenburg wouldn't concede [*Eine Beschränkung der Gültigkeit des Satzes vom Widerspruch ist unannehmbar und undenkbar. Hätte er klar den Gedanken festgehalten, den das Gesetz des Widerspruchs besagt, dass nämlich dasselbe nicht zugleich wahr und falsch sein könne (denn dies bedeutet ja hier sein und nicht sein, nicht aber eine ruhende Realität), so hätte es ihm unmöglich in den Sinn kommen können, er sei auf die Bewegung ohne Anwendung. Wäre dies wirklich nicht der Fall, so müsste das Bewegte zugleich nichtbewegt sein können, was selbst Trendelenburg nicht zugeben würde.*]" (M 96/3186.) While Brentano no doubt learned from Trendelenburg and held him in high regard, his enthusiasm for Clemens (as we shall see in the first chapter) seems to have been greater, though Brentano's orientation in logic also differs in important respect from the neo-scholastic one that he had learned from Clemens, as this will be apparent in the analysis of Brentano's logic.
14   Clemens distinguished himself with a study of Giordano Bruno and Nicholas of Cusa (1847) and also defended orthodox Catholic teaching while Brentano was attending his lectures. See Clemens 1860. There will be further considerations of Clemens on logic in the following chapter.

Aristotle based on the philological advances that had been made by extraordinary work of August Immanuel Bekker (also in Berlin) in the pioneering critical edition of the Aristotelian corpus. From this corpus Trendelenburg also provided readers with a volume of excerpts pertaining to logic.[15] Brentano's dissertation (1862) on the various meanings of "being" was, to be sure, primarily concerned with Aristotle's ontology, but it also involved an interpretation of the doctrine of categories which traditionally belonged to the domain of logic.[16]

Brentano began lecturing in Würzburg in 1867. Unlike many teachers and professors of philosophy, who are often content to impart to their students little more than what the great thinkers have said, he took pains not only to do this, but also systematically to develop his own philosophical views and convey them in his lectures. He succeeded in doing so by drawing upon an uncommonly extensive erudition in the history of philosophy, as his earliest lectures already make clear. As a young priest and as the author of two books on Aristotle, he of course could have simply taught neo-scholasticism, but from the very start of his academic career he did not follow this path, but rather developed theories that also had links with other philosophical currents such as British Empiricism. According to his approach to the philosophy of history, modern philosophy peaked with authors such as Descartes and Locke, whose names are to be found in the *Index Librorum Prohibitorum*.

Unfortunately Brentano's published work represents only a mere fragment of the philosophical views that he formulated in lectures and inspired many a student either to embrace them or at least to make them a starting point for further philosophical reflection. Already in the earliest phase of his academic career, when he was lecturing at the University of Würzburg, he very persuasively presented his philosophy to students such as Carl Stumpf, Anton Marty, Herman Schell, and Georg von Hertling.

During this time, the school of Brentano came into existence with the hallmark of logical rigor as one of its special features.[17] Stumpf testifies to

---

15   Trendelenburg 1868, which was translated into English in Trendelenburg 1898.
16   There was already a very thorough-going study of this doctrine published in Trendelenburg 1846, 196–380.
17   See Ueberweg 1902, 313: "Brentano, scholastically well trained, has continually inspired many by his acute dialectic and by the persuasive formulation of his new statements and by the fact that he often left the grounding of them more to be anticipated than he really provided it." Here of course we see a criticism, namely that Brentano apparently promised more than he actually delivered. This criticism is indeed justified if only the materials that he himself published are taken into account. (Of course Ueberweg and other critics could

Brentano's effect as a teacher in Würzburg: "Only Brentano's iron discipline made the need of logical clarity and consistency second nature to me."[18] If indeed we assess Brentano's achievements, we may at least say on the basis of such testimonies that he is among the great philosophical teachers. The question remains whether he is among the great thinkers. Not until his unpublished writings are made substantially accessible without corruption is it possible to answer this question. This volume will provide the reader with at least some of the tools necessary for answering it. While various aspects of Brentano's philosophy will have to receive similar treatment before this answer is reached, his logic (which includes much of his epistemology) will be relevant to deciding whether he is in fact "one of a handful of towering geniuses in the history of philosophy, on a par with the likes of Aristotle and Kant."[19] His candidacy for this status, however, is already assured by his deep and extensive influence not only on the aforementioned Würzburg students, but also on such outstanding philosophers and thinkers as Alexius Meinong, Edmund Husserl, Kasimir Twardowski, Thomas Masaryk, and Sigmund Freud who attended his lectures during his Vienna years (1874–1895). Brentano's effect as a teacher in Vienna is also supported by such testimonies as the following:

> I too soon admired the acuteness with which Brentano guided us ... in solving ancient sophistries. All our attempts to solve them he could show to be insufficient with few words. I had never up to that time encountered such formal meticulousness in philosophical matters.[20]

---

hardly be blamed for not knowing unpublished materials.) Nevertheless, Brentano gave his students a lot more through his lectures, which are yet to be published in a philologically sound manner.

18 Stumpf 1924, 208. Cf. Stumpf 2019: "Brentano's lectures won me over to philosophy due to the rigour and acuteness of their train of thought."

19 Kriegel 2018, 13 f. At least we can say that a deflationary view of Brentano, e.g. as merely the teacher of Edmund Husserl, does not by any means do justice to his philosophical work. While one does not usually state such a view explicitly, it is easily impressed on a student of philosophy who comes under the influence of one of the two camps, "analytic" and "continental," which have prevailed for a good many decades. The fact that intentionality has become increasingly focal opens up the possibility of Brentano's status being upgraded in future assessments, for he was, after all, the one who introduced the concept of intentionality into modern philosophy.

20 Höfler 1921, 120. Just as Meinong came to conclusions that evoked considerable contempt from Brentano, the same was true of much of Höfler's work, which was indeed Meinongian in large measure. Yet, as we see from the quotation in the text, Höfler acknowledges the great intellectual gain that accrued to him through Brentano's lectures.

In view of the logical skill that Brentano displayed in application to philosophical matters,[21] it is of considerable interest for us to gain access to what he had to say about the discipline of logic.

Brentano began teaching logic quite early in his career, although the concern in his first efforts as a teacher was rather the history of philosophy. In 1867 he obtained the right to lecture, as was the custom, though his *Habilitation*, which is a procedure whereby the post-doctoral candidate submits an extensive written work and formulates a number of theses which he must defend in public. The work that he wrote in this connection was concerned with Aristotle's psychology, particularly the Aristotelian concept of the "agent intellect."[22] In his defense of the theses, in opposition to some of the last remaining defenders of German Idealism, Brentano made a great impression not only as a highly erudite individual, but also as a very skillful debater. The following are the theses that he defended:

1. Philosophy must protest against the division of sciences into speculative and exact ones and the justification of this protest is its very right of existence.
2. Philosophy must protest against the demand that its principles should be drawn from theology and against the assertion that a fruitful philosophizing becomes possible only from the existence of a supernatural revelation.
3. It is nevertheless correct to say that the theologically established truths may serve philosophical research as pointers.
4. The true method of philosophy is none other than that of the natural sciences.
5. The plurality in the world refutes pantheism, while the unity in it refutes atheism.
6. Kant is wrong in asserting that the physico-theolgical proof yields no creative intelligence, but an ordering one.
7. And he was also wrong in saying that, if God as creator is proven, his infinite perfection does not follow from this.

---

21 Cf. Husserl 1919, 154, where the "utterly unique clarity and dialectical acuteness of his arguments" is mentioned. Both Husserl and Höfler attended at least one lecture course together, namely *Die elementare Logik und die in ihr nötigen Reformen* (1884/85). Husserl also attended seminars with Brentano on Hume, Helmholtz, and du Bois-Reymond and says of his mentor in this connection, "Brentano was a master of Socratic maieutics." (Ibid., 155).

22 Brentano 1867. For a discussion of Brentano's relation to Aristotle, see George 2004. His interpretation of Aristotelian philosophy had considerable impact on his students, as exhibited in von Hertling 1871 and Schell 1873.

8. There is neither an unlimited number nor even a multiplicity of worlds, nor is the world infinitely extended.
9. The assumption of an empty space, as taught by older and more recent atomism, is impossible, because the concept of an empty space would contain a contradiction and because an effect through empty space is impossible.
10. Zeno's paralogisms, more precisely the first three of them, are deceptive in that they treat the continuum as a discrete magnitude.
11. Whoever assumes the immortality of the soul of an animal must also assume that there are animals with many, indeed infinitely many souls.
12. There are as many faculties of fantasy as there are of sensory faculties, and the fantasy images are in the senses themselves.
13. There is nothing in the understanding that was not earlier in one of the senses, except the understanding itself.
14. While some deny of man every cognitive faculty outside of the senses, others ascribe to him a multiplicity of supersensory cognitive powers. Both are wrong.
15. The νοῦς ποιητικός [agent intellect] of Aristotle is not a cognizing, but rather an effective power.
16. It is wrong to say of genus and difference that one could not contain the other. Rather every specific difference contains the genus, and the ultimate difference is equal to the whole definition.
17. There is not any definition of accidents in the strict sense of the word, though defining a substance is completely impossible for us.
18. We do not fully think what we speak, and even the most rigorous thinkers usually do not do this, even in conducting the most precise proofs.
19. Far from being beneficial to us only as a means of communication, but becoming an obstacle to us in thinking, as Herbart believes, language is rather an essential aid also for thought.
20. The disjunctive judgment is a complex hypothetical judgment, and thus the disjunctive inference not a special form, but rather an imperfect representation of a hypothetical inference.[23]
21. There are inferences from one premise.[24]
22. It is wrong to think that man is by nature an egoist such that he could not love something more than himself.

---

23 Brentano later revised this early understanding of disjunctives and hypotheticals. See below, pp. 113f.
24 See below, p. 344.

INTRODUCTION

23. Via metaphysical considerations many, such as Spinoza, have thought that belief in free will involuntarily forces itself on us. On the contrary metaphysical consdierations serve to confirm this belief.
24. The concepts of the good and the beautiful are distinguished in that we call something good insofar as it is desirable, but beautiful insofar as its appearance is desirable.
25. That which by preference is peculiarly attractive in tragic representations is primarily the glimpse into the inward beauty of man and into the reign of a higher divine power. Secondarily, however, the movements that are painfully aroused in the soul of the spectator nonetheless guarantee double enjoyment, first because they are noble and sublime, secondly, however, also because a guarded sadness pours out in them and finds relief.[25]

Although some of Brentano's habilitation theses are plainly relevant to a time when German Idealism was still rather pitifully lingering on and some of them, due to subsequent scientific developments, could hardly even be upheld in our time, others may well prove to be viable, such as the fourth thesis in particular, which was indeed to have great impact on such gifted young men as Stumpf and Marty. They were so inspired by this thesis that they were subsequently willing to make great sacrifices in their decision to follow Brentano in both philosophy and religion.[26] Once he became a lecturer in Würzburg he began presenting his system, including not only a unique approach to the history of philosophy,[27] but also in the course of time a metaphysics,[28]

---

25 Brentano 1929, 136–141. This edition provides us with the theses in both Latin and German. Though the Latin version was the one initially presented, the German one is "in essence" Brentano's own.

26 Stumpf 1919, 88 f. Stumpf was actually present at Brentano's *Habilitation* defense, whereas Marty soon joined Stumpf as a fellow student and later became the most outstanding orthodox follower of Brentano. Upon coming to Würzburg Marty was already preparing for the priesthood. Though Stumpf likewise began to do so, he decided to terminate this endeavor when Brentano left the priesthood in 1873. Marty, however, had already become ordained by that time, though he was soon to follow Brentano in quitting his clerical practice. Though Brentano married in 1880, causing a great upheaval in connections with his family and in his academic career (for he was indeed still regarded as a priest), Marty remained celibate.

27 The history of philosophy was what Brentano started lecturing on in Würzburg. His lectures on historical topics were informed by his "four phase" theory, a brief statement of which he later published in Brentano 1895.

28 In Brentano's manuscripts there are notes for at least one complete lecture course (i.e. for a single semester) on metaphysics M 96, consisting of transcendental philosophy and ontology. (These notes stem from his Würzburg period). According to the conception of

a psychology,[29] and a logic.[30] Though the young Brentano, singularly unimpressed with the "mysticism" of his idealist predecessors (i.e. Schelling, Fichte, Hegel, Schleiermacher, and their many disciples), but also finding vast shortcomings in the more contemporary thought of his positivist and neo-Kantian contemporaries,[31] embarked on his philosophical career by following Aristotle[32] and also drawing from "the acute commentaries of Thomas Aquinas,"[33] the results of his investigations retained only some elements of Aristotelianism, albeit highly significant ones. In these early days of his career it was Brentano's logic that bore the stamp of originality more than other aspects of his system and thereby played a key role in the great intellectual movement that ensued from his teaching, the effects of which are still with us today, though not all are aware of them.

metaphysics that is presented in these notes, however, metaphysics has two remaining parts: theology and cosmology. Brentano's theology, i.e. his proofs for the existence of God, was presented in lectures on many occasions during both his Würzburg period (1867–1873) and Vienna period (1873–1895). The material for theological lectures is to be found under signatures Th 31 and Th 32 and edited in Brentano 1929. This edition, however, is very freely constructed from a very complex set of manuscripts.

29 Brentano first lectured on psychology in the winter semester of 1872/73 (the last semester in which he lectured in Würzburg). Though the lecture notes for this course are not to be found in his manuscripts, an extensive plan for it (Ps 62) is extant. See Rollinger 2012. As will be seen in the present study, however, Brentano's early logic contains much of his psychology. In Vienna Brentano continued to develop his psychology, particularly its descriptive branch. The notes for his last lecture course on psychology (EL 74) have been published in Brentano 1982, which is not a critical edition.

30 The two complete sets of lecture notes on logic are to be found in Brentano's manuscripts under signatures EL 72 and EL 80. There will be more to say about this material in the main text.

31 The neo-Kantian movement had been initiated by Liebmann 1865. As for positivism, the work of Auguste Comte was receiving considerable attention, e.g. in Mill 1865. See Brentano 1926, 99–133. Brentano's most concentrated critique of positivism is to be found in a lecture course from the winter semester 1893/94 (LS 20).

32 Kraus 1919: 4: "Though he could find no teacher among the living who met his demands, he sought him in the past and found him in Aristotle, who initially became a guide for him and in whose work he immersed himself in spirit of congeniality." See also Brentano 1911b: iv.

33 Brentano 1911c, 1f. As Brentano indicates here, the Thomistic interpretation of Aristotle was generally not held in high regard outside of Catholic circles. Through his early work on Aristotle, he was able to convince Trendelenburg of the value of Aquinas' commentaries and apparently those of other scholastics. Aquinas in particular, however, is regarded by Brentano as the philosopher who most eminently represents the phase of ascendency in the middle ages (Brentano 1895). For further considerations of early Brentano's relation to Aquinas, see Hedwig 2012.

It is clear not only from Brentano's appeciation of the value of logic (to be discussed in the second chapter of my analysis), but also from considerations of his personal circumstances, why he was driven to formulate criteria for distinguishing truth from falsehood, the known from the unknown, which is indeed the ultimate concern of logic on his view. Though he had been raised in a family that was steeped in Roman Catholic teachings and practices, he already experienced a crisis of faith when he was seventeen years old.[34] He was, to be sure, to overcome this crisis and eventually to be ordained as a priest. The issue of Papal Infallibility that arose during the early years of his academic career and was resolved in 1870 with a declaration of the well-known doctrine on this matter, however, prompted Brentano to engage in reflections, not only on this issue but also on other articles of faith, such as the Holy Trinity, the Incarnation, and "the very concept of faith itself."[35] In view of his failure to defend Christianity on these points, Brentano decided finally to leave his clerical vocation in 1873 and his affiliation with Roman Catholicism altogether in 1880, though he continued to be a theist as his repeated lectures on the existence of God make clear. His inner struggle to come to a judgment on matters that were of such grave importance to him could not allow for indifference with regard to logic as the art of judgment. Logic was indeed something more than a mere frivolity for him. Though some philosophers *entertain* doubts, Brentano actually *experienced* them with regard to matters of the most profound seriousness. Even if one finds it difficult to understand anything other than indifference toward religion, one can at least appreciate the social consequences that had to be faced. Brentano's relation to his family and also his academic circumstances were to be deeply affected. Moreover, the future careers of his young followers were also at stake. While we may all appreciate Brentano's religious doubts with respect to such external ramifications, historical empathy for him is possible perhaps only for those who have had similar experiences. Unlike so many for whom logic is little more than a fascinating technical toy, Brentano felt the need for it "not only [as a product] of intellectual work, but rather of deep struggles of the soul."[36]

As Brentano was reflecting on issues that were to be of momentous importance for the rest of his life, he began his very first lecture course on logic, under the title *Deductive and Inductive Logic* for the winter semester 1869/70 in Würzburg. At the scheduled time for the beginning of this course, however, he started lecturing instead on the immortality of the soul and continued to do

---

34   Kraus 1919, 4.
35   Stumpf 1919, 110.
36   Husserl 1919, 154.

so until after Christmas break.[37] The discussion of immortality was meant to be a "preparation, exercise in psychological reflection."[38]

It would take us too far afield to discuss the details of Brentano's argument in favor of the doctrine of immortality of the soul, although some aspects of the contents of his lecture course on this topic are worth mentioning in the present context. It may be somewhat of a surprise to some to see that the very concept of a soul has a presence in his philosophy, since he later seemed to endorse a "psychology without a soul" in his most widely read work: *Psychology from an Empirical Standpoint*. We should however bear in mind that the published volume of this work (1874) is but a torso of a larger treatment of psychical phenomena.[39] At no time did Brentano regard a psychology without a soul as the final word, but rather only set out from such a psychology as a methodological starting point or perhaps only in order to accommodate contemporaries who dismissed discussions concerning the soul as unduly "metaphysical." In the lectures of 1869 that prefaced Brentano's first lectures on logic, he defined the soul as "what is in us the bearer of thinking, willing, sensation, in short of all *inwardly conscious acts*."[40] These so-called acts are indeed the psychical phenomena that he later classified as presentations, judgments, and love or hate. Nonetheless he concedes that this definition is a nominal definition and that it thus does not actually assert anything. In order to argue for the immortality of the soul, he finds it necessary to dismiss two perspectives from which one will not allow for a soul, namely materialism and Humeanism.

37 Stumpf 1919, 105.
38 Brentano, LS 23/29670: "*Vorbereitung, Übung in psychologischer Reflexion.*" It is of course also possible that at a time when doctrines of revealed theology were undergoing doubt, he wanted to emphasize all the more that he stood on the side of tradition in matters of natural theology in opposition to materialism and positivism. His lecture notes on immortality from 1869 were later revised, most likely in 1873 (since in these revisions Brentano refers to the lectures on psychology and proofs for the existence of God, both of which were held in the winter semester 1872/73). There is thus a strong indication that he was intending to lecture on immortality in the summer semester 1873. Though Brentano resigned from his post in Würzburg prior to this semester, he planned a lecture course entitled *Deductive and Inductive Logic with Applications to the History of the Sciences of Nature and Mind* (*Deduktive und induktive Logik mit Anwendungen auf die Geschichte der Natur- und Geisteswissenschaften*). Since this is the only lecture course announced for the semester in question, it appears that he meant to utilize the lecture notes on immortality once again to supplement a course in logic. (Brentano used some of the material in LS 23 in the winter semester 1875/76. The main manuscript for his lectures on immortality given at that time is LS 22.)
39 Rollinger 2012.
40 Brentano LS 23/29676: "die in uns die *Trägerin* des Denkens, Wollens, Empfindens, kurz aller innerlich bewussten Akte ist."

INTRODUCTION

Against materialism, Brentano takes a Cartesian position, according to which the doubts that may arise about external objects cannot arise concerning consciousness. Such things may *be* other than what they *seem* to be. "The acts of consciousness *are*," he says by contrast, "and *are as they seem to us*."[41] This is of course an appeal to inner perception, an appeal that Brentano also makes in his rejection of the Humean view that we cannot allow for a substantial bearer of psychical phenomena. Among Brentano's contemporaries at the time of his lectures on immortality in 1869 was John Stuart Mill who quite explicitly rejected materialism and at the same time defended the Humean view. Thoughts, feelings, and the like occur in bundles, on this view, but no substantial bearer of them is identifiable in our experience. Gustav Fechner, among the Germans, also insisted on this perspective, which Brentano rejects as follows:

> He [Fechner], too, rejects altogether the assumption of substances as bearers of the phenomena perceived by us, because [it is] nowhere given by experience. But the very contrary is the case. Experience everywhere offers us the concept of substance. In every one of our perceptions it is co-grasped. As in the presentation of color [we have] that of extension, in both [we have] the thing in the proper sense, the substance. Foundation. Therefore [it is] evident: no extension without something extended, no motion without something moved. Thus also in the perception of our own thinking. "I think, therefore I am," Descartes could justly say. Perception is of our own thinking is the perception of a something thinking ([a] thing) that we call "self."

> [Auch er verwirft überhaupt die Annahme von Substanzen als Träger der von uns wahrgenommenen Phänomene, weil nirgends durch die Erfahrung gegeben. Aber gerade das Gegenteil ist der Fall. Die Erfahrung bietet den Begriff der Substanz überall. In jeder unserer Wahrnehmungen wird er miterfasst. Wie in der (Vorstellung der) Farbe die (der) Ausdehnung, so in beiden das Ding im eigentlichen Sinn, d.i. die Substanz. Fundament. Daher evident: keine Ausdehnung ohne Ausgedehntes, keine Bewegung ohne Bewegtes. So denn auch in der Wahrnehmung des eigenen Denkens. "Ich denke, also bin ich" konnte Descartes mit Recht sagen. Die Wahrnehmung des eigenen Denkens ist die Wahrnehmung eines Denkenden (Dinges), das wir Ich nennen.][42]

---

41   LS 23/29677: "*Die Akte unseres Bewusstseins* sind, *und* sind, wie sie uns scheinen."
42   LS 23/29677. The agreement with Descartes here is of course of great importance. The

This appeal to inner perception is of the utmost importance in relation to the logic to be analyzed in the present volume. We shall see that for Brentano logic is as much concerned with immediately evident judgments as it is with judgments that are made evident through inference from other judgments. It is in fact a frequent occurrence, on his view, for people – for philosophers no less – to judge (or at least to express judgments) that are contrary to what we know immediately. Thus it is no surprise that the immaterial substantial bearer of psychical phenomena is not universally accepted.

Crucial to Brentano's argument for immortality is the premise that man is elevated far above the rest of the animals because he has abstract presentations (*abstrakte Vorstellungen*). In his lecture notes for the 1869 he makes this point as follows:

> When we run through our presentations, we find that some are concrete-sensible, others abstract presentations, which we call "intelligible." Examples of concrete-sensible ones are offered by every sensory perception. Imagination as well. By contrast, abstract ones are, for instance, a quality without determinate size, shape, etc. Pure quantity without quality. Genus without differentia (in the case of simple and complex things). Thing without property. Number. Man has the first-mentioned in common with the animals, namely the higher animals that do not lack any of the senses. Animal presentations. The last-mentioned are peculiar to him.
>
> [Wenn wir unsere Vorstellungen durchmustern, so finden wir, dass sie teils konkret-sensible, teils abstrakte Vorstellungen sind, die wir intelligible nennen. Beispiele von konkret-sensiblen bietet jede Sinneswahrnehmung. Ebenso die Phantasie. Abstrakte dagegen sind z.B. eine Qualität ohne bestimmte Größe, Gestalt &c. Reine Quantität ohne Qualität. Gattung ohne Differenz (bei einfachen und komplizierten Dingen). Ding ohne Eigenschaft. Zahl. Die ersten hat der Mensch mit den Tieren,

---

subtitle of Descartes' most celebrated work, *Meditations on First Philosophy*, was at first "in which are demonstrated the existence of God and the immortality of the soul," though it was changed in a second edition to "in which are demonstrated the existence of God and the distinction between the human soul and the body" (Cottingham 1984, 1). The just-cited passage from Brentano's lectures on immortality indicates a very definite affinity between his view and the one that we find in Descartes' *Meditations* regarding the soul, although we must not infer that Brentano is generally in agreement with Descartes. Brentano also thinks that the existence of God is demonstrable, but not by means of the ontological argument that Descartes puts forward in the *Meditations*.

INTRODUCTION   17

> namentlich den höheren, welche keinen Sinn mangelt, gemein. Animalische Vorstellungen. Die letzten sind ihm allein eigentümlich.][43]

Abstract presentations are, as we shall see, a matter of concern for logic and will accordingly be discussed further below.

"No animal," says Brentano in an early manuscript, "has interest in truth as such, which logic serves."[44] This statement and its concomitant appreciation for the abstract as a peculiarity of human cognition put him at odds not only with the prevailing Darwinistic climate, in which the overwhelming tendency was to minimize the difference between man and the higher animals, but also with the nominalistic orientation among British philosophers, such as Berkeley and Mill (though certainly not Locke), who denied the existence of abstract presentations. Brentano's early logic was thus something that arose amid controversies which excede ones that many would regard as purely "logical" in contemporary terms. Questions such as the one concerning whether there are abstract presentations nowadays find their home in epistemology or perhaps philosophy of mind, not logic. As already indicated, however, we are concerned with logic as Brentano understands it. We are not attempting to process his philosophy, his logic in particular, through a grinder that one nowadays deems as "cutting edge" equipment.

After the Christmas break of the winter semester 1869/70, Brentano in fact managed to lecture on logic as such for the remainder of the semester. In the winter semester of the next academic year Brentano used the same lecture notes, though partly revised, for a lecture course, again under the title *Deductive and inductive Logic*. Though he announced the same lecture course again for the summer semester 1873, he had little choice but to leave his post in Würzburg because he ceased to be a practicing priest. After Brentano left Würzburg, his most important publication appeared, namely the first volume of his *Psychologie vom empirischen Standpunkte*, in which he announced a plan to publish the logic lectures from the winter semester 1870/71.[45] Yet, this plan, like his plan to publish the second volume of the work in which he made the announcement in question, never came to fruition. Nonetheless, he continued to revise the same notes and use them in lecture courses in Vienna (apparently still for the summer semesters 1875 and 1877) under the title *Alte und neue Logik* ("Old and New Logic," the old being the neo-scholastic logic, to be discussed in the

---

43   Brentano, LS 23/29724 f.
44   Brentano, LS 1/29007: *"Kein Tier hat Interesse an der Wahrheit als solcher, der die Logik dient."*
45   Brentano 1874, 302 n.

following chapter, and the new being Brentano's logic, to be analyzed in the second, third, and fourth chapters). When we speak of Brentano's early logic, the textual basis under consideration will be first and foremost this set of lecture notes, henceforth called the *Logik*.[46]

According Carl Stumpf, who actually attended the lecture course on logic in the winter semester 1869/70, the lectures proceeded as follows after the prologue on immortality:

> ... here Brentano thrust himself head on into a complete revision of the old traditions. He sets out from considerations of thoughts and their expression in language and distinguishes in the case of both names and statements that which they *express* (the mental functions which they manifest) from what they *mean*. A statement means that something is to be accepted or rejected. Brentano called this the *content of judgment*. It can be expressed linguistically in infinitival form or in "that"-clauses. This concept (later designated by me as "state of affairs"[47]) because *inter alia* the whole class of indirect judgments (it is possible, necessary, probable true, false that –) concern themselves, according to his presentation at that time, with such contents of judgment. Brentano called the *matter* of a judgment all of the presentations underlying the judgment. The *form* or *quality* of a judgment is finally affirmation or negation of the judgment's matter. This was Brentano's basis for his doctrine of the existential sentence as the simplest form of statement. Thus we get only general negative and particular affirmative judgments, and there is no other opposition between judgments besides this one: contradiction. All judgments, when expressed correctly (hence the so-called general affirmative ones, for instance, expressed as general negative ones), can be simply converted. Brentano thus saw himself compelled to overthrow and to simplify in an extraordinary way the whole doctrine of judgment, which we listeners heard with growing astonishment and admiration for the inexorable consistency of the exposition. It got no further than this, for the semester was over.[48]

These points and many others will receive due consideration in the following chapters.

---

46 Most of these notes are catalogued under the signature EL 80 in Brentano's manuscripts. There will be more about the relevant manuscript material in the third chapter below.
47 See Rollinger 1999, 313.
48 Stumpf 1919, 106 f.

The lecture notes which we now have from this course and its revisions in subsequent years contain much more than what Stumpf's sketch indicates,[49] including considerations of both immediate and mediated knowledge. The two types of immediate knowledge for Brentano are inner perception and purely conceptual cognition, whereas mediated knowledge is also of two different kinds, namely deduction and induction. Though we shall only give attention to deduction which is indeed the part of logic that is to be reformed on the basis of a new theory of judgment, we note here that Brentano's early logic provides us with elucidations of both types of inference.

In 1870/71, when Brentano again lectured on logic, he also developed an extensive outline of theology which was for him part of metaphysics, though hardly tied to revelation.[50] The connection between his theology and logic comes to the fore in his critique of the ontological argument. In his terms, this argument is actually an attempt to assert the evidence for the existence of God as immediate and therefore not an inference at all, for an inference provides evidence through mediation. Notions that he draws from the *Logik* in his critique of the ontological argument are the theory of judgment and the distinction between real and nominal definitions. The proponents of this argument in some cases take a nominal definition to be a real one, while in others they construe a negative judgment as an affirmative one.[51] This critique found expression in various lecture courses on metaphysics and theology which Brentano delivered in subsequent years. The rejection of the ontological argument and the defense of the teleological, cosmological, and psychological arguments (not to mention the less widely discussed one from motion) in favor of theism were firmly held positions in Brentanian metaphysics during his academic career. While it is indeed arguable that he later revised his the-

---

49   In a letter to Marty (1 February 1871) Brentano explains that he again used a large portion of the logic course in the winter semester 1870/71 for expounding on proofs for the existence of God. The interruption due to the Franco-Prussian War, however, put limitations on Brentano's lectures on both logic and metaphysics at that time. The letter to Marty (just cited) also indicates that he did not have the lecture notes fully worked out. Thus Marty, who was teaching on a secondary level in Schwyz and had asked to see the notes, could not obtain everything that would be expected from a lecture course on logic. In another letter to Marty (3 March 1871) Brentano states the three rules of syllogistic that we will discuss in Chapter Four. While it is very difficult to identify the various layers of revision in EL 80, it seems that most of the lecture material on mediated evidence had not been worked out until the last year or two of Brentano's time in Würzburg or perhaps even when he was in Vienna.
50   Brentano Th 22.
51   Brentano Th 22/80229. In particular he accuses Descartes of the error in the theory of judgment and Anselm of the error of confusion between the two kinds of definition.

istic arguments somewhat, he nonetheless continued to reject the ontological argument for the same reasons that he had formulated in 1870/71. Brentano's system is indeed deeply theistic in a sense that is comparable to the systems of Aristotle and Aquinas.[52] From this standpoint the existence of God is to be proved from the world as it is empirically given and is in no sense axiomatic. We can however say little more of this aspect of his system in connection with the *Logik*. Further elaborations in this regard must await a profounder study of his metaphysics.

The logic that Brentano developed is an alternative to the Aristotelian syllogistic. This deviation was due to his rejection of the Aristotelian view that all deduction is determined by the subject-predicate structure of the premises and conclusion of an inference. Brentano's non-Aristotelian logic, as well as the other aspects of his philosophical system, continued to evolve and became supplemented with aesthetics and ethics in his lectures at the University of Vienna.[53] This increasingly complex and extensive philosophical system was presented to students who came to be outstanding as philosophers and public figures, e.g. Thomas Masaryk, Alexius Meinong, Christian von Ehrenfels, Anton Marty, Edmund Husserl, and Kasimir Twardowski.[54] The focus of the present

---

[52] Here I can only say in passing that Brentano's does in fact have a system, more particularly a deeply theistic one, whatever the "general opinion" about his theories may be. This system, however, is not easily amenable to labels, certainly not to ones that are imported from alien systems, such as "immanent realism" (Albertazzi 2006). Brentano is often labeled a nominalist, and yet he emphatically rejects this label in application to his theory of universals. There will be more on this point below. Theism and perhaps dualism, albeit of peculiar characters, are certainly crucial building blocks to the Brentanian system. Another label that could well be applicable to this system is "foundationalism" (Kriegel 2018, 27, 141), provided that one exercises due caution.

[53] Brentano first presented his ethics in a lecture course in the winter semester 1875/76 and subsequently in every winter semester up to his retirement. This material has been partly published in Brentano 1952. Of course the short work in ethics that he himself published (Brentano 1889) is an important source for his views on ethical matters. As for his aesthetics, this was presented in a lecture course during the winter semester 1885/86 (Ps 78), which is partly published in Brentano 1959. In Brentano 1892a and 1892b we also encounter aesthetics and thus the doctrine of presentations in application to specific issues, which lie outside of the purview of the present study.

[54] For elaborations on Brentano's relation to Marty, see Rollinger 2009. The relation between Brentano and Meinong is examined in Rollinger 2005, which is revised and expanded in Rollinger 2008a, 157–188. The relation between Brentano and Husserl is examined in Rollinger 1999, 13–67 and again in Rollinger 2004. In Rollinger 2008b the relation between Brentano and Twardowski is discussed. In all of these cases considerations of more manuscript material may yield further revisions and expansions of the relevant discussions.

study, however, will not be the entire Brentanian system in his Vienna period, but rather the logic – the *Logik* as we are calling it – that he first presented in Würzburg and continued to develop for over a decade during his Vienna years, for this is indeed the logic that elaborates on his views on concepts and judgments, including inferences. At the same time, connections with other aspects of his system, especially with his psychology, cannot be avoided here.

There are yet other lecture notes besides the *Logik* which to a lesser extent provide source material in the present study. These are notes which were the basis for his Vienna lecture course entitled *Die elementare Logik und die in ihr nötigen Reformen*, as this was given in the winter semester 1884/85.[55] Though Brentano begins in these notes with his attempt to define logic and to defend its value against critics, just as he had done in his earlier lectures on logic, he proceeds to set out on a path that is very different, though in no way opposed to his previously adopted positions. Brentano's lengthy discussion of the continuum problem in these Vienna lectures presents serious problems for the interpreter, for it still remains to be examined how this discussion belongs in a lecture course on logic as he conceives of this discipline.[56] It is best left for a detailed treatment in another study that can do justice to such extensive and difficult manuscripts (which is indeed still unedited). However, the notes that Franz Hillebrand took from the lectures of 1884/85 on logic are accessible in German (in the fifth chapter) and in English (in the sixth chapter).

The various lecture notes on psychology which we find among Brentano's manuscripts will also be useful here, for it is clear that throughout Brentano's treatment of logic that psychology is the chief underlying theoretical discipline.[57] I shall not make any attempt here, however, to consider Brentano's later thought which especially involves the thesis that only real entities are conceivable.[58] In his early logic he was indeed willing to allow for such non-things

---

[55] This material is catalogued under the signature EL 72 in Brentano's manuscripts and still needs to be properly edited and published. Some of the notes contained therein (EL 72/12007–12020, 12027–12031) stem from a lecture that was delivered in the summer semester 1878/9, simply entitled *Logik*.

[56] Brentano's treatment of the continuum problem is one of the few instances in which he explicitly deals with Bernard Bolzano, who came to be a great influence among his students. As for Bolzano's extensive work in logic and epistemology, namely Bolzano 1837, Brentano has nothing to say about this in his lectures on logic.

[57] As we shall see, there are other theoretical disciplines, e.g. mathematics and metaphysics, which also belong to the foundation for logic as a practical discipline.

[58] The present volume is accordingly restricted to a consideration of writings from the nineteenth century.

as the contents of presentations and of judgments (already mentioned in the above quotation from Stumpf).

It will become apparent throughout the following discussions that Brentano is as much concerned with epistemological issues in his Modest Logic as he is concerned with rules of deduction and such matters to which logicians nowadays usually restrict their inquiries. Rules of deduction are indeed of interest to him, insofar as they can be of use in testing whether a judgment is evident or not. At the very outset of Brentano's logic the distinction between two types of "evidence" (hence two types of knowledge or cognition) is made focal, namely between immediate and mediated evidence. As he conceives of logic, it is in fact to be concerned with *both* of these. Brentano's *Logik* may indeed be regarded as an attempt to develop an *Essay concerning Human Understanding* suitable for his time. This is not to say, however, that the following will be exhaustive concerning Brentano's epistemology even in its early phase. Further considerations of theory of knowledge would best be left for a study of his metaphysics.[59] In view of the fact that he was indeed first and foremost a metaphysician, it is best that his ideas in that area should be treated in the framework in which he took the pains to elaborate on them.[60]

Brentano's ontology, however, will to some extent come into consideration in the present analysis. This is because the *Logik* has some bearing on ontological matters. In Brentano's early ontology certain entities are regarded as real and certain others as non-real. We shall see that the *Logik* cannot dispense with the talk of the non-real objects, particularly ones that have come to be known as states of affairs, as indicated in the above quotation from Stumpf. This will particularly come to light in his treatment of disjunctive judgments. Indeed, in view of the fact that objects of this kind were no longer allowed for in Brentano's later ontology,[61] the plan of publishing the *Logik* eventually became altogether unrealizable for him. Another respect in which ontological issues

---

[59] Notes from the lecture course on metaphysics (M 96) regarding epistemological matters, under the heading "transcendental philosophy," are published in Baumgartner 2003, 31–49.

[60] For a study of the second part of his metaphysics, i.e. ontology in the narrow sense, see Chrudzimski 2004. Contemporary philosophers are most likely to be interested in this part and not nearly as much in theology or cosmology. As for epistemology, this is indeed of some interest in contemporary philosophy, although Brentano's foundationalism will at present be objectionable to many, though not to all.

[61] Here I am referring to Brentano's rejection of the non-real altogether. This rejection apparently began early in the twentieth century, hence some years after his retirement from academic life. See also Brentano 2020 (forthcoming), which is a reliable edition of a manuscript that Brentano dictated in 1908.

arise in the *Logik* concerns the general theory of parts. Nonetheless, it must be born in mind that ontology for Brentano is followed by two additional parts of metaphysics, namely theology and cosmology. These domains of inquiry lie outside of the scope of the present study.

Be this as it may, the present study is by no means irrelevant to any other part of the philosophical system that Brentano was developing in his Würzburg and Vienna periods. His introductory remarks to his early work on Aristotle's psychology should be heeded in this regard:

> In the consideration of any philosophical system the theory of the powers of cognition deserves very special attention, not only because its subject matter belongs to the most sublime things with which the human mind can concern itself, and because many of the most important questions ... are intimately tied up with these researches, but also because in this part more than in others a secure standard of measure for the assessment of the whole is given.[62]

Accordingly the study of Brentano's views in the domain of the logic and epistemology should be of service in further studies of other aspects of his system of philosophy, for it provides the means whereby these can be assessed by his own standards. Here we are in effect dealing with the instrument that is applied throughout his philosophical investigations.

Moreover, Brentano held the view that education on the level of both secondary school and the university should primarily be concerned not with filling students with knowledge, but rather with making them "capable of learning and doing research."[63] As we shall see, logic is of great value to Brentano precisely because he thinks that it helps to develop such a capacity. The importance of logic from his standpoint can therefore hardly be called into question.[64]

The goal of the present study is to focus on the above-mentioned lecture notes on logic, the *Logik*, and thereby attempt to enter Brentano's intellectual

---

62   Brentano 1986, 1.
63   Brentano, EL 64/10859: *"fähig zum Lernen und Forschen."*
64   This naturally raises the question why he stopped offering courses in logic in the late 1880s. Did he do so because he changed his views on the goals of education? Another possibility is that he changed his conception of logic. Far more likely, however, is that he thought that he was giving the students the logic that they needed in his philosophical lectures on ethics, psychology, metaphysics, etc. As interesting as this question is, the present study is not primarily a contribution to the intellectual biography of Brentano. Consequently no further attempt will be made here to decide the matter.

world first and foremost during the last few decades of nineteenth century. Consequently the primary and supplementary literature that will be cited here will for the most part be restricted to considerations of this world of philosophy. However, in view of the impact of Husserl's critique of psychologism, for instance, it will be desirable at least briefly to discuss whether Brentano's early logic is among the logics that fall prey to this critique. The attempt here is accordingly to gain historical empathy (not necessarily sympathy or agreement) with Brentano on the topics at hand within the time-frame of his academic career. By no means am I dismissing the possibility of a less historically oriented study of Brentano's logic and epistemology. Though the reader may perceive a lack of consideration of certain secondary materials, this is only because those writings on Brentano which do not share in historical empathy are of little use here. The more such materials rely on poor editions and the more they involve anachronistic comparisons, the less relevant they are to the present endeavor.[65] If there is any future of such comparisons or if any of Brentano's ideas should prove themselves to be philosophically viable, however, the present study will hopefully prove to be of great use for further considerations of these ideas.

---

65 A very good example of a study of this kind is Albertazzi 2006. Even Rancurello 1968, which was a solid work of scholarship at least for its time and within its limited horizons, contains an annotated bibliography where the posthumously published editions of Brentano's manuscripts are regarded as respectable publications. Almost three decades ago it was true to say of Brentano that "it will take decades to overcome the 'creative' editing of the followers who hoped to convert a generation to their master's view." (Simons 1992, 5.) In the series of *Primary Sources in Phenomenology* (Springer), however, new and improved editions of Brentano's writings, along with English translations, are soon to appear.

CHAPTER 1

The Neo-Scholastic Background

As is commonly known, the scholastic philosophical tradition that had developed in the middle ages fell into disrepute in modern philosophy, especially through the rise of Cartesianism and its offshoots in continental Europe and through the rise empiricism in Britain. In these modern tendencies the old logic, by and large derived from Aristotle's *Organon*, became an object of contempt. In 1620 Francis Bacon published his *Novum Organum*, in which induction rather than syllogistic inference was to become the chief instrument in testing and gaining knowledge. Less than a century later, John Locke openly regarded deductive logic as little more than the art of wrangling which is in fact detrimental wherever the learned have applied it to their discourses.[1] Although Gottfried Wilhelm Leibniz had considerable respect for logic and wished to develop it as a calculus, his ideas about this were not influential until much later. His vision of logic is indeed the chief inspiration for the Great Logic that emerged in the nineteenth century. Nonetheless, by Brentano's time (and indeed long before that) a neo-scholastic logic had become well established, as it was of course taught primarily, though not exclusively, in Catholic seminaries. There was indeed hardly any other logic to teach for quite a long time.

As a young man preparing for the priesthood, Brentano was schooled in neo-scholastic logic. In Münster he took extensive notes from the lectures of the deeply orthodox neo-scholastic Clemens on logic (1859/60).[2] Though it is of great importance that Brentano had already come under the influence of Adolf Trendelenburg in Berlin, the influence of Clemens in Münster is perhaps just as important, if not more so. Brentano wrote to his aunt Kunigunde von Savigny (May 1, 1859), "Clemens is altogether a professor after my own heart [*Clemens ist ganz ein Professor nach meinem Herzen*]."[3] Under the guidance of Clemens, Brentano planned to write a dissertion on the late scholastic Francisco Suaréz, although he could not realize this plan because Clemens fell ill (and passed away in 1862, the year in which Brentano finished his dissertation on Aristotle).

---

1 *An Essay concerning Human Understanding*, III.x.6–13.
2 One notebook (FrSchr 41) consists of detailed notes, while another one consists of an abstract of the lecture course (*Auszug*) (FrSchr 42). Although Brentano never mentions Clemens in the *Logik*, we can have no doubt that the young seminarian studied Clemens' neo-scholastic logic very carefully.
3 Quotation in Russo 2014, 28, n. 51.

Nonetheless, Brentano was able to receive instruction from Clemens not only in logic, but in psychology as well. Here, however, we shall restrict our discussion to Clemens lectures on logic.[4]

The logic that Clemens taught is indeed the logic that is nowadays frequently called "term logic." Here I shall briefly indicate the essentials of this logic, primarily as they are accessible in Brentano's notes from the lectures of Clemens, but only as far as they have any bearing on Brentano's *Logik*. This means that the discussion will focus on the tasks of logic and the doctrines of concepts, judgments, and inference.[5]

1 The Tasks of Logic

According to Clemens, the tasks of logic are the following:

> If logic is exhautively to fulfill its purpose, it obviously may not leave unconsidered any of the essential moments which come into play in the striving for knowledge of the truth. 1. Above all, by means of elaboration of the fundamental conditions without which it is simply impossible for a human being to reach his goal, it must therefore elevate us to the standpoint from which alone we may promise ourselves secured success for our researches. 2. It must furthermore make us acquainted with the sources from which a human being draws his knowledge and demonstrate the justification thereof. 3. It must thoroughly investigate and illuminate

---

[4] I have also taken the liberty to draw upon other neo-scholastic works, particularly the logical part of Balmes 1847, which was translated into both German (Balmes 1852) and English (Balmes 1876) and widely used in Catholic circles in the second half of the nineteenth century. Although there is no copy of any work by Balmes in the remains of Brentano's private library, Balmes 1852 is cited extensively in Marty IIIa/19. This indicates that this textbook was in use in the Münster seminary that Brentano had attended while he was taking notes from Clemens' lectures. Without entering into a discussion of medieval logic (i.e. the school-logic in the proper sense) in comparison with the original Aristotelian logic, we only say here that there are noteworthy differences. The traditional logic to which Brentano was responding, however, was neo-scholastic, as this is discussed in the current chapter.

[5] These doctrines together make up elementary logic (drawing in principle from the first three works of the Aristotelian *Organon*: *Categories, Interpretatione, Prior Analytics*). Beyond this was a doctrine of method (drawing in principle on the fourth work of the Aristotelian *Organon: Posterior Analytics*), which corresponds to the logic of discovery in Brentano's terms, and finally dialectic (drawing in principle upon the remaining two works of the Aristotelian *Organon: Topics* and *Sophistical Refutations*). In the *Logik*, however, Brentano restricts himself to elementary logic.

that form of thought in which alone we possess the truth and fall prey to error, namely judgment. 4. Finally, it must shed light on error, its nature, its causes and types, as well as the means of avoiding it and refuting it. Accordingly logic for us falls into four parts which we shall treat under the following headings:
1. Of the standpoint that a person has to adopt in the examination of the truth.
2. Of the sources of knowledge or the criteria of the true.
3. Of judgment.
4. Of error.

[Soll nämlich die Logik ihren Zweck vollständig erfüllen, so darf sie offenbar keines der wesentlichen Momente, welche bei dem Streben nach Erkenntnis der Wahrheit in Betracht kommen, unberücksichtigt. Sie muss uns 1. daher vor allem durch Erörterung der Grundbedingungen, ohne welche es dem Menschen schlechterdings nicht möglich ist, sein Ziel zu erreichen, auf den richtigen Standpunkt erheben, von welchem aus allein wir uns einen sicheren Erfolg für unsere Forschungen versprechen dürfen. Sie muss uns ferner 2. mit den Quellen, woraus der Mensch seine Erkenntnis schöpft, bekannt machen und die Berechtigung derselben nachweisen. Sie muss 3. jene Form des Gedankens, in der allein wir die Wahrheit besitzen oder dem Irrtum unterliegen, nämlich das Urteil nach allen Seiten hin untersuchen und beleuchten. Sie muss uns endlich 4. über das Irrtum, seine Natur, seine Ursachen und Arten, sowie über das Mittel ihn zu vermeiden und zu widerlegen Aufschluss geben. Demgemäß zerfällt die Logik in vier Teile, die wir unter folgenden Überschriften behandeln wollen:
1. Von dem Standpunkte, den der Mensch bei der Erforschung der Wahrheit einzunehmen hat.
2. Von den Erkenntnisquellen oder die Kriterien des Wahren.
3. Vom Urteile.
4. Vom Irrtum.][6]

While all of these tasks are in some way acknowledged in Brentano's *Logik*, the one that stands out the most saliently is the third. Among the forms of thought, Clemens singles out only one as the bearer of truth and error, for he says, "Judgment is, generally speaking, the form of thought in which we possess the true

---

6 Brentano, FrSchr 41/101415f.

and succumb to error."[7] We shall see that for Brentano the examination of judgment has the same priority in logical inquiry. While many other logicians were saying that logic is concerned with thinking or inferring, the conception of logic as the doctrine of correct judgment was already within the grasp of the young Brentano due to his exposure to the lectures of Clemens.[8]

2 Concept

Nonetheless, Clemens does have something to say about concepts. Here we note the following:

> The concept is the thought-determination of a thing in accordance with the essential marks which distinguish it.
>
> In order for an object to be knowable, it must stand in a real relation with our mind either by means of sensation and sensory presentation or of spiritual feeling and intelligence.
>
> By means of abstraction and reflection, mere perceptions and intuitions are put into a fixed form of thought, for the sake of proper knowledge. The thought which is formed by special activity, which disregards external and accidental features and retains essential ones, is the *concept*.
>
> From this arise consequences: 1. The concept is the general form of determinate and clear thinking. 2. As an imitation that depends on the trustworthiness of perception it is deficient. 3. It is something general. 4. In the formation of the concept, free will is active.
>
> As a unity of thought the concept has 1. a content, 2. an extension ...

> [*Der Begriff ist die Denkbestimmung eines Dings nach den es unterscheidenden wesentlichen Merkmalen.*
>
> *Damit ein Gegenstand erkennbar sei, muss er mit unserem Geist in einer realen Beziehung stehen entweder mittels der Empfindung und sinnlicher Vorstellung, oder des geistigen Gefühls und der Intelligenz.*

---

7 Cf. Brentano, FrSchr 42/101551: "[*Das Urteil ist im Allgemeinen gesprochen die Denkform, worin wir das Wahre besitzen oder dem Irrtum verfallen.*]."
8 On this particular point Clemens is not necessarily representative of neo-scholasticism in which the conception of logic was variously formulated. As for the other topics to be covered in this chapter, however, he is very much in line with neo-scholastic teaching.

> Durch die Abstraktion und Reflexion werden die bloßen Wahrnehmungen und Anschauungen in eine feststehende Gedankenform gebracht, zum eigentlichen Wissen. Der so durch eigene Tätigkeit gebildete Gedanke, welcher von allen rein äußerlichen Merkmalen absieht und nur die wesentlichen festhält, ist der Begriff.
>
> Daraus ergeben sich Folgerungen: 1. Der Begriff ist die allgemeine Form des bestimmten klaren Denkens. 2. Als Nachbildung, die von der Treue der Perzeption abhängt, ist er mangelhaft. 3. Er ist etwas Allgemeines. 4. Bei der Bildung des Begriffs wirkt der freie Wille mit.
>
> Als Gedankeneinheit hat der Begriff 1. einen Inhalt, 2. Einen Umfang ...][9]

Most important for us here is the characterization of concepts as general (as distinct from sensation), as resulting from abstraction, and as consisting in each case of a content and an extension.

The distinction between content and extension, according to Clemens, is to be elucidated as follows:

> The former consists in the sum of the essential marks of the thing that is presented by it [the concept]; the second in its reference to the phenomena encompassed by it; for [although] the concept in itself is something abstract, it can refer to a single object and to a plurality of objects; in terms of both its content and its extension the concept can be taken apart and determined more closely; the taking-apart of the content of a concept in the form of a proposition is the *definition*, and of the extension the *division*.
>
> [Der erstere besteht in der Summe der wesentlichen Merkmale der durch ihn vorgestellten Dinge; der zweite in der Beziehung desselben auf die von ihm umfassten Erscheinungen; denn [wenn] der Begriff an sich etwas abstraktes ist, so kann er sich ebensowohl auf einen einzelnen Gegenstand, als auf eine Mehrheit von Gegenständen beziehen; sowohl seinem Inhalte als seinem Umfange nach kann nun der Begriff in seine Bestandteile auseinandergelgt und näher bestimmt werden; die Auseinanderlegung des Inhalts eines Begriffs in der Form des Satzes ist die Definition, und des Umgfanges die Einteilung.][10]

---

9   Brentano, FrSchr 42/101557.
10   Brentano, FrSchr 41/101489.

The content is thus all the marks that must be mentioned in a definition. If a triangle, for instance, is defined as a plane closed figure with three straight lines as its sides, these marks make up the content of the concept of a triangle. The extension of this concept, however, consists of all the triangles. When we classify triangles into right ones, acute ones, and obtuse ones, we are dividing the extension of this concept.

Clemens makes distinctions between concepts in terms of their content and their extension:

> In terms of content, simple and complex ones. The complex ones are absolute or relative; proper (proprium) or common; abstract or concrete. In terms of extension (or in terms of quantity) individual (singular – particular) or general (species-concepts and genus-concepts).
>
> [Dem Inhalt nach einfache und zusammengesetzte. Die zusammengesetzten sind absolut oder relativ; eigentümlich (proprium) oder gemeinsam; abstrakt oder konkret. Dem Umfange nach (oder der Quantität nach) individuelle (singuläre – partikuläre) oder allgemeine (Art- und Gattungsbegriffe).][11]

The distinction between content and extension as well as the divisions between concepts based on the one or the other will prove to be of importance for Brentano, though we shall see that he felt compelled to treat these matters somewhat differently from the way in which Clemens had done so.

Clemens also advocated the familiar view concerning the inverse relation of content and extension: the greater the content, the smaller the extension, and vice-versa.[12] The concept of an equilateral triangle contains more features (or mentions more features in its definition) than the concept of a triangle, while at the same time fewer objects fall under the concept of an equilateral triangle than under that of a triangle. This inverse relation was in fact hardly contested during the nineteenth century.

We find in Clemens lectures on logic a distinction between concepts in terms of their relation to each other. They can be either identical or different. When concepts differ from each other, we can further divide them into 1) opposite, 2) subordinate, and 3) separate ones. If they oppose each other, they are a) con-

---

11 Brentano, FrSchr 42/101557.
12 Brentano, FrSchr 41/101492f.

tradictory, b) contrary, or c) relative.[13] Again, we shall find similar divisions in Brentano's *Logik*, though not exactly the same.

As already indicated, Clemens regards the definition of a concept as the taking-apart (i.e. analysis) of its content, which consists of marks (*Merkmale*). He also adheres to the traditional distinction between real and nominal definitions. Insofar as the definition tells us what the essence of a real thing is, it is a real one. Otherwise it can just as well be a replacement for a certain name and therefore nominal. In either case it must meet the following requirements:

> ... the definition ... must be clearer than what is defined, for otherwise it would have no purpose. It must not explain the same thing by the same thing or, in other words, the definiendum may not occur in the definition; for if something is explained by the same thing that requires explanation, nothing is gained by the definition. It must furthermore explain everything that is contained in the definiendum and nothing more. That is to say, it must belong to the definiendum, as regards its entire extension, but only to it, and if it contained more, the definiendum could be confused with things different from it.

> [... die Definition ... muss klarer sein, als das, was definiert wird, denn sonst hätte sie keinen Zweck. Sie darf nicht dasselbe durch dasselbe erklären oder mit anderen Worten das Definierte darf nicht in der Definition nicht vorkommen; denn wenn etwas durch dasselbe erklärt wird, was die Erklärung bedarf, so ist mit der Definition nichts gewonnen; sie muss ferner alles, was in dem zu Definierendem enthalten ist, erklären und nichts weiter, d.h. sie muss dem, was definiert wird, seinem ganzen Umfange nach, aber auch nur ihm allein zukommen; enthielte sie nämlich nicht alles, so wären sie unvollständig, und enthielte sie mehr, so würde das zu Definierende mit anderen von ihm verschiedenen Dingen verwechselt werden können.][14]

A good deal of this neo-scholastic orientation regarding definitions as well as concepts in general re-appears in Brentano's *Logik*. However, with respect to the conception of judgment and inference, matters will prove to be quite different.

---

13 Brentano, FrSchr 41/101493 f.
14 Brentano, FrSchr 41/10198.

3 Judgment

Now let us consider the neo-scholastic view of judgments as we find this in the lectures of Clemens. Again he asserts that truth and error belong to judgment: "Only when we affirm or negate something concerning a matter, hence ascribe to or deny of a subject a predicate, i.e. make a judgment, is there truth or error in our thinking."[15] Here we see that the already observed characterization judgment as the bearer of truth, but Clemens adds that a judgment involves affirming or denying a predicate of a subject. Judgments accordingly manifest themselves in a subject-predicate form. This must especially be highlighted, for it is not only a point where he sides with a longstanding tradition in logic, but a point from which Brentano diverges, as will especially be seen in the fourth and seventh chapters of the present volume.

Clemens also says that judgments have quality, i.e. that they are either affirmative or negative.[16] He also divides judgments by quantity into universal and particular ones. We shall see that Brentano maintains that the notion of a quantity of a judgment can be fully accounted for in terms of quality.

The quality and quantity of judgments are crucial in the neo-scholastic theory of inference. Judgments are divided into four classes: affirmative and universal (A), negative and universal (E), affirmative and particular (I), and negative and particular (O). These may be exemplified by the following instances:

A: Every philosopher is mortal.
E: Every philosopher is not mortal. (Or: No philosopher is mortal.)
I: Some philosophers are mortal.
O: Some philosophers are not mortal.

We shall see that in his *Logik* Brentano also divides judgments into four classes, although he formulates them differently due to the fact that he does not make use of the concept of quantity.

The relations among the various types of propositions, provided that the terms are uniform, are classified in the following ways according to the neo-

---

15 Brentano, FrSchr 41/101483: *"Erst wenn wir etwas von einer Sache bejahen oder verneinen, also einem Subjekte ein Prädikat beilegen oder absprechen, d.h. ein Urteil fällen, ist Wahrheit oder Irrtum in unserem Denken vorhanden."*

16 The quality of a judgment is sometimes contrasted with the matter. If an affirmative judgment and a negative judgment have the same terms in common, these judgments may be said to have the same matter. We shall see that Brentano proposes to analyze judgments strictly in terms of quality and matter, without any need to determine the quantity of the judgment.

scholastic theory. If A is true, O is false, and vice versa. A and O accordingly stand in a "contradictory" relation to each other. E and I also stand in such a relation. A and E cannot both be true, but they can both be false. A and E accordingly stand in a "contrary" relation to each other. I and O, however, stand in a "subcontrary" relation to each other, because both can be true whereas both cannot be false. Finally, I follows from A, but not vice-versa, while O follows from E, but not vice-versa. A and I accordingly stand in a "subaltern" relation to each other, as do E and O. These relations (sometimes called "oppositions") have been represented for many centuries by means of the square of opposition:

In the *Logik* this view concerning the oppositions among judgments will be quite drastically altered. Although Brentano's interpretation of categorical judgments will allow him to view A and O as contradictory in relation to each other and likewise E and I in the same relation, the other oppositions will no longer remain.

4 Syllogism

The neo-scholastic theory of inference is primarily concerned with a single type of argument, known as the categorical syllogism,[17] consisting of two premises, each one of the above four types (A, E, I, O), and a conclusion, again of one of these four types. The conclusion consists of a minor term as the subject ("philosopher" in the above examples) and a major term ("mortal") as the predicate. While one of the premises includes the minor term in either the subject or predicate position and the major term in one of these positions, each premise also includes a middle term in one of these positions. If we take the above example of A as a conclusion, we can see that it follows from two other judgments of this type:

---

17   When we simply use the term "syllogism," it will be either the categorical syllogism or Brentano's revision thereof that is meant.

Major Premise:[18] Every human being is mortal.
Minor Premise: Every philosopher is a human being.
Conclusion: Every philosopher is mortal.

The major term is "mortal," the minor term "philosopher," the middle term "human being." While the conclusion of this argument follows from the premises, this is not the case for every syllogism. If, for instance, we retain the same premises and make the conclusion "Some philosophers are not mortal," this conclusion (O) obviously does not follow from the two premises (both A).

In Clemens' lectures on logic we find the following rules for determining whether the conclusion of a syllogism follows from its premises:

1. The simple syllogism contains three terms: the middle, the major, and the minor.
2. A term that is not distributed in the premises may not be distributed in the conclusion.[19]
3. The middle term must be distributed either once or twice.
4. The middle term must not enter into the conclusion.
5. Two affirmative premises cannot yield a negative conclusion.
6. The conclusion must be negative if one of the premises is negative and must be particular if one of the premises is particular.
7. From two negative premises no conclusion follows.
8. From two particular premises no conclusion follows.

[Terminus esto triplex: medius, majorque, minorque.
Latius hoc quam praemissae conclusio non vult.
Aut semel aut iterum medius generaliter esto.
Nequaquam medium capiat conclusio fas est.
Ambae affirmantes nequeunt generare negatem.
Pejorem. sequitur semper conclusio partem.
Utraque si praemissa neget, nil inde sequetur.
Nil sequitur geminis ex particularibus unquam.][20]

---

18 The major premise is the one that contains the major term, whereas the minor premise is the one that contains the minor term.
19 The notion of distribution is a rather difficult one in the history of logic. Here we may suffice it to say that the subject term of A, both terms of E, and the predicate term of I are distributed, whereas the predicate term of A, the subject term of I, and both terms of O are not distributed.
20 Brentano, FrSchr 41/101512. Brentano, FrSchr 42/101560. The rules are loosely translated into English here for the sake of elaboration.

If we consider the syllogism whereby the conclusion "Some philosophers are not mortal" is drawn from the two premises "Every philosopher is a human being" and "Every human being is mortal," we see at once that it violates the fifth rule listed above. Since the premises are both affirmative and the conclusion is negative, the conclusion does not follow from the premises.

The syllogisms are also classified by mood and figure. The mood is determined by the quantity and quality of the propositions. If the conclusion "All philosophers are mortal" is drawn from the premises "All philosophers are human beings" and "All human beings are mortal," the resulting syllogism has the mood AAA. That is to say, the premises and the conclusion are universal affirmatives. The figure is determined by the positions of the major, minor, and middle terms in the premises (while by definition the minor term is always the subject, the major term always the predicate of the conclusion). If we represent the major term with S, the minor term with P, and the middle term with M, we see that the following four figures are possible (the conclusion always being S is P):

1) M is P.
   S is M.
   ―――――
   S is P.

2) P is M.
   S is M.
   ―――――
   S is P.

3) M is P.
   M is S.
   ―――――
   S is P.

4) P is M.
   M is S.
   ―――――
   S is P.[21]

The above-considered argument, whose mood has been determined as AAA, belongs to the first figure. Any syllogism in the first figure, consisting of the mood AAA, is called "Barbara" for the sake of memorization. Other proper names were given to other syllogistic forms. We shall consider these further

―――――――――

21   Brentano, FrSchr 42/101560.

when we discuss Brentano's critique of neo-scholastic logic. Suffice it to say that neo-scholastic logic continued along Aristotelian lines in allowing for inferences in the first three moods only.

5   Concluding Remarks

Clemens' logic is for the most part representative of neo-scholastic logic. Brentano's alternative to this logic is, as we shall see, very different in its views on judgments and syllogism. This is mainly because Clemens adheres to the traditional view that judgments are essentially predications, whereas Brentano arrived at the characterization of them as acts of acceptance or rejection, to be formulated in existential sentences, and made this the foundation for an alternative syllogistc, as this will be elaborated on in the fourth and seventh chapters of the present volume. Be that as it may, it does seem that Brentano at least took from Clemens his focus on judgments, as opposed to other acts of mind, as the guiding thread of logical inquiry.

CHAPTER 2

Definition and Value of Logic

In the posthumously published editions of Brentano's writings we find one that is meant to represent his logic. This volume bears the title *Die Lehre vom richtigen Urteil*.[1] It is partly, but not entirely based on the manuscripts that we have designated as the *Logik*, from which Brentano lectured in Würzburg and probably also in Vienna. The analysis that we shall pursue is based on these manuscripts and not on the just-mentioned published edition, for this volume in fact contains passages from later manuscripts and even extensive insertions from the editor's own hand. As is usually the case with posthumously published editions of Brentano's writings, it is meant to accommodate his philosophy as it was developed just before his death. Attention to his earlier philosophy, however, brings out themes which help us better to understand the motives behind such later developments and also relations between Brentano and his students, while at the same time avoiding anachronism. The most salient case of a theme that characterizes his early philosophy is that of the content of judgment, which will become prominent in the fourth chapter of the present analysis. We have already seen that Stumpf regards this as a topic of the utmost importance, whereas the editor of Brentano's posthumously published logic deliberately suppresses all references to it.[2] The question as to how Brentano could conceive of logic in accordance with his later philosophy must be left aside, as we now analyze the logic that he actually taught in his years of academic employment.

1 The Relevant Manuscripts

There is first and foremost one set of manuscripts that we shall examine here. This consists of the archival material designated under the signature EL 80. The manuscript pages were numbered posthumously from 12955 to 13492. There are accordingly in principle 538 pages of this particular set of manuscripts, although we should take such calculations with a grain of salt. Many of the

---

1 Brentano 1956. No English translation of this volume is available.
2 See the editor's remark in Brentano 1956, 311 n. 21.

pages belong to folded sheets. In a good number of these cases a sheet is folded in the middle, creating two pages on the outside and two on the inside, though the two on the inside were often posthumously numbered as a single page. Moreover, many of the pages are duplicates, as Brentano apparently rewrote some of the earlier notes without discarding the older pages. While some of these notes were written very early, perhaps 1869 or 1870, if not earlier, we find a reference to Wilhelm Windelband that can be no earlier than 1884.[3] As we have already seen, Brentano at some point planned to publish the *Logik*. This means that some of his later insertions could be explained in light of this fact. Due to the bulk of the material, it is indeed unlikely that he ever managed to use all of it in a single semester.

Moreover, some of the earlier and even later written pages of the *Logik* are to be found under other signatures, most notably EL 75 and EL 81. In my analysis I shall sometimes utilize this material as well and sometimes notes from students. Occasionally I shall stray somewhat from the *Logik* a bit into additional manuscript material, but in all cases my analysis will be based on what Brentano actually said or what his students wrote down from his lectures and not on what a later editor constructed as Brentano's "doctrine of correct judgment."

2   Logic as the Art of Judging

As already indicated, the *Logik* is meant to be a Modest Logic. Traditionally a logic of this kind has been characterized as an instrument. There are, however, various possibilities of conceiving of logic as an instrument or art. Brentano finds that some define this art too broadly and others define it too narrowly.[4] In Port Royal logic, for instance, it is called "the art of thinking" (*l'art de penser*), whereas many during the nineteenth century opted for characterizing it as the art of inferring, reasoning, and the like. This characterization is represented by John Stuart Mill's *System of Logic*, which appeared in many editions after its original publication (1843) and was translated twice into German. From Brentano's standpoint, we may not characterize logic as the art of thinking or the art of reasoning, but rather we must characterize it as the art (and not the science) of judging. This art, according to him, is of great value even for people who have a natural talent or developed skill for judging correctly, for all of us

---

3   EL 80/13006. See p. 114 below.
4   Brentano, EL 80/12956.

DEFINITION AND VALUE OF LOGIC

are at times prone to error. In this chapter we shall look more closely at this conception and evaluation of logic.

From the outset we must get clear about Brentano's acceptance of Aristotelian foundationalism.[5] On this view, there cannot even be any sort of knowledge by inference unless there is non-inferential or, as he usually says, immediate knowledge (*unmittelbare Erkenntnis*). "It is impossible," Brentano argues in his lectures on practical philosophy,

> to prove every assertion that is set forth in science, for every proof rests on certain presuppositions from which the proof is made. If one proves them, one does this in turn from certain presuppositions. Here one cannot go on into infinity. ... Science must therefore start from what is unproved. It must make certain assumptions immediate.
>
> [Es ist unmöglich, jede Behauptung, die in der Wissenschaft aufgestellt wird, zu beweisen, denn jeder Beweis ruht auf gewissen Voraussetzungen, aus denen bewiesen wird. Beweist man sie, so tut man dies wieder aus gewissen Voraussetzungen. Dabei kann man nicht ins Unendliche gehen ... Die Wissenschaft muss also von Unbewiesenem ausgehen. Sie muss gewisse Annahmen unmittelbar machen.].[6]

Moreover, assumptions on Brentano's view can be immediately evident in two ways: "Both single facts of experience and general propositions can be immdiately evident."[7] While we can know that we are thinking, which is a fact of experience, we can also know that it is impossible for a judgment to be both true and false. Inner perception (*innere Wahrnehmung*) and the grasp of axioms are thus the two ways in which we can have knowledge that requires no proof.

With this view of knowledge in mind, let us now cite the introduction to the *Logik* as Brentano delivered it before his students in 1875:

> Our task is the exposition of the rules of logic. It will above all be necessary to make clear the concept and its place in relation to other ones.
>
> Logic is defined diversely by different people. Some say that it is the art of thinking, while others call it the art of inferring, of reasoning in the broadest sense.

---

5   Aristotle, *Posterior Analytics*, 72 b 1–15.
6   Brentano, Y 4/14 f.
7   Brentano, Y 4/16: "*Sowohl einzelne Tatsachen der Erfahrung als auch allgemeine Sätze können unmittelbar einleuchtend sein.*" The tendency that some have nowadays to think of assumptions simply as beliefs utterly devoid of evidence is a corruption.

However, Hegel defines: Logic is the science of the pure Idea, the scientific development of the pure concepts of reason, which are the foundation of all thought and being. It is, on his view, the exposition of the truth, as it is by itself without any encasement, or as he also says, the exposition of God, as he is in his eternal essence prior to the creation of the world and of a finite mind. It is thus of course a realm of schadows, but these shadows are, on the other hand, the simple essences which are freed of all material and in whose diamond net the entire universe is built.

These are certainly very elevated determinations. Nonetheless, you will escuse [me] if I do not take them into further consideration.

Aside from erroneous philosophical views that reveal themselves in his definition, Hegel changes the entire concept of logic by transferring the name to metaphysical investigations.

It would be altogether unjustifiably arbitrary if we follow his example in this and were not rather to understand by logic what one has designated with the name from time immemorial. This, however, is a practical discipline, as this reveals itself also in the two other definitions that I have cited.

They define logic as an art. One of them says that it is the art of thinking, the other the art of inferring.

Maintaining in a certain way the middle ground between both designations, I would like [to call it the art of judging].

[1. Unsere Aufgabe ist die Darstellung der Regeln der Logik. Es wird vor allem nötig sein, den Begriff dieser Disziplin und ihre Stellung zu anderen klar zu machen.

2. Die Logik wird von Verschiedenen verschieden definiert. Einige sagen, sie sei die Kunst des Denkens, andere nennen sie die Kunst des Schließens, der Folgerung im weitesten Sinne. Hegel aber definiert: Die Logik sei die Wissenschaft von der reinen Idee, die wissenschaftliche Entwicklung der reinen Vernunftbegriffe, die allem Denken und Sein zugrunde liegen. Sie ist nach ihm die Darstellung der Wahrheit, wie sie ohne Hülle für sich ist, oder, wie er auch sagt, die Darstellung Gottes, wie er in seinem ewigen Wesen vor Erschaffung der Welt und eines endlichen Geistes ist. So ist sie allerdings ein Reich der Schatten; aber diese Schatten sind andererseits die einfachen von aller Materiatur befreiten Wesenheiten, in deren diamantenes Netz das ganze Universum hineingebaut ist.

Das sind gewiss sehr erhabene Bestimmungen. Dennoch werden Sie entschuldigen, wenn ich nicht weiter auf sie Rücksicht nehme.

> Abgesehen von irrigen philosophischen Anschauungen, welche sich in seiner Definition zu erkennen geben, verschiebt Hegel den ganzen Begriff der Logik, indem er den Namen auf metaphysische Untersuchungen überträgt.
>
> Es wäre eine ganz ungerechtfertigte Willkür, wenn wir hierin seinem Beispiele folgen, und nicht vielmehr das unter Logik verstehen wollen, was man von Alters her allgemein mit dem Namen bezeichnet hat. Das aber ist eine praktische Disziplin, wie dies auch in den beiden anderen Definitionen, die ich anführte, sich zu erkennen gibt.
>
> Sie definieren die Logik als Kunst. Die eine sagt, sie sei die Kunst des Denkens, die andere die Kunst des Schließens.
>
> Ich möchte sie lieber, zwischen beiden Bezeichnungen, in gewisser Weise die Mitte [haltend, die Kunst des Urteilens nennen].][8]

Let us now look at why Brentano chooses this middle ground in his definition of logic.

Logic is not the art of inferring, Brentano argues, because the knowledge that requires no proof should be included within the scope of logic.[9] More particularly, he maintains that immediately evident judgments are of concern to the logician because there are cases where certain people believe that they have immediate evidence and yet they do not. There are also cases where such knowledge is available and yet some people are convinced by sophistry that it is not. In his treatment of sophistry in the domain of politics, for example, Brentano identifies one of the main classes of sophisms as pertaining to immediate cognition.[10]

Among the instances where we believe that we have immediate evidence is of course outer perception. While we ordinarily think that we have access

---

8   Brentano EL 81/13599–13600. The insertion in square brackets at the end of the quotation is taken from Brentano EL 80/12957.
9   Brentano, EL 80/12957. On this point Brentano seems to be reacting to John Stuart Mill, who maintains that questions concerning "the original data, or the ultimate premises of our knowledge" "are partly not a subject of science at all, partly that of a different science [i.e. one other than logic]." The science which turns out to be concerned with them, as when the question arises whether an instance of knowledge is inferred (perhaps too rapidly to be noticed, at least under normal conditions) or not, is a "perfectly distinct department of science, to which the name metaphysics more particularly belongs" (*A System of Logic*, Introduction, § 4). While non-inferential knowledge for Brentano can certainly belong to a science other than logic, e.g. to metaphysics and certainly to psychology, this in no way prevents him from considering it in the art of judging.
10 Brentano, EL 82/14005.

to an external world consisting of things with sensory properties such as colors and sounds, the external world that we come to know through science is actually very different. It is an instinct, according to Brentano, to accept whatever we present. In particular, we accept what we present through our senses. We instinctively accept the colored things we see, for instance, but it turns out that our sensations of color are caused by light waves. The colors do not really exist in the external world. They exist phenomenally or "in the mind." We also instinctively accept what memory presents to us. Obviously we do not have immediate access to the past, for the past is gone forever. Nor is memory a case of mediated knowledge, on Brentano's view, for in memory we do not know the past by means of inference from immediately evident judgments.[11]

As regards cases where we believe that we know something to be true as if it were an axiom, Brentano tells us that the history of philosophy offers a number of these. One of these is the belief that like causes like. Due to this belief, which indeed prevailed for quite a long time, the interaction between mind and body posed a problem, for such interaction was unacceptable unless one was willing to concede that two things very different from each other could stand in a causal relation to each other. Yet, from the empiricists, such as Hume and Mill, this belief was subject to doubt. We are also familiar with cases in the history of philosophy such as the denial of the law of non-contradiction. Hegel's system, as Brentano understands it, is based on such a denial. However much philosophers may confuse and perplex us, we nonetheless have the ability to know that a judgment cannot be true and false at the same time and in the same respect.

Among the causes of delusion with respect to immediately evident judgments Brentano lists the following:

---

11   Cf. Marty B7/24990: "Every outer perception and every memory deceives us. All is not quite correct. Space is not, time is not, but rather something analogous. We leave this for metaphysics. [*Jede äußere Wahrnehmung und jedes Gedächtnis belügt uns. Alles ist nicht ganz richtig. Der Raum ist nicht, die Zeit ist nicht, sondern etwas Analoges. Das überlassen wir der Metaphysik.*]" While Anton Marty was faithful to Brentano's teachings during the nineteenth century, Alexius Meinong stands out among Brentano's students as one who challenged the master's epistemological assessment of memory by attributing "immediate evidence of surmise" (*unmittelbare Vermutungsevidenz*) to the faculty under consideration (Meinong 1886). In a letter (15 February 1886) to Meinong (Meinong 1965, 23), Brentano expressed extreme disapproval of Meinong's theory of memory (cf. Brentano 1970: 251). The relation between Brentano and Meinong is discussed at length in Rollinger 2005 and more extensively in Rollinger 2008a, 157–188.

1. Instinct (original inclination to assent to every presentation).
2. Habit (*post hoc ergo propter hoc*).
3. Influence of inclinations.
4. Overlooking differences. Lack of sharpness. Confusion ...
5. Overestimatination and underestimation of differing easiness of distinguishing (comparing). (Noticeability of distinction).
6. Unattentiveness or division of attention (narrowness of consciousness).
7. Other causes that create a weakened state of mind: exhaustion, [emotional] affects, etc.
8. Properly to be contained in the foregoing items: deceptions of the senses in the case of abnormal relations; deceptions of the imagination; deceptions of memory (forgetting counter-examples, *petitio principii*, uncommonly easy retention); deceptions through language: homonymy, synonymy, amphiboly, etc., scholastic distinction, meaninglessness; deceptions of relations of thoughts to objects (confusing the distinctions *re* and *ratione*), *sophisma accidentis*.

[1. Instinkt (ursprüngliche Neigung jeder Vorstellung zuzustimmen).
2. Gewohnheit (post hoc ergo propter hoc).
3. Einfluss der Neigungen.
4. Übersehen kleiner Differenzen. Mangel an Schärfe. Konfusion ...
5. Überschätzung und Unterschätzung bei verschiedener Leichtigkeit der Unterscheidung (Vergleichung) (Merklichkeit des Unterschieds).
6. Unaufmerksamkeit oder Zerteilung der Aufmerksamkeit (Enge des Bewusstseins)
7. Andere Gründe, welche einen geschwächten Geisteszustand schaffen: Ermüdung, Affekte &c.
8. Eigentlich in den vorigen enthalten, doch besonders zu nennen: Täuschungen der Sinne bei anormalen Verhältnissen; Täuschungen der Phantasie; Täuschungen des Gedächtnisses (Vergessen der Gegenfälle, petitio principii, ungleich leichtes Behalten); Täuschungen durch die Sprache (Verhältnis zum Gedanken): Homonymie, Synonymie, Amphibolie &c., Scholastische Distinktion, Sinnlosigkeit; Täuschungen der Verhältnisse der Gedanken zu den Gegenständen (Verwechslung der Unterschiede re und ratione), Sophisma accidentis.].[12]

---

12 Brentano, EL 82/14007.

Of course this list pertains to mediated evidence as well, but here it is important for us to see that for Brentano these various deceptions lead us to accept principles that are not really principles and to reject ones that are really so. Some of these causes of deception have to do with language, which will be discussed further below.

In view of the fact that it is possible to go astray in our immediate evidence as well as the evidence which we obtain by means of inference, Brentano maintains that there is a need for logic to elaborate on both kinds of evidence. As a result, he defines logic as the art of knowledge or the art of correct judgment.[13] Logic is accordingly for him a practical discipline that helps us in our endeavor to arrive at knowledge. For this reason it cannot, at least as Brentano conceives of it, be distinguished from epistemology. While this concept of logic certainly diverges from the mainstream in contemporary logic, it is all the more contrary to contemporary philosophy to regard logic as a discipline that in any way involves psychology. We shall return to this point below.

Logic cannot be defined as the art of thinking,[14] Brentano argues, because thinking can be construed so broadly that it includes not only judgments (*Urteile*), but also presentations (*Vorstellungen*).[15] Though he maintains that judgments in all cases have a foundation in presentations and are to this extent of interest to logic, the art of presentation is in fact aesthetics, which he takes to be clearly a discipline outside of the scope of logic.

---

13   In an earlier manuscript we find Brentano speaking of assent (*Zustimmung*) rather than judgment (EL 75/12921[21]). In yet another old manuscript Brentano makes a distinction between affirmation or acceptance (*Anerkennung*) and assent (*Zustimmung*): "The object is accepted, whereas we assent to the content of the judgment [*Der Gegenstand wird anerkannt, dem Inhalt des Urteils zugestimmt*]" (EL 75/12921[35]). His terminology in such manuscripts may suggest that he was influenced by Cardinal Henry Newman. Though the latter's *Grammar of Assent* was first published in 1870, the notion of assent had already been thematized in his *Apologia Pro Vita Sua*, first published in 1864. While Brentano was a priest and indeed concerned with apologetics, it was only natural for him to be interested in the work of Newman. Moreover, even after he ceased his practice as a clergyman, he made a point to attend lectures by Newman when he visited England (see Stumpf 1872).

14   In Brentano EL 75/12921(78) Thomas Aquinas is mentioned in addition to Arnauld as an advocate of the conception of logic as the art of thinking.

15   Brentano, EL 80/12958. The term *Vorstellung* is here translated as "presentation," since this allows for a corresponding verb for *Vorstellen*. At the same time, it should be kept in mind that the term *Vorstellung* came into philosophical usage as a translation of the English term "idea" and its Latin and French cognates. Accordingly Brentano's theory of presentations is comparable to the treatment of ideas in *Logic or the Art of Thinking* discussed above.

3 Logic, Psychology, and Philosophy

The epistemological distinction between immediate and inferential knowledge is accordingly crucial to understanding how Brentano conceives of the tasks of logic. While his treatment of logic in connection with epistemology already sets him apart from many contemporary logicians, his epistemology is also very different from what we find in the work of some contemporary epistemologists. Like Aristotle, Descartes, and indeed the vast majority of philosophers up to his own time, Brentano is a thorough-going foundationalist. That is to say, our immediate knowledge – which for Brentano includes two kinds: inner perception and the grasp of axioms[16] – is conceived of in Brentano's epistemology as the foundation for all other knowledge, in the sense that any other knowledge must be derived by inference from immediate knowledge. It is difficult to know what he would say about the rejection of foundationalist epistemology, for during his day there was hardly anything else around (unless we count the Hegelian system, which he considered to be most reprehensible, as exemplifying non-foundationalist epistemology).[17]

---

16 While this epistemology of immediacy may be deemed as "classical," it must be acknowledged that it was by no means universally accepted by Brentano's contemporaries. Here we may compare it with two of the most prominent epistemologically oriented logics in the nineteenth century. In Mill's *System of Logic* (v.iii.§1.) there are only two views of immediate knowledge that are considered: "The one recognizes no ultimate premises but the facts of our subjective consciousness; our sensations, emotions, intellectual states of mind, and volitions ... The opposite school hold that there are other existences, suggested indeed to our minds by these subjective phenomena, but not inferrable from them, by any process either of deduction or of induction; which, however, we must, by the constitution of our mental nature, recognize as realities; and realities, too, of a higher order than the phenomena of our consciousness, being the efficient causes and necessary substrata of all Phenomena." In Ueberweg's *System of Logic* (§1), by contrast, we find the passage: "The immediate act of knowing is partly immediate or inner or outer perception, partly mediated or thinking." For Brentano there is an immediate act of knowing that is not inner or outer perception (contrary to Ueberweg) and does not as such recognize realities as efficient causes or necessary substrata of all phenomena (contrary to Mill). We may, for instance, know that something cannot be and not-be at the same time and in the same respect, though this is neither perception nor the recognition of realities of the kind mentioned by Mill.

17 Another exception may be Charles Sanders Peirce, whose life (1839–1914) more or less ran parallel to Brentano's. Though they never refer to each other, they were both familiar with much of the same literature, but stood in opposition in many ways which would be worthy of an interesting comparative study. Such a study, however, lies far beyond the purview of the present volume.

Insofar as Brentano saw his epistemological orientation in contrast with others, these would be of two kinds: 1) skepticism (the rejection of genuine knowledge), and 2) dogmatism (acceptance of various tenants without actually knowing them). While Hume is the most prominent skeptic of modern philosophy, Brentano sees the adherence to common sense, as we find this in the philosophy of Thomas Reid, to be a good representative of dogmatism. The Kantian synthetic *a priori* judgments, as presented in the *Kritik der reinen Vernunft*, are also dogmatic in character, according to Brentano. This is not to say that he is skeptical about such assertions as the law of causality (that every event is caused), but rather that they are not in any way supported by characterizing them as synthetic *a priori* or indeed by any of the stratagems employed by Kant and his followers.[18] In his *Logik* Brentano attempts to formulate the alternative epistemological position that the only generalities which are knowable besides analytic judgments are to be tested either by the rules of deduction or induction.

Granted that logic is an art that provides us with such rules, the question arises whether logic is also a science. Brentano was aware that such an outstanding logician of the nineteenth century as Richard Whately had characterized logic "as the Science, and also the Art, of reasoning."[19] Although Brentano does not dismiss the possibility of a discipline as being both an art and a science, he does not allow for it in the case of logic. As a practical discipline, logic is unified by its goal and not by the affinity of its truths. A theoretical discipline is unified in the latter way. Physics, for instance, is a theoretical discipline because all of its truths pertain to the physical. Brentano's characterization of a practical discipline, by contrast, allows for a large variety of theoretical disciplines to be used for the sake of its goal. A reliance on a variety of theoretical disciplines is to be found in arts such as that of building and that of medicine. It is obvious from Brentano's perspective that logic as the art of correct judgment will have to involve psychology. This is simply due the fact that judging is in fact a psychical act. Yet, logic also involves considerations from linguistics and mathematics, again insofar as they are applied to the end of instructing us in our pursuit for knowledge.[20]

---

18 See p. 130 below.
19 Whately 1855, 1.
20 Contrary to Mill's statement that the determination of what characterizes a psychical act as "one of the most intricate of metaphysical problems" (*System of Logic*, I.v.1), this is for Brentano in essence a psychological problem and, as we shall see, one that lies at the very heart of logic. Here it should be added that logic for Brentano still remains of great significance for metaphysics as it does for all areas of philosophical inquiry, for he remains in

It is nowadays almost a cliché to indicate a lack of precision or certainty of an endeavor by saying that it is an art and not a science. Though this may well be true in certain cases, Brentano makes it clear that he does not at all mean this in his characterization of an art and not a science. He only means that logic is not unified by an intrinsic affinity of its truths, as psychology (at least on his view) and presumably any of the natural sciences are, but rather by a goal.[21]

The fact that logic involves psychology, Brentano maintains, is what makes logic a philosophical science. This is because he defines philosophy precisely as the whole range of disciplines which rely on concepts derived from inner perception. Psychology can indeed be defined as the science which deals in such concepts. The other theoretical discipline which is included in philosophy, according to Brentano, is metaphysics, which involves both concepts of outer perception and ones of inner perception. In addition, he identifies two other practical disciplines besides logic, namely aesthetics or the art of presentation and ethics or the art of love and hate. Other branches of philosophy are extensions of these, as politics, for instance, is an extension of ethics.

In a single semester Brentano had to limit himself to a treatment of the elementary part of logic. This discipline can indeed be understood in a sense in which it is concerned only with how the individual is to obtain knowledge, but it is also possible to develop a communicative logic which is concerned with didactics, dialectic, and rhetoric.[22] The *Logik*, however, is restricted to individual logic. There is yet another sense in which it is restricted. What Brentano ultimately aimed at in this lecture course was to provide his students with a means of testing (*Prüfung*) whether certain judgments are genuine instances of knowledge. Beyond this logic of testing, however, Brentano – in accordance with tradition and contemporaneous logics – is willing to allow for a logic of discovery (*Entdeckung*), although there is no text among his writings in which he offers a logic of the latter kind.

The following passage from his above-mentioned lectures on logic from 1884/85 elaborates on the reasons for making the logic of testing the initial part of logic and therefore prior to the logic of discovery:

---

the Aristotelian tradition to the extent that he regards logic as an "instrument." Moreover, Brentano does maintain that metaphysics is one of the theoretical sciences from which logic draws, as this is already evident in the Aristotelian *Organon* which begins with the *Categories*, a work in metaphysics. See below, p. 220.

21   Carl Stumpf, by contrast, speaks of logic as a "practical science" (Q 14). The (very difficult to translate) term (*Kunstlehre*) is also used by him in reference to logic. Though this term was frequently used in the logical literature of the second half of the nineteenth century, Brentano chooses instead to simply speak of logic as an art (*Kunst*).

22   Brentano, EL80/12963. Cf. pp. 72 f. below.

The task of testing the prior one (as regards time):

1. At first glance someone might perhaps think that the reversed order is the more reasonable and natural one, since testing of an already given item of knowledge presupposes discovery.

However, this is not (generally) correct, since many items of knowledge are rather given to us without having to be discovered previously or at least discovered by us.

This is true of immediately evident truths that offer themselves, without being sought after, and of what others teach us.

Hence, the argument gets reversed: The part that concerns the testing of given items of knowledge appears naturally as the earlier one because we must first adopt given items of knowledge and appropriate them by testing in order then perhaps to set out towards discoveries.

a) For us and our time (and any time where there was logic, for [it] arose late) clearly; b) But also [it was] necessary for the first thinkers that certain items of knowledge had to be given to them in order for them to set out towards the discovery of other ones.

And the easier [task]:

2. The task of judging given items of knowledge, however, is at the same time the easier one. This is accepted so much that it goes without saying.

The more general [task]:

3. Furthermore, [it is] the more general [task]. We are often in a position to test. a) Not everyone has to make new discoveries. b) And whoever [makes discoveries] in fact learns from others. "The living [are] ruled more and more by the dead." c) [This is so,] completely leaving aside from the *immediate* items of knowledge. d) And if someone discovered more, he would nonetheless often be in the position of judging given items of knowledge because this task is included in that one [of discovery].

4. It is thus also clear how the task of the tester is not only the more general one, but also the *simpler* one.

5. And the rules for what he must otherwise do are altogether dependent on the rules that serve testing and cannot be understood without them. If someone does not know what belongs to an item of knowledge, how is he to grasp what he must do in order to obtain what belongs to it?

Please note: For similar reasons, also in the theory of discovery itself one will first treat the discovery of the proof of a given truth, [and] only only then the finding of the truth, [and] only then of the formulation of the questions.

6. The first part of logic in the narrower sense is called "logic" in the narrowest sense.

[Die Aufgabe der Prüfung die frühere (der Zeit nach):
1. Auf den ersten Blick könnte vielleicht einer meinen, dass die umgekehrte Ordnung die vernünftigere und natürlichere sei, da die Prüfung einer bereits gegebenen Erkenntnis ihre Entdeckung voraussetze.

Allein dies ist nicht (allgemein) richtig, da vielmehr viele Erkenntnisse, ohne dass sie zuvor endeckt oder wenigstens von uns entdeckt werden müssten, uns gegeben sind.

Dies gilt von unmittelbar einleuchtenden Wahrheiten, die ungesucht sich uns darbieten, und von dem, was andere uns lehren.

So verkehrt sich das Argument in sein Gegenteil: Der Teil, der von der Prüfung gegebener Erkenntnisse handelt, erscheint naturgemäß als der frühere, weil wir zunächst gegebene Erkenntnisse aufnehmen und (prüfend uns aneignen) müssen, um dann vielleicht auf Entdeckungen auszugehen.

a) Für uns und unsere Zeit (und alle Zeit, wo es Logik gab; denn spät entstanden) klar. b) Aber auch bei den ersten Denkern nötig, dass ihnen gewisse Erkenntnisse gegeben sein mussten, um auf die Entdeckung anderer auszugehen.

Und die leichtere [Aufgabe]:
2. Die Aufgabe, gegebene Erkenntnis zu beurteilen, ist aber zugleich auch die leichtere. Dies so sehr anerkannt, dass es keiner Worte bedarf.

Die allgemeinere [Aufgabe]:
3. Ferner [ist es] die allgemeinere [Aufgabe]. Wir sind öfter in der Lage zu prüfen. a) Nicht jeder hat neue Entdeckungen zu machen. b) Und wer [sie macht], lernt doch mehr von den anderen. "Die Lebenden [sind] mehr und mehr von den Toten beherrscht." c) Von den unmittelbaren Erkenntnissen ganz abgesehen. d) Und wenn einer mehr entdeckt, so würde er dennoch öfter in der Lage sein, gegebene Erkenntnis zu beurteilen, weil diese Aufgabe in jener eingeschlossen liegt.

Die einfachere [Aufgabe]:
4. Darum ist es auch klar, wie die Aufgabe des Prüfenden nicht bloß die allgemeinere, sondern auch die einfachere ist. Was der Prüfende tut, muss der Forschende alles auch tun und noch mehr. Denn wer z.B. einen Beweis entdeckt, muss ihn als Beweis erkennen, aber noch mehr.

Die unabhängigere [Aufgabe]:
5. Und die Regeln für das, was er sonst tun muss, sind durchaus von den Regeln, welche der Prüfung dienen, abhängig und können ohne sie nicht verstanden werden. Wenn einer nicht weiß, was zu einer Erkenntnis gehört, wie soll er wissen, was er tun muss, um das zu ihr Gehörige zu erlangen?

Notabene: Aus ähnlichem Grund wird man auch in der Lehre von der Entdeckung selbst, zuerst von der Entdeckung des Beweises einer gegebenen Wahrheit, denn erst von dem Aufsuchen der Wahrheit, dann erst von der Aufstellung der Fragen handeln.

6. Der erste Teil der Logik im engeren Sinn wird im engsten Sinn Logik genannt. So sagt Mill: die Logik gebe nur die Regeln der Prüfung (obwohl er dann in seiner [Logik] manchmal weiter geführt wird). Dehnt man die Logik weiter aus, so ist sie der relativ elementare Teil. Daher [bezeichnen] wir [sie als] "die elementare Logik."]²³

The logic of testing is the first part of logic to be developed because it has advantages over the logic of discovery in priority, easiness, generality, simplicity, and independence. While individual logic (i.e. logic in the narrower sense) can be divided into a logic of testing and a logic of discovery, the former is elementary logic, i.e. logic in the *narrowest* sense.

Brentano may well at one time have thought that he could present a wider scope of logical topics than what elementary logic encompasses. In this regard one may consider some of the outlines that are included among his preparations for the *Logik*. In one of these 1) he defines logic as the art of knowledge or cognition (*Erkenntniskunst*)²⁴ and divides up its subject matter just as he does in the *Logik*. 2) Following this introduction, there is to be a section on psychological matters. 3) The third section concerns the testing of both immediate and mediated knowledge. An additional section, however, is presented as follows:

4. Of Discovery
    a) In general
        1) Of finding the proofs of given truths
        2) Of finding truth
        3) Of formulating questions
            a. Of the possibility or impossibility of a question
            b. Of easiness or difficulty
            c. Of dependence and cohesiveness
            d. Of importance
            e. Of the discovery of gaps

---

23 EL 72/12033–12034.
24 Since knowledge is successful judging and an art of a thing aims at its success, the art of judgment and the art of knowledge turn out to be the same.

                    f.   Of the division of labor (of many not only, but also of the individuals)
                    g.   Of systematization
                    h.   Of the classification of the sciences
            b)   In Particular
                1)   Mathematical science
                2)   Natural science
                    a.   Simple
                    b.   Complex
                3)   Humanities
                4)   Metaphysics

[4. Von der Entdeckung
       a)   Im Allgemeine
              1)   Von der Auffindung der Beweise gegebener Wahrheiten
              2)   Von der Auffindung der Wahrheit
              3)   Von der Aufstellung der Fragen
                    a.   Von Möglichkeit oder Unmöglichkeit einer Frage
                    b.   Von der Leichtigkeit oder Schwierigkeit
                    c.   Von der Abhängigkeit und Zusammengehörigkeit
                    d.   Von der Wichtigkeit
                    e.   Von der Entdeckung der Lücke
                    f.   Von der Teilung der Arbeit (vieler nicht bloß, sondern auch der einzelnen)
                    g.   Von der Systematisation
                    h.   von der Klassifikation der Wissenschaften
       b)   Im Besonderen
              1)   Mathematische Wissenschaft
              2)   Naturwissenschaft
                    a.   Einfache
                    b.   Komplizierte
              3)   Geisteswissenschaft
              4)   Metaphysik.][25]

Accordingly Brentano did apparently at some time (probably in the late 1860s) plan to encompass a logic of discovery within the scope of his lecture course on

---

25 Brentano, EL 75: 12821[85]. Minor corrections in Brentano's numbering have been made. While most of this passage is written in ink, there are some additions in pencil, not all of which could be read.

logic. Since no manuscript in which he further elaborates on this logic of discovery has surfaced, we shall not venture further into a discussion of it. From the above outline we may nonetheless at least get a glimpse of the topics which were to be covered in Brentano's this domain of logic. This should make it clear enough that logic and epistemology belong together for Brentano. Yet, as our discussion advances, we shall see that their unity is still evident in the *Logik*, within the confines of the logic of testing on an individual level.

4   The Value of Logic

Among the critics who Brentano had to face were of course those who found logic to be of no value. In support of their position it could be pointed out that certain great thinkers in both science and practical life have in many cases not been schooled in logic. Their skill in arriving at correct judgments is rather to be attributed to instinct and practice. Though Brentano fully concedes that a natural inclination and a certain amount of practice are to be highly valued in our endeavor to obtain knowledge, he points out that the most naturally gifted and well-practiced among us can nevertheless go wrong in our judgments. If science had an index, as is the case in theology, says Brentano, "the names of the greatest researchers would be on it,"[26] for all of them have somewhere along the line run into errors which could have been corrected by the application of logic.

In his lectures of 1884/85 on logic he cites a number of instances of such mistakes in the history of philosophy. Plato, for instance, put forward his theory of Ideas, which he conceived of as entities existing apart from concrete instantiations and in which these instantiations somehow "share." Though Aristotle as a student in Plato's academy had refuted this theory, this apparently did not keep Plato from espousing it.[27] In his lectures on practical philosophy Brentano continues to cite other examples as follows:

> It is similar with regard to the so-called ontological proof for the existence of God. Anselm of Canterbury formulated it. When his attention was drawn to the fact that it contained a fallacy, he still did not want to concede this point. Later on, to be sure, Descartes came along and

---

26   Brentano, EL 80/12969: "*so kämen gerade die Werke der größten Forscher alle darauf zu stehen.*"

27   Yet, we must not overlook the fact that some of Aristotle's criticisms, most notably the "third man" argument, are already prefigured in Plato's *Parmenides*.

rejected the form that Anselm had given the proof, but still accepted it and never saw the error.

Furthermore, Kant asserted that we may apply the law of causality only within experience and yet applied it to the "thing in itself," which is not an object of experience. His attention was drawn to this, but he did not see his error. Something similar happened to him in the case of the antinomies. Many of them are pure paralogisms.

Something similar happened to Herbart. He wanted to find contradictions in our experiential concepts: experience, ego, etc.

These examples can be piled up. Up to the present day many statements are in dispute, not as to whether they are correct or incorrect, but rather as to whether they are proved or not. A precise knowledge of logic should eliminate such dispute at once. I mentioned the ontological proof and consider it to be a fallacy. But there are still people today who consider it to be correct.

[Ähnliches gilt bezüglich des sogenannten ontologischen Beweises vom Dasein Gottes. Anselm von Canterbury stellte ihn auf; aufmerksam gemacht, dass darin ein Fehlschluss enthalten sei, wollte er das doch nie zugeben. Später kam Descartes, verwarf zwar die Form, die Anselm dem Beweis gegeben, nahm ihn aber doch an und hat den Fehler niemals eingesehen. Und doch haben wir es hier mit Männern allerersten Rangs zu tun.

Weiter. Kant behauptete, dass man das Kausalgesetz nur innerhalb der Erfahrung anwenden dürfe und wendete es doch auf das "Ding an sich", das kein Gegenstand der Erfahrung ist, an. Man machte ihn darauf aufmerksam, er sah seinen Irrtum aber nicht ein. Ähnlich erging es ihm mit seinen Antinomien; darunter sind manche reine Paralogismen.

Ähnlich ging es Herbart. Er wollte in unseren Erfahrungsbegriffen Widerspruch finden: Erfahrung, Ich etc.

Diese Beispiele ließen sich häufen. Bis zum heutigen Tage wird über viele Sätze Streit geführt: nicht darüber, ob sie richtig sind oder unrichtig, sondern darüber, ob sie bewiesen sind oder nicht! Eine genau Kenntnis der Logik müsse diesen Streit doch sofort heben. Ich erwähnte des ontologischen Beweises, und ich halte ihn für eine Fehlschluss, aber es gibt Leute, die ihn heute noch für richtig halten.][28]

---

28 Y 2, 20f.

It is of course obviously the case that philosophical disputation on many of these issues rages on. Regarding the ontological argument for the existence of God, there have been outstanding thinkers who have upheld it well after Brentano's death. Up to the present there are still philosophers who regard it as a logically sound argument.[29] The objections raised by Gaunilo, by Kant, and by Brentano himself against this proof have not convinced all philosophers and theologians that it is unacceptable. While it is quite possible that there are things that we cannot know, it would seem that we could at least agree on what counts as a proof and what does not. Though this point may well indicate the need for logic, the many failed attempts to develop a logic that can perform such a task may well, contrary to Brentano, lead us to the conclusion that this is a futile endeavor. Amid our contemporary developments in logic, we still find ourselves in the situation decried by Kant, in which metaphysics has not enjoyed the fate of "having entering upon the secure path of a science," while few of us seem to share his confidence in the completeness of logic.[30] Yet, we cannot help but examine this situation further and explore the possibilities which outstanding thinkers have opened up.

The question may of course be raised why philosophical issues of great importance have been left unsettled if indeed logic is as useful as Brentano claims it to be. Here we must bear in mind that he maintains that logic should be reformed. As we know from his *Psychology from an Empirical Standpoint*,[31] Brentano proposes reforms in deductive logic. These will be discussed further below. Moreover, it should be mentioned here, without going into Brentano's metaphysics (which is a topic that would require a much lengthier treatment, again in connection with abundant unpublished manuscript material), that he did try to settle most of the matters enumerated above. In his lectures he rejected the ontological argument,[32] whereas he went into great elaborations in defense of the teleological argument.[33] According to the original plan for his *Psychologie vom empirischen Standpunkte*, he also intended to address the question concerning the immortality of the soul.[34] In his manuscripts there are extensive lecture notes on this topic.[35] While he did abandon the attempt

---

29 Oppy 2019.
30 Kant, *Critique of Pure Reason*, B xiv.
31 Brentano 1874, 302 ff.
32 Brentano 1929, 19–59.
33 Brentano 1929, 214–299.
34 Brentano 1874, v.
35 His arguments for immortality and his closely related treatment of the mind-body problem are already outlined in his plan for a lecture course on psychology for the winter semester of 1872/73 in Würzburg (Ps 62/54011–54012). This plan corresponds to what was

to defend Christianity as such, he nonetheless upheld many of its teachings as rational, particularly those which do not involve revealed theology. He also devoted much energy to developing a theory of space and time, not to mention a treatment of the vexing problem concerning the continuum as such.[36] Finally, as regards causality, he contended that it is indeed immediately evident in inner perception, though he also held the view that a law of causality could only be a matter of inference.[37] In short, Brentano was fully confident in the extensive and penetrating power of his logic to such an extent that we may hesitate to call it a Modest Logic. Indeed, he is open to expansions of logic in that he says, "Usually one imagines logic as complete. In this case one does it too great an honor, as one scorned it in other cases."[38]

None of Brentano's students, however, went on to expand his logic or even to become logicians. The impressive achievements of such thinkers as Meinong, Marty, Stumpf, von Ehrenfels, Twardowski, and Husserl are most certainly worthy of the attention of present philosophers and will no doubt be so for future generations, but we must concede that these achievements are hardly ones in the domain of logic as such. Some may indeed reply that Husserl did achieve something in this domain. Already in the nineteenth century he began giving lecture courses on logic and continued to do so for the rest of his academic career, which he ended with the publication of his *Formale und transzendentale Logik*.[39] Yet, most of Husserl's thoughts on logic were programmatic at best, as we would indeed more readily classify them as "philosophy of logic" rather than logic itself. Moreover, by the early twentieth century his thoughts on this

---

partly executed and also planned in Brentano 1874. In Brentano's manuscripts there is also a plan for the continuation of the work just mentioned. This plan also encompasses the topic of immortality, again in connection with the mind-body problem (50/52143). Insofar as Brentano's actual attempt to execute his plans to continue the work that was published in 1874, this can be found in Ps 53, which does not go beyond an elaboration of his theory of presentations. All of this material, incidentally, indicates that the work in question was meant to go in an entirely different direction than the one that is published in Brentano 1968, which is merely a collage of bits and pieces from later manuscripts, written long after the original project had been abandoned.

36 As already mentioned, EL 72 contains an extensive discussion of this problem. See the the fifth and sixth chapters below.
37 The theory of causality which Stumpf later worked out, as discussed in Rollinger 2008a, 263–299, was presumably in large measure taken from Brentano, although a reliance on Stumpf cannot in any way be substitued for an exploration of manuscript material relevant to this topic.
38 Brentano EL 80/12174: "*Gewöhnlich denkt man sich die Logik wie fertig. Man tut ihr hier zu große Ehre an, wie man dort ihre Ehre schmälerte. Viel ist mangelhaft.*"
39 Husserl 1929.

topic took a very different direction from the one that his mentor had taught him. A short book by one of Brentano's students, Franz Hilleband, in defense of Brentano's logic appeared in 1891 (and is translated in the seventh chapter of the present volume), perhaps as a response to the logical propaedeutic of Alois Höfler (also a student of Brentano) in collaboration with Meinong,[40] a work that was also in many ways alien to the thought of the author's mentor. In short, in spite of Brentano's confidence in his reform of logic, it had very little success among his students and therefore – since the reform primarily found expression in lectures rather than publications – among his contemporaries. Still, aside from the fact that his philosophical achievements are worthy of attention in their own right, these achievements, particularly his logic, become so all the more in the light of his students' praise for him for teaching them how to think accurately.

As regards people who are successful in practical life, Brentano says, "The most intelligent often act unintelligently and their smaller and less frequent mistakes are rendered harmless and covered up by other, greater and more numerous, things [they did]."[41] There is certainly room for improvement in their reasonings. Brentano's sees logic as the means for making such improvement in practical as well as theoretical matters. Accordingly, Brentano has no doubt about the value of logic. Philosophers such as Hume who advocate No Logic are alien to Brentano's entire philosophical enterprise.

5 Psychologism

Here we may briefly consider whether Brentano's *Logik* is subject to the criticisms that Husserl was later to put forward against psychologism. Certainly Brentano was by no means a relativist at any time in his philosophical development.[42] Nor did he ever accept the non-real in the sense in which Husserl was to do so.[43] According to Husserl's view, the non-real is timeless, but we encounter

---

40 Höfler 1890. Later another student of Brentano, Kasimir Twardowski, gave a lecture course on logic which was influenced by this propaedeutic. See Twardowski 2016.

41 Brentano, EL 80/12970: *"Die Verständigsten handeln oft unverständig und ihre kleineren und selteneren Fehler werden nur durch die größeren und zahlreicheren der Übrigen unschädlich gemacht und verdeckt."* In Brentano's lectures *Ausgewählte Fragen aus der Ästhetik und Psychologie* the same point is made in favor of aesthetics. Although aesthetic rules for the production and appreciation of the beautiful cannot be a replacement for artistic genius, this does not mean that such rules are useless (Ps 78/59245).

42 See Brentano 1911, 165 ff.

43 This is particularly the case in Husserl 1901, not in Husserl 1900 and Husserl 2001.

no timeless objects in Brentano's early (or late) ontology. Yet, Husserl insists that we have to accept timeless entities in order to overcome relativism. Without this requirement, his whole case against psychologism has no force.

When Husserl visited Brentano in 1907, they discussed their disagreements. According to Brentano, Husserl exonerated him from psychologism.[44] Yet, we may doubt that Husserl was sincere in expressing this exoneration. It is simply incompatible with the thrust of his whole argument against psychologism, for this argument involves the conception of logical objects as timeless entities ("ideal").

Another angle from which the question under consideration here can be approached is by considering the status of logical laws rather than logical objects. Psychologism often involves a conception of such laws as psychological laws. According to this conception, the law of non-contradiction, for instance, would simply state the psychological impossibility of contradictory beliefs existing simultaneously in the same mind (as strongly suggested in Höfler 1890). This is most emphatically not how Brentano conceives of the law of non-contradiction. Moreover, nowhere does he say that logical laws are psychological laws.

In an early manuscript, apparently written in the late 1860s as a preparation for the *Logik*, Brentano characterizes the laws of logic as "laws of states of that which is (can be)."[45] In his lectures entitled *Deskriptive Psychologie odor beschreibende Phänomenologie* (winter semester 1888/89) we find the following passage which is highly relevant to the issue at hand:

> As logical rules, the laws of logic, e.g. the law of non-contradiction, of course concern judgment alone; to this they turn and they tell it: You may not, under any circumstances, regard contradictories as true at the same time. But as a law of nature, as a universal incontrovertible fact, the law of non-contradiction concerns all that *is*. It is true of hydrogen and oxygen and of heat and motion and even of sensation. It is impossible for something to be given in sensation and not given in sensation at the same time.

---

44 Brentano 1946/47, 93. Husserl's advocacy for timeless objects had of course been expressed in the second volume of his *Logische Untersuchungen* (1901), a work that was accepted with great enthusiasm in Munich.

45 Brentano, EL 75/12921(3): "*Gesetze der Verhältnisse dessen, was ist (sein kann).*" Not only does the style of handwriting (in pencil) on this page indicate that it was written before 1870, but on an adjacent leaf (EL 75: 12921[5]) we find similar handwriting (again in pencil) on an announcement of a dissertation defense for 30 November 1867. All of the leaves included in EL 75 in fact appear to be fragments from about this time.

> It is impossible for the same lines in the same appearance to be straight and broken, whole and disrupted at the same time.
>
> [Als logische Regel gehen die Gesetze der Logik z.B. das Gesetz des Widerspruchs allerdings nur das Urteil an; an dieses wenden sie sich und sagen ihm: Du darfst unter keinen Umständen Widersprechendes zugleich als wahr gelten lassen. Aber als Naturgesetz, als allgemeine unumstössliche Tatsache geht das Gesetz des Widerspruchs jedes Seiende an. Es gilt von dem Wasserstoff und Sauerstoff und von der Wärme und Bewegung und ebenso von der Empfindung. Es ist unmöglich, dass etwas zugleich empfunden und nicht empfunden wird. Es ist unmöglich, dass dieselben Linien in derselben Erscheinung zugleich gradlinig und gebrochen, ganz und zerrissen sind.]⁴⁶

The law of con-contradiction is not about what can be thought or judged at any time, but rather a law that tells us that it is impossible for something to *be* and also not to *be* at the same time and in the same respect. Brentano's view on this point is reminiscent of Aristotle's elaboration of this law in Book Γ (Chapter Three) of the *Metaphysics*, where it properly finds in place in first philosophy. The laws of logic from this perspective grounded in reality or "nature."

We may of course be troubled from the standpoint of contemporary sensibilities that the law of non-contradiction is characterized above as a law of nature. The question arises whether these laws are to be known just as other laws of nature, e.g. the law of gravity, is to be known. If this is the case, our knowledge of laws of logic would be arrived by means of induction and experiment. Aside from extreme absurdities which might thereby be suggested, the question arises what the limits of logic are. If its laws are known by induction and experiment just as the law of gravity is known, perhaps its laws include not only this one, but also laws of the other natural sciences. Brentano, however, states in the above cited manuscript from the late 1860s, "All [laws of logic] are *a priori*. Not all laws of circumstances of that which-is, however, are *a priori*. Consequently logic does not have to employ all laws of states of that which is."⁴⁷ This

---

46 Brentano, EL 77/59038–59038. The occurrence of the term "descriptive phenomenology" in the title of the cited lecture course naturally invites comments and speculations in view of the fact that it places Brentano at the beginning of the phenomenological movement. In the present context, however, we can only say that the term is meant as synonym of "descriptive psychology" or "psychognosy (*Psychognosie*)" which is of course present throughout Brentano's *Logik*.

47 Brentano, EL 75: 12921(78): "*Alle sind apriorisch. Nicht alle Gesetze der Verhältnisse dessen, was ist, sind aber apriorisch. Somit hat die Logik nicht alle Gesetze der Verhältnisse dessen,*

quotation leaves no room for doubt that he, at least at one time, conceived of the laws of logic as distinct from laws of nature as ordinarily understood. The laws of logic are for Brentano in fact the *a priori* laws of nature.

Yet, Brentano does not think that logic is merely concerned with stating such laws. Logic for him is rather normative and accordingly states rules rather than laws. Since these rules are meant to regulate our judgments, logic inevitably demands elaborations on judgments as such and also on those psychical phenomena on which judgments are based. Yet, we may ask, what is the theoretical discipline which concerns itself with the *laws* of logic? In an early manuscript written in preparation for the *Logik* Brentano says, "There is a science of logic. This [is] only a part of the art." To this statement he adds the following important points concerning the method of logic:

a) The science of logic [is] *a priori*. [It has an] affinity with mathematics. Some call the latter an immense expansion of logic towards a certain side.

b) The art of logic combines *a posteriori* elements with this. Yet, it proceeds deductively here too, only from *a posteriori* established premises.

It takes these from: 1) psychology, e.g. the association of ideas, habit, more easily aquivocating in more abstract concepts, 2) in the special logic of the particular (inductive) sciences from these themselves.

[Es gibt eine Wissenschaft der Logik. Diese von der Kunst nur Teil.

a) Die Wissenschaft der Logik [ist] apriorisch. [Sie hat eine] Verwandschaft mit der Mathematik. Manche nennen diese eine immense Ausdehnung der Logik nach einer Seite hin.

b) Die Kunst der Logik verbindet damit Aposteriorisches. Doch verfährt sie auch hier deduktiv, nur aus a posterirori festgestellten Prämissen.

Sie entnimmt dieselben: 1) der Psychologie, z.B. Ideenassoziation, Gewohnheit, Leichtere Äquivokation in abstrakteren Begriffen, 2) in der speziellen Logik der einzelnen (induktiven) Wissenschaften diesen selbst.][48]

---

was ist, anzustellen." The verb "employ" (*anstellen*) in this context may seem odd, but it must be kept in mind that logic for Brentano states *rules*, ultimately rules about how we may judge. The law of non-contradiction is accordingly employed by logic in that logic tells us that we may not judge that something *is* and at the same time and in the same respect is *not*.

48 Brentano, EL 75/12921(3).

Here we encounter thoughts which are highly suggestive of the direction that Husserl later took in the formulation of the notion of a pure logic. The close affinity between this science of logic and mathematics is also noteworthy. Yet, perhaps Brentano did not find the formulation of such thoughts to be satisfactory, for he did not include them in the *Logik*. In 1878/79 and again 1884/85, however, he plainly says of logic, "It must also adopt metaphysical truths [*Auch allgemeine metaphysische Wahrheiten muss sie entlehnen*],"[49] though without telling us which truths these are. Nevertheless, he continued to think, as the above quotation from his lectures on psychology from the winter semester 1888/89 makes clear, that corresponding to the rules of correct judgment there are *laws of being*. The law of non-contradiction, according to Brentano's conception, accordingly seems to be a law of being, i.e. a natural law of the *a priori* kind, which we might also call a metaphysical law.

If the law of non-contradition is such a law, the logical laws of inference are apparently so as well. This topic continued to be on Brentano's mind as late as 1890, when he delievered a lecture on it before the Philosophical Society at the University of Vienna.[50] The *a priori* status of these laws is, contrary to John Stuart Mill and other moderns, not called into question. Yet, in this public address Brentano is very cautious regarding this matter and does not take the further step of regarding the knowledge of these laws as belonging to metaphysics. Epistemologically, however, there is no doubt that he is as distant as possible from the psychologism that Husserl was to condemn a decade later. Never, however, did Brentano see the necessity of positing timeless entities in order to account for the "objectivity" of logic, for the laws of logic are for him laws of the real things, e.g. hydrogen, oxygen, sensations, and other temporally existing entities. Logic is thus derived from a metaphysics that is in a very broad sense naturalistic.

We may conclude that Brentano does not fall prey to psychologism insofar as he is not a relativist and he sees the laws of logic, at least the law of non-contradiction, as pertaining to what *is* as such, not as psychological laws. In a word, he whole-heartedly subscribes to the objectivity of logic, without allowing for a special class of logical objects, as Husserl does. In short, there was no disagreement between Brentano and Husserl as regards the epistemological status of logic, but they could not see eye-to-eye regarding its ontological presuppositions. However objectionable one might find Brentano's conception of logic as "nominalistic,"[51] such a conception cannot rightly be called psychologistic.

---

49 Brentano EL 72/12020.
50 Brentano 2013a and Brentano 2013b.
51 This term here refers only to the rejection of a class of abstract or, in Husserl's terminology,

Nevertheless, from a contemporary standpoint Brentano's reason for saying that logic is a philosophical discipline, namely because it involves concepts taken from inner perception and therefore involves psychology, will not be acceptable in many quarters of the present intellectual climate. In the twentieth century logic has of course become highly formalized and closely related to mathematics, indeed often characterized as a branch of mathematics. While Brentano, as the above quotation from his early manuscripts shows, was well aware of such possibilities, he was in fact opposed to the mathematization that was gaining ground in the nineteenth century.[52] Purely mathematical or symbolic logic, as it is often called, is hardly philosophical in the Brentanian sense. Proponents of mathematical logic would in many cases be inclined to call his position "psychologistic" and dismiss it out of hand. While I cannot argue at greater length that such a dismissal is much too hasty, I have hopefully at least shown that he does not fall prey to psychologism when we understand this notion precisely. Since he thinks that the laws of logic are laws of states of what is (or can be), it might indeed be more appropriate to call his philosophy of logic "ontologism" or even "metaphysicalism" if such terms terms would not suggest something utterly atrocious and indeed alien to the whole spirit of Brentano's philosophical orientation. He most certainly does not wish to posit any weird entities, as various students of his felt compelled to do.

6   Language

As a practical discipline, logic can draw on various theoretical sources in order to reach its goal. Among these sources is the study of language as well as psychology and metaphysics. The concern with language in logical matters is of course one that has a deep historical background. Brentano points out that Aristotle concerned himself with language in the *On Interpretation*, as did the stoics after him and also later the scholastics, not to mention that language occupies an entire book of Locke's *Essay concerning Human Understanding*.[53] Among more contemporaneous philosophers who see a treatment of language

---

"ideal" objects. As Brentano uses the term, he does not consider himself to be a nominalist. There will be more about this issue below.

52   See Brentano 1911, 158 ff.

53   Brentano is of course thinking of Book III of this work, which is, incidentallly, not a logic, although we may very well consider it to be an epistemology. Here again we see that Brentano's concern in the *Logik* is as much epistemology as it is logic.

as necessary for logic John Stuart Mill is mentioned.[54] The fact that such great thinkers preface their elaborations on knowledge with considerations of linguistic expressions, Brentano says, already indicates that such a procedure is fully justifiable.

The primary purpose of language, according to Brentano, is to facilitate communication, primarily the communication of judgments and of phenomena of love and hate, although he concedes that presentations are also communicated.[55] Due to the communicative purpose of language it may seem appropriate to treat it only in communicative logic, which is explicitly not the concern of the *Logik*. The purpose of elementary logic is rather to put forward a logic of testing for individuals rather than communities. Brentano points out, however, that language has a great influence on our thinking, apart from its use in communication, and can thereby be both a help and a hindrance in the endeavor to judge correctly. It is helpful, he tells us, insofar as it performs a mnemonic function and thereby allows us to distinguish thoughts which we might easily confuse with each other. While we may have difficulties in distinguishing the thoughts of nine and ten and even more difficulties in distinguishing between a million and the same number with a unit added to it, it is easy for us to distinguish between the signs for these numbers. Moreover, language aids our thinking generally as signs are helpful to the mathematician, i.e. insofar as we can replace extremely complex thoughts with signs and thereby make thinking much easier.

Other advantages of language are of course ones that accrue to us through communication, as mentioned in the following quotation from Alexander Bain, which is cited by Brentano with approval:

> All extensions of human knowledge, all new generalizations, are fixed and spread, even unintentionally, by the use of words. [a)] The child growing up learns, along with the vocables of his mother tongue, that things which he would have believed to be different are, in important points, the same. [d)] Without any formal instruction, the language in which we grow up teaches us all the common philosophy of the age. [b)] It directs us to observe and know things which we should have overlooked; [c)] it supplies us with classifications ready-made, by which things are arranged (as far as the light of by-gone generalizations admits) with objects to which they bear the greatest total resemblance. [e)] The number of general names in a language, and the degree of generality of those names,

---

54   Mill, *A System of Logic*, I.i.1.
55   EL 80/13008.

afford a test of the knowledge of the era, and of the intellectual insight which is the birthright of anyone born into it.

[Alle Erweiterungen der menschlichen Erkenntnis, alle neuen Generalisationen werden, sogar unabsichtlich, durch den Gebrauch von Wörtern fixiert und verbreitet. A) Das aufwachsende Kind lernt mit den Wörtern der Muttersprache, dass Dinge, welche es für verschieden gehalten haben würde, in wichtigen Punkten dieselben sind. d) Ohne einen förmlichen Unterricht lehrt uns die Sprache, in der wir aufgewachsen sind, die ganze allgemeine Philosophie des Zeitalters. b) Sie veranlasst uns, Dinge zu beobachten und zu erkennen, die wir übersehen haben würden; c) sie versteht uns mit schon fertigen Klassifikationen, durch welche die Dinge mit den Gegenständen, mit denen sie die größte Ähnlichkeit haben, zusammengeordnet werden (soweit es die Aufklärung vergangener Geschlechter zulässig macht). e) Die Zahl der Gemeinsamen einer Sprache und der Grad von Allgemeinheit dieser Namen bieten ein Mittel, um das Wissen des Zeitalters und die geistige Einsicht zu prüfen, welche das Geburtsrecht eines Jeden ist, der in demselben geboren ist.][56]

At the same time, however, Brentano also thinks that language has its disadvantages. The chief disadvantage is to be found in cases where one and same name is used for different thoughts. This is equivocation. While this is often harmless, namely where the thoughts involved are very different, as we can use the word "bark," for instance, to designate the covering of a tree and also the sound a dog makes, the danger arises when the thoughts in question closely resemble each other, especially in cases of "abstract and reflexive concepts." "Most fallacies," says Brentano, occur "perhaps as a result of equivocation. Particularly the metaphysics of the most famous thinkers are teeming with such sophisms, and one of the main tasks of a conscientious ontology lies, for instance, in a precise differentiation of the meanings of 'being,' 'part,' 'cause,' etc."[57] Mathematics, he

---

56   Brentano, EL 80/12993. Brentano cites this passage in German translation from Mill's *System of Logic*, IV.3.1. The passage, however, does not occur in Bain 1870 or in any other published text by that author. Mill is apparently quoting from a manuscript that Bain made available to him. The letters from a to e are inserted by Brentano in the order in which they appear in the original quotation, apparently as an indication of the sequence in which he meant to discuss them in his lectures.

57   EL 80/12995: *"Die meisten Fehlschlüsse warden vielleicht in Folge von Äquivokationen begangen. Namentlich wimmelt die Metaphysik der berühmtesten Denker von solchen Sophismen; und eine der Hauptaufgaben einer gewissenhaften Ontologie besteht z.B. in einer genauen Unterscheidung der Bedeutungen des Seienden, des Teils, der Ursache u. dgl."* EL 75/12921(9):

says, is not nearly as bad off in this regard as metaphysics is, for in mathematics the technical usage of language excludes equivocation.

Synonymity (in the normal sense, not in the Aristotelian one) can also hinder thinking. This of course occurs where there are two different expressions in language for a single thought. In such cases we may believe that there is a distinction where there is really none. Such a danger is, as in the case of equivocation, the greatest where abstract and reflective concepts are under consideration.

Due to the hindrances which are found again and again in natural language, it is of great interest, Brentano concedes, to be wary of them. Other philosophers, such as Aristotle, Leibniz, Mill, Boole, and Lange, have found it advisable to construct an artificial language in order to deal with the dangers of equivocation and synonymity. Nonetheless, it is clear that he too thought that the philosopher should reshape language in light of the discoveries that accrue to us through descriptive psychology (also called phenomenology or psychognosy).[58]

While language is of great interest to logic, insofar as it poses dangers through equivocation and synonymity, Brentano also identifies a second reason why logicians have made language focal in their logical investigations. They have often maintained that language, as the expression of thought, actually somehow mirrors thought. If this is so, the examination of language will indeed yield great profit. The prevailing assumption here is that, while there are vast differences among languages, they also have aspects in common. These aspects, some have assumed, reflect thinking or are in is some way a picture (*Abbild*) thereof. "The consideration of *thinking* in itself," Brentano explains, "is, like all reflection, very difficult, while the *consideration of language* is not subject to this difficulty, and it can often replace the former."[59] Brentano, however,

---

"The most general concepts are most easily confused. Language ties them to concrete presentations. Herien [lies] the most advantageous assistance of language in thinking itself. [*Die allgemeinsten Begriffe werden am leichtesten verwechselt. Die Sprache bindet sie an konkrete Vorstellungen. Hierin die vorzüglichste Hilfeleistung der Sprache beim Denken selbst.*]" Cf. Brentano 1862, 5, where a reference to *Posterior Analytics*, 97 b 29 is made on this point.

58   Brentano 1895a, p. 35: "My school distinguishes a *psychognosy* and a *genetic psychology* (remotely analogous to geognosy and geology). The first of these makes known all the ultimate psychical elements, from the combination of which the totality of psychical phenomena and the totality of words from letters results. Its execution could serve as the basis for a *characterica universalis*, as Leibniz and before him Descartes had this in mind. The other informs us about the laws by which the appearances come and go." Cf. Brentano 1982, 77. It should be born in mind that the psychology that we find throughout Brentano's epistemology and logic is indeed psychognosy, not genetic psychology.

59   EL 72/12998: "*Die Betrachtung des Denkens in sich ist schwierig, wie jede Reflexion. Die*

insists that the common features of language do not at all mirror thinking any more than a cry, for example, is a picture of pain. Moreover, he maintains that great errors have been committed in psychology, logic, and metaphysics due to the assumption of a mirroring function of language. It will be seen below that for Brentano the prominence of the subject-predicate structure in statements has indeed misled logicians to characterize judgments by means of the same structure, as if judging were actually predicating. This, he tells us, has misled them in formulating the unreliable rules of deduction. Hence, dispelling the conception of language as a mirror of thought has great consequences in logic for Brentano.[60] It is accordingly no wonder why one of his early critics exclaimed, "If these doctrines can be made out, obviously all logicians from Aristotle downwards have been sheer imposters ..."[61]

A case in point is particularly the impersonals, i.e. sentences such as "It is raining" and "It is cold," which some have understandably regarded as subjectless. If we strictly adhered to the view that language mirrors thought, we would not consider the impersonals to be subjectless. The "it", according to the mirror theory, would indeed have to mirror a thought (or a presentation) no less than what is predicated of it, e.g. raining. There were indeed some who maintained that such mirroring does occur. Not only linguists, but outstanding philosophers, psychologists, and logicians, such as Hermann Lotze, Christoph Sigwart, and Wilhelm Wundt attempted to construct theories to account for impersonals as cases of genuine predication, whereas Brentano and especially Marty argued relentlessly that the "it" was not a genuine subject and therefore has no predicate in the strict and proper sense.[62] A noteworthy specialist in Slavic languages fully supported the Brentanian view on impersonals.[63] When we say that it is raining, all that we are thinking of and accepting is the event of raining. That is to say, "It is raining" is just another way of saying that the event in question really does exist. An impersonal is only superficially comparable to a sentence like "He is running," where we can plainly identify a subject

---

Betrachtung der Sprache unterliegt dieser Schwierigkeit nicht und sie kann vielfach jene ersetzen."

60   Brentano 1874, 302 ff.
61   Flint 1876, 122. It seems unlikely that Brentano would have ever said that Aristotle was an imposter, for he consistently held Aristotle in the highest regard. Nonetheless, Brentano's consistent reverence for Aristotle does not exclude criticisms of some of the central points of Aristotelian doctrines. Flint is nonetheless right to stress the revolutionary character of Brentano's theory of judgment.
62   Marty 1884, Marty 1894, and Marty 1895. Sigwart 1888 in particular stirred up considerably bitter disputes with Marty, which lie outside the scope of the present analysis. Concerning this matter, see Varga 2016.
63   Miklosich 1883. 111–122.

that runs. The impersonals are thus merely special cases of existential sentences and do not express the ascription of a predicate to some abstruse subject (e.g. reality, the universe, Zeus, or merely an altogether indeterminate subject).

Impersonals are of course a product of natural language. The question of course arises as to what extent the logician should rely on these products or rather attempt to reformulate them. While Adolf Trendelenburg went so far as to characterize logic as "a grammar immersed in itself,"[64] there is of course the opposing tendency, according to which logic is to develop its own artificial language. The *characteristica universalis*, at least as Leibniz and others have understood it, was indeed to be a language of this kind. In the nineteenth century the idea of a logical language apart from natural language especially received attention in the algebraic systems of George Boole and William Stanley Jevons. The latter's proposal in particular, to formulate all statements as ones concerned with identity (a = b), became subject to criticism from Brentano, though not in the *Logik*.[65]

In speech (*Rede*) we communicate our psychical phenomena to each other. However, Brentano points out that not all that we utter in language is speech:

> Rather what we speak is of three kinds: 1) In isolation it can be completely meaningless, signative only in connection with something else. For instance, particles, declensions of substantives, etc. ... In the case of the *suppositio materialis* what we have is not a sign, but the signified: "But" is a conjunction ... 2) What is spoken can presumably be something already signative, but only *naming* something and not a proper full-fledged utterance (an instance of speech), e.g. every name that we speak (categorematic expressions, also names consisting of multiple words. 3) Something can be meaningful and a full-fledged utterance (an instance of speech). For instance, statement, exclamation, request.

> [Vielmehr ist das Gesprochene von einer dreifachen Art: 1. Es kann für sich allein ganz bedeutungslos, nur mit einem anderen verbunden etwas bezeichnend, sein. Z.B. Partikeln, Beugungsfälle von Substantiven u.s.w. ... Bei der suppositio materialis liegt nicht ein Zeichen vor, sondern ein bezeichnetes: Das „Aber" ist eine Konjunktion ... Oder ein Name für das

---

64 Trendelenburg 1870, vol. I, 28.
65 See pp. 155 f., 227 f. below.

> Partikel, nicht das Partikel selbst (synkategorematisch Ausdrücke). 2. Das Gesprochene kann wohl bereits etwas bedeutend, aber nur etwas benennend, und nicht ein eigentlicher fertiger Ausspruch (eine Rede) sein, wie z.B. jeder Namen, den wir sprechen (kategorematische Ausdrücke, auch vielwörterige Namen). 3. Es kann etwas bedeutend und ein fertiger Ausspruch (eine Rede) sein. Z.B. Aussage, Ausruf, Bitte.][66]

The third class consists of speech, including statements, which will prove to be of special importance to logic. The second class, however, consists of names. A name, as Brentano understands it, is not as such an item of speech. Simply by naming something we are not speaking. We do not speak until we say something about what we name, or perhaps ask something about it or make a command or request about it. The first of these classes consists of syncategorematic expressions, which are exemplified by particles ("and," "the," etc.) and inflections ("man's"). Of course we can name syncategorematic experession. We speak of the word "and," but in this case the word designates a conjunction and is not itself a conjunction. This is what the scholastics called *suppositio materialis*. A conjunction, however, does not have any meaning in isolation, but obtains meaning together with other words. A name has meaning in isolation, but is not as such a unit of speech. Statements, questions, commands, and requests are all units of speech and as such manifest acts of judgment or acts of loving or hating.

The question arises concerning the *meaning* of expressions in language. Brentano attempts to answer this question with regard to names and statements. According to an early version of the *Logik*, the meaning of a statement, in contrast with the meaning of a name, is to be understood in the following way:

> If someone makes a statement, this a sign for the fact that he has a certain judgment.
>
> What statements mean, however, is not thereby established. If the judgment, as many teach, were nothing but a combination of two presentations, the question would be easily decided according to earlier discussions. The meaning of a statement would thus be the object of the judgment.
>
> However, this is not correct [...]: a) Combined presentations give a complex presentation, but no judgment. For a judgment and a complex

---

66   EL 80/13001.

presentation are by no means identical. b) A judgment is a psychical phenomenon of a genus completely different from a presentation. If this were not the case, if judgments were only a special kind of presentation, the expressions of judgment, though perhaps something else, still mean something in the same sense in which those names which are expressions of other presentations do. But they mean [...] what they mean in a completely different sense. The statements notify what they mean, give notice (knowledge thereof), whereas names do not do this. The names name, while the statements state: It therefore does not follow that, because the names mean the objects of the psychical phenomenon of which they are the expression, the same is also true of statements: that these must therefore mean the objects of the relevant judgments.

Indeed, this is not even possible. For a judgment and the underlying presentation have the same object, and also affirmation and denial have the same one as love and hate when they refer to the same thing. Consequently the name and the two opposing statements would mean the same thing; i.e. affirmation and denial would make the same thing known, which is obviously ridiculous. We might rightly say that they give an indication concerning the same thing, but they obviously do not notify the same.

How do we therefore find the answer to our question what statements mean? Let us look at what is established: that a statement is the expression of our judgment. The affirmation is the expression of our acceptance, the negation the expression of our rejection of an object and indicates this. What does someone do who makes a judgment, who accepts or rejects something? Obviously he treats that which he judges as something which is to be judged as he judges it. If he accepts it, he treats it as something that is to be accepted, and if he rejects it, as something that is to be rejected.

If we therefore pose the case that it would be given to someone that he immediately perceived the judgment of another person, and of a person in whose insight he trusts, this judgment would indicate to him at the same time how he is to judge, whether he is to accept or reject.

In like manner, however, it will do this if it is discerned in mediated way, via a linguistic expression, rather than immediately perceived. It will also make known to us how we are to judge. And this, which the judgment makes known to us in this way, we call the *content of the judgment*.

While the judgment in such a case indicates its content, the linguistic expression of the judgment obviously indicates in a twofold manner: 1) the judgment whose expression it is, 2) by means of the judgment that the object is to be judged in a certain manner, to be accepted or rejected, in a word: the content of the judgment.

[Macht einer eine Aussage, so ist dies ein Zeichen dafür, dass er ein gewisses Urteil hat.

Das aber, was die Aussagen bedeuten, ist damit noch nicht festgestellt. Wäre das Urteil, wie gar viele lehren, nichts anderes als eine Zusammensetzung zweier Vorstellungen, so wäre die Frage nach unseren früheren Erörterungen leicht entschieden. Die Bedeutung der Aussage würde dann der Gegenstand des Urteils sein.

Allein dies ist nicht richtig [...]: a) Verbundene Vorstellungen geben eine komplizierte Vorstellung, aber kein Urteil. Denn ein Urteil und eine komplizierte Vorstellung sind keineswegs identisch. b) Ein Urteil ist ein psychisches Phänomen von einer ganz anderen Gattung als die Vorstellung. Wäre dies nicht der Fall, wären die Urteile nur eine besondere Art von Vorstellungen, so würden die Aussagen, die Ausdrücke der Urteile, wenn auch vielleicht etwas anderes, doch in demselben Sinne etwas bedeuten wie die Namen, die Ausdrücke anderer Vorstellungen sind. Aber sie bedeuten [...], was sie bedeuten, in ganz anderem Sinne. Die Aussagen zeigen an, was sie bedeuten, geben es kund (Kenntnis davon), während dies die Namen nicht tun. Die Namen nennen, die Aussagen sagen aus. Es folgt also nicht, dass, weil die Namen die Gegenstände des psychischen Phänomens bedeuten, dessen Ausdruck sie sind, dasselbe auch bei den Aussagen der Fall sei, dass also diese die Gegenstände der betreffenden Urteile bedeuten müssen.

Ja, es ist auch dies gar nicht möglich. Denn das Urteil und die ihm zugrunde liegende Vorstellung haben denselben Gegenstand, und denselben haben auch Bejahung und Verneinung wie Liebe und Haß, wenn sie sich auf dasselbe Objekt beziehen. Somit würden der Name und die beiden entgegengesetzten Aussagen dasselbe bedeuten, und namentlich Bejahung und Verneinung dasselbe kundgeben, was offenbar lächerlich ist. Über dasselbe mögen wir mit Recht sagen, dass sie Anzeige machen, aber dasselbe zeigen sie offenbar nicht an.

Wie finden wir also die Antwort auf unsere Frage, was die Aussagen bedeuten? Blicken wir auf das, was feststeht, dass die Aussage der Ausdruck unseres Urteils ist. Die Bejahung ist der Ausdruck unserer Anerkennung, die Verneinung der Ausdruck unserer Verwerfung eines Gegenstandes und zeigt sie an. Was tut nun der, der ein Urteil fällt, etwas anerkennt oder verwirft? Offenbar behandelt er das, was er beurteilt, als etwas, was so zu beurteilen ist, wie er es beurteilt. Wenn er es anerkennt, behandelt er es als etwas, was anzuerkennen, wenn er es verwirft, als etwas, was zu verwerfen ist.

Setzen wir also den Fall, es würde einem gegeben, dass er das Urteil eines anderen, und eines solchen, auf dessen Einsicht er vertraute, unmittelbar wahrnähme, so würde ihm dieses Urteil zugleich anzeigen, wie sein Gegenstand zu beurteilen, ob er anzuerkennen oder zu verwerfen sei.

In gleicher Weise wird es dies aber tun, wenn es statt unmittelbar wahrgenommen zu werden, mittelbar durch den sprachlichen Ausdruck erkannt wird. Es wird uns dann auch kundgeben, wie wir über seinen Gegenstand urteilen sollen. Und dieses, was uns in solcher Weise das Urteil kundmacht, nennen wir den Inhalt des Urteils.

Während uns aber das Urteil in einem solchen Fall seinen Inhalt anzeigt, zeigt uns der sprachliche Ausdruck eines Urteils, die Aussage, offenbar ein doppeltes an: 1. das Urteil, dessen Ausdruck es ist, 2. mittels des Urteil, dass der Gegenstand in einer gewissen Weise zu beurteilen, anzuerkennen oder zu verwerfen ist, mit einem Worte: den Inhalt des Urteils.][67]

While Brentano here thinks that the meaning of a name is in fact no different from the named object (i.e. the object of the presentation which is expressed by the name), he also maintains that a statement has a meaning in a very different sense. A statement, on this view, expresses a judgment, and the meaning (which is the content of the expressed judgment) is what the listener of the statement is to judge. By making a statement we convey the meaning to our listeners in precisely this sense. If, for instance, I make the statement in the present volume that Brentano started lecturing on logic in 1870, the meaning of this statement is what I want the reader to believe, in this case that Brentano started lecturing on logic in 1870. In contemporary terms Brentano's theory of meaning, as we find it in the above-quoted passage, is a pragmatic one, at least as it pertains to statements, for it concerns linguistic practice rather than language as an abstract system of signs.

The pragmatic theory of language does not for the most part find an echo in the work of his students. Hence it is no surprise that Husserl's early approach to

---

67 Brentano, EL 80/13127, 13130–13131. Brentano later removed this passage from the *Logik*, because he altered his theory of meaning (to be considered below). See the following quotation from Brentano's plan for the *Logik* (EL 73/12595): "The meaning of a statement is the content of the judgment which it expresses, that the object is to be judged as the expressed judgment judges it. [*Die Bedeutung der Aussage ist der Inhalt des Urteils, das sie ausdrückt, dass der Gegenstand so zu beurteilen ist, wie ihn das ausgedrückte Urteil urteilt.*]"

language in the *Logical Investigations*, for instance, does not involve any extensive treatment of communication.[68] The one student of Brentano who did not only accept the pragmatic theory of language, but also continued to develop it further was Marty,[69] who had copied detailed notes from Brentano's the Würzburg version of the *Logik*.[70]

The theory of meaning in the Logik also incorporates aspects of scholasticism. As is well known, the scholastics had maintained that a name is systematically ambiguous. 1) *Suppositio realis*: It can name an object, as this is normally thought of. The name "dog," for instance, can name an individual dog. 2) *Suppositio materialis*: A name can also, however, be used to name itself, as when we say that dog has three letters. 3) *Suppositio simplex*: Finally, it can be used to name the relevant species, as we may indeed speak of the dog, the cat, the fish, etc. 4) According to Brentano, there is an additional case, which he also draws from scholastic sources.[71] This occurs whenever any name "X" is used as equivalent to "something called X" or "someone called X." This may be made clear in the case of proper names. Various individual people are called John, for instance. This is not a case of ambiguity or equivocation, since we have here only various individuals and not various meanings.[72] Nor is this name a general one, as the names of "dog," "cat," etc. are. It is possible, however, to say that this person is John and that person is also John as well. In such a case the name is equivalent to "someone called John." There are indeed many instances in which a proper name means hardly anything more than someone who bears that name. Consider, for instance, the following conversation:

---

68 Husserl 1901, 23–104.
69 The most elaborate version of this theory is expounded in Marty 1908. In Rollinger 2009 I argue that this theory originated with Brentano, as the passage cited from EL 80/13127, 13130–13131 indicates. Cesalli 2013, however, argues that Brentano's early pragmatic theory of meaning is lacking any notion of the *intention* to communicate whereas Marty's mature version of this theory does involve this notion. This point seems to be worth considering, although it would take us too far afield to discuss it further in the present context, as the focus of this analysis Brentano's relation with Marty or other students of his.
70 Marty B7. Marty did not attend Brentano's lectures on logic. His notes were apparently in large measure copied from Stumpf's notes and perhaps also from Brentano's lecture manuscript. One must confuse these notes with Marty's own notes (or notes of a student) from Prague (Log 20/58).
71 Brentano, EL 80/13018. In this connection Brentano (EL 80/13063) cites a medieval puzzle concerning a dog (*Hund*) and seal (*Seehund*) in a bag. One who sees that something is moving in the bag, may say in German that a *Hund* is moving. Here it is *ein Hund Genanntes* under consideration. Cf. Marty 1888, 248–249. Another example is: "I am traveling to Frankfurt" (Marty 1908, 509).
72 John Stuart Mill held the view that such a proper name, strictly speaking, does not have a meaning. Brentano does not address this issue in the *Logik*.

> A: John was here to see you today.
> B: Who is John?
> A: I have no idea. All I know is that it was someone called "John."

Hence a name, including a proper name, can be used in this sense which is yet an additional kind of *suppositio* besides the other three.

Thus far we have a picture of Brentano's theory of language in the *Logik* at a very early stage of development, but we must add that the lectures under consideration involve a revision in his theory of meaning. This will be more fully discussed below, but for now we should highlight a shift in perspective on the meaning of a statement. Though he continues to speak of it as a content of judgment, he characterizes it differently. It is, according to this revised theory, the content of the judgment which is expressed by the statement. This content of judgment is also called "the judged as such."[73] Here the question is particularly important whether this content is an immanent object in the sense of existing in the mind. Yet, it is difficult to come to a decision on this question on the basis of the text of the *Logik* or related texts. Moreover, our concern with the judged as such is increased by the passage that we have cited above from Stumpf's memoires: "It can be expressed linguistically in infinitival form or in 'that'-clauses."[74] If the judgment under consideration is "God is," this would mean that the content of the judgment is the being of God or that God is.[75] Although we find little in the *Logik* about the content of a judgment in this sense, we shall see in Brentano's treatment of disjunctive judgments he finds himself compelled to speak of the being (or existence) of an object.

7 Dialectic

As we have already stressed, the *Logik* gives us a doctrine of correct judgment as a means to testing rather than discovering and restricts such testing to the judging individual rather than the community. We should point out, however, that Brentano did devote some of his teaching activity to at least one of the domains of communicative logic, namely dialectic. This domain corresponds to Aristotle's *Topics* and *Sophistical Refutations* and accordingly concerns applications of logic to areas where prevalent opinions or perhaps opinions of the more educated people are under discussion. Although Brentano did not devote full-

---

73 Brentano, EL 13020: *"Das Geurteilte als solches ist die Bedeutung."*
74 Stumpf 1919, 106.
75 Here we must make allowances for differences between German and English grammar.

fledged lectures to dialectic, he did conduct two seminars on dialectic. These will briefly be discussed here in chronological order.

The first of these was a seminar entitled *Von den Sophismen und ihrer Anwendung auf politische Gebiet*. The notes for this seminar (EL 82) bear the date 3 May 1876, but they were used a year later for the summer semester 1877. They were first written in ink, but then heavily revised in pencil, possibly during the course of the seminar. They are however sketchy on many points. Like many of his predecessors, he maintains that there are bad as well as good arguments, some of the latter not merely mistakes, but genuine attempts to deceive. However, as we have already seen, the sophisms that concern Brentano are not only arguments (consisting of at least one premise and a conclusion), but also faulty claims to axioms, such as the inadequately understood inalienable rights that were declared in the French Revolution and ultimately resulted in blood baths. Here, however, the political philosophy of Brentano would take us too far afield from the concerns of the *Logik*, which are central to the present study.

The following statements are designated as prejudices (*Vorurteile*) in the manuscript under consideration here:

> The ground of knowledge must be the ground of the real.
> [The statement] that space [is] infinite.
> Change must be enduringly based on something.
> The psychological [is] physiological [and thus cannot be immediately known].
> All general laws must be induced.
> Everything must be proved or proof is better than immediate assumption.
> Everything must be explained from one principle (also the physical phenomena [from] motion, radically different phenomena conceived of in the same thing).
> Everything that is inferred with assurance must have existed at some time in experience.

> [Der Erkenntnisgrund müsse der Realgrund sein
> [Der Satz,] dass der Raum unendlich [sei].
> Es müsse etwas bleibend dem Wechsel zugrunde liegen.
> Das Psychologische [sei] physiologisch.
> Alle allgemeinen Gesetze müssten induziert [und können also nicht unmittelbar erkannt] werden.
> Die ersten Eindrücke müssten die einfachsten sein.
> Alles müsse bewiesen werden oder Beweis sei besser als unmittelbar[e] Annahme.

Alles müsse aus einem Prinzip erklärt werden (auch die psychisichen Phänomene [aus] Bewegung, radikal verschiedene Phänomene in dasselbe aufgefasst).
Alles, was mit Sicherheit erschlossen werde, müsse irgendwo in der Erfahrung vorgelegen haben.][76]

These principles are all given axiomatic status in various philosophical orientations, even the ones which deny the status of axioms as such (e.g. the prejudice that all generalizations are induced or that everything must be proved). Again we find Brentano giving particular attention to false principles as the source of error rather than invalid inferences.

Brentano conducted a seminar on disputation in the winter semester 1876/77. The notes for this seminar (EL 64) consist only of a nine-page manuscript. In a letter to Stumpf, Brentano writes:

> I am at present reading [i.e. lecturing on] logic and give in addition appendices to the psychology of the previous semester and exercises in disputation, which have as their basis in succession the most essential statements of the *Meditations* by Descartes.[77]

While it is impossible to reconstruct such rigorous step-by-step Cartesian-oriented exercises from the short and sketchy lecture notes, which are apparently only preparatory, we once more find Brentano taking his starting point from immediate cognition, both inner perception and a genuine grasp of axioms, and criticizing other positions in their failure to do precisely this.

By no means, however, should we take Brentano to be giving a whole-hearted endorsement to Descartes' *Mediations* as such, for these contain a version of the ontological argument which Brentano had already rejected in his Würzburg days and continued to reject for the rest of his life. We may remark also that, besides the previously noted problems in the ontological argument, an additional one from Brentano's perspective comes to light in Descartes' attempt to demonstrate the existence of God by using the axiom according to which the cause is more perfect than the effect. For Brentano this axiom is no more a genuine item of cognition than Spinoza's fourth axiom, according to which knowing the effect involves knowing the cause.[78]

---

76   EL 82/14001.
77   Brentano 1877, 184. The manuscript from which Brentano was lecturing on logic was of course EL 80, i.e. the *Logik*.
78   See below, pp. 145, 218.

Among the interesting points which we can find in the notes on disputation is the suggestion of topics for disputations (*Vorschlag der Thematen*), which includes the following:

> 1. Evidence of inner perception: evidence of the psychical phenomena. 2. Origin of law: Origin positive or natural or a priori truths. 3. Determinism. 4. Ontological argument. 5. Are there axioms? Are there evident judgments? 6. What [is] judgment? 7. Abstract concepts. 8. Unconscious consciousness. 9. Unity of consciousness. 10. Darwin and teleology. 11. Limits of the knowledge of nature. 12. Hume's theory of providence. 13. Smaller credibility of intrinsic improbabilities. Hume on the miracles.
>
> [1. Evidenz der inneren Wahrnehmung: Evidenz der psychischen Phänomene. 2. Ursprung des Rechts: Ursprung positiv oder natürlich oder apriorische Wahrheiten. 3. Determinismus. 4. Ontologisches Argument. 5. Gibt es Axiome? Gibt es evidente Urteile? 6. Was [ist] das Urteil? 7. Abstrakte Begriffe. 8. Unbewusstes Bewusstsein. 9. Einheit des Bewusstseins. 10. Darwin und die Teoleologie. 11. Grenzen der Naturerkenntnisse. 12. Humes Lehre von der Providenz. 13. Geringere Glaubenswürdigkeit der in sich Unwahrscheinlichkeiten. Hume über die Wunder.][79]

Many of these topics are indeed ones that Brentano brings up in the *Logik* as well as his other lectures, as themes which are to receive further treatment with the tool of a properly reformed logic. Indeed, all of them turn up in various areas of his system of philosophy in one way or another.

8 Concluding Remarks

In sum, Brentano conceives of logic as the art of judging and contrasts this concept with two others that he rejects: that of logic as the art of thinking and that of logic as the art of reasoning. What we find in the *Logik*, however, is only part of the art of judging (though never designated by him as a *Kunstlehre*, as we find this designation recurring among many of Brentano's contemporaries, including even some of his students). The *Logik* is an individual logic, not a communicative logic. Nor does it include the logic of discovery, though Brentano apparently originally planned to encompass a logic of discovery in the *Logik*. What we have in these lectures is only the logic of testing, also called "elementary logic." Such a logic, on Brentano's view, in fact has great advantages over a

---

79 Brentano EL 65/10869.

logic of discovery and must be treated first. While logic, according to Brentano's conception, is not to replace natural talent or exercise, he nonetheless regards it as a discipline of great value. For natural talent and exercise do not always suffice in keeping us from falling prey to error. There is obviously much psychology in the *Logik*, for logic is the art of judging, and judging is a function of mind. Yet, he does not succumb to psychologism, because he gives logic an *a priori* status, which seems to be connected to metaphysics according to him. The law of non-contradiction and perhaps the laws of inference have their theoretical home in metaphysics, their practical home in logic. In the former case they are laws, in the latter rules. This need not at all be alarming, for it is in fact very much in line with the Aristotelian view of the matter. Language also falls within the purview of logic, though restricted to the consideration of two classes of categoramatic linguistic expressions: names and statements. While Brentano thinks that language serves communication and facilitates thought in important ways, he also thinks that it can in some instances be detrimental. The chief obstacle that language puts before our judging is to be found in equivocation. Though this can be removed in certain disciplines, e.g. mathematics, it is a much greater threat to judgment in other disciplines, especially in metaphysics. The topic of language in the *Logik* will continue to receive attention in the following two chapters. What emerges time and again throughout Brentano's treatment of logic is its intimate tie with psychology and metaphysics, which we should keep in mind throughout the present analysis.

CHAPTER 3

Concept

The largest section of Brentano's *Logik* is an elaboration on "thoughts and their expression in language." In the preceding chapter we have already entered this territory somewhat. In this chapter, however, we shall particularly concern ourselves with Brentano's views on those thoughts that he calls "concepts" (*Begriffe*). As we have seen, logic for him must involve some consideration of presentations. While some of these presentations are sensations (*Empfindungen*) or intuitions (*Anschauungen*), these are not the presentations that are properly involved in thinking. Concepts are rather derived from these.[1] Hence, our concrete intuition of red allows us to form a concept of red. When one judgment movitates another one, we have an intuition of cause and effect, according to Brentano. However, he does not provide us with a strict definition of a concept. Here we shall venture to say that a concept for him is a thought in which a distinction can be found between the content on the one hand and the extension on the other. The extension consists of the objects that fall under the concept, even if this extension does not exceed beyond a single object, whereas the content consists of those marks (*Merkmale*) that must belong to all these objects. For the most part, Brentano identifies a concept with a content of a presentation rather than the act of presenting. We must of course bear in mind that Brentano does not always work with strict definitions and precise terminology in the *Logik*. It is, after all, a set of lecture notes which were constantly undergoing revision and not a finished book.

In the *Logik* Brentano is basically working with the same psychology that he elaborated on in his *Psychologie vom empirischen Standpunkte*. According to this psychology, "All psychical phenomena have in common a relation to a content. This is what distinguishes them from everything else."[2] The usage of the term "content" in this context is rather troublesome. It does not seem to be the same as the content in the sense which has just been indicated, namely in contrast with extension. As is well known, Brentano also spoke of the immanent object of consciousness in contrast with the external object. He also spoke of the "intentional inexistence" (*intentionale Inexistenz*) of an object.[3] Some think

---

1   Brentano 1889, 50 f.
2   Brentano EL 80/13003: "*Alle psychischen Phänomene haben gemeinsam eine Beziehung auf einen Inhalt. Das ist, was sie von jedem anderen unterscheidet.*"
3   Brentano 1874, 115 ff. In his preparatory manuscripts for the *Logik* he says regarding the three

that what Brentano meant in this early doctrine of intentionality is that there is an object in the mind, whether or not there also an object outside of the mind.[4] Intentionality would thus in fact be a relation in the proper sense and not merely in a manner of speaking. According to this view, his later statement that intentionality is *not* a proper relation, but rather "relation-like" (*Relativliches*), insofar as the foundation (the act of consciousness) can exist and the term (the object of consciousness) need not exist,[5] represents a substantive shift in doctrine. According to a more recent interpretation, however, Brentano never, even when he spoke of immanent objects, actually did think that there is an object that exists in the mind. On this view, the later statement is only a *reformulation* of the early doctrine.[6] While I do not propose to settle this matter definitively here, I shall address this issue below in connection with Brentano's already briefly discussed theory of the meaning of a name as it is put forward in the *Logik*.

1 Presentations and Names

As we have already pointed out, Brentano refuses to characterize logic as the art of thinking because he regards the term "thinking" as one that can refer to both presenting and judging. These in fact belong to two different basic classes of psychical phenomena and are thus to be most rigorously distinguished. Yet, he adds, "This is not to say that a judging without presenting [is] possible. This is indeed also not [possible] in the case of desiring [i.e. loving or hating]. Whoever judges presents what he judges."[7] Presentations are accordingly regarded as the fundamental psychical phenomena and are as such unavoidable in the treatment of judgments, which is of course a focal concern in logic as the art of judging.

---

different functions of consciousness "that [they involve] a mental inexistence, but in different ways [*dass eine mentale Inexistenz, aber in verschiedener Weise*]." (EL 75/12921[54].) Again, after distinguishing between three classes of psychical phenomena, Brentano adds, "But [they have this in] common: that [they have] a mental in existence [*Aber gemeinsam, dass eine mentale Inexistenz*]." (EL 80/13514.) In these manuscripts he also speaks of "objective inexistence" (*objektive Inexistenz*) (EL 75/12921[21]). Such statements are perhaps the earliest ones of the doctrine of intentionality to be found in Brentano's writings. In this regard it appears that he actually formulated this doctrine in the context of logic rather than psychology.

4 Smith 1994 and Chrudzimski 2001.
5 Brentano 1911, 123.
6 Antonelli 2000 and Antonelli 2012.
7 Brentano, EL 80/13004–13005: "*Damit* [*wird*] *offenbar nicht gesagt, dass ein Urteilen ohne ein Vorstellen möglich* [*sei*]. *Dies* [*ist*] *ja auch nicht* [*möglich*] *beim Begehren. Wer urteilt, stellt das, was er beurteilt, vor.*"

We have also already seen that Brentano regards names as the linguistic expressions that properly express presentations. Although we might expect an account of the meaning of a name, we have seen in the previous chapter that his earliest theory of meaning attributes meanings to statements, but not to names. Brentano, however, did not continue to put forward such a theory in the *Logik*. He did continue to speak of the content of a judgment and maintained that this content is the meaning of the statement whereby the judgment is expressed. Yet, he also arrived at the view that the content of a presentation is the meaning of the name whereby the presentation is expressed. The revised theory of meaning is moreover no longer a pragmatic one. Let us consider this revised theory further.

In this theory of meaning, apparently presented in his logic lectures as early as the winter semester 1870/71, he argues that the meaning of a name cannot be identical with the named object. While some attach great significance to Frege's distinction between sense (*Sinn*) and reference (*Bedeutung*) as a great innovation,[8] Brentano was making precisely a distinction of this kind a couple of decades before Frege was doing so, although their terminology differs. Brentano says that the meaning of a name is made clear in cases where there are two names that differ in meaning and at the same time name the same object. The names "the son of Phaenerate" and "the wisest among the Athenians" are for him examples of this: two different meanings and yet only one named object.[9] The meaning of a name, as it turns out, is the content of the presentation which the name expresses rather than the named object. This content is moreover also, according to Brentano, what is presented *as* it is presented.[10] The name "the founder of logic" expresses a presentation that presents its object *as* the founder of logic, whereas the name "the teacher of

---

8   Frege 1892.
9   The example is changed in Mayer-Hillebrand's edition of Brentano's logic (an edition compiled very freely from various sources, including lecture notes that Franz Hillebrand allegedly took from Brentano in the late 1880s, though these – not to be confused the notes published in the material of the present volume – have not been found). There we find the distinction between "the founder of logic" and "the teacher of Alexander the Great" to illustrate a case of two different meanings and yet only one object (Brentano 1956, 47). It is nonetheless wrong to assert that Brentano lacks "Frege's machinery" of sense and reference (Kriegel 2018, 31). However, I do not wish to say that Brentano was the first philosopher or logician ever to acknowledge such a distinction.
10 In Brentano's plan for the *Logik* (EL 73/12593) and other related manuscripts for the *Logik* he also speaks of the presentation (*Vorstellung*) as distinct from both the act of presentation (*Vorstellungsakt*) and what is presented (*das Vorgestellte*). In these cases the presentation seems to be the presented as such. This terminology, however, is not used in the *Logik*. Moreover, in Brentano 1874, 103, he explicitly says that he understands the presentation to be the "act of presenting."

Alexander the Great" expresses a presentation that presents the same object *as* the teacher of Alexander the Great.[11] The presented *as* what is presented therefore differs, and thus the two names differ in meaning. Here we should point out that the meaning a name in this sense does not share in the presentational character of the act. It is strictly a distinction that is made on the side of the object,[12] and yet the meaning is not itself the object as long as we understand the object to be what is presented *simpliciter*.

In view of Brentano's early descriptions of the intentional relation of a psychical phenomenon to an object as the "intentional inexistence" of the object and his related contrast between the actual and the immanent object, the question arises whether the presented *as* what is presented is in fact the same as the immanent object. This question becomes all the more difficult in the face of different interpretations of Brentano's concept of the immanent object. If the immanent object and the presented as such are identified, it would seem wrong to ascribe to him the view that the immanent object is something existing in the mind. What we present *as* the son of Phaenerate and what we present *as* the wisest man among the Athenians would be distinguishable from external objects, and yet they happen to be identical with a certain external object (or at least were so at one time). We would accordingly regard the doctrine of intentional inexistence more appropriately neither as a psychological theory nor as an ontological one, but rather as a semantical theory.

Nonetheless, this interpretation is not completely satisfying when we look at other manuscripts which are closely related to the *Logik*. In a passage that was removed from these lecture notes, Brentano says that there are "objectless presentations" (*gegenstandslose Vorstellungen*) in the sense that they have no external object, but they still have an immanent one.[13] One might take such a statement as a support for the view that immanent objects are in fact objects in the mind. Moreover, the following passage was written for the *Logik*, though perhaps never used in Brentano's lectures:

---

11   The same strategy for distinguishing between the meaning of a name and the named object again turns up in Husserl 1901, 47 ("the victor of Jena" and "the vanquished of Waterloo"), though Husserl gives the concept of meaning a Platonic twist which could never be acceptable for Brentano.

12   In this regard the presented as presented, according to Brentano's conception, is not to be identified with the noema, which is highlighted in Husserl 1913 and is indeed characterized as sharing in the act-character. A comparison between Brentano and Husserl, however, would take us far afield of the topic of our analysis no less than a comparison between Brentano and Frege would.

13   Brentano, EL 80/13016.

The name *makes known* a psychical phenomenon, *means* the content of a presentation as such (the immanent object?), *names* that which is presented *via* the content of a presentation. Of this [content] we say: The name belongs to it. The possible real object of the presentation [is, by contrast to the content,] that which an external object of the presentation is if it does exist. (We name [something] via mediation of the meaning.)

(Man is a species = the content of the presentation of a human being is species = the meaning of the word "man" is a species.)

[Der Name *gibt kund* ein psychisches Phänomen, *bedeutet* den Inhalt einer Vorstellung als solchen (den immanenten Gegenstand?), *nennt* das, was durch den Inhalt einer Vorstellung vorgestellt wird. Davon sagen wir: Es kommen ihm der Namen zu. Der etwaige wirkliche Gegenstände der Vorstellungen [ist im Gegensatz zum Inhalt], was, wenn er existiert, äußerer Gegenstand der Vorstellung ist. (Man nennt [etwas] unter Vermittlung der Bedeutung.)

(Mensch ist eine Spezies = der Inhalt der Vorstellung eines Menschen ist eine Spezies = die Bedeutung des Wortes "Mensch" ist eine Spezies.)][14]

While passages from the final version of the *Logik* may have greater exegetical weight than this, they occur in a context which does not lend them the definitiveness which one would like in support of the interpretation under discussion. A final reason why the semantic interpretation of the doctrine of intentional inexistence may be subject to doubt lies the fact that Brentano's assertion that Aristotle's notion of the form of the sensed object being received without its matter is already an expression of this doctrine.[15] If this is so, inexistence applies to cases outside the scope of semantics, namely sensation.

In sum, the *Logik* apparently does not allow us to solve the problem of how to interpret Brentano's doctrine of intentional inexistence. If anything, it makes this problem more complex, for it also introduces the notion of contents of judgment as distinct from contents of presentation, whereas the previously discussed pragmatic theory of meaning allows for the contents of judgments, but not contents of presentations. Here we stress that Brentano does not explicitly characterize contents of judgment as immanent objects. While it may be unsatisfying that the *Logik* does not solve the problem we have been discussing, one must bear in mind that the lectures in question were ultimately meant for

---

14   Brentano, EL 80/13528.
15   Brentano 1874, 115–116 n.

teaching his students the art of judging, particularly in the domain of testing whether a judgment is evident or not. What Brentano will ultimately have to say about such testing does not turn on how intentional inexistence is to be understood.

Yet, another question that arises concerning Brentano's view that the meaning of a name is the content of the corresponding presentation concerns how early he put forward this view. The earliest manuscript that is relevant here is his plan for the *Logik*, most likely written in 1869 and certainly no later than 1870 (as can be seen from the older handwriting). There he says that a name means "the presented, but not as something presented, but rather what it is presented as."[16] Brentano's distinction between content and object was already in place long before his students, such as Twardowski, began to utilize it for their own purposes.[17]

Brentano's main concern with presentations in the *Logik* is to make distinctions between certain kinds of them, insofar as these distinctions are of course relevant to the art of judging. By no means, however, is this treatment of presentations intended to be exhaustive. Aesthetics rather than logic, after all, is the practical discipline which especially deals with presentations. Brentano is primarily concerned with the semantic aspects of names and presentations, i.e. with concepts.

Brentano's treatment of concepts in the *Logik* might be compared with Aristotle's *Categories*, although such a comparison would be rather superficial. The categories which Aristotle enumerates and elaborates on in that work turn up again in a metaphysical context.[18] In the *Logik*, however, the treatment of concepts does not explicitly have such a metaphysical application. Brentano's doctrine of concepts in these lectures would be more favorably compared with the second book of Locke's *Essay concerning Human Nature*, although Locke's interest in the *origin* of ideas in that part of his classical work is not the prevailing interest in the *Logik*. That is to say, while Brentano examines concepts primarily from a *descriptive* point of view in his lectures on logic, Locke investigates them primarily from a "genetic" point of view as well. Nevertheless, we shall see that the *Logik* is not completely indifferent to the origin of ideas.

---

16 Brentano, EL 73/12594: "*das Vorgestellte, aber nicht als Vorgestelltes, sondern als was es vorgestellt wird.*" The phrase "not as something presented" confirms our thesis that the content of a presentation on Brentano's view does not share in the act of presenting.
17 Twardowski 1894. The manuscript from 1869 or 1870 that is cited in the previous footnote suffices to show that Betti 2013 is wrong in asserting the thesis that Brentano formulated the content-object distinction in the 1880s in reaction to Sigwart.
18 In Brentano 1862 the context in which the Aristotelian categories are discussed is plainly a metaphysical one.

2 Distinctions among Concepts

Let us consider, first of all, some of the distinctions that Brentano makes among various concepts in the *Logik*. Here we shall discuss only a selection of these distinctions, for Brentano only mentions some of them in passing.

First of all, Brentano divides concepts into ones which are *individual* and ones which are *universal* (or general). "A general concept," says Brentano, "is one to which different objects can correspond, while an individual is one to which only one object can correspond, e.g. Socrates, the wisest among all Greeks who have lived."[19] The concept of a dog, by contrast with the presentation of Socrates, may have many different individuals corresponding to it.[20] Here of course we may be reminded of ancient disputes about whether there are actually universals which somehow exist beyond our concepts. The realists say that there are, whereas the nominalists say that only individual objects (so-called "particulars") exist. While Brentano certainly does not embrace realism regarding universals, he also concedes that it is correct in rejecting nominalism. "For 'universal' and 'individual' in the proper sense," he explains, "only pertain to the contents of psychical phenomena, e.g. universal judgment, universal love of man."[21] This passage seems to indicate that it would, strictly speaking, be

---

19   EL 80/13025: "Ein allgemeiner Begriff ist ein solcher, dem verschiedene Gegenstände entsprechen können, individuell ein solcher, welchem nur ein Gegenstand entsprechen kann. z.B. Sokrates, der weiseste unter allen Griechen, welche gelebt haben." We may note here that "the wisest among all Greeks, which apparently names only one individual," has a meaning on Brentano's view. Meaning is therefore not restricted to general names, although it would be amiss to ascribe meaning to sensations.

20   While the correspondence of more than one individual to a concept makes that concept universal, Brentano says in an earlier manuscript (EL 81/13509) (first written in ink and heavily revised in pencil) that a universal concept has "one, but an indeterminate meaning, such that there possibly corresponds to the presentation several objects [*eine, aber eine unbestimmte Bedeutung, so dass der Vorstellung möglicherweise mehrere Gegenstände entsprechen*]," or that the concept is universal when something is presented "as what can be presented and named as multiple [*als etwas, als was Mehreres vorgestellt und genannt sein kann*]." Even if there is only one, the concept "founder of logic" is nonetheless universal, according to this older definition, because there could have been more than one.

21   EL 80/13025: "*Denn universell und individuell im eigentlichen Sinn gelten nur von Inhalten psychischer Phänomene, [z.B.] allgemeines Urteil, allgemeine Liebe.*" Cf. Masaryk 1875 (no signature), 15: "Only our psychical phenomena relate to many or single objects. It is therefore better to say, instead of universal – individual objects, a universally – individually presented object [*Nur unsere psychischen Phänomene beziehen sich auf viele oder einzelne Gegenstände. Es ist daher besser anstatt: universelle – individuelle Gegenstände zu sagen: ein universell – individuell vorgestellter Gegenstand.*]" The application of the distinction under

wrong to describe anything outside of such contents as individual or particular. It would accordingly be wrong to say, as Locke does, that only particulars exist.[22] The dispute involving realism, nominalism, and other conceptions of universals, however, is not a focal concern of the *Logik*, for that dispute involves more extensive metaphysical and psychological considerations.

Secondly, Brentano distinguishes between *simple* and *complex* concepts. Here we find an early statement of his theory of parts and wholes, which came to have great impact on some of his students, particularly on Stumpf,[23] Twardowski,[24] and (through Stumpf) on Husserl.[25] When we say something is complex, this means that it has parts. According to the *Logik*, there are three ways in which a thing can consist of parts, namely "of 1. physical, 2. metaphysical, 3. logical parts."[26] Examples of the first kind of complexity are a herd, a house, mind and body (*Leib*), or indeed a body (*Körper*). Metaphysical parts, however, are properties (*Eigenschaften*), such as humanity and braveness as parts of a hero. Logical parts are something colored in relation to something red, for instance, or a figure in relation to a circle.[27]

---

consideration here is of great importance not only to presentations, but to judgments and acts of love and hate as well. It will be seen below how Brentano deals with universal judgments, though the distinction between universals and invidiuals in the realm of acts of love and hate lies beyond the scope of this study.

22   Locke, *Essay concerning Human Understanding*, III.iii.§ 6.
23   Stumpf 1873.
24   Twardowsk 1894.
25   Husserl 1901, 222–285. This investigation was preceded by a similar one that Husserl had published in 1894. See Husserl 1979, 92–100.
26   Brentano, EL 80/13027: "*aus 1. physischen, 2. metaphysichen, 3. Logischen Teilen.*" To this list could be added: collective parts. See pp. 195, 263 below. The members of a herd would in this case more properly be designated as collective rather than physical parts.
27   Already in Brentano 1867, 55 ff. distinguishes between physical and logical parts in his interpetation of the Aristotelian doctrine of the soul. In his early lectures on metaphysics he explains his usage of these terms (M 95). Logical parts are called "logical" not because they are exclusively the concern of logic. Indeed, he maintains that metaphysics is likewise concerned with such parts. They are rather logical in the sense that they pertain to the *logos* of the thing under consideration. Strictly speaking, the *logos* is the definition, though it can be understood in a broader sense as well. "The metaphysical parts too are indeed called metaphysical, not because [only] metaphysics is concerned with them, but in contrast to the physical ones, which, at least insofar as they are parts of substances – and these are precisely the most prominent ones – are found only in connection with corporeal entities, whereas the metaphysical ones, substance as well as accidents, belong also to minds. We call them metaphysical because of this greater universality, as indeed metaphysics is also the most universal science, more universal than physics which is only concerned with the corporeal [*Heißen ja auch die metaphysischen Teile nicht darum metaphysisch, weil von ihnen [nur] die Metaphysik handelt, sondern im Gegensatz zu den physischen, welche,*

With regard to logical parts in particular Brentano points out that there is in their case a one-sided separability (*Trennbarkeit*). Color and red, for instance, can be parts of a whole. Color can be separated from red, for it can also be a part of green whereas something red can never exist separately from color. The separable logical part is the genus. Yet, parts need not only be parts of things, for by analogy a non-thing can also have parts, "e.g. something called ψυχή by the Greeks and *anima* by the Romans (metaphysical), a quantity of six feet, a journey from Aschaffenburg to Würzburg, an army (physical), redness (logical)."[28]

While Brentano's pioneering work in the theory of wholes and parts is certainly praiseworthy, it is disturbing that in this context he speaks of simple and complex *concepts*. A concept for him seems to be either a presentation or a content of a presentation, whereas such examples as a house, a hero, and something colored might indicate objects to which concepts (or the relevant names) refer and not to the concepts themselves. It is, in other words, unclear whether the complexity or simplicity of a concept under discussion here belongs to its content or to its extension. In his 1884/85 lectures on logic Brentano does in fact deal with this problem. There he maintains that the metaphysical parts together individuate the content.[29]

Another division that Brentano makes is the one between *relative* and *non-relative* concepts.[30] The presentation of a cause, for instance, is the presentation of something in relation to something, namely to its effect. Cause and effect are indeed *correlativa*, just as master and servant, top and bottom are. When Brentano speaks of relations, he in fact often has in mind cases of these kinds. Here we only note that status of objects as *correlativa* is entirely a con-

---

    *wenigstens soweit sie Teile von Substanzen sind – und diese gerade sind die vornehmsten – nur an körperlichen Wesen gefunden werden, während die metaphysischen, Substanz sowohl als Akzidenzen, auch Geistern zukommen. Darum nennt man sie metaphysisch wegen dieser größeren Allgemeinheit, wie ja auch die Metaphysik die allgemeinste Wissenschaft ist, allgemeiner als die Physik, die bloß von dem Körperlichen handelt.]" (M 95/31567). The characterization of physical parts here, however, cannot be definitive, for in his lectures on the immortality of the soul, which were a prologue to the *Logik* in 1869, Brentano came to the conclusion that the soul itself is a physical part of a human being (Ps 62/54011–54012; see Rollinger 2012, pp. 272 f., where the relevant passage is quoted). This means that the soul is separable from the corporeal part, not that the soul is itself is corporeal.

28   Brentano, EL 80/13028: "*z.B. ein von den Griechen Psyche, von den Römern Anima Genanntes (metaphysisch), eine Größe von sechs Fuß, eine Reise von Aschafffenburg bis Würzburg, ein Heer (physisch), Röte (logisch).*"

29   In this regard one should consult the fifth and sixth chapters below which will have to suffice until a proper edition of Brentano EL 72 is published.

30   Brentano, EL 80/13029.

ceptual issue, for even though an effect has a cause in a strictly necessary sense, this is not so, for instance, regarding the relation of a chicken to an egg. We can only know from experience that the latter is the cause of the former, whereas we can know that every effect has a cause simply by having the concepts of cause and effect.[31]

Concepts can also be positive or negative, although Brentano provides no examples in this case. However, when we see how Brentano reformulates the four classes of judgments in traditional logic (A, E, I, and O), it will become clear that he will need negative terms and accordingly negative concepts.[32] Logically, this doesn't seem to be a problem. Although the issue can arise in a more psychological and metaphysical context, we mention it here only in passing since Brentano does not provide elaborations on it in the *Logik*.

According to the *Logik*, we can also divide concepts according to their origin, namely from inner or outer perception, from imagination, or from any combination of these. We have said that Brentano's concern with concepts in the *Logik*, in contrast with Locke's concern with ideas in Book II of the *Essay concerning Human Understanding*, is primarily descriptive rather than genetic. In his division between concepts with regard to their origin, however, he does address some of Locke's concerns. As Locke had identified some concepts as originating in reflection, others as originating in sensation, and others still as originating from both sources, Brentano likewise identifies the same sources, though with his own terminology. The *Logik* does not provide us with examples of such originations, but it is not difficult to see what he has in mind. Our concepts of presentations, judgments, and emotions, for instance, originate in inner perception (reflection), whereas our concepts of color and extension originate in outer perception (sensation). Color and genus, moreover, belong together as species of the same genus, namely sensory quality. While we get this concept from our sensations, it is not to be confused with quality in a completely different sense, namely the quality of judgments, whereby one judgment is an affirmation and yet another judgment is a negation. We get our concept of quality in this sense from inner perception. Our concept of a metaphysical part has its origin in both inner and outer perception. However, Brentano also lists imagination (*Phantasie*) as one of the sources of concepts.

---

31 In an older manuscript (EL 81/13543) Brentano gives the following examples of *correlativa*: "parents – children, greater – smaller, husband – wife, cause – effect, knowing – known [*Eltern – Kinder, größer – kleiner, Mann – Weib, Ursache – Wirkung, Erkennen – erkannt*]." While some treat such pairs as opposites, this way of viewing them requires considerable qualification, as indicated below (pp. 210–214, 276–280).

32 See Enoch 1893, 437 f.

In this regard he diverges from Locke. Here Brentano is no doubt thinking of his doctrine of original association, according to which the temporal features of an object can only be presented imaginatively.[33] A sensory content may have location, intensity, and quality, but any feature that involves time does not come from sensation, but rather from imagination. According to Brentano, we do not actually see motion, for instance, for at any instant we can only see the moving object at its present location. We associate ideas of the object at previous locations, however, and this provides us with a presentation of the motion.

As already seen, in the *Logik* Brentano allows for presentations of non-things as well as things. Here we see yet another division between presentations, although Brentano maintains that we can present even a fiction, such as a person living on Mars, as a thing.[34] Its existence or non-existence is thus irrelevant to its status as a thing, just as the presentation may very well be one of a non-thing (e.g. of redness).

It is important to note here that the name which expresses a presentation need not always indicate whether the presented object is a thing or a non-thing. Some names, according to Brentano, are indeterminate in this respect. These are *aorista*, which are explained as follows:

> We present something as something undecided (*aoriston*), where if it is accepted nothing is determined as to whether it ia thing or not. These are, for instance, negative, paeterita and future, as also wherever nothing is decided about present, past, and future, e.g. "someone living at some time," *objectiva, signitiva, possibilia*, and the like. (*Hypothetica* and *disjunctiva*.) Many *relativa* (equal, cause). (An *aoriston* can be an individual, e.g. "something called Homer.") ... A particularly important and curious *aoriston* is that which [remains] undecided as to whether [it is] included in nothing, one, or collective, such as a number [like] 0 and 1.
>
> [Als ein Unentschiedenes (Aoriston) wird genannt und vorgestellt, wobei, wenn es anerkannt wird, nichts darüber bestimmt wird, ob es ein Ding ist oder nicht. Solche sind z.B. Negativa; Päterita und Futura, so wie auch wo über Gegenwart, Vergangenheit und Zukunft nichts entschieden wird, z.B. ein Irgendwann-Lebender; Objektiva; Signativa; Possibilia u.dgl. (Hypothetika und Disjunktiva). Viele Relativa (gleich, Ursache).

---

33   Brentano 1982, 19. See Rollinger 2019, 178.
34   Brentano, EL 80/13030.

> (Ein Aoriston kann Individuum sein, z.B. ein Homer Genanntes.) ... Ein besonders wichtiges und merkwürdiges Aoriston ist das, wo es unentschieden [bleibt], ob [es] nichts, eins oder Kollektiv wie z.B. eine Zahl 0 und 1 eingerechnet ...][35]

While these are all extremely interesting cases, Brentano unfortunately doesn't enter into further detail about them in the *Logik*. The most salient examples are of course the *negativa*, which have already been considered. If we further consider Brentano's elaborations on genera in his 1884/85 lectures, we note a view that is highly relevant here.[36] He tells us that the genus of a thing is not actually the same as the genus of an imagined thing or a past or future thing. A present king, a past king, and a future king are not all kings. Only a present king is a king. The same could be said of a thing in general. If we speak of a past or future thing, we are not properly thinking of a thing. Accordingly if we leave the time to which something belongs undecided, it is also left undecided whether it is a thing.[37]

Presentations or concepts are further divided into ones according to an *essential* determination and ones according to an *inessential* determination.[38] Of this division Brentano says the following in the *Logik*:

> a) ... if we are dealing with relations among the things we present, the ones that are commonly presented via a presentation have, besides one determination also yet other ones too that distinguish them from others that are not subsumed thereunder.
>
> b) Two cases: In the case of some general presentations the things subsumed thereunder differentiate themselves from the ones not subsumed thereunder only in certain particulars that one can enumerate, whereas others differentiate themselves in more particulars than we can enumerate or even than we might expect ever to know ...

---

35 Brentano, EL 80/13031.
36 See below, pp. 212, 278.
37 Here we are restricted to Brentano's philosophy during the nineteenth century, primarily to the *Logik*, but we should remark in passing that this problem as well as many others are viewed from a rather different perspective in his late philosophy, according to which a non-thing cannot be presented and therefore not correctly accepted. Statements in which *aorista* occur as grammatical names would accordingly be reformulated into statements in which the only names would be the names of things, "logical" rather than "grammatical" names.
38 Brentano, EL 80/13032.

c) Examples of the first kind: e.g. white, two feet long; of the second by contrast: animals, plants, oxygen, phosphorous. Hundreds of generations have not exhausted the common properties of these, as we also do not presuppose that they are exhaustible, but rather we again and again make new observations and experiments in full confidence of discovering new properties that were not by any means included in the previously known one.

If, however, someone were to endeavor to investigate the common properties of all things that have the same shape, the same color, or the same specific weight, this would be an obvious absurdity. No other ones are common to them besides the ones included in the name itself or derivable (through a law of causation).

d) Some have often interpreted this as saying that in the former presentations the things are presented in their substantial determinations (substantial differentia). This, however, is wrong. 1. These are in no single case at all accessible. "Thing" is the only substantial concept that we might have. Demonstration from the definition of "human." 2. Such a determination is often intrinsically of very little significance: a taste, smell, a crystal formation different by a small angle …

e) It is inappropriate to say, however, that of these two classifications the one corresponds to a more radical distinction in the things themselves. If such determinations are themselves not substantial ones, they are still signs of a special substantial affinity that is not in itself observable. What makes these innumerable peculiarities inseparable, such that wherever the one is the others also occur, and where the one is lost innumerable [peculiarities] are eliminated?

From the determinations themselves there does not shine forth such a necessity, but a necessitating ground must exist, and this will lie in the lie in the particularity of the substance hidden from us on which the peculiarities depend. If we were to be familiar with it, we would grasp the necessity of the concomitant peculiarities. Thus while the inessentials have a multiplicity of causes, the other, essential ones have a common cause.

But this is a matter of concern for ontology, not for logic. It belongs to the points concerning which the metaphysicians of different schools dispute most of all. Whether there are substances and substantial differentiae and whether the determinations that we have just discussed indicate them or not, it suffices that they are themselves certainly undeniable.

[a] ... wenn wir von den Verhältnissen des Vorgestellten handeln, ... haben Dinge, die durch eine Vorstellung gemeinsam vorgestellt werden, außer der einen auch noch andere Bestimmungen gemein, welche sie von anderen, nicht darunter begriffenen unterscheiden.

b) Ein doppelter Fall: Bei manchen allgemeinen Vorstellungen unterscheiden sich die darunter begriffenen Dinge von den nicht darunter begriffenen nur in gewissen Einzelheiten, die man aufzählen kann, während sich andere in mehr Einzelheiten unterscheiden als wir aufzählen können oder sogar als wir jemals zu wissen erwarten dürfen ...

c) Beispiele der ersten Art: z.B. weiß, 2 Schuh groß; der zweiten dagegen: Tiere, Pflanzen, Sauerstoff, Phosphor. Hunderte von Generationen haben die gemeinsamen Eigenschaften davon nicht erschöpft, auch setzen wir gar nicht voraus, dass sie zu erschöpfen seien, sondern wir machen immer neue Beobachtungen und Experimente in der vollen Zuversicht, neue Eigenschaften zu entdecken, welche in den vorher gekannten keineswegs eingeschlossen lagen. Wenn sich aber Jemand vornehmen wollte, die gemeinsamen Eigenschaften aller Dinge zu untersuchen, welche dieselbe Gestalt, dieselbe Farbe oder dasselbe spezifische Gewicht haben, so wäre dies eine handgreifliche Absurdität.

Keine anderen sind ihnen gemeinsam als die in dem Namen selbst eingeschlossenen oder (durch ein Kausalgesetz) ableitbaren.

d) Vielfach hat man dies so gedeutet, dass man sagte, in den ersteren Vorstellungen würden die Dinge ihren substanziellen Bestimmungen (substanziellen Differenzen) nach vorgestellt. Allein dies ist falsch. 1. überhaupt keine sind zugänglich. „Ding" ist der einzige substanzielle Begriff, den wir etwa haben. Nachweis, an der Definition des Menschen. 2. Eine solche Bestimmung ist oft in sich selbst von sehr geringer Bedeutung: ein Geschmack, Geruch, eine um einen kleinen Winkel verschiedene Kristallbildung ... e) Allein dennoch ist es gewiss nicht unpassend zu sagen, dass von diesen zwei Klassifikationen die eine einer viel radikaleren Unterscheidung in den Dingen selbst entspreche. Wenn solche Bestimmungen selbst keine substanziellen sind, so sind sie doch Zeichen einer besonderen substanziellen Verwandtschaft, die in sich selbst nicht zu beobachten ist.

Was macht diese unzählbaren Eigentümlichkeiten unzertrennlich, so dass, wo die eine ist, auch die anderen sich finden, und wo die eine verloren geht sofort unzählige aufgehoben werden?

Aus den Bestimmungen selbst erhellt sich eine solche Notwendigkeit nicht, aber dennoch muss ein nötigender Grund bestehen, und dieser wird in der uns verborgenen Besonderheit der Substanz liegen, von der die Eigentümlichkeiten abhängen. Würden wir sie kennen, so würden wir die Notwendigkeit der begleitenden Eigentümlichkeiten einsehen. So während die einen Unwesentlichen eine Vielfachheit der Ursachen haben, haben die anderen Wesentlichen eine gemeinsame.

Doch dies geht die Ontologie, nicht die Logik an. Es gehört zu den Punkten, über die am meisten die Metaphysiker verschiedener Schulen sich streiten. Mag es Substanzen und substantielle Differenzen geben und mögen auf sie die von uns eben besprochenen Bestimmungen hindeuten oder nicht – genug, dass sie selbst jedenfalls nicht zu leugnen sind.]³⁹

Here we see Brentano once again on the precipice of metaphysics in his logical inquiries. For logic, however, it suffices to point out the difference between the two sets of properties and to designate the one as essential determinations and the other as inessential determinations. We note however that Brentano is careful here not to trace the essential ones to substance and therefore does not embrace the Lockean doctrine of the real essence, though he does suggest it as a solution to the question concerning what makes the difference between them. Suffice it to say that Brentano at least appreciates the motive behind this doctrine. We shall see below that he allows for real definitions, but not in the sense that they entail the real essence.

While our analysis of the *Logik* is not as such concerned with Brentano's relation to his students or critics, his distinction between essential and inessential determinations invites an irresistible comparison with Husserl, who developed the idea of phenomenology as a discipline that is concerned with the essence of acts of consciousness.[40] Here we must bear in mind, however, that in this regard Husserl limits the discipline in question to a concern with strictly *a priori* matters. Brentano, by contrast, conceives of essential determinations much more in the spirit of the empiricist tradition and ultimately the Aristotelian orientation. The essence of something, according to this conception, belongs to a thing of the given genus or species either necessarily or *for the most part*. There are thousands upon thousands of essential determinations of a human being. Every (or almost every) individual that belongs to this species has a heart, a brain, lungs, etc., all of which are distinct from those of another species. Yet, there are sometimes exceptional cases where an individual diverges from the essence. This empirical model is not at all the same as Husserl's mathematical model. Every right triangle is, without exception, subject to the Pythagorean

---

39 Brentano, EL 80/13032.
40 Husserl 1950.

theorem. Brentano's essential determinations do not have such exceptionlessness as a necessary condition, although there are cases where he does find it among the acts of consciousness (e.g. intentionality, presentations as the foundation of acts of all other kinds, and the division of judgments into affirmations and negations). Here we are of course leaving aside Husserl's unbridled metaphysical extravagance in asserting that the ideal objects truly exist,[41] for metaphysics as such is not the focus of the present analysis.[42]

There is also a distinction, according to the *Logik*, between *true* and *false* concepts.[43] The former are concepts to which an object corresponds, whereas no object corresponds to the latter.[44] Yet, Brentano gives us no examples of such concepts in the *Logik*. The concept of a unicorn would presumably be a false one, whereas a concept of consciousness would be a true one. A concept can also be a *necessary*, an *impossible*, or a *non-necessary* one. The concept of a round square would perhaps be an impossible one, whereas the concept of any contingent entity would presumably be a non-necessary one, the concept of God a necessary one.

An extremely important division among concepts as regards their contents is that between knowable and non-knowable ones. "*Knowable*," Brentano explains, "is that which is presented if we can possibly form a true and justified judgment about whether or not it is. Otherwise it is unknowable."[45] The knowable concept need not be the foundation for an act of cognition, i.e. a judgment whereby we actually know something. As long as it is a concept of the potentially knowable, this will suffice.

Brentano continues with epistemological elaborations by telling us that the knowable may be "knowable with absolute certainty, with physical certainty, or with probability."[46] Sometimes we know something as necessary, though what we thereby mean is that we know with absolute certainty, as is the case for much of mathematics. Yet, there may very well be matters of necessity which

---

41   Husserl 1901, 124.
42   See the chapter on the metaphysical triad of Austrian phenomenology in Rollinger (forthcoming).
43   Brentano, EL 80/13032–13034.
44   Cf. Brentano 1862, 25. The terms "true" and "false" are of course characterized as equivocal. As we shall see below, their application to judgments rather than concepts is of the utmost importance for the *Logik*.
45   Brentano, EL 80/13037: "*Erkennbar ist das Vorgestellte, wenn es möglich ist, ein wahres und berechtigtes Urteil darüber zu bilden, ob es sei oder nicht sei. Sonst [ist es] unerkennbar.*" We may note here that Brentano in effect defines knowledge here as true justified judgment.
46   Brentano, EL 80/13037: "*... mit absoluter Sicherheit erkennbar oder mit physischer Sicherheit erkennbar oder mit Wahrscheinlichkeit erkennbar.*"

no human being can know, as we can also know some things with abolute certainty that are quite accidental. We may say, for instance, that we are thinking and that this is knowable with absolute certainty, although the contrary is not as such an impossibility. Our thinking is only a contigent fact. There is moreover a distinction, says Brentano, between what is knowable with precision and what is knowable with absolute certainty. Whether a person is dead or not, for instance, is a matter of precision, although it is sometimes difficult to ascertain.

When we say that something is knowable as a matter of probability, this is, says Brentano, not entirely accurate.[47] What is knowable is in such cases merely a certain probability. We are not justified in saying, for instance, that someone rolling a die will not roll a six. What is knowable in this case is only that rolling a six is less probable than rolling any one of the five other numbers. Here Brentano follows Pierre-Simon Laplace in the determination of the probability of something by discerning the number of possible outcomes (in the case of a die: six) as a demominator and the number of favored outcomes (in the case of rolling a six: one) as a numerator. If the resulting fraction is at least ½ it is possible to speak of the probability of the favored outcome, whereas it is otherwise to be called improbable.[48] Knowing that a certain outcome is probable, however, is not equivalent to knowing that the outcome will occur.

It is possible in some cases, says Brentano, to have "physical assurance," which he defines in the following way:

> Something presented that is knowable with physical assurance is that in the case of which the circumstances allow for a correct judgment that is not necessary, but is infinitely probable, i.e. one in which the possiblity of error disappears (the intrsinically conceivable cases of error disappear). And indeed it disappears in a sense so strict that we can say that that which is presented a judgment that is as good as absolutely infallible.
>
> [Ein mit physisicher Sicherheit erkennbares Vorgestelltes ist ein solches, bei welchem die Umstände ein zwar nicht notwendig aber unendlich wahrscheinliches richtiges Urteil gestatten, i.e. ein solches, bei welchem die Möglichkeit des Irrtums verschwindet (die an und für sich denkbaren Fälle des Irrtums verschwinden). Und zwar verschwindet sie in einem so strengen Sinn des Wortes, dass man in der Tat sagen kann, das Vorgestellte gestatte ein so gut wie absolut unfehlbares Urteil.][49]

---

47   Brentano, EL 80/13039.
48   Brentano, EL 80/13040f.
49   EL 80/13042f.

Certainty of this kind is to be found wherever the probability of the unfavored outcome is $1/\infty$ and that of the favored outcomes is consequently $1 - 1/\infty$. An example of this would be the probability that a ball that we throw will not land at a given point.

"That which is knowable with physical certainty," Brentano adds, "is knowable in the *proper sense of the word*,"[50] whereas what is knowable by mere probability "is not knowable in the strict and proper sense."[51] While some like to speak of absolute certainty as metaphysical certainty, Brentano tells us that such people have a wrong view of metaphysics. "Its most important statements," he says, "can be established either not at all or by the method of natural science, and hence their objects also have no other knowability besides physical certainty."[52] There is accordingly no difference between physical and metaphysical necessity when properly understood. Obviously the type of certainty under discussion here is likely to meet resistance. Although the example of a ball not landing at a given point nicely illustrates physical certainty insofar as it will not meet with controversy, it involves a kind of precision due to the idealization resulting from applying geometrical concepts to the physical world. This kind of precision is difficult to arrive at in metaphysical reflections. In our analysis of Brentano's *Logik* we may only note his extreme epistemological optimism in this regard, which is indeed why he finds it crucial to his philosophical enterprise to take into account probability theory. In face of scepticism towards metaphysics as a science, so prevalent since Hume and Kant and consequently still very much in vogue in the neo-Kantian atmosphere of the late nineteenth century in the German speaking world, Brentano pays special tribute to Laplace, the one who provides us with the basic theory of probability which will allegedly change this sceptical climate. Whether or not such

---

50   EL 80/13044: *"Das mit physischer Sicherheit Erkennbare ist ein im eigentlichen Sinn des Wortes Erkennbares."*
51   Brentano, EL 80/13039: *"nicht eigentlich und im strengen Sinne des Wortes erkennbar."*
52   Brentano, EL 80/13038: *"Die wichtigsten ihrer Sätze sind entweder gar nicht oder nach derselben Methode wie die der Naturwissenschaft festzustellen, und darum haben ihre Gegenstände auch keine andere Erkennbarkeit als die mit physischer Sicherheit."* Here we are of course reminded of Brentano's thesis that the method of philosophy is to be no different from that of natural science. See p. 9 above. Included among the "physically certain" statements that Brentano endorses are: 1) There is an external spatio-temporal world for which our sensations are signs. 2) Every occurrence does have a cause. 3) God, as an infinitely powerful, wise, and benevolent creator of the world exists. Here we must of course forgo a detailed discussion of these statements, not only because our concern here is Brentano's logic rather than metaphysics, but because much of Brentano's metaphysics, especially as it was formulated during the years in which he lectured on logic, remains unpublished.

optimism is ultimately justified, Brentano was able to communicate it to his students with great effect.

"The knowable, especially what is knowable with certainty (whether mathematical or physical)," according to Brentano, "is further divided into the the knowable through mediation – the immediately knowable."[53] Moreover, each of these is divided into into the *a priori* and the *a posteriori* knowable.[54] We can have immediate *a priori* knowledge from mere presentations. From our presentation of the number 2, for instance, we can know that by multiplying it by 2 the result is 4. We have immediate *a posteriori* knowledge of our own psychical phenomena. The Cartesian *cogito* is knowable with absolute certainty, but it is still *a posteriori* or, in Humean terms, a matter of fact: by no means a necessity.

The forgoing divisions among presentations are presumably ones which Brentano makes in terms of contents and are thus distinctions among concepts in the proper sense, although it sometimes seems that it is rather the presented object that is actually under consideration. In this respect Brentano may well be open to criticism, but we must bear in mind the pioneering nature of his logical endeavor. If students of his, such as Twardowski, Meinong, and Husserl, managed to get clearer about the distinction between content and object, it is only because they stood on Brentano's shoulders.

A very important point regarding the *Logik* is that he does not thematize the distinction between abstract and concrete concepts. To be sure, he sometimes speaks of abstract and concrete concepts, presentations, or names. We find the following claims about them in the *Logik*: 1) that in mathematics signs are connected with abstract concepts,[55] 2) that equivocation is especially dangerous in the case of abstract concepts,[56] 3) that synonymity is especially dangerous in the case of abstract concepts,[57] 4) that there is a correspondence between certain concrete and certain abstract names, e.g. "beautiful" and "beauty",[58] 5) that in some cases the reference of an abstract name is a *concretum*,[59] 6) that statements can have correlative material that is abstract in one and concrete in

---

53   Brentano, EL 80/13047: *"Das Erkennbare, insbesondere das mit Sicherheit Erkennbare (sei diese nun eine mathematische oder physisische) wird ferner eingeteilt in das mittelar – unmittelbar Erkennbare."* Here we may note that by "mathematical certainty" Brentano means "absolute certainty."
54   EL 80/13048.
55   Brentano, EL 80/12978.
56   Brentano, EL 80/12995.
57   Brentano, EL 80/12996.
58   Brentano, EL 80/13118 f.
59   Brentano, EL 80/13339. The word for reference here is *Bedeutung*, which is in this case used in an unusual manner.

the other,[60] and 7) that "abstraction" is to be considered together with the "perception of the understanding."[61] While we have already considered the first of these three claims, we have yet to consider the others (except the final one, since Brentano does not elaborate on it in the *Logik*).

It would seem that, in view of these interesting claims about mind and language involving the abstract, we should expect Brentano's *Logik* to contain an elucidation of the distinction between the abstract and the concrete. Since Brentano's student, Stumpf, does explicitly tell us that concepts can be divided into abstract and concrete ones and moreover emphasizes that this distinction is not at all the same as the one between universal and individual concepts,[62] we would very much like to know what Brentano's view on this matter is. We have already considered his notions of metaphysical and logical parts which pertain to the matter at hand. The red of the colored patch is a metaphysical part. Color is a logical part of red. In both cases we are apparently applying abstract concepts. However, in Hillebrand's lecture notes from Brentano's *Die elementare Logik und die in ihr nötigen Reformen*, we do find the claim that logical parts are individualized by metaphysical parts, particularly location (*Ort*).[63] Thus, we should be cautious about saying Stumpf took a step beyond Brentano regarding the matter at hand, although Stumpf certainly does state his case much more sharply.

3 Distinctions among Modes of Presentation

Having discussed Brentano's divisions of concepts with regard to their content, we now turn to his divisions between them in terms of *mode of presentation*. Such divisions are those between clear and unclear, proper and improper, and finally dissected and non-dissected presentations.[64]

"What is clearly presented," says Brentano, "is presented with a great intensity of consciousness, such that, as a result, a confusion can less easily come about (than under equal circumstances)."[65] "With a great intensity of consciousness" here means "attentively," as is made plain by the statement: "A com-

---

60 Brentano, EL 80/13339.
61 Brentano, EL 80/13351: "*die Wahrnehmung des Verstehens.*"
62 Rollinger 2015.
63 See pp. 178, 185, 201, 214, 249, 254, 274, 280 below.
64 Brentano, EL 80/13057.
65 Brentano, EL 80/13059: "*Klar vorgestellt wird, was mit einer großen Bewusstseinsstärke vorgestellt wird, so dass in Folge davon eine Verwechslung minder leicht statt haben kann (als unter gleichen Umständen).*"

plex object can be presented in part clearly, in part unclearly, or more or less clearly (as in the case of attention to special parts)."[66] We are of course accustomed to the notions of clarity and distinctness from Descartes. For Brentano distinctness belongs to the presentation of a complex object when the different parts of these objects are not confused with each other.

The distinction between proper and improper presentations is of particular importance. An improper presentation is the presentation of a surrogate (*eines Surrogates*), which he further characterizes in the following way:

> We improperly present that of which we do not have and often cannot have a precisely corresponding presentation. We name it, but we do not quite understand the name while we name it.
>
> a) Here belongs, for instance, the inadequate way in which we present God by means of analogies which we take from created things. We designate with the name "God" that at which analogies aim. We do not properly know what "God" means. God is a necessary concept. The denial of him would be for the person who had it immediately absurd. However, we presumably speak "God is" without discerning the truth at once and from the concept.
>
> Similarly, a blind person may speak of color, as we speak of substantial differences.
>
> b) It is, however, also similar when we name objects and could presumably grasp single features, which are, however, no longer presentable to us due to their complication.
>
> A million, a billion we can presumably no longer properly present, and we name them without precisely understanding the name.

> [Uneigentlich stellen wir solches vor, wovon wir keine genau entsprechende Vorstellung haben und oft auch haben können. Wir nennen es, verstehen aber selbst den Namen nicht recht, während wir ihn nennen.
>
> a) Hierher gehört z.B. die inadequate Weise, wie wir Gott vorstellen durch Analogien, die wir kreatürlichen [Dingen] entnehmen.
>
> Wir bezeichnen mit dem Namen "Gott" das, worauf unsere Analogien zielen. Was das aber ist, entzieht sich unserer Vorstellung. Wir verstehen eigentlich nicht, was "Gott" heißt, den Sinn des Namens "Gott" nicht. Gott ist ein notwendiger Begriff. Seine Leugnung würde für den, [der] ihn

---

66   Brentano, EL 80/13059: "*Ein zusammengesetzter Gegenstand kann zum Teil klar, zum Teil unklar, oder mehr und minder klar vorgestellt werden (wie bei besonderer Aufmerksamkeit auf besondere Teile).*"

> hätte, unmittelbar absurd sein. Wir aber sprechen wohl "Gott ist," aber ohne sofort und aus dem Begriff die Wahrheit einzusehen.
>
> Ähnlich mag der Blinde von der Farbe sprechen, wir von den substantiellen Differenzen.
>
> b) Ähnlich ist aber auch, wenn wir Gegenstände nennen, [deren] einzelne Merkmale wir wohl fassen könnten, die aber wegen ihrer Komplikation für uns nicht mehr vorstellbar sind.
>
> Eine Million, eine Billion können wir nicht eigentlich mehr vorstellen, und nennen sie, ohne den Namen genau zu verstehen.][67]

This distinction between proper and improper presentations is of course important for Brentano's own investigations. It is already clear from the above passage that it comes into play in the theological part of his metaphysics. It is also of use to him in his theory of imagination, since it does not suffice for him that a phantasm is less vivid than a corresponding sensation. The imagined object is also to some extent presented improperly, though to a degree that approaches intuition.[68]

As for the modes of presenting objects in dissected and non-dissected ways, Brentano finds it hardly possible to clarify such modes except by means of examples. Everyone inwardly experiences the difference.

> A glance puts something I see before me in a non-dissected way. If, however I present a body to myself as warm and black, the presentation is dissected. It is the same when I present to myself a king and a future beggar. This is best shown in the case of contradictories. They are not presentable in a non-dissected way, e.g. rectangular sphere ...

> [Ein Blick stellt mir, was ich sehe, unzergliedert vor. Wenn ich dagegen einen Körper mir warm und Schwarz vorstelle, so die Vorstellung gegliedert. Ebenso wenn ich mir einen König und künftigen Bettler vorstelle. Am besten zeigt sich das beim Widerprechenden. Das ist nicht unzergliedert vorstellbar, z.B. eckige Kugel ...][69]

It should be obvious that only complex objects can be presented in a dissected way, though these can also be presented in a non-dissected way. What one sees

---

67 Brentano, EL 80/13060.
68 See Rollinger 1993, revised in Rollinger 2008a, 29–50.
69 Brentano, EL 80/13060.

in a glance may obviously be complex (consisting, for instance, of various colors), but it is nonetheless presented in a non-dissected way. When we conceive of two contradictories together there is no way for us to join them together in a presentation, even though we present them simultaneously (for if we did not, we could not judge, for instance, that there cannot be a rectangular sphere).

4   Distinctions among Names

Brentano distinguishes various classes of presentations not only by content and mode, but also by *expression*. As we have already seen, the categorematic expressions whereby presentations are conveyed are names.

A presentation, says Brentano, can be expressed by an *equivocal* and *univocal* name.[70] Moreover, he identifies various types of equivocal names.[71] Some of them are identified as equivocal merely by accident. While his examples are peculiar to German, there are abundant examples of this type of equivocation in English, e.g. "bark" in reference to the bark of a tree and also the sound that a dog makes. Names can also be equivocal by analogy. We say, for instance, that a light is brilliant, but also that a person is brilliant. All metaphors fall under this heading. A name can also be equivocal by relation (*Beziehung*), as we can speak of a healthy exercise, but also of a healthy person. Finally, we may use a name like "philosopher" as a general term, but also strictly applied to a single philosopher, as Aquinas designates Aristotle. Equivocation by analogy and by relation, Brentano tells us, is especially important.[72] We may indeed call cases of this kind "systematic ambiguity," though he does not use this term. However, we may extend this term to other cases of ambiguity, which have already been identified, i.e. a name in reference to some thing (a lion) or non-thing, a name in reference to the name itself (the name "lion"), a name in reference to a species (the lion as a species), and a name as a universal term in reference to anything named by it (something-called-lion). To what degree, we may ask, should equivocal names be tolerated in science and philosophy? Brentano's answer to this question will be considered shortly.

Another distinction which Brentano considers is that between presentations expressed by *sharp* and *vague* names. What he means by a sharp name is "one whose meaning (or also whose meanings) is precisely established, a

---

70   Brentano, EL 80/13061.
71   Brentano, EL 80/13062.
72   Brentano, EL 80/13062.

vague one where this is not the case."[73] Technical terms in art and science are of course sharp in this sense. Sometimes this is not the case in philosophy for certain thinkers, but Brentano expresses doubt whether their thinking should really count as philosophy. He concedes, however, that much of our everyday communication takes place by means of vague expressions. We may say that someone or some action is civilized, for instance, but very few of us has precisely established what this means. "Science must attempt," says Brentano, "to transform these vague expressions into sharp univocals or equivals."[74]

Here we see that Brentano does allow for equivocals in science and of course philosophy (which for him should be a science). We must not forget that he follows the model of Aristotle, who was not only the first philosopher to have identified equivocation as a pervasive feature of language, but also the one who gave us an impressive body of philosophical work that is full of equivocal names, such as "substance" (οὐσία), "cause" (αἰτία), and "principle" (ἀρχή). His celebrated fifth book of the *Metaphysics* is sometimes regarded as a philosophical glossary, which indeed it is; to be more precise, however, it is a glossary of equivocals which are used throughout the *Metaphysics* and his other works. These equivocals are indeed cases of systematic ambiguity. As long as the equivocals are sharp rather than vague, they can be of great philosophical use. It may indeed be argued that they must not be eliminated by neologisms which avoid equivocation altogether, for otherwise certain systematic interconnections will no longer be thematic. As long as medical science, for instance, gives sharpness to the expression "healthy," it should proceed, as we do in ordinary language, to apply this name to the bearer of health, the cause of health, and to the symptom of health.

At the same time, however, Brentano says that science cannot absolutely without exception make all of its expressions sharp, as we find terms such as "large" and "small" to be very useful.[75] There are indeed even cases, e.g. in botany, where science finds it necessary to coin vague expressions.[76]

A presentation can also be expressed, according to Brentano, by a simple name or a complex one.[77] Yet another distinction that Brentano makes

---

73   Brentano, EL 80/13063: "*ein solcher [Ausdruck], dessen Bedeutung oder auch Bedeutungen genau festgestellt sind, ein verschwommener wo dies nicht der Fall ist.*"
74   Brentano, EL 80/13064: "*Die Wissenschaft muss suchen, diese verschwommenen Ausdrücke in scharfe Univoka oder Äquivoka zu verwandeln.*"
75   Brentano, EL 80/13065.
76   Brentano, EL 80/13066, where an instance of this in Mill's *System of Logic* Book IV, Chapter VII, §4 is cited.
77   Brentano, EL 80/13067.

between presentations is the one corresponding to the distinction between colorful and colorless names.[78]

5 Relations among Presentations

Various *relations among presentations* (including ones among their corresponding names and objects) are identified in the *Logik*. Presentations can consist of equal features or marks (*Merkmale*), in which case we make speak of identical concepts.[79] They may of course also be unequal (or non-identical) in various ways. The concepts of God and creature, for instance, completely exclude each other, while in other cases one name includes another or they can intersect. The fully unequal concepts can moreover be opposed to each other, but they can also be different without opposition (e.g. white and warm). When they are opposed, they can be so in a contradictory way (e.g. human and non-human), but also by privation (e.g. seeing and blind). They can moreover be positively opposed (e.g. white and black). In addition to relations of equality and inequality, including opposition, yet another one that Brentano discerns among presentations is that of analogy. In this case there is a relation of equality between the objects, such as the relation between spatial and temporal length.[80]

While the relations just considered are ones among presentations in and of themselves,[81] Brentano also considers "relations of presentations to each other considered in application to their objects."[82] As far as general presentations are concerned, it is the extension of concepts that is under consideration here.

Concepts can be equipollent in their extension. These are "ones which are mutually inseparable, thus [having] the perfectly equal sphere of extension," although "sometimes those which occur separately only as an exception" are also considered equipollent.[83] Brentano does not provide us with examples here. The concepts of equilateral and equiangular triangles would, however, seem to fit his description well. The sphere of extension in this case is the same without exception. If concepts are not equipollent, they are fully disjunctive or

---

78 Brentano, EL 80/13069.
79 Brentano, EL 80/13072.
80 Brenano, EL 80/13073.
81 Brentano, EL 80/13072.
82 Brentano, EL 80/13073: "*Verhältnisse der Vorstellungen zueinander in ihrer Anwendbarkeit auf die Gegenstände betrachtet.*"
83 Brentano, EL 80/13086: "*solche, welche gegenseitig untrennbar sind, also die vollkommen gleiche Sphäre des Umfangs ... Manchmal auch solche, welche nur ausnahmsweise getrennt vorkommen.*"

partly unified, and if partly unified, then superordinate, subordinate, or intersecting. The genus is superordinate to the species, the species subordinate to the genus.

As regards relations among names, Brentano pays special attention to "the relations of names which belong to one and the same [thing] in one and the same sense."[84] If the two names are not identical, they are synonyms, e.g. "human being" and "rational animal." "Between such perfectly synonymous expressions," Brentano further explains, "some differences do occur":

> a) One of them can be *more familiar*, the other less familiar, b) one of them univocal, the other equivocal, c) one sharper, the other more vague, and d) one can finally be more suitable than the other for calling into consciousness powerfully (directing attention to) the parts of what is presented in detail or also one or the other single parts thereof.
>
> [Zwischen solchen vollkommen synonymen Ausdrücken finden aber doch manche Unterschiede statt. a) Der eine kann bekannter, der andere minder bekannt, b) der eine univok, der andere äquivok, c) der eine schärfer, der andere verschwommener sein, d) der eine endlich kann mehr als der andere geeignet sein, die Teile des Vorgestellten im einzelnen oder auch den einen oder anderen einzelnen Teil des Vorgestellten kräftig ins Bewusstsein zu rufen (die Aufmerksamkeit darauf zu richten).][85]

In this case we are dealing with definitions. That is to say, the more familiar, univocal, sharper, or suitable name can function as the definition of the name that is less familiar, univocal, sharp, or suitable.

6 Definition

A definition occurs wherever a name helps us to understand its synonym. While a definition in this sense can be merely "nominal" rather than "real" (in the classical sense of identifying genus and differentia), in either case it can be of great service in the advancement of knowledge, as long as the following points are heeded:

---

84   Brentano, EL 80/13094: "*die Verhältnisse der Namen, die ein und demselben in ein und demselben Sinn zukommen.*"

85   Brentano, EL 80/1398.

1) The definition is not to have either excess or lack, namely in comparison with the defined. It is to indicate all the features, though not more features than the defined name. This is included in our requirement that the definition must be equi-significant with the defined.
2) What is true of the definition must also be true of the defined and vice-versa. Others express the same thing by saying that it should not be too broad and too narrow. This is self-evident if it is to have the same content. Identical concepts are indeed always and in the strictest sense equipollent.
3) The definition may contain none other but essential features. This rule (which repeats only one part of the first one) is consequently also included in our requirement that the definition must be equi-significant with the defined.
4) The definition is to be clearer than the defined. This is the same thing we also have said. It must in some sense make the defined more intelligible and be more intelligible either in and of itself or as a definition.
5) Something similar goes for the rule: the definition is to contain only perfectly familiar or already explained expressions (Pascal). This is included in our rule of the perfect definition.
6) The definition may not repeat the defined name (either fully or partly). (*Idem per idem.*) This rule does not apply with complete universality. It applies when the definition of completely unfamiliar things is at stake, but not equally when the definition of equivocal names is under consideration ... It is of course self-evident that the mere repetition of one and the same name can never be a definition.
7) The definition is to be multi-membered (or also): it is to be an analysis of the defined name (in which the third rule is included). This rule might be attributed as a confusion of the nominal definitions (of the concept, properly speaking, which is the meaning of the defined name) with the definitions of species concepts. It is, however, also relevant also in the case of nominal definitions, though it is not here universally valid, The multi-membered names are usually eminently suited for nominal definitions.

[*1*. Die Definition soll nicht Überfluss noch Mangel haben. Nämlich mit dem Definierten verglichen; sie soll die sämtlichen Merkmale, aber nicht mehr Merkmale als der definierte Name anzeigen. Dies ist eingeschlossen in unserer Forderung, die Definition müsse dem Definierten gleichbedeutend sein. Dasselbe gilt:

2. Was von der Definition gilt, muss auch vom Definierten gelten, und umgekehrt. Andere drücken dasselbe so aus, dass sie sagen, die Definition dürfe nicht zu weit und nicht zu eng sein, d.h. sie muss den gleichen Umfang mit dem Definierten haben. Was sich, wenn sie den gleichen Inhalt hat, von selbst versteht. Identische Begriffe sind ja immer und im strengsten Sinn äquipollente Begriffe.

3. Die Definition darf keine anderen als wesentliche Merkmale enthalten. Unter wesentlichen Merkmalen versteht man aber in dem Begriff des Definitierten inbegriffene Merkmale. Somit ist auch diese Regel (die nur einen Teil der ersten wiederholt) in unserer Forderung, dass die Definition dem Definierten gleichbedeutend sein müsse, eingeschlossen.

4. Die Definition soll klarer als das Definierte sein. Das ist dasselbe, was auch wir, nur mit näheren Erläuterungen, gesagt haben. Sie und also entweder an und für sich oder doch als Definition verständlicher sein.

5. Ähnliches gilt von der Regel: die Definition soll nur vollkommen bekannte oder bereits erkläre Ausdrücke enthalten (Pascal). In unserer Regel von der vollkommenen Definition ist diese eingeschlossen.

6. Die Definition darf nicht den definierten Namen (ganz oder teilweise) wiederholen. (Idem per idem.) Diese Regel gilt nicht ganz allgemein. Sie gilt, wenn es sich um die Definition ganz unbekannter, nicht aber in gleichem Maß, wenn es sich z.B. um die Definition äquivoker Namen handelt. Zum Beispiel könnte einer wohl den Ausdrück trüb, den er metaphorisch gebraucht, erklären als trüb gestimmt. Ebenso könnte einer, um das, was der Name Röte bedeutet, seinem allgemeinen Merkmal nach markierender zu bezeichnen, sagen, Röte heißt rote Farbe. Dass natürlich die bloße Wiederholung eines und desselben Namens niemals eine Definition sein kann, versteht sich von selbst.

7. Die Definition soll mehrgliedrig (oder auch:) sie soll eine Analyse des definierten Namens (worin die dritte Regel mitinbegriffen ist). Diese Regel könnte auf eine Verwechslung der Nominaldefinition (eigentlich des Begriffs, der die Bedeutung des definierten Namens ist) mit den Definitionen von Artbegriffen gedeutet werden. Indessen ist sie auch bei der Nominaldefinition häufig am Platze, wenn sie auch hier nicht allgemein gültig ist. Die mehrgliedrigen

Namen sind meistens in vorzüglicher Weise für Nominaldefinitionen geeignet.][86]

As Clemens had taught Brentano, any instance in which the usage of certain words helps us to clarify other words is acceptable as a definition in the *Logik*. Explanations in words without conceptual analysis may accordingly count as definitions, but Brentano still thinks that real definitions have a special logical and metaphysical significance, as this is evident in his theory of parts and wholes (which we have already seen elaborated in his distinctions of physical, metaphysical, logical, and collective parts).[87]

7   Concluding Remarks

This chapter will suffice as an analysis of Brentano's theory of concepts presentations in the *Logik*. A concept for him is a presentation in which there is a distinction between content and extension, but in some cases it seems to be the content as opposed to the extension. There is yet another way in which he speaks of the content of a presentation. In this sense the content is the meaning of the name that expresses the presentation, although it is not entirely clear whether the content in this sense is equivalent to the immanent object. Here we confront issues that should be futher investigated in psychology and metaphysics rather than in logic. In the *Logik* Brentano rather proceeds to establish distinctions among presentations and their various modes and the names that express them, whereas he also gives some attention to relations among presentations and definitions. Much of Brentano's epistemology is stated in his theory of concepts, for there is a distinction between knowable and unknowable concepts. Yet, knowledge is properly to be found in judgment, as this will be the central topic of the following chapter which concerns the most important domain of the *Logik*.

---

86 EL 80/13103–13108.
87 Regarding this issue, see the materials below (pp. 185 , 249).

CHAPTER 4

Judgment

"A peculiar, cleverly thought-out theory of judgment," says one of the lesser known followers of Brentano, "we owe to Franz von Brentano which Marty and Hillebrand in particular have followed."[1] Although there was a tendency among some logicians and linguists to use the terms "judgment" (*Urteil*) and "statement" (*Aussage*) synonymously, Brentano demands that we make a very sharp distinction between them. One of his chief reasons for rejecting certain alternative theories of judgment is cystalized in his assessment of the most prominent theory at the time of the *Logik*: "... Kant, e.g., cited what in truth is only [a set of] distinctions of the *expression* among the main distinctions of the form of understanding of the judgment."[2] *Judgments* are for Brentano psychical acts, alongside presentations on the one hand and phenomena of love and hate on the other, whereas he regards *statements* as the linguistic expressions whereby we convey judgments. As we have seen in the previous chapter, he distinguishes these expressions from names, which are for him the linguistic expressions whereby we convey presentations. Statements have meanings which are likewise distinguishable from the meanings of names. According to Brentano's initial theory of meaning in the *Logik*, the meaning of a statement is what the speaker announces or communicates by uttering the statement, namely that whoever he addresses is to judge as the speaker does. A name in this sense does not have a meaning. It only has an object. However, Brentano developed a second theory of meaning, according to which a difference of meaning is exemplified by "the son of Phaenerate" and "the wisest of Athenians". The meaning of a name in this sense is the content of the presention that the name expresses. According to this second theory of meaning, a statement has a meaning in an analogous sense. The meaning of a statement in this sense is the content of the judgment that the statement expresses, but Brentano unfortunately does not elaborate on this point further in the *Logik*. We might indeed think that he is speaking of judgments as analogues of concepts, hence not the acts of judging, but rather the contents of these acts. It is not always

---

1 Kreibig 1909, 194. The insertion of "von" in Brentano's name here is not erroneous. This indicates aristocracy, which he chose not to flaunt in public. This author was in fact one of the students who attended Brentano's lectures on logic during the winter semester 1884/85.
2 Brentano EL 81/13546: "... Kant z.B. hat, was in Wahrheit nur Unterschiede des Ausdrucks sind, unter den Hauptunterschieden der Verstandesform des Urteils aufgeführt."

entirely clear whether he is speaking in this manner. Here we are left with no choice but to tolerate such ambiguity, just as we so often do in the various treatments of logical topics.

1   Critique of Kant's Table

The theory of judgment that we are to consider is expounded first and foremost through a critique of the table of judgments that Kant gives in his *Critique of Pure Reason*:[3]

I
Quality of Judgments
Universal
Particular
Singular

II
Quality
Affirmative
Negative
Infinite

III
Relation
Categorical
Hypothetical
Disjunctive

IV
Modality
Problematic
Assertoric
Apodeictic

As we have seen in the first chapter, the quality and quantity were of central focus in neo-scholastic logic. The entire syllogistic doctrine is built upon the consideration of these aspects of judgment. Brentano's reformed syllogistic doctrine is in turn based on a new conception of quality and quantity.

In the *Logik* neither the singular judgments nor the infinite judgments receive special attention, as indeed Kant concedes their insignificance for formal logic, though he says that for the purposes of transcendental logic it is important to discern them in classes of their own. Of course so-called transcendental logic is a project that does not concern Brentano, for whom logic is

---

3   Kant, *Critique of Pure Reason* A 70/B 95. The table, as presented here, is taken from Norman Kemp Smith's translation (Kant 1929, 650).

a practical philosophical discipline and by no means a critique of pure reason. Moreover, disjunctive judgments for him do not make up a special class any more than singular or infinite judgments do. While Kant maintains that there is a special class of disjunctive judgments because he regards them as exclusive, Brentano points out that there are cases of disjunction which are clearly inclusive. When we say that people are motivated to act either through fear or hope, we clearly do not mean to say that there are no instances where people are motivated by *both* fear and hope. (EL 80/13137.) We shall see below in greater detail how Brentano wishes to deal with disjunction.

While Brentano thus thinks that some of the members of Kant's table are to be omitted, he also thinks that that it is not complete. Thus he says:

> In order to convince ourselves of this, we need only think back [to our thesis] that there are sentences that add to a single name an "is" or "is not", which contains no predicate. The existential sentence is thus not categorical. Still less, however, [is it] hypothetical or disjunctive.
>
> [Wir brauchen, um uns davon zu überzeugen, nur an den Nachweis zurückzudenken, dass es Sätze gibt, die zu einem einzigen Namen ein "ist" oder "ist nicht" hinzufügen, welches keinen Prädikatbegriff enthält. Der Existentialsatz ist also nicht kategorisch. Noch weniger aber hypothetisch oder disjunktiv.][4]

Since Brentano here contrasts the existential sentence with the categorical, hypothetical, and disjunctive sentences, one might think that such a sentence would be included along with them under the heading of "relation" in his table. We shall see, however, that he rather thinks that all of the judgments which Kant puts under that heading are existential for Brentano.[5] Other criticisms of Kant's table of judgment will also come to light in the present chapter.

---

4 EL 80/13185.
5 While one may here be reminded that Kant criticized the ontological argument by asserting that existence is not a predicate and accordingly by implication allows for existential judgments as distinct from predicative or categorical judgments, we must bear in mind that in the *Logik* Brentano is concerned only with Kant's table of categorical judgments as this is formulated at the outset of the transcendental logic. In the present context an examination of Kant's theory of existential judgment as it unfolds in his rejection of the ontological argument would take us much too far afield.

2 Complexity and Simplicity

As presentations divide into the complex and the simple, one might also suggest that there is likewise such a division among judgments. The judgments "Not a man, but rather a virgin liberated France from England" and "Ceasar is dead, but Brutus lives" would thus be candidates for the class of complex judgments. Brentano concedes that in each of these instances there is indeed a plurality of judgments. The question, however, is whether a plurality of judgments should count as a complex judgment.

On this point Brentano critically encounters John Stuart Mill's argument that we should not in fact regard a plurality of judgments as one judgment just as we should not regard a team of horses as a complex horse or a street as a complex house. Brentano replies:

> Such a nomenclature would indeed not seem so absurd to me. And the best proof against this lies in what we do in the case of presentations, and what Mill as well does in their case. If it is not absurd to call a presentation composed of several a presentation, why should it be absurd to speak of a judgment composed of several judgments? This is ... justified, as the same intimate combination which occurs among certain (part-)presentations can occur among judgments. We can at the same time have many presentations at the same time and in one act of presentations. Likewise many judgments, as inferring in particular clearly shows. And this is common to all three classes of psychical functions, for we are also able to will simultaneously and in one act of volition several things; to love one, to hate the other, etc. Since [there is] no absurdity in the case of the presentations, also none in the case of the judgments.

> [So absurd schiene mir eine solche Benennung wohl nicht. Und der beste Beweis dagegen liegt in dem, was wir bei den Vorstellungen tun, und was bei ihnen auch Mill tut. Wenn es nicht absurd ist, eine aus mehreren zusammengesetzte Vorstellung eine Vorstellung zu nennen, warum soll es absurd sein, von einem aus mehreren Urteilen zusammengesetzten Urteil zu sprechen? Die ist ... berechtigt, als dieselbe innige Verbindung, welche zwischen gewissen (Teil)vorstellungen auch zwischen Urteilen statt haben kann. Wir können viele Vorstellungen zugleich und einen Vorstellungsakt haben. Ebenso viele Urteile, wie das Schließen namentlich deutlich zeigt. Und es ist dies allen drei Klassen der psychischen Funktionen gemein, denn wir sind im Stande, auch gleichzeitig und in einem Willensakt Mehreres zu wollen; die eine zu lieben, die andere

zu hassen u.s.f. Da also bei den Vorstellungen, auch bei den Urteilen keine Absurdität.][6]

This is of course a psychological argument in favor of the concept of a complex judgment. It is the intimate combination in consciousness which makes several judgments a single complex judgment. Brentano's indication of an inference is particularly noteworthy. When the judgments "All philosophers are human beings" and "All human beings are mortal" are for me premises and I conclude from them that all philosophers are mortal, the entire inference is one single act of judging in my consciousness and in this sense a complex judgment.

However, Brentano also notes that the analogy between presentations and judgments does not hold up perfectly with regard to the instance of complexity. While there occurs a one-sided separability for presentations in the case of logical parts, for instance, each of the judgments in a plurality of judgments can occur separably. Moreover, after we leave aside complex presentations, there are not many simple ones left over, whereas there are many simple judgments, e.g. "A human being is" and "Jupiter is not." Moreover, Brentano finds it unacceptable to break with tradition by calling a plurality of judgments a judgment and accordingly restricts the treatment of judgment in the *Logik* to simple judgments.

Yet, in Brentano's notes to his lecture *Vom Usprung sittlicher Erkenntnis*, he allows for the possibility of complex judgments that we cannot, through linguistic formulation, actually dissolve into simple ones.[7] We obtain examples of these from both Marty and Hillebrand.

Marty gives attention to complex judgments of this kind under the heading "double judgment" as follows:

> ... we have without any question a double judgment before us in statements such as:
> "This is red."
> "This flower is blue."
> "I am well."
> "My brother has gone away."
> "Some of my fields are rented."
> "Some flowers of your garden have been subject to frost."

---

6   EL 80/13188 f.
7   Brentano 1889, 57 ff.

In these cases and all similar ones the meaning of the statement is a peculiarly complex affirmative judgment which cannot be dissolved into a sum of simple assertions. Simply by saying "I" or "this flower" the acceptance of an object is given. But on this basis there is built a second acceptance which would not be conceivable without the first. This second acceptance involves in a certain way the first one. The first one is its necessary foundation, from which it is indissoluble. One may distinguish in the judgment that is thus compounded a subject-part and a predicating part or speak of a subject-judgment and predicting judgment or partial judgment. For here are in truth not merely two concepts, but rather two concepts, where only the second, predicating one is such that it involves the first as the thought of red includes the thought of color, and thus there is only a one-sided detatchability between the elements.[8]

We may note that all of the statements that Marty indicates as expressions of double judgment are indexical. Statements of this kind had not usually been assimilated to logic.

While Franz Hillebrand reflects orthodox Brentanism on this point as it developed into the 1890s,[9] as Marty does as well, they do not see the acknowledgement of double judgments as an insurmountable challenge to Brentano's logic. A judgment of this kind can be expressed by using other statements which at least express equivalent judgments, though not in some cases identical ones. The reader may of course consult Hillebrand's attempt to deal with this matter in the seventh chapter of the present volume. Our concern here is Brentano's views as these are expounded in the *Logik*. We shall accordingly leave aside the question how a logic that accommodates double judgments should look. Brentano simply did not develop such logic of this kind after his discovery double judgments, as his interests turned more to psychology and metaphysics.

A simple judgment is not necessarily a judgment that does not have a complex matter. The matter of a judgment is whatever is judged (i.e. accepted or rejected) and thus presented. Accordingly, as far as complexity and simplicity are concerned, whatever holds of the presentation that underlies a judgment holds of its matter. At the same time, however, Brentano cautions against certain errors that might arise by acknowledging the matter under the heading

---

[8] Marty 1895, 63.
[9] The allowance for universal judgments that affirm the existence of the subject is perhaps a concession to criticism put forward in Land 1876a and 1876b, although Brentano continued insist on the artificial character of logic in opposition to Land's criticisms. In both of those short articles Land had maintained that Brentano's logical reform was unnatural.

of presentations. When a complex matter belongs to a negative judgment, this does not entail that the matter is rejected in all of its parts. If, for instance, we judge that a white raven does not exist, this is not the same as rejecting a raven and rejecting what is white.

The most fundamental distinction that Brentano makes in a judgment is indeed the distinction between quality and matter. As we have often had occasion to note, he thinks that a judgment always has an underlying presentation. While the judgment has the quality of affirmation insofar as it accepts the presented object, it has the quality of negation insofar as it rejects the presented object. Brentano, however, often speaks of the matter and the content interchangeably.

3   Form

Brentano frequently refers to the quality of a judgment as its form. "In this respect," he tells us, "there is only one single [form]: the familiar [one]: a) accepting, b) rejecting judgments."[10] While Kant's infinite judgments are accordingly affirmative and thus do make up a third class of judgments under the aspect of quality, some have gone astray by regarding a *negativum* in the matter as qualifying the judgment as negative. For instance, if we judge that there is something that is not mortal, the negative element here belongs to the matter and not to the judgment as such, which is in fact an acceptance. As long as the expression of the judgment is an existential sentence, there should indeed be no difficulty in determining whether it has the form of affirmation or negation.

The statements "All human beings are mortal," "All triangles have 2 R as the sum of their angles," and "A human being is not learned" are outstanding examples of how the linguistic expression may mislead us in the identification of the form of a judgment. Brentano accordingly says, "The logicians who are familiar to me have all declared the first two as affirmations, the third one as a negation. The opposite is correct."[11] Brentano accordingly thinks that all the judgments which are clothed in predicative garb, so-called categorical judgments, are to be reformulated in existential statements for the purposes of logic. Accordingly the judgments which logicians have previously classified as universal are all

---

10   EL 80: 193: *"In dieser Beziehung gibt es nur eine einzige: die bekannte: a) anerkennende, b) verwerfende Urteile."*

11   EL 80: 194: *"Die Logiker, die mir bekannt sind, haben sämtlich die ersten zwei für Bejahungen, die dritte für eine Verneinung. Das Gegenteil ist richtig."*

negative, while the ones classified as particular are affirmative. Though A and O of the square of opposition are still contradictories in relation to each other, as are E and I, all the other oppositions (contrary, subcontrary, are subalternation) are unacceptable in the *Logik*.

As the following passage indicates, not only the so-called categorical judgments, but indeed all the judgments that Kant had classified under the aspect of relation are better to be classified under the aspect of form (or quality):

> a) "If the sun sets beautifully, there is beautiful weather!" It is negative.
> b) Or: "Gone is gone." It is negative. c) Or: Either there is a God, or there is no true happiness. It is positive. (One of the two, the existence of God and the non-existence of a true happiness, is. So disjunctives in general.) Whoever does not know what to do with these manners of expression will not easily arrive at a correct grasp. Indeed, regarding the first two examples [one will] most probably speak the very contrary of the truth with great confidence. With regard to the last one, however, he might be misled by the twofold nature of the forms and be tempted, in spite of what has been said, to accept a partially affirmative, partially negative quality. But incorrectly; [for] there is indeed no judgment composed from several ones here.

> [a) "Wenn die Sonne schön untergeht, so gibt es schönes Wetter!" Es ist negativ. b) Oder: "Hin ist hin." Es ist negativ. c) Oder: Entweder es gibt einen Gott, oder es gibt kein wahres Glück. Es ist positiv. (Eines von beiden, die Existenz Gottes und die Nichtexistenz eines wahren Glückes, ist. So überhaupt die Disjunktiva.) Wer sich nicht auf diese Ausdrucksweisen versteht, wird hier nicht leicht zu einer richtigen Einsicht kommen. Ja, in Betreff der ersten zwei Beispiele höchst wahrscheinlich mit aller Zuversicht das gerade Gegenteil der Wahrheit aussprechen. In Betreff des letzteren aber könnte aber er an der Zweizahl der Formen irr werden und versucht werden, trotz des Gesagten, eine partial bejahende, partial verneinende Qualität anzunehmen. Allein mit Unrecht; liegt ja doch kein aus mehreren zusammengesetztes Urteil vor.][12]

A conditional statement accordingly expresses a negative existential judgment. "If A is, then B is" conveys the judgment that there is no A without B. A disjunctive statement expresses an affirmative existential judgment. "Either A is or B

---

12   EL 80/13194. In this passage, the disjunctive judgment was initally designated as "negative" (*negativ*), whereas this designation was later changed to "positive" (*positiv*). The characte-

is not" conveys the judgment that one of the two, the existence of A and the non-existence of B, is not.

The treatment of disjunctives is particularly noteworthy here. We have seen above that, according to Stumpf, Brentano was making use of the concept of states of affairs in his logic. The existence of God and the non-existence of true happiness are indeed examples of what Stumpf had in mind under this heading. The concept of a state of affairs turns out to be crucial to the treatment of disjunctive judgment, for the being of one thing and the non-being of another thing must be named when we properly express such a judgment.

Among Brentano's neo-Kantian contemporaries, one in particular, namely Wilhelm Windelband, directly criticized his theory of judgment. Instead of defending the Kantian table of judgments, Windelband maintains that the division between affirmative and negative judgments is actually no different from the division of corresponding emotions. In both cases, according to him, there is an assessment (*Beurteilung*).[13] In the *Logik* Brentano, however, asserts that judgments are clearly distinct from feelings, for we can see "incomparability with regard to intensity," as "It is ridiculous thus to compare: This is half as certain to me as that is precious to me."[14]

4 Form and Matter

Brentano considers further divisions among judgments not under the aspect of form alone, but rather under the aspect of form together with matter.[15]

---

rization of disjunctives as positive (or affirmative) existential judgments will be discussed further immediately after this quotation and later in the present chapter (pp. 127, 137).

13 Windelband 1884, translated in Windelband 2019.
14 EL 80/13006–13007: "*hinsichtlich der Intensität Unvergleichlichkeit ... Es ist z.B. lächerlich, so zu vergleichen: Dies ist mir halb so gewiss als mir jenes lieb ist.*" In Hillebrand's work on Brentano's logic, however, we find another defense of Brentano on this point, namely that it is wrong to assimilate judgments to the practical side of life as Windelband does. (See pp. 304 ff. below. In this regard Hillebrand actually appeals to yet another opponent of Brentano, namely Sigwart.) Moreover, Hillebrand maintains that the issue has no bearing the theory of logical inference. Brentano's own reference to Windelband's essay on negative judgment clearly indicates that he was still revising the manuscript of the *Logik* as late as 1884, though it is difficult to say in what connection. Perhaps at that time he was still planning to publish the *Logik*. Another possibility is that he still somehow used the *Logik* in his lectures of the winter semester 1884/85 and the following summer semester. Still other possibilities are not to be dismissed here.
15 In view of this division and the others to be considered below, it would be wrong to assert, "Since all other distinctions of judgments [besides acceptance and rejection] concern only their matter, the affirmative and the negative are the only two kinds of judgment." (Enoch 1893, 434.) Cf. the criticisms of Brentano's theory judgment that are made from another

Such a division for him is the one between true and false judgments. We are of course familiar with the traditional definition of truth as *adaequatio rei et intellectus*, i.e. the correspondence between the judgment with the thing (*Sache*). On this point Brentano says:

> This definition is correct, but not very clear. Confusion into which I have fallen at the moment (both because of the expression and because of a lack of understanding of the formulas. Not everything is a thing, e.g. something in the future, negations, then in the case of hypotheticals and disjunctives). Others too have fallen into confusion without knowing how to reply.
>
> ... We have heard earlier that the presented is divided into what is to be accepted and what is to be rejected (objects – non-objects). According to the just-given definition, a true judgment is accordingly that which accepts an object or rejects a non-object.

[Diese Bestimmung ist richtig, aber nicht sehr deutlich. Verwirrung, in die ich augenblicklich gekommen bin (sowohl durch den Ausdruck als durch Mangel an Verständnis der Formulare. Nicht alles ist eine Sache, z.B. Zukünftiges, Negationen, dann bei hypothetischen und disjunktiven). Auch Andere wurden in Verwirrung gebracht, wussten nicht zu antworten.

Übereinstimmung in zwei Fällen: d.h. ein Urteil ist wahr, wenn es je nachdem der ihr zu Grund liegenden Vorstellung entspricht oder nicht, anerkennt oder verwirft ... Sie besagt nichts anderes als: dass das Urteil wahr ist, welches das Beurteilte so beurteilt, wie [es] zu beurteilen ist. (In diesem Sinn ist Wahrheit die Güte des Urteils.)

... Wir haben früher gehört, dass das Vorgestellte eingeteilt wird in ein solches, welches anzuerkennen und in ein solches, welches zu verwerfen ist (Gegenstände – Nichtgegenstände). Nach der eben gebebenen Bestimmung ist demnach ein wahres Urteil dasjenige, welches einen Gegenstand anerkennt, oder einen Nichtgegenstand verwirft.][16]

---

perspective in Jerusalem 1895 and the incisive rejection of that perspective in Husserl 1903, 523–531. See also Hillebrand's response (in the seventh chapter of the present volume) to various critics of Brentano's theory of judgment. In my analysis, however, the focus is concept and judgment as this is represented in Brentano's logic lectures, not criticisms of his views, many of which are based on insufficient materials (through no fault of their own of course). Those criticisms could indeed very well be the topic of a separate volume.

16　EL 80/13197. Cf. the lecture in Brentano 1930, 3–18 that is mentioned in the comment that immediately follows this quotation.

This is a very curious passage, for Brentano here uses the very unusual term "non-object", which apparently means the same as "non-being." His criticism of the traditional definition of truth as correspondence is further elaborated on in a lecture that he held some years later and has been subject to discussion in the literature. To say that a true negative judgment rejects a non-object, however, is hardly helpful. Brentano wrestled with the concept of truth for many years and finally came up with the definition of a true judgment that involves judging as a knower judges. This later definition lies far beyond the purview of the *Logik*.

Yet another division among judgments under the aspect of form together with matter is: necessarily true – not necessarily true, absurd – not absurd judgments. Brentano elaborates on this division as follows:

> An affirmative judgment with necessary, a negative judgment with impossible matter are necessarily true. An affirmative judgment with impossible matter, a negative judgment with necessary matter are absurd. That same can also be expressed thus: A true judgment with necessary necessary or impossible matter is necessarily true. A false judgment with necessary or impossible matter is absurd.
>
> [Ein bejahendes Urteil mit notwendiger, ein verneinendes Urteil mit unmöglicher Materie sind notwendig wahr. Ein bejahendes Urteil mit unmöglicher Materie, ein verneinendes Urteil mit notwendiger Materie sind absurd. Dasselbe kann auch so ausgedrückt werden: Ein wahres Urteil mit notwendiger oder unmöglicher Materie ist notwendig wahr. Ein falsches Urteil mit notwendiger oder unmöglicher Materie ist absurd.][17]

Brentano adds that there is a further distinction between immediately necessary and inferentially necessary truths. There is also a closely related distinction to be made between axioms (*Grundsätze*) and basic laws (*Grundgesetze*). This issue will receive further attention below.

According to Brentano, some judgments judge their matter in its entire extension.[18] Such a judgment occurs when the matter is determinate, as in the case of an individual. If, however, the matter is indeterminate (i.e. universal), only the negative judgment judges it in its entire extension, whereas the affirmative one does not. Although the *Logik* only indicates that examples of this division were to be given in the lectures, Brentano does not provide them in his lecture notes. However, Marty gives the example of "There are no human

---

17 EL 80/13198 f.
18 EL 80/13199 f.

beings" as an example of a judgment that judges the matter in its entire extension, "There is a human being" as one that does not judge in this manner.[19]

Another division that Brentano considers is the one between judgments that judge their matter in its entire content.[20] If the matter is simple, both affirmative and negative judgments judge it in this manner. If, however, the matter is complex, only the affirmative judgment judges the matter in all of its parts. If we judge that there are white flowers, both whiteness and flowers are accepted, whereas if we judge that there are no black flowers we do not reject both blackness and flowers. These are again examples that Marty provides in his lectures on logic which by and large run parallel with the *Logik*. Here we may note, however, that Brentano makes the point that the division under consideration applies to parts and wholes of all kinds. Thus, if the judgment is affirmative, it accepts all the parts of the matter, whether these be physical, metaphysical, logical, or collective parts, and the same goes for negative judgments. If their matter is complex, the rejection does not pertain to all the parts of the content, of whatever kind these parts may be.

The presented might also be knowable or not knowable, which for Brentano indicates a division among judgments.[21] All the distinctions that he had made between knowability in the domain of presentations apply here. He does however stress the difference between immediately and inferentially knowable truths. The former are principles of knowledge, whereas the latter are provable truths. If the principle is *a priori*, it is an axiom. If, however, it is *a posteriori*, it is guaranteed by experience. Although Brentano does not mention Kant in this context, it is clear that his rejection of the synthetic *a priori* is relevant here. The *Logik*, however, is not a polemical document.

In this connection we may also observe the important distinction between axioms (*Grundsätze*) and basic laws (*Grundgesetze*).[22] They are both knowable and indeed necessary. The axioms, however, are immediately knowable, whereas the basic laws are not. And yet, both are immediately necessary. When Brentano speaks of immediate necessity as opposed to mediated necessity, he means this in a metaphysical sense. It is not an epistemological distinction. The existence of God, he tells us, is not immediately knowable, but it is immediately necessary.

---

19 Log 20/58: 148.
20 EL 80/13200.
21 EL 80/13201–13207.
22 EL 80/13208 ff.

5 Intensity

When Brentano speaks of the intensity of a judgment, what he means is its decisiveness (*Entschiedenheit*).[23] Judgments are accordingly confident (*zuversichtlich*) or conjecturing (*vermutend*). While the latter may have a tinge of doubt, the former do not. Here one may also speak of conviction (*Überzeugung*), which has certainty (*Gewissheit*). He points out, however, that we must not confuse this with assurance (*Sicherheit*), which involves actually knowing. To speak in contemporary terminology, certainty is accordingly purely psychological, whereas assurance is epistemological. The intensity of a judgment, as Brentano understands it, has absolutely nothing to do with whether the judgment is an actual instance of knowing. A person can have absolute and doubtless conviction without the slightest degree of actual knowledge. The distinction between this and actual epistemic assurance in fact pertains to the one between the motives of a judgment.

6 Motive

"The motive," says Brentano, "is ... that cause of the judgment to which our question is properly directed when we say to someone: Why do you take that to be true?"[24] There are however unmotivated judgments, according to Brentano. These include instinctive judgments, such as outer perception and memory. Habitual judgments also count as unmotivated for him. Moreover, as we find that vanity moves a person to judge in a certain way, such a judgment is unmotivated. Religious faith also belongs among judgments of this kind. "Also in these cases," Brentano explains, "the judgment is not motivated as judgment, but rather only perhaps as an action (insofar as one calls an action motivated which arises from a motivated will)."[25] While it may seem arbitrary for Brentano to call instinctive, habitual, and volitional judgments "unmotivated," we may consider that one does not adequately answer the question "why" by saying that one is merely inclined to judge in such and such a way.

Brentano distinguishes between immediately motivated judgments and inferentially motivated ones. Both of these are also called "judgments of the understanding" (*Verstandesurteile*). If the judgment is inferentially motivated

---

23 EL 80/13174 ff.
24 EL 80/13211: "*Das Motiv ist ... jene Ursache des Urteils, auf die eigentlich unsere Frage gerichtet ist, wenn wir zu jemandem sagen: Warum hältest du das für wahr?*"
25 EL 80/13211: "*Auch in diesen Fällen ist das Urteil nicht als Urteil, sondern nur etwa als Handlung motiviert (insofern man eine Handlung motiviert nennt, welche aus einem motivierten Willen hervorgeht.)*"

it has its motive in another judgment (or other judgments), whereas if it has its motive in a presentation it is immediately motivated.[26] He elaborates on this point as follows:

> In the last case, the judgment is an immediate judgment of the understanding, an immediate grasping, e.g. the perception of one's own acts [of consciousness], or the grasping of the proposition "The whole is greater than the part." ... If, however, the motive lies in other already made assumptions, it is called a concluded judgment, a conclusion, e.g. "Since so many thousands and millions of the most diverse human beings have died and none of them has lived beyond a certain age, I too, who am related to them in my nature, shall die." The judgments that have become motives we call "premises," the process that draws the conclusion from them (the emergence of the conclusion from the premises) "concluding" or "inferring," and the premises together with the conclusion "inference."

> [Im letzten Falle ist das Urteil ein unmittelbares Verstandesurteil, eine unmittelbare Einsicht, wie z.B. die Wahrnehmung der eigenen Akte, oder die Einsicht des Satzes "Das Ganze ist größer als der Teil." ... Liegt dagegen das Motiv in anderen bereits gemachten Annahmen, so heißt es ein gefolgertes Urteil, eine Folgerung, z.B. "Da so viele Tausende und Millionen der verschiedenartigsten Menschen gestorben sind und keiner ein gewisses Alter überschritten hat, so werde auch ich, der ich ihnen meiner Natur nach verwant bin, sterben." Die Urteile, welche Motive geworden sind, nennt man Prämissen, das Verfahren, welches aus ihnen die Folgerung zieht (den Hervorgang der Folgerung aus den Prämissen) Folgern oder Schließen, und die Prämissen mit der Folgerung zusammen nennt man Schluss.][27]

While inner perception and the grasping of axioms are thus instances of immediately motivated judgment, the inferentially motivated judgments are the conclusions that are derived from premises. The question accordingly arises whether motivated judgments are simply the same as evident judgment.

Since Brentano distinguishes between correctly and incorrectly drawn conclusions, the answer to this question must be "no", as far as the *Logik* is concerned. They are correctly drawn, he explains, "if the relation of the premises to the conclusions is such that never, in the case of a similar relation of certain judgments to other judgments, the former judgments are true, but the latter are

---

26   EL 80/13215.
27   EL 80/13225.

false" adding: "this relation is the ground of the assumption of the concluded judgment."[28] We shall see more plainly what he means by "a similar relation" in our consideration of his syllogistic. Here in fact we encounter his version of what we at present call the logical form of an argument. In contemporary terms, he is saying that certain arguments are valid when their logical form is valid.

The reasonings may moreover be pure judgments of the understanding. These occur, Brentano explains, "only if the premises also and, in case they are mediated reasonings, the premises, all the way up to the first and immediate assumptions, are judgments of the understandings."[29] If this condition is not met, the conclusion is of course an impure judgment of the understanding. The inference is a proof in the strict sense if the premises are instances of immediate grasping and the conclusion is correctly drawn from them. Otherwise it is inexact or incorrect.

7   Modality

The question remains as to how Brentano deals with modality, the aspect under which Kant classified problematic, assertoric, and apodictic judgment. He raises this question in connection with the above-considered divisions:

> 1. Is the aspect perhaps identical with the one in the case of our division of judgments into necessarily true – not necessarily true, absurd – not absurd? Obviously not! (The proposition "God is" is not apodictic. Likewise "A is A.") 2. Or perhaps with the one in the case of our division into *a priori* and *a posteriori*? Newton grasped *a posteriori* the binomial proposition, and yet he could assert it apodictically in the Kantian sense. A is A, though *a priori*, is not apodictic. 3. Or into absolutely assured, physically assured, probable? Here too it would be easy to show that the division is a different one, e.g. "I am" is not apodictic. 4. Or does the apodictic judgment coincide with the apodictically demonstrated [judgment] of which we have spoken? This too is not the case, for otherwise, just to mention one point, only what is inferentially known could be asserted apodictically in the Kantian sense, which is by no means the case. The

---

28   EL 80/13225 f.: *"wenn das Verhältnis der Prämissen zu den Folgerungen ein derartiges ist, dass nie bei einem ähnlichen Verhalten gewisser Urteile zu anderen Urteilen, die ersten wahr, die anderen aber falsch sind; und dieses Verhalten Grund der Annahme des gefolgerten Urteils ist."*

29   EL 80/13228: *"Reine Verstandesurteile sind sie nur dann, wenn auch die Prämissen und, im Falle sie mittelbare Folgerung sind, auch die Prämissen der Prämissen bis hinauf zu der ersten und unmittelbaren Annahmen Verstandesurteile sind."*

name is related and therefore adopted, but the sense is a very different one that Kant would have hardly given it, if he would have borne in mind its derivation. 5. Or finally does Kant's division correspond to our division according to intensity? Sometimes it seems to suggest this. Still, by no means. "I am," for instance, [is] not apodictic, though certain with all decisiveness.

[1. Ist der Gesichtspunkt vielleicht identisch mit dem bei unserer Einteilung der Urteile in notwendig wahre – nicht notwendig wahre, absurde – nicht absurde? Offenbar nicht! (Der Satz "Gott ist" ist nicht apodiktisch. Ebenso "A ist A.") 2. Oder vielleicht mit dem bei unserer Einteilung in apriorische und aposteriorische? Newton erkannte a posteriori den binomischen Satz, und doch konnt er ihn im kantischen Sinn apodiktisch behaupten. A ist A, obwohl a priori, ist nicht apodiktisch. 3. Oder in absolute sichere, physisch sichere und wahrscheinliche? Auch hier wäre es leicht zu zeigen, dass die Einteilung eine verschiedene ist, z.B. "Ich bin" ist nicht apodiktisch. 4. Oder trifft das apodiktische Urteil mit dem apodiktisch erwiesenen zusammen, von dem wir sprachen? Auch dies ist nicht der Fall, sonst könnte, um nur eins zu erwähnen, nur mittelbar Erkennbares im kantischen Sinn apodiktisch behauptet werden, was keineswegs der Fall ist. Der Namen ist verwandt und daher genommen, aber der Sinn ein ganz anderer, den Kant ihm wohl kaum gegeben hätte, wenn er seine Abstammung sich vergegenwärtigt haben würde. 5. Oder endlich entspricht vielleicht die Einteilung Kants unserer Einteilung nach der Intensität? Manchmal scheint sie hinüberzuspielen. Aber doch keineswegs. Zum Beispiel "Ich bin" nicht apodiktisch, obwohl gewiss mit aller Entschiedenheit.][30]

Accordingly it appears at first that Brentano cannot find a place for modality in his divison of judgments. This is indeed a problem for him because this aspect has been enshrined in traditional logic, not only in Kantian and Cartesian logic, but in scholasticism and all the way back to Aristotle.

After engaging in extensive polemics against various accounts of modality, Brentano tells us that there is no place for modality in a legitimate classification of judgments. "The modal ones," he says, "are those judgments that are made about a judgment."[31] Whenever we say that it is true, false, necessarily true, necessarily false, etc., that such and such is the case, our judgment is modal. If we judge that God exists, for instance, our judgment is not modal, whereas

---

30   EL 80/13249.
31   EL 80/13259: *"Die modalen sind solche Urteile, welche über ein Urteil gefällt werden."*

if we judge that it is necessarily true that God exists we are judging about the judgment that God exists. For this reason the judgment that it is necessarily true that God exists is a modal one. The matter in this case is itself a judgment. Modality is accordingly not one of the main aspects under which Brentano classifies judgments because it concerns the matter of the judgment. Kant seems to think that all judgments are modal because from his perspective (as Brentano interprets the Kantian view) we first present a judgment and then actually pass the judgment, whereas Brentano makes the assertion, "Sometimes the presentation of a judgment certainly precedes the passing of the judgment, but this is not generally necessary; rather, it suffices when the presentation of the judged is present."[32] A modal judgment is accordingly a judgment that has the presentation of a judgment as its foundation. Otherwise the judgment is not modal.

Kant's table of judgments is in fact based on the presupposition that presented judgments are to be treated as judgments. Brentano argues against this presupposition in the following passage:

> The division that Kant gives here of the judgments is like someone dividing the horses into the painted horses, the horses that are horses, and the saddled horses. For in fact a presented judgment is no more a judgment than a painted horse [is] a horse. And as every horse is a horse that is a horse, every judgment is an assertoric judgment, i.e. a judging judgment, a really asserting assertion.
>
> [Die Einteilung, die Kant hier von den Urteilen gibt, ist so, wenn etwa einer die Pferde in die gemalten Pferde, die Pferde seienden Pferde und die gesattelten Pferde einteilen würde. Denn in der Tat is ein vorgestelltes Urteil so wenig ein Urteil als ein gemaltes Pferd ein Pferd. Und wie jedes Pferd ein Pferd seiendes Pferd, so ist jedes vorgestellte Urteil so wenig ein Urteil als ein gemaltes Pferd ein Pferd.][33]

The question arises, however, whether the judgment that is presented in modal judgments should actually be called a "judgment." In this regard we confront notions such as "proposition" and "state of affairs."

Here again we are reminded of what Stumpf was later to say about Brentano's theory of modality in the *Logik*, namely that it involved the conception

---

32   EL 80/13259: "*Manchmal geht gewiss die Vorstellung eines Urteils dem Fällen des Urteils voraus, nicht aber ist dies allgemein notwendig; vielmehr genügt es, wenn die Vorstellung des Beurteilten vorhanden ist ...*" We note here that Brentano here speaks of the *Vorstellung des Beurteilten* and not of the *Vorstellung des Geurteilten*.
33   EL 80/13265.

of modal judgments as judgments about contents of judgments (in his terminology – not Brentano's – states of affairs).[34] And indeed Brentano does say, for instance, "'That a lion is, is (true)' has the content of the judgment 'A lion is' as its matter."[35] Such a statement is not as such among the modals that Kant lists, but it is, like them, an indirect or reflexive judgment. When Brentano speaks of the presented judgment, it is actually the content of judgment under consideration. Again, if we say, "That a Chameleon is *not* and that a lion *is* is true," we have a similar case, only that "Here the matter is the content of two other judgments."[36] The matter of a modal need not be an actual judgment at all. We might, for instance, say that it is false that a circle is not a circle, but this does not involve the judgment that anyone judges that a circle is not a circle. We can say that the modal judgment is a judgment about a judgment, but it is in fact a judgment about a *content* of a judgment. This is an extremely important and difficult point, for it indicates not only a motive for theories of states of affairs such as Stumpf's (also Husserl's and Meinong's), but also a motive for Brentano's later metaphysics, which involved the rejection of such theories. In this connection we note that Brentano's mention of the sentence "That a lion is, is (true)" contains *the word "true" in parentheses*.[37] It makes an enormous difference whether one takes "is true" as equivalent to "is" *simplicter*. While the *Logik* evades this issue, Brentano later came to think that these are not equivalent and also that we are wrong to think that a name of the form "that a lion is" or "the being of a lion" is merely a grammatical name, not a name in the proper sense (a logical name), whereas a good many of his students – even the otherwise faithful Marty – were willing to allow for names of this kind as genuine names and the named objects as genuine entities. We have already seen that the same issue arises in Brentano's theory of disjunctives. Though the focus of the present analysis is not his later philosophy or his relation to his students, it is nonetheless a point of considerable interest to make it clear that the motives for later divergences between him and his school are present in the *Logik*. His students who embraced the non-real did so, at least in part, because they set out with his views. After he saw that this leads to absurdity he attempted to establish an ontology that excluded the non-real.

---

34 Stumpf 1919, 116 f.
35 EL 80/13262: "'*Dass ein Löwe ist, ist (wahr)' hat den Inhalt des Urteils 'Ein Löwe ist' zur Materie.*"
36 EL 80/13263: "'*Dass ein Chamäleon nicht ist und ein Löwe ist', ist wahr. (Hier ist die Materie der Inhalt zweier anderer Urteile.)*"
37 Cf. the marginal note in EL 80/13262: "That A is, is (true). That A is not, is not (is false). [*Dass A ist, ist (wahr). Dass A nicht ist, ist nicht (ist falsch).*]"

As for Brentano's critique of the Kantian table of judgments is concerned, we may say in sum that it involves not only problems in the conception of quality, quantity, and relations, but that it puts modal judgments on a par with these others and thus fails to take into account that they are in fact indirect while the others are direct. This point, according to Brentano, was clear to the medieval philosophers and even to the authors of the Port Royal logic, written well before Kant's time.[38] Accordingly we see Brentano taking an opportunity to disparage Kant as a philosopher of decline.

8 Expression of Judgments

The expression of a judgment is a statement, according to Brentano. He maintains that judgments can be classified with respect to statements under the aspects: 1) sincerity or insincerity, 2) the form of the expression, 3) clarity or unclarity.

A statement is sincere if it actually conveys the speaker's judgment. A lie is of course insincere. But the statement need not be a lie. If a student guesses in an examination the resulting statement is insincere, but not a lie.

Brentano concerns himself with only two forms of statement, namely existential and non-existential. Of these he says the following:

> The existential form is the most important one of all for the logician. And this [is the case] for two reasons: 1) Because it is the most general one in its applicability. It must be possible to express every unitary judgment in an existential sentence. For … every judgment consists in the acceptance or rejection of something presented. Please note, however: This is not to say that the existential form is also the one used most frequently. It is only the most frequently usable one. All others are suited only for certain cases; they [the existential sentences] alone [are] altogether exceptionless. 2. Because it is the simplest and the one that most corresponds to the psychical occurrence. Thus it serves most of all in general for making clear the essence of judgment and its relation to the presentation (whose denial has become most disadvantageous for logic and metaphysics) and for discerning especially the special character of judgment.

> [Die existentiale Form ist für den Logiker die wichtigste unter allen. Und dies aus einem doppelten Grund: 1) Weil sie in ihrer Anwendbarkeit die allgemeinste ist. Jedes einheitliche Urteil muss in einem Exis-

---

38 EL 80/13266 ff.

tentialsatz ausgedrückt werden können. Denn ... jedes Urteil besteht in der Annahme oder Verwerfung des Vorgestellten. Notabene. Damit ist aber nicht gesagt, dass die existentiale Form auch die am häufigsten gebrauchte ist. Sie ist nur die am häufigsten brauchbare. Alle anderen taugen nur für gewisse Fälle; sie allein ganz ausnahmslos. 2) Weil sie die einfachste und dem psychischen Vorgang entsprechendste ist. So dient sie am meisten sowohl im Allgemeinen das Wesen des Urteils und sein Verhältnis zur Vorstellung klar zu machen (dessen Verkennung für Logik und Metaphysik von größtem Nachteil geworden) als auch insbesondere den speziellen Charakter des Urteils zu erkennen.][39]

We shall see that Brentano makes use of the existential form of statement in his syllogistic.

9 Relations between Judgments

There are cases of identity of judgments, as Brentano notes in his conversion of all universal judgments into negative existentials and all particular judgments into affirmative existentials. There are of course other cases, such as ones where a name is replaced by a synonymous one. He notes the traditional theory of conversion, however, only in passing,[40] apparently because these are unnecessary for his syllogistic and indeed in some cases erroneous. "It can occur," he stresses, "that someone at first glance doubts whether or not [the judgment that one statement expresses] is identical [with what another one expresses]."[41] This doubt is certainly one that he had to face in view of his theory of judgment which was to overturn the whole tradition of logic.

As regards relations of opposition, the older logics represented these in the square of opposition, according to which A and O are opposed as contradictories, E and I also as contradictories, A and E as contraries, O and I as contraries, A and I as subalterns, and finally E and O as subalterns. As we have already noted, however, in the *Logik* Brentano identifies only one kind of opposition between judgments, i.e. the opposition of contradictories.

Yet another relation between judgments is equivalence which occurs "when one or more judgments say as much as one or more other judgments do, even

---

39   EL 80/13290.
40   EL 80/1338.
41   EL 80/1338–1339: *"Es kann geschehen, dass einer auf den ersten Blick zweifelt, ob identisch oder nicht."*

if they are perhaps not identical with them."[42] He finds various kinds of equivalence. These are as follows:

> 1) Indirect equivalence, e.g. "A is" – "It is true that A is" – "It is false that A is not."
> Belonging here are also the contrapositions, e.g. "Some human being is not just" – "Someone who is not just is not not a human being." "All human beings are living beings" – "All non-living beings are not human beings."
> Belonging here are also the hypothetical and the corresponding disjunctive [judgments].
> 2) Equivalence of sentences with correlative matter (including *concretum* and *abstractum*), e.g. "A cause is" – "An effect is." "A is moved by B" – "B moves A," etc.
> 3) Equivalence of affirmative sentences one of which indeterminately affirms one of two terms which are formed by adding contradictory determinations to the matter of the other, e.g. "A is," "A [which is] B or A [which is] not-B is."
> 4) Equivalence of absolute and relative determinations or also of relative determinations with each other, as these occur in mathematics, e.g. "2 × 2 [objects] are," "There are 4 [objects]." ... (Or identical? And only due to not connecting in our thought? This seems correct!)

> [1] Indirekte Äquivalenz, z. B. „A ist" – „Es ist wahr, dass A ist", – „Es ist falsch, dass A nicht ist".
> Hieher gehören auch die Kontrapositionen, z. B. „Irgend ein Mensch ist nicht gerecht" – „Irgend ein nicht Gerechter ist nicht nicht Mensch", „Alle Menschen sind lebende Wesen" – „Alle nicht lebenden Wesen sind nicht Menschen".
> Hieher gehören auch die hypothetischen und die entsprechenden disjunktiven.
> 2) Äquivalenz von Sätzen mit korrelativer Materie (dazu Konkretum und Abstraktum), z. B. „Eine Ursache ist" – „Eine Wirkung ist"; „A wird von B bewegt" – „B bewegt A" usw.
> 3) Äquivalenz von affirmativen Sätzen, von welchen der eine unbestimmt eines von zweien Termini affirmiert, die durch Hinzufügung

---

42 EL 80/1339: *"wenn ein oder mehrere Urteile so viel sagen, wie ein oder mehrere andere Urteile, wenn sie auch vielleicht nicht mit ihnen identisch sind."*

kontradiktorischer Bestimmungen zur Materie des anderen gebildet sind, z. B. „A ist," „AB oder A nicht-B ist."

4) Äquivalenz von absoluten und relativen Bestimmungen oder auch von relativen Bestimmungen untereinander, wie sie in der Mathematik vorkommen, z. B. 2×2 sind; es sind 4; es sind 4 + 5 ... (Oder identisch? Und nur wegen des Nichtverbindens der Begriffe in unserem Denken verschieden? – Dies scheint richtig!)][43]

We see here in the fourth case an instance where there is uncertainty whether the equivalence in question is actually a case of identity. A discussion pertaining to mathematics, however, would take us much too far afield here. It is nonetheless the first case of equivalence that is of particular interest in the context of the present analysis of the *Logik*.

There can certainly be an indirect equivalence between judgments (actually an equivalence of an indirect judgment with a direct one). We have already observed that Brentano identifies the traditional modal judgments as indirect, as he also includes judgments expressed in the forms of "it is true that" and "it is false that" as judgments of this kind. These are judgments about judgments, or more precisely they are judgments about the *contents* of judgments. Any judgment that is expressed in the form of "A is" is equivalent to one expressed in the form of "It is true that A is" (also "It is false that A is not"). We have already noted that for Brentano a judgment about the content of a judgment has a different matter from that of direct judgments. "A is" and "It is true that A is" are thus not identical judgment, but they are rather equivalent. Brentano says that hypothetical and disjunctive judgments also belong here. If, for example, we say that A exists or B exists, the judgment that we express in this case is equivalent with the one that we express when we say, "One of the two, the existence of A and the existence of B, exists." Yet, we have noted the peculiar case of "A exists or B does not exist," which is the same as "One of the two, the existence of A and the non-existence of B, exists." This is, it seems, strictly a judgment about the contents of judgment and cannot be equivalent with a direct judgment.

Inclusion (*Einschluss*) is, in addition to identity and opposition, an additional way in which a judgment can stand in relation to others. It occurs, says Brentano, "when a judgment is contained in one or several ones; either explicitly ... (in a plurality of judgments one of which is identical) or implicitly ..., potentially, if it can be inferred from the one of which one says that this

---

43   EL 80/1339.

contains it."⁴⁴ While inclusion is explicit when the affirmation of the whole includes the affirmation of the parts or when the denial of a part includes the denial of the whole, it is implicit when "A is" contains "AB is not A which is not B."⁴⁵ Cases of inclusion indeed account for immediate inferences.

10   Evidence

While Brentano regards all evident judgments as motivated, he thinks that a judgment can be motivated without actually being evident. Leaving aside motivating factors besides evidence, we now turn to Brentano's concept of evidence. The evidence that motivates us to make a correct judgment, however, need not lie in the evidence of another judgment (i.e. a premise). Some judgments are rather immediately evident. These are no less a concern for logic than are judgments that are evident through mediation.

There are two ways we can go astray regarding immediate evidence:

> Here one can be mistaken 1) by trusting immediately in compulsion of an entire class that is not knowledge, 2) by thinking that something belongs to one class belongs to another: a) [mistaking] outer [perception] for inner, e.g. pain [in the phantom limb] ([after] amputation), b) memory for perception in the usual sense: obvious and yet one thinks that one sees motion, that one perceives the progression of one's own thoughts, the inner changes. (Hence time is not immediately certain (as Ueberweg [thinks]) no more than space [is]).
>
> ... We can also be mistaken by seeking to mistrust something perceived with immediate evidence, for [this is] actually impossible (cf. practical philosophy). For this reason [we are] to leave to the metaphysician this investigation against the skeptics.
>
> [Hier kann man fehlen 1) indem man auf den Drang hin unmittelbar einer ganzen Klasse vertraut, die nicht Einsicht ist; 2) indem man etwas, was zur einen Klasse gehört, zur anderen gehörig denkt: a) äussere für innere,

---

44   EL 80/1341: "*Wenn ein Urteil in einem oder mehreren anderen enthalten ist; entweder explizite ... (in einer Mehrheit von Urteilen, von welchen eines identisch ist) oder implicite ..., der Kraft nach, wenn es aus dem, wovon man sagt, dass dieses es enthalte, gefolgert werden kann.*"

45   EL 80/1341 ff.

> z. B. Schmerz [im Phantomglied] ([nach] Amputation), b) Gedächtnis für Wahrnehmung im gewöhnlichen Sinne: Auffallend und dennoch, man meint man sehe Bewegung, man nehme durch inneren Sinn das Fortschreiten der eigenen Gedanken, die inneren Veränderungen wahr. Aber dies ist nicht der Fall. (Daher ist die Zeit nicht unmittelbat gewiss (wie Überweg), so wenig wie der Raum.)
> ... Wir können auch fehlen, indem wir etwas evident unmittelbar Wahrgenommenem misstrauen oder zu misstrauen suchen, denn eigentlich unmöglich (cf. praktische Philosophie). Ebendarum diese Untersuchung gegen die Skeptiker dem Metaphysiker zu überlassen.][46]

Here again we see the *Logik* as just a short step away from metaphysics. It is best however to leave further considerations of this issue for another occasion.

Inner perception, excluding both outer perception and memory, is for Brentano a clear-cut instance of immediate evidence. We need to be particularly careful about misclassifying. We perceive pain by inner perception, whereas we often perceive what is painful, such as a sting of a needle or extremely bright light, by outer perception. Our judgment that things move or even that there is change in our own consciousness, however, is the product of memory and therefore not inner perception. It is of course understandable that some of Brentano's students, particularly Meinong and Husserl, were very dissatisfied with his very extreme restrictions on what we can know about our own consciousness. Epistemological theories of time-consciousness and of memory were in fact central topics in his school, which lie outside the scope of the present analysis.

Besides inner perception, other cases of immediate evidence, according to the *Logik*, are purely conceptual. We can immediately know axioms to be not only true, but necessarily true.[47] We can know that if A is A is or that A either is or is not. If we confront skeptics about such a law, "we turn them over to the metaphysician."[48] This remark is in itself highly significant, as we

---

46   EL 80/13352.
47   In Brentano 1889, 78–84, we find an attack on a concept of evidence as a "feeling of necessity" (*Gefühl der Notwendigkeit*) which is expressed in Sigwart 1889, 16. While Brentano's critique of the view that logic is concerned with evidence in this sense (or indeed that this is an adequate understanding of evidence) falls outside of the present analysis, it is interesting to note that Husserl (1900, 181 ff.) later came to criticize the same view as belonging to psychologism. Accordingly at least this aspect of the rejection of psychologism is already prefigured in Brentano's philosophy during the nineteenth century.
48   EL 80/13360: „*diese überlassen wir dem Metaphysiker.*"

have already seen that the science of logic for Brentano comes into close contact with metaphysics.

Kant and his followers, however, have tried to show that metaphysics cannot be a science. The initial stage of their case for this thesis lies in the claim that we have knowledge which is synthetic on the one hand and *a priori* on the other. Synthetic judgments, according to them, occur wherever the predicate is not contained in the subject. Accordingly, 5 < 12 is an example of a synthetic judgment, for "less than 12" is not contained in "5." At the same time, however, it is necessary and universal and therefore on the Kantian view *a priori*. The necessity and universality of such judgments on this view is however limited to the domain of experience. Brentano objects to this view in the *Logik* as follows:

> But Kant's doctrine is nonetheless wrong: Not from the subject alone, but from subject and predicate does the relation arise analytically, and from this it follows that a 12 that is not greater than 5 cannot exist. For this reason [it is] also unconditional and valid not merely within the limits of experience.
>
> [Aber dennoch Kants Lehre falsch: nicht aus dem Subjekt allein, aber aus Subjekt und Prädikat zusammen ergibt sich das Verhältnis analytisch, und daraus folgt, dass ein nicht kleiner als 12 seiendes 5 nicht existieren kann. Darum auch unbedingt und nicht bloß innerhalb der Grenzen unserer Erfahrung gültig.][49]

The implication here is that the Kantian objection to metaphysics as science is an utter failure. Our immediate knowledge of axioms, according to Brentano, is just as applicable to what lies beyond our experience as it is to the phenomenal sphere, though this matter is not of further concern in the present context as it pertains more to metaphysics than to logic.

In the *Logik* Brentano is also interested in dealing with philosophers who call into question the immediacy of our knowledge of logical truths of the kind under consideration. Such a philosopher is John Stuart Mill,[50] against whom Brentano argues as follows:

---

49   EL 80/13371.
50   *A System of Logic*, II.vii.5: "I consider it [the law of non-contradiction] to be, like other axioms, one of our first and most familiar generalizations from experience."

He asserts that they are established by experience and induction. Even the proposition "If A is, then A is" would be based on an experience, infinitely multiplied, that something never is and is not at the same time. 1. It is easy to show the untenability of this view. If we establish our so-called axioms, e.g. the law of non-contradiction, by means of induction from particular cases, we can obviously do this only if it comes to light that what is true in all possible cases is universally and necessarily true. 2. It even seems that, by allowing induction to be self-justifying, the proposition must come to light that what has been found by us as true in certain cases may be asserted as universally and necessarily true, although our observations do not exhaust the number of possible cases. For in fact induction is not exhaustive. 3. In both cases the knowledge of the law of non-contradiction would thus presuppose the knowledge of another universal necessary principle, in the latter ... even the knowledge of one that does not seem to come to light as much as the law of non-contradiction itself does. 4. Yet, aside from this, this principle itself would in any case have to be proved again by induction. However, that could be only if it already were to come to light prior to the proof. And consequently one gets ensnared in a circle. 5. Hence, all assurance of universal principles is gone, and all science for which Mill wants to establish rules is impossible.

[Er behauptet, sie würden durch Erfahrung und Induktion festgestellt. Selbst der Satz "Wenn A ist, ist A" beruhte auf einer ins Endlose vervielfältigten Erfahrung, dass niemals etwas zugleich sei und nicht sei. 1. Es ist leicht, die Unhaltbarkeit dieser Ansicht zu zeigen. Wenn wir unsere so genannten Axiome, z.B. den Satz des Widerspruchs, durch Induktion aus einzelnen Fällen feststellen, so können wir dies offenbar nur tun, wenn es einleuchtend ist, dass, was in allen möglichen Fällen wahr ist, allgemein und notwendig wahr ist. 2. Ja es scheint sogar, dass, damit unsere Induktion sich rechtfertigen lasse, der Satz einleuchtend sein müsse, dass, was in gewissen Fällen von uns als wahr befunden worden ist, als allgemein und notwendig wahr behauptet werden dürfe, obwohl unsre Beobachtungen die Zahl der möglichen Fälle nicht erschöpfen. Denn in der Tat ist die Induktion nicht erschöpfend. 3. In beiden Fällen würde also die Erkenntnis des Satzes des Widerspruchs die Erkenntnis eines anderen allgemeinen notwendigen Prinzips voraussetzen, in dem letzteren (und es ist dies, wie gesagt, der eigentlich vorliegende) sogar die Erkenntnis eines solchen, das keineswegs so einleuchtend scheint, wie der Satz des Widerspruchs selbst. 4. Doch auch davon abgesehen, müsste jedenfalls dieses Prinzip selbst wieder durch Induktion bewiesen werden. Das könnte aber nur sein, wenn es schon vor dem Beweis einleuchtend wäre. Und somit verfängt man sich in einem Zirkel. 5. So ist denn alle Sicherheit allgemeiner Prinzipien dahin, und die ganze Wissenschaft, für die Mill die Regeln feststellen will, ist unmöglich.][51]

While Brentano thus sees Mill's inductive theory of axioms as self-refuting, he also identifies Friedrich Ueberweg, who wrote a very important work in the history and system of logic, as a proponent of the view that we do not know axioms with immediacy.[52] Our knowledge of them, according to this logician, is mediated by concepts. Brentano argues that "mediated knowledge" refers to cases where a judgment is mediated by other judgments, not by concepts. This theory of axiomatic knowledge is accordingly unacceptable, according to the *Logik*.[53]

Brentano also allows for evidence by mediation. In this case we have premises that either guarantee the conclusion or make the conclusion highly probable. The theory of probability for Brentano, however, would require a separate study. Although he does give it attention in the *Logik*, that part of his manuscript is yet to be properly edited. Moreover, that part of his logical reform, unlike his theory of deduction, is not based on his theory of judgment. In the following section we shall briefly consider Brentano's theory of deduction as an alternative to the traditional syllogistic.

11   Syllogism

In the *Logik* Brentano develops his syllogistic by using his own peculiar and quite simple notation. Of anything that we may designate as "A", there are

---

51   EL 80/13360f.
52   Ueberweg 1871, § 77.
53   EL 80/13362f. In this connection I take the liberty to quote from a letter that Brentano wrote to Ernst Mach (18 November 1903): "There are three classes of universal judgments that come to light from mere concepts: 1) judgments of contradictional opposition, e.g. 'No human is a non-human,' 'No stone is a non-body,' 2) judgments of positive opposition, e.g. 'If something is red, it is not blue,' and 3, judgments of correlative inseparability, such as 'No cause without effect,' 'Nothing greater without something smaller,' etc. Kant thought that a scientific edifice cannot be built upon such judgments, but in contradiction with this view would have it that all formal logic is based on statements of non-contradiction. I am convinced, however, that all *pure* mathematics is erected from such analytic statements. I stress the word 'pure' with the greatest emphasis, which I want to be taken very strictly." (Brentano 1988: 207.)

basically two judgments that can be made: "A exists" and "A does not exist." Brentano indicates the latter by "Ax", whereas he has no special sign for the former except "A" by itself.[54] Moreover, "AB" indicates the judgment that A which is B exists, whereas "ABx" indicates the judgment that A which is B does not exist. He also strikes a letter through to indicate the negation of a term. Thus "A̶B" means that A which is not B exists, whereas "A̶Bx" means that A which is not B does not exist. We must strictly bear in mind the difference between the negation of a term on the one hand and negation as a negative judgment on the other.

As the traditional syllogistic worked with A, E, I, O, Brentano does so as well. His notation in the *Logik* for these classes is as follows:

Traditional formulation	Existential formulation	Brentano's notation
A: All A is B.	There is no A that is not B.	A̶Bx
E: No A is B.	There is no A that is B.	ABx
I: Some A is B.	There is A that is B.	AB
O: Some A is not B.	There is A that is not B	A̶B

The syllogistic of the form Barbara (AAA in the first figure) would accordingly look as follows:

Traditional formulation	Existential formulation	Brentano's notation
All A is B.	There is no A that is not B.	A̶Bx
All B is C.	There is no B that is not C.	B̶Cx
All A is C.	There is no A that is not C.	A̶Cx

---

54 The fact that Brentano does not use a special sign for affirmation is of course in accordance with natural language. In this regard as well as the use of a small letter for term negation, the notation in the *Logik* differs from what we find in Hillebrand's work on Brentano's logic (see p. 343 below) or in Brentano 1956, 200–226 (Cf. Kastil 1951, 201–209), which is repeated in Simons 2004, 52–63. Nor is the notation that occurs in Simons 1987 (and in Simons 1992) what we actually find in the *Logik*.

Here we may note that the Brentanian syllogism actually has four terms (A, B, B̵, and C̵), whereas the traditional syllogism has three. This requires a change of syllogistic rules which in turn alter the evaluation of certain syllogism.

As we know from Brentano's *Psychology*, the rules for syllogistic inference are to be revised in accordance with three of his own, which I cite here from the *Logik*:

> 1. Every so-called syllogistic inference, in order to be valid, must contain four terms, two of which are contradictorily opposed to each other, wheras the other two occur twice in it.
> 2. If the conclusion is negative, each premise has the quality and one term in common with it (and consequently the two premises contain the contradictory terms).
> 3. If the conclusion is affirmative, one of the premises has the same quality and one of the same terms, whereas the other has the opposite quality and an opposite term.

> [1. Jeder sogenannte kategorische Schluss muss, um gültig zu sein, vier Termini enthalten, von denen zwei kontradiktorisch einander entgegengesetzt sind, die beiden anderen aber zweimal in ihm zu stehen kommen.
> 2. Ist der Schlusssatz negativ, so hat jede Prämisse die Qualität und einen Terminus mit him gemein (und folglich enthalten die beiden Prämissen die beiden Prämissen die beiden kontradiktorischen Termini).
> 3. Ist der Schlusssatz affirmativ, so hat jede Prämisse die gleiche Qualität und einen gleichen Terminus; die andere aber die entgegengesetzte Qualität und einen entgegengesetzten Terminus.]⁵⁵

Since the conclusion of Barbara is *negative*, the third rule has no bearing on it. It has four terms, two of which (B and B̵) are opposed to each other whereas the other two (A and C̵) occur twice in it. Barbara thus meets the requirement of the first rule. The conclusion is negative and each premise has the quality (negation) and one term (A in the first premise, C̵ in the second premise) in common with it. One of the two contradictory terms (B and B̵) is contained

---

55 EL 80/13412 f. Cf. Brentano 1874, 303. In Simons 2004, 57–58, the first of these rules is stated in the definition of the syllogisms, whereas the second is called "negative syllogism" and the third "positive syllogism." These two rules, abbreviated as NEG and POS, are formalized by Simons, whereas I simply quote them from the *Logik*.

in each premise. Barbara is thus valid in accordance with Brentano's first two rules and is therefore valid. Other traditional syllogisms that are valid in accordance with these rules are Celarent (EAE in the first figure), Cesare (EAE in the second figure), Camenes (AEE in the fourth figure), and Camestres (AEE in the second figure).

An example of a syllogism that has an affirmative conclusion is the following:

> Nothing that has justified remorse as a consequence is desirable.
> Some enjoyment has justified remorse as a consequence.
> Therefore, some enjoyment is not desirable.

A syllogism of this form (Ferio: EIO in the first figure) would be symbolized as follows in Brentano's notation:

ABx
CA
--
C$\bar{\text{B}}$

Of course we have four terms (A, B, C, and $\bar{\text{B}}$) here. The second premise and the conclusion have the same quality (affirmation) and one of their terms (C) in common, whereas the quality of the first premise (negation) is the opposite of the conclusion's quality and one of this premise's terms (B) is the opposite of one of the conclusion's terms ($\bar{\text{B}}$). The other two terms (A and C) occur twice in the syllogism. Ferio is accordingly no less valid than Barbara. However, it is, unlike Barbara, a syllogism that is confirmed by the first rule and the third one. Other syllogisms that are confirmed by these rules are Darii (AII in the first figure), Datisi (AII in the third figure), Dimaris (IAI in the fourth figure), Bocardo (OAO in the third figure), Disamis (IAI in the third figure), Baroco (AOO in the second figure), Festino (EIO in the second figure), Ferison (EIO in the third figure), and Fresison (EIO in the fourth figure).

According to Brentano, there are accordingly ten valid syllogisms in accordance with the first rule and the third one, whereas there are five valid syllogisms in accordance with the first rule and the second one. Yet, according to the logic that he had learned from Clemens and perhaps from neo-scholastic textbooks, there are at least five more and sometimes as many as nine more valid syllogisms. Wherever a syllogism essentially involves subalternative inference, i.e. from the universal to the particular, it is invalid for Brentano, whereas such inference was acceptable in the neo-scholastic logic. For further discussion of this point, one may consider Hillebrand's discussion of four types of syllogism (below, pp. 355 f.) which were acceptable in traditional logic, though not in Brentanian logic because they violate the third rule. This is likewise the case regarding five additional types left unmentioned by Brentano and Hillebrand (and indeed by many other modern commentators on term logic), namely Barbari (AAI in the first figure), Celaront (EAO in the first figure), Cesaro (EAO in the second figure), Camestros (AEO in the second figure), and Camenos (AEO in the fourth figure). It is easy to see that they all involve negative premises (A or E) and an affirmative conclusion (I or O) and thus violate the third rule. Essentially they are expansions of subalternation which is unacceptable according to the *Logik*.

From Brentano's point of view there is no need for extensive mnemonics or the analysis of syllogisms into moods and figures. The simple application of his three rules is all that is needed in a syllogistic in accordance with the *Logik*, although this reformed syllogistic does not take into account the vexing problem of double judgment. This is perhaps the main reason why Brentano never did publish the *Logik*, as he had planned at one time. In the seventh chapter one can also find further details regarding Brentano's reformed logic with respect to its syllogistic constructions and the theory of double judgment.

12   Concluding Remarks

In this chapter we have elaborated on the theory of judgment that Brentano espouses in the *Logik*. The central thesis of this theory is that a judgment is an acceptance or rejection of an object, most accurately formulated in a statement that the object exists or does not exist. In the former case it is an affirmation, in the latter a negation. Although affirmation and negation had a place in the old logic under the heading of quality, so did universality and particularity under the heading of quantity. For Brentano, however, there is no need in the syllogistic for quantity. While a judgment has other aspects, e.g. intensity and motivation, though not necessarily modality (which pertains to judgments about contents of judgment), the aspect of quality is the only one that Brentano uses in his syllogistic. The Kantian table of judgments not only goes awry in failing to see that quantity is reducible to quality, but that conditionals and disjunctives, no less than universal and particular judgments, are to be reformulated as affirmative and negative existential judgments, whereas not all judgments have modality and are thus to be classified by another principle of division (indirect as opposed direct). The result of Brentano's theory of judgment is a theory of deduction which requires four terms, not the traditional three, for valid syllogisms, and a much simpler set of rules as compared to neo-scholastic logic.

Yet, for whatever reasons, Brentano was not driven to develop this logic further after the mid 1880s. By the end of that decade he was finished with lecturing on logic and rather gave attention to descriptive psychology in his lectures. After delivering three distinct lecture courses on that topic (1887/88, 1888/80, 1890/91), he planned to publish a book on it, apparently as an alternative to the previously planned second volume of *Psychologie vom empirischen Standpuntke*.[56] However, his interest then shifted more towards metaphysics. The discovery of double judgment, as we have already emphasized, introduced difficulties in formulating his particular version of a Modest Logic. In addition to this, his contentment with brief dismals of algebraic logic could hardly suffice in face of the Great Logic of algebra that Ernst Schröder was developing in the 1890s, in part under the influence of Charles Sanders Peirce. Though Brentano boldly declared, "On the basis of new psychological results I flatter myself in having reformed elementary logic …,"[57] there is a world of difference between such self-flattery and actually publishing the alleged results and their consequences in logic. The problem of publishing Brentano's Modest Logic is of course compounded in the wake of the Fregean logic that Bertrand Russell and others were developing in the twentieth century and now outshines all of the term logics of the past. Be this as it may, those who find Brentano as an important philosopher in other domains of inquiry, such as psychology (particularly descriptive psychology or phenomenology) and metaphysics, will profit from knowing about the *Logik* (just as one might profit from knowing about Kant's logic in order to understand other aspects of Kant's philosophy).

The above-described Modest Logic is a product of Brentano's academic activity in the nineteenth century. Further developments in his own system of philosophy in the twentieth century may also serve to explain why it never made its way into publication beyond his manuscripts, lecture courses, and correspondence. As early as 1902 or thereabouts, he began to think that we cannot even conceive of anything but a real entity. In the *Logik*, however, he was compelled to formulate the disjunction of A or not B as "one of the two, the existence of A and the non-existence of B, exists." His Modest Logic accordingly demanded that we conceive of not only real entities, but also of their existence and non-existence: states of affairs in the terminology of Stumpf and Husserl. The same issue is again plainly apparent in Brentano's view that indirect judg-

---

56 Rollinger 2012, 298–303. The plain fact of the matter is that Brentano in general found it difficult to prepare manuscripts for publications, as this involves much tedious labor rather than pure philosophizing.

57 Brentano 1895, 39.

ments (including modals) are judgments about *contents* of judgment.[58] This issue most certainly calls for further investigations, though it would take us far beyond the purview of the *Logik* to pursue these matters further. It is however of considerable importance for us to see that Brentano's theory of judgment and his theory of concepts (which allows for concepts of non-things) indicate powerful motives for developing yet further theories which inevitably involve metaphysical considerations rather than merely logical ones.

---

58 In Morscher 1986 we find the thesis that Brentano's theory of contents of judgments was motivated by an attempt to give an account of the objectivity of logical properties, whereas Fréchette 2014 argues instead that the motivation behind this theory is the empiricist view of the origin of concepts. The analysis of the *Logik*, however, does not at all support either of these interpretations, but it rather supports the thesis that Brentano finds himself compelled to speak of contents of judgments in connection with the meanings of statements and, above all, in order to account for problematic cases for one of his most cherished doctrines, namely that all judgments are the acceptance or rejection of an object as this can be formulated in affirmative or negative statements ("A exists" and "A does not exist"). While the theory of meaning is a marginal concern in the *Logik*, the conception of judgments as existential in character is absolutely central to Brentano's concerns in the lecture notes under examination in the present analysis.

Materials

∴

Preparatory Note to Materials

The analysis of Brentano's logic that is conducted in the present volume is first and formost oriented in the set of notes contained in EL 80 of his manuscripts, the so-called *Logik*. Though this material is recognizably a logic from the standpoint of tradition and, at least partly, even from a more contemporary perspective, this is not at all so with regard to the other extensive set of lecture notes which Brentano used for *Die elementare Logik und die in ihr nötigen Reformen* (EL 72), which were lectures delivered in Vienna in the winter semester 1884/85. Neither these notes nor the *Logik* have been edited and published as they are in Brentano's manuscripts. The present volume will hopefully meet a need in this regard by at least providing an analysis of the *Logik* and also an edition and translation of lecture notes that a student took from the lectures on logic of 1884/85. The following texts consist of such an edition (the fifth chapter) and translation (the sixth chapter). The student in question was Franz Hillebrand, whose notes in Gabelsberger stenography have been preserved. Here I have transcribed these notes for an edition in German and also provided an English translation of them.

The notes are included in a single notebook. In view of the fact that Brentano's own notes of these lectures and also notes from other students have been preserved, I have taken the liberty to draw from such notes as well, though I have in all cases clearly marked where I have drawn upon them, often in editorial footnotes and sometimes in square brackets in the main text. The notes from other students are drawn from two notebooks in the hand of Eduard Leisching and from a single notebook in the hand of Alois Höfler. The notes from Leisching and Höfler are in both cases more elaborate than the ones from Hillebrand and will hopefully be edited and translated at a later date. Of course Brentano's own notes of the lectures in question should be made available to readers, but for the time being the notes from Hillebrand will have to suffice. There is indeed an advantage in seeing this material in a condensed form. One must always, to be sure, bear in mind the possibility of being confronted with a corrupt text, but I have in many cases compared the text with the other abovementioned materials and found Hillebrand's notes for the most part highly accurate.

Among the students who attended the lectures of 1884/85 on elementary logic was Edmund Husserl, whose notes on these lectures filled three notebooks. Unfortunately, however, these notebooks along with other extensive materials from Brentano's lectures were lost in the German invasion of Czechoslovakia in 1938.

Brentano divided his own notes corresponding to the ones that are published here into four chapters. Hillebrand, however, only designates the first two of these explicitly as chapters, whereas on the basis of Brentano's and Leisching's notes I have been able to discern where the other two chapters begin in Hillebrand's notes. Though there are further chapters in Brentano's notes, he apparently lectured from these in the summer semester 1885. Husserl did not attend Brentano's lectures at that time. Nor do we have notes from Hillebrand or Höfler beyond the winter semester 1884/85. It will be a great benefit to researchers to have the notes from those lectures in an acceptable edition and English translation, particularly because Brentano there provides a solution to the controversy of nominalism. For the time being, however, we will have to be content with the following edition and translation, as limited as they are.

While Brentano begins here with a definition of logic and continues for some time afterwards in a way that is comparable to his procedure in the *Logik*, he elaborates much more extensively on his theory of wholes and parts. It is moreover clear from these elaborations that they are absolutely essential to his concept of his logic. Here we will not find any exposition of his theory of deduction or induction, but rather a detailed treatment of the concept of the continuum, including a critical discussion of Bernard Bolzano's attempt to deal with this concept, not to mention the attempt of Georg Cantor's criticism of Bolzano and his own attempt to fufill the same task. Brentano's treatment of the concept of the continuum, however, is not purely mathematical. He is much rather concerned with continua as they actually appear among the physical phenomena, including the continua of tones and colors as well as those of space and time. While the notes from Leisching end with Brentano's discussion of the concept of a continuum, the notes from Hillebrand continue from that point into another area which is of great interest to logic as Brentano conceives of it, namely the theory of relations and opposition.

Although the German text is not a full-fledged critical edition, indications of some of the details in the manuscripts are given wherever they prove particularly interesting. The editor also makes corrections, which he indicates in footnotes. All editorial insertions and remarks are put in square brackets. The editor's remarks are moreover italicized, whereas the German passages in the remarks are not italicized (contrary to the practice in the analysis).

The English translation does not significantly diverge from the terminology that I have used in the analysis of the *Logik*. In some cases the text-critical remarks which are given in the German edition are also given in the translation, but the translator does not deem this to be always appropriate. In some cases I have managed to provide references to some of the texts that Brentano cites, though they were not attainable in certain other cases. This is hardly a problem where Brentano is dealing with very familiar authors, whereas in other cases there will no doubt be a lack of interest among many readers, since there is generally a lack of interest in figures who have faded through time, however lamentable such an ahistorical (or anti-antiquarian) attitude may be.

Finally, the seventh chapter of the present volume is a translation of Hillebrand's monograph that he published in defense of Brentanian logic against some of its critics, e.g. Wilhelm Windelband and Christoph Sigwart, with respect to the "idiogenetic" theory of judgment, but also against some of the contemporaneous trends in logic stemming from the work of such important figures as William Hamilton, George Boole, and William Stanley Jevons. Although Hillebrand's symbolism for syllogisms diverges from Brentano's, I have left them both intact as they are. Hillebrand's account of Brentano's syllogistic fills in some of the gaps which are not covered in my own analysis. His source here is apparently from lecture notes, but not from those made available in the other materials in this volume.

Robin D. Rollinger

CHAPTER 5

Franz Hillebrand, *Die elementare Logik und die in ihr nötigen Reformen nach den Vorlesungen des Dr. Franz Brentano* (Wintersemester 1884/85, Wien)

1 I. Vorlesung, d. 25. Oktober 84

Die Logik wird sehr verschieden definiert. Die einen nennen sie Kunst, die anderen Kunst und Wissenschaft. Die ersteren nun bezeichnen sie entweder als Kunst des Schließens oder Kunst des Denkens. Hegel sagt:[1] Die Logik sei die Wissenschaft von der reinen Idee, die wissenschaftliche Entwicklung der reinen Vernunftbegriffe, die allem Denken und Sein zugrunde liegen. Die Logik ist die Darstellung der Wahrheit, wie sie ohne Hülle für sich ist, die Darstellung Gottes, wie er in seinem ewigen Wesen vor der Erschaffung der Welt und eines endlichen Geistes ist; es ist ein Reich der Schatten, die aber andererseits die einfachen, von aller Materiatur freien Wesenheiten sind, in deren diamantenes Netz das ganze Universum hinein gebaut ist.[2]

Vor allem ist daran festzuhalten, dass die Logik eine *praktische Disziplin* ist, und in Hinblick darauf wird sie auch von manchen als Kunst definiert. Brentano definiert sie als Kunst des Urteilens. Sie soll uns das Verfahren lehren, das uns zur Erkenntnis der Wahrheit führt, d. i. zum richtigen Urteil.

Sie ist nicht die Kunst des richtigen Schließens.

Wenn man sagt, die Logik sei die Kunst des Schließens, so ist dazu Folgendes zu bemerken: Jeder, der schließt, urteilt, indem er schließt, aber nicht jeder, der urteilt, zieht auch schon eine Folgerung. Dennoch ist der Unterschied beider Definitionen nicht eben so groß, denn, wenn auch unser Urteil häufig nicht

---

1 [*Der übrige Text dieses Absatzes ist anscheinend eine Darstellung eher als ein exaktes Zitat aus einem Werk Hegels.*]
2 [*Kritik dieser Auffasung der Logik in Brentano El 72/12008:* „Abweisung Hegels: Das sind gewiss sehr hochtönende, erhaben klingende Worte. Dennoch werden Sie entschuldigen, wenn ich nicht weiter auf sie Rücksicht nehme. Abgesehen von fundamentalen Irrtümern seines Systems, mit welchen die von ihm gegebene Definition der Logik zusammenhängt, verschiebt Hegel die hergebrachte Bedeutung des Namens vollständig, indem er ihn auf gewisse metaphysische Untersuchungen überträgt. Es wäre eine durch nichts gerechtigfertigte Willkür, wenn wir hierin seinem Beispiele folgen, und nicht vielmehr das unter Logik verstehen wollten, was man allgemein und von Alters her mit dem Namen bezeichnet hat."]

ein Schließen ist, so kann man doch sagen, dass die Kunst des Urteilens fast ganz und gar in der Kunst des Schließens liegt. Die richtigen Schlüsse sind uns vermittelnde Erkenntnisse. Die unvermittelten bieten nicht dieselbe Schwierigkeit; ja, man könnte glauben, dass die Erkenntnis der unmittelbar einleuchtenden Wahrheiten für eine Kunst gar keinen Raum lässt, und so würden denn Kunst des Urteilens und Kunst des Schließens zusammenfallen. Wäre dem so, so würde die Definition der Logik als Kunst des Schließens den Vorzug verdienen, indem sie deutlicher wäre. Doch steht die Sache in Wahrheit anders. Es kommt vor, dass man etwas, was nicht unmittelbare Erkenntnis ist, ja etwas, das vielleicht geradezu falsch ist, für eine unmittelbare Erkenntnis annimmt. Beispiele: die Evidenz der äußeren Wahrnehmung, des Gedächtnisses, des Satzes: *effectus cognitio a cognitione causae dependent et eandem involvit* (Spinoza, *Ethik*, 4. Axiom),[3] oder der Sätze: „Ähnliches wirkt Ähnliches,"[4] „Die Ursache muss vorzüglicher sein als die Wirkung."[5] | Hierher gehören auch viele „Axiome" der französischen Aufklärungsphilosophie, so der Satz von unveräußerlichen Menschenrechten, von der Volkssouveränität etc. etc.[6]

---

3 [*Kritik in Brentano* EL 72/12011: „Die Konsequenz [dieses Axioms ist] keine geringere als, dass alle Erkenntnis deduktiv [sei]. Gottes Existenz [sei aber] unmittelbar einleuchtend." *Vgl. Leisching Y 2/3:* „Das wird als Axiom, als unmittelbar einleuchtender Satz hingestellt. Nun ist das gewiss kein einleuchtender, auch kein wahrer Satz. Die Konsequenz desselben wäre, dass alle Erkenntnis deduktiv sein müsse, keine induktiv. Und endlich in letzter Konsquenz: Gottes Existenz ist unmittelbar einleuchtend, wenn anders er die Ursache aller Dinge ist. Spinoza führt auch tatsächlich das ontologische Argument – was nichts ist als ein gewöhnlicher Paralogismus – als Beweis für das Dasein Gottes an."]
4 [*Kritik in Brentano* EL 72/12011: „Dinge, die nichts miteinander gemein haben, können nicht aufeinander wirken (Körper – Geist)." *Vgl. Leisching Y 3/3:* „Das soll einleuchtend sein! Gott könne daher nicht auf die Welt wirken, Körper nicht auf den Geist. Wenn der Satz richtig ist, kann er nur auf Erfahrung beruhen, einleuchtend ist er nicht."]
5 [*Kritik in Leisching Y 2/4:* „Aus dem Ei entwickelt sich das Huhn. Ist das Ei vorzüglicher als das Huhn?"]
6 [*Kritik in Leisching Y 2/4:* „Z.B. ,volle persönliche Freiheit' sei ein solches. Sofort wurde dann gepredigt: Aufhebung der Klöster, der Ehe. Ja, jede Vertragspflicht wird aufgehoben, denn sie beschränkt die volle persönliche Freiheit. So auch der Satz: ,Alle Menschen sind gleich'. Daran knüpft sich die Gleichheit der Rechte. Damit wäre dann der Privatbesitz aufgehoben, aber auch wenn dies geschähe, wären doch nicht alle gleich. Beispiel: Beethoven und sein Bruder gerieten in Streit, sie verkehrten nur schriftlich miteinander. Letzterer unterschrieb sich ,Gutsbesitzer', ersterer antwortete darauf mit der Unterschrift ,Hirnbesitzer'. Jenem hätte man aufgrund jener Folgerung wohl sein gut wegnehmen können; diesem aber sein Gehirn? – So auch das Dogma der ,Volkssouveränität'. Dies beruht auf groben Verwechslungen. Man verwechselt den richtigen Satz ,Der höchste Zweck des Staates soll das Beste des Volkes sein' mit dem Satze ,Das Volk soll der höchste Regent sein'." *Vgl. Fortsetzung der Kritik in Brentano* EL 72/12012: „Traurige Folgen: Bruderliebe gepredigt – Guillotine; Freiheit gepredigt: Cäsarismus und Despotism, Militarismus und so auch was in dem Gedanken der *Gleichheit* Wahres

Umgekehrt kommt es auch vor, dass tatsächlich unmittelbar einleuchtende Sätze nicht als solche anerkannt werden; dies geschieht in Betreff der inneren Wahrnehmung oder des Satzes des Widerspruchs, wessen Evidenz Epikur und Hegel nicht nur bezweifelte, sondern sogar leugnete. Auch für diesen Teil der Erkenntnisse sind also gewisse Regeln nicht ohne Wert, nicht nur für die vermittelnden; dann aber ist es auch unrichtig, diese Regeln von der Logik auszuschließen, und das würde die Definition der Logik als Kunst des Schließens tun. Streng genommen, richtig also ist die Bestimmung der Logik als Kunst des Urteilens oder der Erkenntnis.

Sie ist auch nicht die Kunst des Denkens.

Andere definieren die Logik, wie bereits erwähnt, als Kunst des Denkens. Unter Denken begreift man das Vorstellen. Die Logik muss sich nun allerdings in eine Erörterung der Vorstellungen einlassen, da das Urteil diese voraussetzt. Handelt nun aber die Logik nur deshalb auch von Vorstellungen, so ist die Definition unrichtig. Dieses aber wird sich auch aus folgender allgemeiner Erörterung ergeben: Jede praktische Disziplin wird nach ihrem Zweck bestimmt. Bei der Logik ist der Zweck einzig und allein die Erkenntnisse, nicht aber die Vorstellungen. Die Ästhetik ist die Kunst der Vorstellungen und strebt darin Vollkommenheit an, nicht aber die Logik. Wie also die Definition der Logik als Kunst des Schließens zu eng ist, so ist sie als Kunst des Denkens zu weit.

11. Vorlesung,
d. 30. Oktober 84

Sie ist auch keine Wissenschaft.

Manche definieren nun die Logik nicht als Kunst, sondern auch als Wissenschaft; sie soll die Wissenschaft sowohl als auch die Kunst des Schließens sein. So sagt Ueberweg: „die Logik ist die Wissenschaft von den normativen Gesetzen der menschlichen Erkenntnis."[7] (Auch Whately ist dieser Ansicht.) Kunst und Wissenschaft sind voneinander unterschieden; zur Kunst gehört, dass ein praktischer Zweck den Wahrheiten Einheit gibt; zur Wissenschaft gehört, dass der Komplex eine intelligible Gattung ausmacht. Die Logik ist nun gewiss eine Kunst. | Schon die Aristoteliker nannten die Schriften ihres Meisters, die sich mit Logik beschäftigen, Organon. Um nun in richtiger Weise Kunst zu sein, darf die Logik gar nicht Wissenschaft sein; sie kann von ganz heterogenen Fragen

---

und Großes liegt ins Gegenteil verkehrt. Der Tyrann nützte alle anderen nur als Werkzeug seiner Zwecke."]

7 [*Ueberweg 1882, 1.*]

handeln. Zweck der Logik ist zur Erkenntnis hinzuleiten, zu lehren, wie wir uns vor Irrtümern bewahren können. Wenn sie diesen Zwecken genügt, indem sie die richtigen Urteile gegenüber den unrichtigen charakterisiert, so könnte man sie vielleicht auch zugleich Wissenschaft nennen, denn diese Normalgesetze könnte als ein Kreis verwandter Wahrheiten angesehen werden. Die Logik kann sich aber nicht in diesen Schranken halten; sie muss außer dem Kanon der Erkenntnistätigkeit noch manches aus anderen psychischen Gebieten beibringen, um uns vor Versuchungen zu bewahren. So muss sie handeln von der Macht der Gewohnheit, von den Gesetzen der Assoziation, vom Einfluss des Willens. Auch auf Sprachliches und Grammatisches hat sie Rücksicht zu nehmen. Auch aus der Metaphysik muss sie Wahrheiten entlehnen, ebenso bei der Schätzung der Wahrscheinlichkeiten die Mathematik herbeiziehen. Auch geht die Logik auf die Verhältnisse verschiedener besonderen Wissenschaften ein, weil alles nicht als geschlossener Kreis innerlich verwandter Wahrheiten gelten kann. Beispiele aus den Schriften bedeutender Logiker können zeigen, mit welchen heterogenen Fragen sich die Logik beschäftigt. Die erste logische Schrift des Aristoteles handelt über die Kategorien, d. h. über die höchsten Gattungen des Seienden. Das gehört in die Metaphysik. Die nächste Schrift, *De Interpretatione*, handelt über Grammatisches. Die *Analytica Posteriora* handeln von den vier Ursachen, dann z. B. über die Gleichzeitigkeit von Ursache und Wirkung. Ebenso verschieden sind die *Topica* und die Schrift *De Sophisticis Elenchis*. Alle diese Schriften schreiten ab von einer einzigen intelligiblen Gattung. Dasselbe zeigt ein bloßer Blick ins Inhaltsverzeichnis der Logik von J. St. Mill. Alexander Bain berücksichtigt sogar das Gesetz der Erhaltung der Kraft; Ähnliches finden wir bei Jevons. Selbst | Pascal, wo er über die Kunst der Überzeugung handelt, gibt unter acht Regeln, die er aufstellt, vier, die über die Definition handeln. (Vgl. Pascal's „Gedanken," übers. von Heinr. Heße, Reclam, pp. 56–57.) Kant allerdings und Herbart wollten eine formale Wissenschaft der Logik aufstellen; allein Albert Lange (*Logische Studien*) wirft ihnen vor, dass das, welches sie tatsächlich bieten, nichts weniger als solche formale Logik sei. Keine Logik hat rein formale Logik sein können, sagt er. Die Logik nötigt eben selbst zur Einmischung anderer Elemente; sie ist also eine Kunst und keine Wissenschaft. Wollen wir aber wirklich eine rein formale Logik haben, was bleibt von ihr übrig? Fast nichts, nur ein kleines Stückchen Psychologie. Es ist nun nicht abzusehen, warum dieses Stückchen für eine besondere Wissenschaft erklärt werden soll. Im praktischen Interesse liegt es gar wohl dieses Stückchen herauszugreifen, aber nur um es mit alledem, was der praktische Zweck sonst fordert, zu verbinden. A. Lange tadelt das, er hatte es aber in seinen eigenen *Logischen Studien* nicht vermieden; namentlich der zweite Teil derselben, der wegen des Autors Todes nicht zur Vollendung kam, zeigt in den erhaltenen Skizzen, wie auch

Lange ganz Heterogenes behandeln wollte. Der kleinere Abschnitt der Logik, welcher der Psychologie entnommen ist und darum heterogene Erkenntnis enthielte, könnte man ja nennen „über den allgemeinen Charakter und die Arten richtig gefällter Urteile."

III. Vorlesung,
am 5. November 84

Wie die Ethik, so kann auch die Logik im weiteren und engeren Sinn gefasst werden. Die erstere lehrt sich selbst und andere zur Erkenntnis zu führen; das war Thomas von Aquin Ansicht, der die Rhetorik und Poetik unter die Logik rechnet. Aristoteles selbst dehnt manchmal die Grenzen der Logik aus, ebenso Pascal („die Kunst zu überzeugen"). | Auch Arnauld nähert sich dieser Auffassung, indem er sagt: „Die Logik ist die Kunst seine Vernunft bei der Erkenntnis der Dinge gut zu handhaben, sei es zur eigenen Belehrung, sei es zur Unterweisung anderer." Die Logik im weitesten Sinn zerfällt in zwei Teile, die individuelle Logik zur Selbsthilfe im Erkennen, und die Logik, welche die Regeln gibt, andere zur Wahrheit zu führen, die kommunikative Logik (sie zerfällt in Didaktik, Dialektik und Rhetorik). Die individuelle Logik ist der frühere Teil und kann selbständig behandelt werden; sie zerfällt in zwei Teile, entsprechend der doppelten Lage, in der wir uns einer zu erwerbenden Erkenntnis gegenüber befinden. Die Kenntnis liegt uns entweder als gegeben vor, oder aber sie ist nicht gegeben. Im ersten Fall müssen wir die gegebene Erkenntnis mit Sicherheit zu beurteilen wissen. Im zweiten Fall müssen wir sie erst aufzufinden wissen. Der erste Teil handelt von der Prüfung gegebener Erkenntnisse, der zweite Teil von der Entdeckung. Viele Erkenntnisse, ohne dass sie von uns entdeckt haben müssten, sind uns gegeben; der erste Teil der Logik, die Prüfung, ist der einfachere und unabhängigere, darum wird er vorangestellt: unmittelbar einleuchtende Wahrheiten bieten sich uns ungesucht da. Auch andere lehren uns Vieles. Darum ist der Teil, der von der Prüfung gegebener Erkenntnis handelt, der frühere. Für uns und unsere Zeit ist das ganz klar. Aber auch bei den ersten Denkern war es nötig, dass ihnen gewisse Erkenntnisse gegeben sein mussten, damit sie auf die Entdeckung anderer ausgehen konnten. Auch sind wir früher in der Lage zu prüfen als zu entdecken. Comte hat das ausgedrückt: „Die Lebenden werden mehr und mehr von Toten beherrscht." Das heißt, das Überlieferte wächst immer, und wer mehr dazu bringt, wird immer ein kleinerer Bruchteil; wenn einer sogar mehr entdeckte, als er von anderen überkäme, würde er dennoch öfters in der Lage sein zu beurteilen als zu entdecken, weil die Aufgabe der Prüfung in der Aufgabe der Entdeckung eingeschlossen ist. Das Prüfen ist auch die einfachere; was der Prüfende tut, muss der Forschende auch tun und noch etwas mehr dazu. Der erste Teil ist auch der unabhängigere; die Regeln für den Entdecker sind von den Regeln des Prüfenden abhängig. | Auch in der Lage von der Entdeckung wird man zuerst von der Entdeckung des Beweises, dann erst von der Auffindung der Wahrheit und dann über die richtige Fragestellung handeln. Der erste Teil wird oft ausschließlich Logik genannt, so von J. St. Mill. Dehnt man die Logik weiter aus, so ist die Logik der Prüfung der relativ elementare Teil. Die Logik der Entdeckung ist der höhere Teil. Unsere Logik ist also die Logik der Prüfung, die elementare Logik (Programm des Semesters).

Wert der Logik.

Was hat diese Disziplin für einen Wert? Die Logik teilt in Bezug auf die Wertschätzung das Schicksal der ganzen Philosophie, aber aus verschiedenem Grund; andere Disziplinen der Philosophie hält man für unzuverlässig, die Logik aber hält man für wertlos. Jede Kunst ist umso wertvoller, je bedeutender der Zweck ist, dem sie dient. Und mit Ausnahme der Ethik lässt sich mit der Logik keine andere Kunst in Bezug auf den Zweck vergleichen. Aber auch praktisch ist die Logik. Wer nicht gut urteilt, ist nicht zu brauchen. Überall müssen wir urteilen und schließen, und es ist nicht gleichgültig, ob wir es in vollkommener oder unvollkommener Weise tun. Dennoch hält man die Logik für wertlos. Man sagt: Gewiss ist die Erkenntnis nicht wertlos, aber dieses Mittel ist verächtlich; es ist dieses Mittel entbehrlich, ja vielleicht nicht einmal förderlich. Natur und Übung machen den scharfen Denker, nicht die Logik. Es gibt viele große Denker, die sich nie mit Logik beschäftigt haben. Die natürliche Anlage ist nun gewiss nicht gleichgültig, kann auch nicht durch Logik ersetzt werden. Ebenso macht auch bei der Erforschung der Wahrheit Übung den Meister. Deshalb aber ist die Logik doch nicht überflüssig, gilt es doch von jedem auch noch so großen und geübten Verstand, dass er durch Talent und Übung allein nicht gegen jeden Irrtum geschützt ist; es zeigt sich, wie alle geirrt haben. Und wenn jede Wissenschaft einen Index hätte, die Werke der größten Männer kämen darauf. Logische Fehler waren es, die oft den einen oder anderen zum Irrtum führten; höchstens bei der Mathematik könnte man das schwer behaupten. Aber auch | im praktischen Leben werden viele solche logischen Fehler vorgefunden. Da nun aber keiner außer Gefahr ist gegen die Gesetze des Urteils zu verstoßen, so ist klar, dass derjenige, der die Gesetze kennt, unter sonst gleichen Umständen dieselben leichter beobachten wird als ein anderer; wer die Gefahren kennt, vermeidet sie leichter. Denn nicht überall bilden die anschaulichen Tatsachen eine Kontrolle für die Richtigkeit der Beweisführung; bei den höchsten Wissenschaften ist eine solche Kontrolle gar nicht gegeben, und mit ihnen hängen oft die höchsten praktischen Zwecke zusammen, so Politik, Pädagogik. Eine genaue Aufmerksamkeit, wird man sagen, richtet hin, um den Fehler zu finden; die besondere Aufmerksamkeit, die die logischen Regeln in Anspruch nimmt, ist nicht wirkungsvoller als eine nochmalige Aufmerksamkeit aufs Argument. Aber auch das ist falsch, und die Erfahrung widerlegt es. Es ist geschehen, dass die größten Denker, sogar auf ihre Fehlschlüsse aufmerksam gemacht, sie oft nicht erkannt haben. Platon stellte seine Ideenlehre auf. Aristoteles zeigte ihm die Fehler der Argumentation, aber Platon hat diese Fehler nie eingesehen. Auch in Betreff des ontologischen Arguments ging es so: Gaunilo macht den Anselm von Caunterbury aufmerksam auf den Fehler, und letzterer hat es nie eingesehen; ebenso wenig Descartes. Kant behauptete, dass man das Kausalgesetz nur in den Grenzen möglicher Erfahrung halten müsse,[8] und dennoch nahm er ein Ding an sich an, das wirkte, und nie hat er den Fehler eingesehen; auch in Betreff der Antinomien gilt dasselbe; er hat hier manche Paralogismen aufgestellt, und die Tatsache einer Antinomie hätte ihn schon aufmerksam machen können. Dasselbe war [der Fall] bei Herbart. Ja, selbst darüber, ob etwas bewiesen sei oder nicht, wird oft bestritten, so in Betreff der Teleologie und die darauf gestützten Gottesbeweise; oder in Betreff der Glaubwürdigkeit eines Wunders (siehe D. Hume über Wunder in seiner *Untersuchung des menschlichen Verstandes*); oder der Beweis der Existenz eines leeren Raumes: die einen beweisen [das], indem sie auf die Ausdehnung durch Wärme aufmerksam machen; andere sagen, auf diese Art könnte man ja auch beweisen, dass man eine Bewegung nicht beschleunigen könne.

8 IV. Vorlesung,
d. 8. November 84

Auch bei dem Auffinden neuer Wahrheiten fördert die Logik; so hat Baco von Verulam durch Aufstellung der richtigen Methode die Naturwissenschaft gefördert. In der Methode liegt die Logik. Aristoteles stellt bei Beginn jedes seiner Werke Reflexionen über die Methode der betreffenden Disziplin an; er beginnt also mit einer logischen Betrachtung. Baco sagt: Der Teil der Philosophie, der die Logik betrifft, ist dem Geschmack vieler nicht angemessen und scheint gar nichts anderes zu sein als ein Fallstrick von spinoser Subtilität; insbesondere wenn wir jedes Ding nach seinem eigentlichen Dienst messen wollen, so müssen wir sagen, dass die logische Wissenschaft der Schlüssel zu den anderen

---

8 [halten müsse *statt* hielte *im Ms.*]

Wissenschaften ist, so wie die Hand das Instrument der Instrumente, so die Logik die Kunst aller Künste (*ars artium*). Auch Leibniz stellte die Logik sehr hoch. [Justus von] Liebig ebenso. Heutzutage allerdings gibt die Logik nicht, was sie [geben] soll, schöpft hingegen einen unnützen Ballast mit sich. Darüber klagte Descartes, ebenso auch Pascal. Auch enthält die Logik, selbst schon die elementare, viele Irrtümer; dennoch glauben manche, sie sei bereits fertig, Weiteres sei aber noch nicht da. Baco meint selbst, ein schwacher Kopf, der im Besitz der Logik sei, könne es einem besseren zuvortun, der sie nicht hätte, wie ein Kind mit einem Lineal eine bessere gerade Linie zeichnen kann als ein guter Zeichner mit freier Hand.

Was die Ansicht anlangt, dass die Logik eine bereits fertige Disziplin sei, so spricht sich schon Leibniz dagegen aus, indem er sagt: „Es gibt nichts Unfertigeres als unsere Logik." „Die Kunst, nach wahrscheinlichen Gründen zu schließen, ist noch nicht ausgeführt."

I. Kapitel
Notwendigkeit gewisser Vorbemerkungen über psychische Phänomene und ihre sprachliche Ausdrücke

Aristoteles sagt in seiner *Nikomacischen Ethik*:

> Ein Politiker hat von der den Menschen eigentümlichen Vollkommenheit zu handeln, denn auf das den Menschen eigentümliche Gute und auf die menschliche Glückseligkeit ist sein Streben gerichtet. Die eigentümliche menschliche Vollkommenheit nennen wir nicht die Vollkommenheit des Leibes, sondern der Seele, und von der Glückseligkeit sagen wir, dass sie in einer Tätigkeit der Seele besteht. Wenn dem so ist, so muss der Politiker in gewisser Weise das wissen, was die Seele betrifft, ähnlich wie derjenige, welcher die Augen oder überhaupt den Leib heilen will, vom Leib Kenntnis haben muss. Wie die Ärzte sich zeitlebens mit der Erforschung des Leibes abgeben, so muss der Politiker Betrachtungen über die Seele anstellen, und das ist umso deutlicher als die Politik ehrwürdiger ist and höher steht als die Heilkunst. Bei dieser Betrachtung wird aber sein Zweck maßgebend sein, und er wird sich nicht tiefer darauf einlassen, als sein Zweck es verlangt; denn die tiefere und genauere Erkenntnis dürfte eine schwierigere Aufgabe sein als der Aufbau der ganzen Politik.[9]

---

9 [*Übersetzung von 1102 a 5–15, nicht genau.*]

Ganz Ähnliches gilt nun von der Logik. Wer Regeln über die Erkenntnis gibt, der muss über das Urteil, aber auch über die psychischen Erscheinungen überhaupt sich einige Bemerkungen nicht ersparen können. Das Urteil gehört zu den psychischen Erscheinungen, aber auch andere psychische Erscheinungen sind mit dem Urteil eng verbunden; so vor allem die Vorstellungen, welche ja die Basis der Urteile sind. Oft hat man behauptet, und noch heute tut man es vielfach, dass das Urteil in einer Verwerfung oder Bejahung von Vorstellungen bestehe. Die übrigen psychischen Erscheinungen stehen allerdings in geringerer Beziehung zum Urteil.

Aber nicht nur über psychische Phänomene, sondern auch über deren sprachlichen Ausdruck pflegen die Logiker Betrachtungen anzustellen. Aristoteles behandelt in in einer | eigenen Schrift über diesen Gegenstand (Περὶ Ἑρμηνείας). Die Stoiker folgten seinem Beispiel; ebenso die Scholastiker, von denen einige (die Nominalisten) sogar in Gefahr kamen, die ganze Logik als eine Untersuchung über die Sprache aufzufassen. John Locke hat das ganze dritte Buch seiner *Untersuchung über den menschlichen Verstand* einer Erörterung über die Worte gewidmet. J. St. Mill beginnt seine Logik mit einer Untersuchung über die Namen. Auch die Logiker, die rein formal sein wollten, sind ohne ihre Absicht in sprachliche Untersuchung gefallen; so Friedrich Albert Lange (*Logische Studien*). Wie erklärt sich nun diese Tatsache? Die Sprache hat den Zweck der Gedankenmitteilung. Durch die Ideenassoziation aber wird der sprachliche Ausdruck mit dem Gedanken eng verknüpft und gewinnt dadurch auf unser Denken selbst großen Einfluss. Dieser Einfluss ist wohl im Ganzen ein fördernder. Wie eng[10] diese Verbindung ist, zeigt wohl am besten den Ausdruck „er denkt französisch." Ja, die Traditionalisten meinen, man könne gar nicht denken ohne zu sprechen (vergleich [die Schrift von] A. Marty über die Entstehung der Sprache).[11] Doch kann in einigen Fällen die Sprache auch für das Denken nachteilig werden. Betrachten wir kurz die Vorteile und Nachteile, welche die Sprache dem Denken bringt.

v. Vorlesung,
d. 11. November 84

Die Vorteile sind folgende:
1. Das assoziierte Wort hindert oft an der Verwechslung der Begriffe, besonders bei solchen, die nur durch Reflexion auf die eigenen psychischen

---

10 [eng *statt* scharf *im Ms.*]
11 [*Marty 1875.*]

Bewegungen erfasst werden, ferner aber auch bei sehr abstrakten Begriffen. Das zeigt sich besonders bei Zahlen. 9 und 10 wären an sich schwer zu unterscheiden, hätten sie nicht verschiedene Namen; noch mehr ist das bei größeren Zahlen der Fall.

2. Auch als Hilfsmittel des Gedächtnisses fördert die Sprache das Denken. Die Verknüpfung der Gedanken mit solchen Zeichen ist das Prinzip der Mnemonik; so ist es für uns beinahe unmöglich, die Gedanken des Vaterunsers in eigenen Worten wiederzugeben, ohne sich beständig den tatsächlichen Wortlaut dieses Gebets zu vergegenwärtigen. |

3. Die Sprache fördert das Denken aber auch in der Weise, in welcher das Zeichen des Mathematikers sein Rechnen fördert, wenn er z.B. für einen langen Ausdruck, den er in seiner Rechnung wiederholt braucht, einen einfachen bezeichneten einsetzt. Dasselbe gilt von den Namen großer Zahlen. Niemand kann sich eine Million vorstellen; denn könnte er es, so müsste er sie von 1,000,001 unterscheiden können, was nicht der Fall ist; er denkt sich nur den Namen oder ein Ziffernsymbol. Ähnliches geschieht fort und fort da, wo eine allzu große Komplikation eintritt.

4. Im Erlernen der Muttersprache allein wird schon ein Reichtum von Mitteilungen gemacht; Alexander Bain hat diesen Vorteil besonders gewürdigt.

Die Nachteile der Sprache sind folgende: 1. Für ungleiche Gedanken gibt es oft gleiche sprachliche Ausdrücke; dieser Umstand bewirkt die Fehler der Äquivokation. Dies ist allerdings nicht immer gleich gefährlich; wenn Begriffe an und für sich durch kräftige sinnliche Merkmale unterschieden sind, so ist eine Verwechslung nicht zu befürchten (so mit dem Worte „Ball" oder „Hahn"). Leicht möglich hingegen ist eine Verwechslung, wenn die Begriffe, die den gleichen sprachlichen Ausdruck haben, an und für sich sehr ähnlich sind; besonders ist das der Fall, wenn der sprachliche Ausdruck in Bezug auf denselben *terminus* gebraucht wird (z.B. beim Worte „königlich," welches immer eine Beziehung zu „König" hat, eine Beziehung, die aber sehr verschieden sein kann, so wenn man sagt „ein königliches Wort," „das königliche Purpur," „der königliche Prinz" etc.). (Vergleich Fr. Brentano, *Von der mannigfachen Bedeutung des Seienden nach Aristoteles*, Freiburg i. Br. 1862, p. 96 ff.) Bei sehr abstrakten oder besonders komplizierten Begriffen ist diese Gefahr ebenfalls sehr groß, weil die Bedeutung dieser Worte überhaupt schwerer zu erfassen ist. Die Mathematik ist allerdings auch abstrakt, aber die einfache Technik ihrer Worte und Schriftzeichen hindert die Fehler der Äquivokation; sobald aber gar ein Fehler hier gemacht wird, ist auch die Äquivokation mit ihrer großen Gefahr vermieden, so wenn man bei einem geometrischen Beweis zwei verschiedene Winkel mit demselben Buchstabe bezeichnet.

2. Aber auch der umgekehrte Fall tritt häufig ein; es wird nämlich oft für gleiche Gedanken ungleiche sprachliche Ausdrücke gebraucht (Synonymie). Hier hindert der Unterschied der assoziierten Worte für die Gleichheit der Gedanken zu erkennen; das geschieht aber besonders da, wo der eine Ausdruck mehr in dieser, der andere mehr in jener Phrase gebraucht wird; oder wenn die Worte selbst äquivok sind; so bei den Ausdrücken „Ort," „Platz," „Stelle," „örtliche Bestimmtheit" etc., die alle in gewisser Weise gleichbedeutend sind, jedoch in verschiedenem Sinn gebraucht werden können und dadurch Äquivokationen veranlassen können. Die Synonymie hat es bewirkt, dass man oft identische Urteile für verschieden hält.

3. Manche sprachliche Ausdrücke sind verschwommen und haben oft gar keinen einheitlichen Gebrauch, so das Wort „Bildung."

4. Auch gibt es viele Lücken in der gewöhnlichen Sprache; manche Begriffe haben keinen völlig adäquaten Ausdruck.

5. Auch ist die gewöhnliche Klassifikation oft unrichtig (vgl. Aristoteles, *Analytica Posteriora* II); so beim Worte Kastanie, welches die wilde und zahme Kastanien wie zu ein und derselben Klasse gehörig hinstellt.

6. Folgendes Vorurteil macht die Sprache oft gefährlich: Das Denken spiegelt sich in der Sprache ab; die verschiedenen Sprachen haben nämlich manches Gemeinsame und in diesem Gemeinsamen ist das Abbild des Denkens zu erkennen. Die Betrachtung der Sprache, meint man oft, könne die des Denkens ersetzen. Das ist nun durchaus nicht richtig. Eine gewisse Gemeinsamkeit erklärt sich daraus, dass das Gleiche durch ein gleiches Mittel bezeichnet werden soll, wenn dies auch im Bezeichneten so unähnlich ist, dass es durchaus nicht als Abbild desselben angesehen werden kann. So z.B. ist der Schrei des Schmerzes bei Menschen der verschiedensten | Sprachen dennoch gleich, und doch wird man nicht behaupten wollen, der Schrei habe mit dem Schmerz eine Ähnlichkeit. Auch daraus, dass man das Denken nach dem sprachlichen Ausdruck beurteilt, ist so mancher Fehler entsprungen; so meinte man, dass das Subjekt eines Satzes früher gedacht wird als das Prädikat, weil der Ausdruck des ersteren dem des letzteren vorhergeht; dies aber ist nicht wahr.

Um derartige Fehler zu vermeiden, meinten daher manche, man solle eine genauere Sprache einführen, bei welcher diese Fehler unmöglich wären; Leibniz beschäftigte sich viel mit einer allgemeinen Schriftsprache durch Zeichen, welche für jeden Unterrichteten verständlich sein sollte, ganz abgesehen von seiner Nationalität; er spricht sogar die Hoffnung aus, wenn er 12 verständige Gehilfen hätte, er diese Sprache fertigbringen wollte. Ein derartiges Unternehmen wäre nun ohne Zweifel sehr nützlich; man müsste aber mit den elementaren Begriffen beginnen und für sie neue Ausdrücke schaffen. (Brentano meint, dass dies auch eigentlich geschehen würde.) Viele Logiker wollten nun wenigstens eine neue Urteilssprache erfinden, für die Begriffe aber die alten Namen beibehalten, so bildeten sie für die Urteile neue algebraische Zeichen (Lambert, Boole, Jevons).

VI. Vorlesung,
d. 22. November 84

Eine gewisse Berechtigung gibt diesen Versuchen auf der einen Seite das Unnötige von vielen Verwicklungen jener Ausdrucksweisen, Synonymien der Urteile; andererseits aber die Zweideutigkeit der gewöhnlichen Sprache im Ausdruck des Urteils; ein und dieselbe Form drückt oft ganz verschiedene Urteile aus. Eine neue Urteilssprache hält Lange für geradezu notwendig. (Zitat aus Langes *Logischen Studien*.)[12] Die Sprache, die Jevons einführt, macht es beinahe unmöglich alle Urteile auszudrücken. Jevons: Alle Urteile seien Identitätssätze und darum könnten sie alle auf Gleichungen zurückgeführt werden. Das ist nun nicht richtig, denn gewiss sind nicht alle Urteile Identitätssätze. Beispiele: Die Guten sind die Glücklichen; Jevons würde | sagen: Die Guten = die Glücklichen ($a = b$). Ein anderes Beispiel: Alle Menschen sind sterblich. Jevons: Die Menschen sind die Mensch-seienden Sterblichen. Mensch = Mensch–

---

12 [*Lange 1876, 146f.*: „Auf zwei sehr verschiedenen Wegen hat man versucht, Sprachen und Logik in Einklang zu bringen. Den ersten großartigen Versuch unternahmen die Logiker des späteren Mittelalters, mit denen im Prinzip die von Überweg nach dem Vorgange Beckers und Trendelenburgs eingeschlagenen Richtung übereinstimmt. Hier wird versucht, alles in der Sprache logisch zu analysieren und für jeden Kasus, jeden Modus, jedes Formwort, Hilfzeitwort usw. eine exakte Formel zu finden, mit deren Hilfe diese Modifikationen der Rede in die logische Analyse aufgenommen werden können. Der andere Weg ist der eben beschriebene, welcher alles in der Sprache als nutzlos und störend beiseite wirft, was sich nicht in eine Gleichung zwischen Subjekt und Prädikat bringen lässt. Dieser zweite Weg hat den Vorteil der Ausführlichkeit, während beiden eine gleiche Verkennung des Wesens der Sprache zugrunde liegt. Durch eine exakte Zeichensprache schafft sich der Logiker ein neues, rein verstandesmäßiges Mittel des Gedankenausdrucks. Dasselbe entbehrt aller Vorzüge der Sprache für das geistige Leben überhaupt, ist aber frei von ihren Nachteilen in Beziehung auf präzises, von allen Zweideutigkeiten freies Urteilen. Ihre Mittel sind die kleinen, beweglichen, streng konventionellen Raumbilder der Buchstaben und der Operationszeichen. Durch *taxis* und *thesis* derselben im Raum wird eine unabsehbare Fülle streng miteinander zusammenhängender Ausdrücke ermöglicht, und es ist eine Grundeigenschaft unserer Erkenntnis, dass jeder streng konsequenter Gebrauch solcher Zeichen durch alle Wandlungen der Identitätsausdrücke hindurch wieder zu streng richtigen, direkt oder indirekt anwendbaren Formen führt."]

seiender Sterblicher. Oder: Kein Stein ist lebendig. Jevons würde sagen: Die Steine = die Stein-seienden Nichtlebendigen. Oder: Es gibt einen Baum. Jevons würde sagen: Der Baum N.N. ist das der Baum N.N.-seiende Existierende. Man sieht, um wie viel der Gedanke komplizierter ist; wenn auch die beiden Urteile äquivalent sind, so sind sie doch nicht dieselben; manche Urteile können [wir] aber auch nicht einmal in äquivalenter Weise in die Sprache Jevons übersetzen. Man muss zusehen, ob bei der Mannigfaltigkeit der gewöhnlichen Sprache nicht vielleicht eine Form gefunden wird, die nicht missverständlich ist; das ist besser als die Erfindung einer neuen Form. Diesen Weg hat Brentano betreten. Land (aus Leiden) verdammt den Versuch Brentanos als unnatürlich. Natürlich und unnatürlich kann hier gar nicht angewandt werden; die Sprache der gemeinen Leute doch nicht als natürlich bezeichnet werden im Gegensatz zu den wissenschaftlichen Terminis; so ist die natürliche Klassifikation nicht die Klassifikation des Volkes, sondern der Wissenschaft.

II. Kapitel
Von den Grundklassen der psychischen Phänomenen

Phänomene sind alles, was wir wahrnehmen. Die Erscheinungen der Phantasie rechnet man nicht dazu.[13] Wir nehmen, wenn wir Farben wahrnehmen, auch das Sehen der Farben wahr; hier ist der Ausdruck Wahrnehmung sogar viel mehr am Platz. Die Farbe wird nur als Phänomen wahrgenommen, das Sehen aber als wirklich Existierendes. Es gibt also keine Farbe, die nicht wahrgenommen werden kann. Hingegen scheint es denkbar, dass einer sieht, ohne dieses Sehen | wahrzunehmen. Dies und Ähnliches haben manche behauptet; wäre nun dies der Fall, so bestände das Sehen eigentlich nicht als Phänomen, sondern nur in der Wirklichkeit; man hat es aber auch in solchen Fällen mit einem modifizierenden als determinierenden Beiwort „unbewusste Phänomene" genannt. [Eduard von] Hartmann hat diese Behauptung gemacht. Wir wollen die Gründe nicht untersuchen, da sie uns nicht angehen. Manche

---

13 [*Vgl. Leisching* Y 2/41: „Was verstehen wir denn unter einem Phänomen? Um es durch einen gemeinüblichen Ausdruck deutlicher zu machen, sage ich: Ein Phänomen können wir alles, was man wahrnimmt, Töne, die wir hören, Farben, die wir sehen, Wärme und Kälte, die wir fühlen, nennen. Anderes gilt von den Tönen und Farben, die wir uns bloß in der Phantasie vorstellen. Man darf aber nicht glauben, dass man diese Phantasiephänomene nicht zu den Phänomenen rechnet deshalb, weil ihnen nichts Wirkliches entspricht. Auch bei den gehörten Tönen etc. ist dies nicht der Fall. Nicht Farbe entspricht in Wirklichkeit dem Phänomen Farbe etc. Dagegen gibt es andere Wahrnehmungen, bei denen das Wahrgenomene allerdings zugleich in Wirklichkeit existiert."]

leugnen nur geradezu, dass wir je das Sehen wahrnehmen. Sie behaupten, alle derartige Phänomene ließen sich analysieren in Töne, Muskelgefühle, Farben etc. etc. (Entgegnung gegen R. Wahle.[14]) Alle Phänomene zerfallen in die Klassen der physischen und der psychischen. [Die physischen sind Phänomene der äußeren, die psychischen aber Phänomene der inneren Wahrnehmung.]

VII. Vorlesung,
d. 26. Nov. 84

Die letztere wurde als „innere Wahrnehmung" bezeichnet, da sie selbst zu den Phänomenen gehört, die wahrgenommen werden. Die physischen Phänomene haben das Gemeine, dass sie räumlich erscheinen; beim Gesichtssinn wird das jeder sämtlich zugeben, beim Gehör mag es einer bezweifeln; aber Aristoteles macht darauf aufmerksam, dass das Phänomen des Hörens lokalisiert wird. [Ernst Heinrich] Weber konnte, nachdem er den Kopf ins Wasser getaucht

---

14 [*Wahle 1884, 68:* „Wer hat das Hören – natürlich nicht separat, sondern zusammen mit dem Tone schon wahrgenommen? Niemand kann neben dem Tone in Verbindung mit ihm noch ein bewusstes psychisches Phänomen entdecken; nur Ton und Leibesbewegung und Leibesempfindung bieten sich dar." *Vgl.* EL *72/12073:* „Diese Lehre widerspricht der unmittelbaren Erfahrung. Und wenn es außerdem noch einer Widerlegung bedürfte, so fänden sich die besten Mittel dazu in der Betrachtung der einzelnen Analysen, die ihre Vertreter selbst versucht haben." *Vgl. die Betrachtung in Leisching Y 2/43:* „Was ist denn das Wollen, wenn wir es auflösen in Farbe, Ton, Muskelempfindung? Es sei ein Wünschen vorhanden mit Muskelempfindung, Muskelgefühl. Freilich wird unterlassen, genau zu beschreiben, was das für Muskelgefühle seien. Und doch dürfte nicht jedes beliebige Muskelgefühl entsprechend sein. Denn sonst wäre es kurios, wenn jedes Wünschen mit einem Muskelgefühl verbunden ist, und ich will einen Spaziergang machen und gehe, so habe ich ein Muskelgefühl in den Beinen usw. Was ist denn das Wünschen? Eine Phantasievorstellung mit Muskelgefühlen. Nun, wenn schon das Wollen ein Wünschen mit Muskelgefühlen ist, so jetzt also Muskelgefühle zur zweiten Potenz! Wenn nun einer zugleich mehrere Phantasievorstellungen hat, wünscht er alles, was er sich vorstellt? Das doch wohl nicht; z.B. aus dem Falle einer Wahl geht doch das Gegenteil hervor. Das eine wünche ich und will es und das andere nicht. So kann es nicht gemeint sein und man müsste es deutlicher ausdrücken, würde dann aber in die größten Schwierigkeiten geraten. Fragt man endlich auch noch Folgendes: ‚Was für Muskelgefühle hätte denn einer, wenn er wünschte, zur Zeit Alexanders des Großen gelebt zu haben?', so sagen sie: Ja, hier ist von Muskelgefühlen gar keine Rede. Das hat sie aber nicht irre gemacht zu glauben, dass im Allgemeinen die Phantasievorstellungen ein Wünschen mit Muskelgefühlen seien. Hier sei *nur* eine Phantasievorstellung. Sie meinen, wenn ein Wunsch auf Unmögliches gerichtet sei, so wäre es bloß eine Phantasievorstellung. Aber nehmen wir den Fall: Einer sagt: Ich wünsche noch einmal auf die Welt zu kommen und ein anderer sagt: Ich wünsche es nicht, so stellen doch beide dasselbe vor."]

hatte, die Richtung, von welcher das Geräusch kam, unterscheiden. Aber selbst hinsichtlich des Gesichtssinns wurde die Örtlichkeit geleugnet, aber nicht mit Recht. Von psychischen Phänomenen gilt nun das Gegenteil; sie scheinen nicht räumlich. Allerdings behauptet man dagegen, dass der Schmerz lokalisiert sei; das ist wahr; aber man muss unterscheiden zwischen der Qualität des Sinnes und der Unlust, die sich daran knüpft. Die psychischen Phänomene haben aber noch ein positives Merkmal gemeinsam, nämlich die Beziehung auf ein immanentes Objekt; und diese Beziehung ist den psychischen Phänomenen ausschließlich eigen; bei den physischen Phänomenen kommt etwas Derartiges nicht vor. Die Beziehung auf das immanente Objekt ist eine mehrfache, und nach Unterschieden dieser Beziehung unterscheidet | man drei Hauptklassen der psychischen Phänomene: Vorstellen, Urteilen, Gemütszustand. Es folgt eine Erklärung dieser drei Klassen der psychischen Phänomene. Wenn unsere Seelentätigkeit nicht weg ist, so ist immer jede dieser drei Klassen in uns vertreten. Wir nehmen diese drei Phänomene aber nicht als drei verschiedene Dinge wahr, aber sie bilden ein einziges Phänomen, welches nicht einfach ist, sondern eine Mehrheit von Teilphänomenen unterscheiden lässt. Die Einteilung der drei Klassen ist nicht anerkannt; man gibt gewöhnlich eine andere Einteilung: Denken, Fühlen, Wollen. Es wird die Behauptung aufgestellt, dass im Urteil eine neue grundverschiedene Beziehung zum immanenten Objekt vorhanden sei und sich diese beiden Klassen [d.h. Urteil und Vorstellung] ebenso sehr unterscheiden wie in der alten Einteilung das Denken und Wollen, was ich hier nicht mitteile (vgl. Brentano [1874], emp. Psych., I. Band). Es wird die Meinung bekämpft, dass das Urteil in einer Trennung oder Verbindung von Vorstellungen bestehe. Als Beweis dagegen: der Existentialsatz „Der Baum ist grün" in Vergleich[15] zu „der grüne Baum." Ferner in dem Akt der Erinnerung haben wir eine Anerkennung von etwas, oder etwas Gewesenem; ist die Erinnerung eine Prädikation? Gewiss nicht. Die erste Wahrnehmung wird schon als evident innerlich wahrgenommen, ohne dass wir Existenz von ihr prädizierten, da wir den Begriff „Existenz" noch gar nicht haben.

---

15 [Existentialsatz „Der Baum ist grün" in Vergleich *statt* Existentialsatz und Vergleich zu „Der Baum ist grün," in Vergleich *im Ms.*]

VIII. Vorlesung,
d. 29. November 84

[III. Kapitel]
Relativität und Zweiseitigkeit aller Phänomene[16]

Jevons meint, dass wir bei jedem Urteil etwas bejahen und etwas verneinen. „Die Guten sind die Glücklichen" heißt zugleich „Die Nichtguten sind nicht glücklich."

Bain stellt folgendes Gesetz auf: Jedes Phänomen der Wahrnehmung und jede Erscheinung der Phantasie ist eigentlich eine Relation, eine Beziehung zwischen zwei positiven Gegensätzen, also zweiseitig; ein Oben gibt es nicht ohne Unten; Wärme nicht ohne Kälte; auch der | Akt, in welchem wir diese Phänomene vorstellen, ist zweiseitig; auch anderen psychischen Akten kommt ein solcher Charakter zu. Wir erkennen immer nur Relationen. Wir freuen uns an der Gesundheit und Besitz nur im Gegensatz zu Krankheit und Entbehrung. Bain kommt dann auch zum Schluss: Der Name des Seienden muss ohne alle Bedeutung sein; denn es lässt sich keinen anderen Gegensatz angeben als das Nichts; das ist aber kein positiver Gegensatz, also ist das Seiende ein Wort ohne Sinn, da es sonst einen positiven Gegensatz haben müsste. Wodurch begründet Bain das Gesetz? Aufgrund von psychologischen und psychophysischen wird über das entschieden, was, wenn es richtig wäre, uns die direkte Erfahrung zeigen müsste; und so kommt er zu jener befremdlichen Konsequenz, die die Erfahrung durchaus nicht bestätigt. Bain weist darauf hin, dass kein Vorstellen ohne Wechsel möglich sei; so sei das deutlich bei den Empfindungen; bei stetig fortdauernden Reizen schwinde das Bewusstsein und werde stärker bei kräftigerem Wechsel. Viele Übergänge geben kräftige Eindrücke. Jede Empfindung muss also die Empfindung des Unterschieds positiver Gegensätze sein. Ähnlich nun wie für die Empfindung muss es auch für die anderen Vorstellungen sein; so bei den Phantasien; so können wir uns nicht Hitze ohne im Gedanken eine Kälte vorzustellen. Ohne im Gedanken einer Gerade ist der einer krummen Linie nicht möglich.[17]

Kritik der Ansicht Bains: Es ist nicht zu leugnen, dass wir, so oft wir vorstellen, einen mannigfaltigen Vorstellungsinhalt haben; wir haben immer psychi-

---

16 [*Titel vom III. Kapitel nach Brentano* EL 72/12002, 12083: „Von den angeblichen Gesetze der Relativität und Zweiseitigkeit aller Phänomene"]
17 [*Vgl. Leisching* Y 2/48–49: „So können wir nicht Hitze denken, außer indem wir in Gedanken Hitze zu Kälte oder von Kälte zu Hitze übergehen; Bewegung nicht, ohne sie auf Ruhe zu beziehen. Kein Oben ohne Unten auch in der Phantasievorstellung. Damnach scheint die Zweiseitigkeit und Relativität eine allgemeine Tatsache für alles, was wir vorstellen."]

sche und physische Phänomene; auch assoziiert sich immer jene mannigfaltige Vorstellung; jede einzelne Anschauung zeigt ein räumliches Nebeneinander verschiedener Teile; und so ist die Mannigfaltigkeit von Unterschieden jener Vorstellungen richtig; deshalb dürfen wir aber nicht glauben, dass alles Vorgestellte eine Relation sei; der Unterschied von Rot und Blau ist eine Relation; aber selbst wenn wir beide vorstellen, ist[18] jedes von ihnen für sich nicht eine Relation, sie sind die Fundamente. | Der ganze Beweis Bains beruht darauf, dass in der Empfindung ein Wechsel nötig sei. Ist es bewiesen, dass ein Wechsel in der Empfindung statt hat, wenn der äußere Reiz wechselt? Könnte es nicht sein, dass durch die Zunahme des äußeren Reizes ausgeglichen würde die zunehmende Stumpfheit meiner Empfindung, und so die tatsächliche Empfindung gleich bleibt. Aber wenn das sogar zugegeben würde, [dass die Intensität wechselt,] genügt es wohl nicht, einen bloßen Wechsel der Intensität anzunehmen ohne Wechsel der Qualität?[19] Nach Bain müssten alle positiven Bestimmungen fort und fort dem Wechsel unterliegen; kein Rot ohne Blau. Ja, Bain behauptet sogar: die Vorstellung des Wechsels sei nicht ohne gleichzeitige Vorstellung der Ruhe möglich; während, wenn alles fort und fort wechselte, eine positive Vorstellung von Ruhe gar nicht statt haben könnte.[20] Wenn ferner Bains Beweis alle diese Mängel nicht hätte, so könnten wir noch das sagen, dass dennoch das Vorgestellte selbst noch immer keine Relation sei.

Jevons und J. St. Mill anerkennen diese Ansicht Bains nicht. Dennoch hatte Mill einen Anklang an eine Wahrheit erkennen wollen; auch er glaubt, dass jede Vorstellung die Vorstellung zweier Gegensätze sei, nur braucht nur der eine Gegensatz positiv zu sein, der andere ist negativ. Wenn ich vorstelle „etwas," so muss ich „nichts" vorstellen. Die Unterscheidung eines Gegensatzes von seinem kontradiktorischen Gegensatz ist nach Mill für sein Bewusstsein notwendig; und ebenso soll auch jedes Urteil ähnliche eine doppelte Beziehung zu kontradiktorischen Gegensätzen haben. Außer Wahrheit des Seins schließen wir nach Mill nicht eigentlich auf die Falschheit des Nichtseins, sondern beide Behauptungen sind wesentlich identisch; und deshalb, meint Mill, kann niemand das Gesetz des „Widerspruchs" anzweifeln können. Auch für Phänomene | der Gemütsbewegung gibt da Ähnliches: wer einen Gegenstand liebt, hasst sein Gegenteil. So würde das Gesetz der Beziehung auf kontradiktorische Gegensätze allgemein gelten.

---

18 [ist *statt* sind *im Ms.*]
19 [*In der Abschrift Hillebrands endet dieser Satz mit einem Punkt. Man könnte den Satz also als eine Behauptung verstehen. In Brentano* EL *72/12087 (auch in Leisching Y 2/50) endet er aber mit einem Fragezeichen.*]
20 [*zwischen* positive Vorstellung *und* von Ruhe *unleserlicher Text*]

Kritik: Wenn man die Behauptung hört, die Leugnung des Seins sei die Anerkennung des Nichtseins, der Hass des Seins die Liebe des Nichtseins, so ist das plausibel; aber „die Anerkennung des Seins sei die Leugnung des Nichtseins" ist eine härter klingende Behauptung. Beginnen wir mit einer Untersuchung über die Vorstellungen: Aber gerade auf dem Gebiet der Vorstellungen steht der Annahme des Gesetzes ein unüberwindliches Hindernis entgegen; wenn es in der Natur der psychischen Phänomenen liegt, dass mit jeder positiven Vorstellung die ihres negativen Gegensatzes verbunden ist, so muss dieselbe auch ursprünglich und bei der ersten Empfindung so gewesen sein; war die erste Empfindung die von Wärme, so muss ich damals die Vorstellung von der Nichtexistenz der Wärme gehabt haben; aber das ist unmöglich, wenn anders das, was Mill sagt, wahr ist, dass der Begriff der Nichtexistenz nur durch Reflexion auf ein verneinendes Urteil gewonnen wird. Die erste Vorstellung im Leben kann aber nicht von einem Urteil, das früher gefällt worden wäre, gewonnen werden. Das Sein und das Nichtsein [als Begriffe] werden überhaupt *erst nach* der Fällung von Urteilen gewonnen. Die erste Vorstellung also war keine Vorstellung eines Gegensatzes, dann ist aber auch nicht abzusehen, warum man nicht auch später eine Vorstellung haben soll, ohne den negativen Gegensatz auszuführen. Wo wir wirklich eigentlich die beiden Gegensätze verbinden, stellt sich ganz anders dar. Wie die erste Vorstellung also keine Beziehung zeigt, so zeigt auch das erste Urteil und das erste Gefühl keine Beziehung auf einen negativen Gegensatz. Überhaupt ist es klar, dass, wenn das Gesetz auf dem Gebiete der Vorstellung nicht mehr zu halten ist, von einer universellen Gültigkeit auf den anderen Gebieten nicht mehr die Rede sein [kann], da die Vorstellungen die Grundlage aller anderen Phänomene bilden. |

20

IX. Vorlesung,
am 3. Dezember 84

[IV. Kapitel]
Natur und Ursprung unserer Vorstellungen[21]

Was unser Vorstellen sei und wie es sich vom Urteil und von den Phänomenen des Gemüts unterscheidet, ist gezeigt worden. Es gibt kein Vorstellen ohne Vorgestelltes, welches letztere oft Vorstellung genannt wird. Zu den Vorstellungen gehören die Vorstellungen der äußeren Wahrnehmungen (Anschauungen), die Vorstellungen der äußeren Phantasie, die Vorstellungen der inneren Wahrneh-

---

21 [*Titel vom IV. Kapitel nach* EL 72/1203: „Von der Natur und dem Urspunge unserer Vorstellungen"]

mung und die der inneren Phantasie. Dazu gehören dann die abstrakten und die apriorischen Vorstellungen, die nicht alle gelten lassen.

Unter den abstrakten Vorstellungen denkt man sich Vorstellungen, die durch eine Art Vereinfachung aus den anderen gewonnen worden sind, und rechnet sie mit zu den Erfahrungsvorstellungen; die apriorischen Vorstellungen hingegen sind von der Erfahrung unabhängig; sie sind entweder individuelle, dann sind sie apriorische Anschauungen, oder allgemeine, dann nennt man sie apriorische Begriffe; zu den apriorischen Anschauungen rechnet man z. B. den Raum (so Kant); zu den apriorischen Begriffen gehört der der Ursache (so Kant). Ganz klar ist die Scheidung der zwei ersteren Klassen von den zwei letzteren, der äußeren Vorstellungen von den inneren. Ebenso ist uns klar die Scheidung der inneren Wahrnehmung von der Vorstellung der inneren Phantasie. Nicht so klar aber ist die Scheidung der Klasse der Vorstellungen der äußeren Wahrnehmung und der der Phantasie. Man kann wohl sagen, dass alles, was etwas als vergangen oder zukünftig vorstellt, zur Phantasie gehört. Das ist oft verkannt worden; so, wenn man meinte, Bewegung oder Ruhe wirklich wahrzunehmen; ebenso die Vorstellungen von Wechsel und Dauer. Wenn etwas als gegenwärtig vorgestellt wird, so ist es hingegen nicht schon deshalb Vorstellung; | hier haben wir also kein Kritierium. Man hat nun ein solches Kriterium in die Intensität verlegen wollen; die Wahrnehmungsvorstellung soll größere Fülle und größere Intensität haben. Allein das ist nicht wahr. Die Phantasievorstellungen haben verschiedene Grade der Intensität. Wo ist nun die Grenze, von der man sagen kann, es sei eine Vorstellung und nicht mehr Phantasie? Die Phantasien von Fieberkranken und Träumenden gehören hierher. Auch die von wachen Menschen manchmal, so von Goethe, auch von Johannes Müller.

Man hat nun gesagt: Eine Wahrnehmungsvorstellung sei da, wo eine Reizung der peripheren Organe vorhanden sei; wenn nun aber der Nerv in der Mitte seines Verlaufs gereizt wird, oder gerade mit dem Eintritt ins Gehirn, so müsste man ihn noch immer peripher nennen? Wir können hier nicht klar unterscheiden; und sicher wurde in früherer Zeit bei geringerer Kenntnis der Physiologie diese Unterscheidung gekannt. Aber auch vor Physiologen sprach [man] vom Augenschwarz; hier wäre also keine Reizung vorhanden und doch gehörte diese Vorstellung zu den Wahrnehmungen. Man hat auch den Unterschied in psychische Vorbedingungen sehen wollen, indem man sagte, über die Phantasievorstellungen habe man willkürliche Macht. Dennoch hat der Wille oft eine sehr unvollkommene Macht über Phantasievorstellungen. Man sagte ferner: Eine Phantasievorstellung sei immer eine Wiederholung eines früheren Eindrucks als Folge desselben; aber auch das ist ungenügend: Die Phantasie zeigt etwas als vergangen, aber die Wahrnehmung zeigt es nie als vergangen, also haben wir eine andere Vorstellung. Man könnte vielleicht sagen, die Phantasievorstellung sei eine Folge einer früheren durch ähnliche Akte erlangter psychischen Dispositionen. Auch das kommt vor, dass gewisse Gebilde weder reine Empfindungsvorstellungen sind noch reine Phantasievorstellungen. | Eine große Verwandtschaft besteht also ebenfalls zwischen den Phantasie- und Wahrnehmungsvorstellungen; und deshalb ist die Unterscheidung zwar für die Psychologie wichtig, nicht aber für die Logik, da ja weder die einen noch die anderen Vorstellungen den Vorzug der Wirklichkeit haben. Wichtiger ist eine Charakteristik des Inhalts dieser ganzen Hauptgattung. Sie sind immer komplizierte Vorstellungen, [denn] sie enthalten [eine Reihe von Elementen]:

1. Sinnliche Qualität: Sie sind von verschiedener Gattung, und nach ihrer Zahl scheidet man die Zahl der Sinne und der entsprechenden Klassen der äußeren Phantasien.

Farbe.

a) Eine solche Gattung ist die Farbe. Sechs Farben sind von besonderer Wichtigkeit: Schwarz, Weiß, Blau, Gelb, Rot, Grün; alle anderen Farben sind durch Abstammung von diesen zu bestimmen. Es folgt der *Farbenkörper*. Die Abstände der einzelnen Eckfarben sind einander nicht gleich; so steht das Blau dem Schwarz näher als das Gelb. Die Methode, um die relativen Abstandsverhältnisse zu erfahren, könnte die „Methode der eben merklichen Unterschiede" sein (so nennt sie [Gustav] Fechner). Diese ist jedoch nicht genau, da bei größerer Übung immer kleinere Unterschiede gemerkt werden; das sieht man klarer bei den Tönen; bei sehr hohen und sehr tiefen Tönen nimmt man nämlich Unterschiede bereits nicht mehr wahr, die man in der mittleren Tonlage noch wahrnimmt; in dieser hat man aber die größte Übung.

X. Vorlesung,
d. 6. Dezember 84

Schall.

b) Der Schall [ist eine zweite Gattung der sinnlichen Qualität]. Es gibt unzählige Arten von Schallen; die wichtigsten sind reine einfache Töne, welche die Skala bilden. Die letztere hat man oft mit einer geraden ansteigenden Linie verglichen, aber sehr mit Unrecht. Die Oktave scheint dem Grundton näher gerückt als jeder andere Ton, nach ihr die Quinte. Man hat die Tonleiter darum mit einer Spirale verglichen; ob in dieser aber jeder Schall liegt, ist sehr fraglich; [Hermann von] Helmholtz glaubt dies nicht hinsichtlich gewisser Geräusche, obwohl man auch von diesen höhere und niedere unterscheiden kann. | Aber auch in Bezug auf die Töne, die nicht rein und einfach sind, kann der Zweifel erhoben werden; so bei den Akkorden und bei Tönen, die eine gesamte Klangfarbe haben. Die letzteren hat man durch die Obertöne zu erklären versucht; es ist immerhin möglich, dass draußen manche[?] Schwingungen verschiedener Art bestehen; die Frage ist aber, ob sie ein einheitliches Schallprodukt erregen oder ob sie als Vielheit wahrgenommen werden. Wenn Helmholtz sagt, er höre aus den einzelnen Vokalen die Obertöne heraus, so würde das, wenn es wahr wäre, so viel beweisen; aber diese Tatsache ist sehr zweifelhaft, ebenso wie es nicht richtig ist, dass man aus dem Orange das Gelb und Rot heraussehe, wie Goethe gemeint hat. Wäre in einem Akkord keine wirkliche Einheitlichkeit gegeben, so könnte man hier nicht einsehen, warum es schwerer ist die einzelnen Töne desselben zu unterscheiden, als wenn man sie in zeitlicher Sukzession hört; ja, man müsste sie im Akkord noch viel deutlicher unterscheiden können, da sie einander zeitlich viel näher gerückt sind. Es besteht ferner ein merkwürdiger Unterschied bei gewissen Akkorden gegenüber anderen. Bei harmonischen Vielklängen erkennt man die Vielheit viel schwerer als bei unharmonischen; die letzteren sind nämlich von einem so unangenehmen Gefühl begleitet, von einem Gefühl, das einfache Töne nie begleitet; es dürfte mancher bei der Beurteilung der Vielheit von Klängen so auf das Gefühl ankommen und darin das Kriterium der Vielheit zu sehen sein. Man sagt, in der Harmonie verschmelzen die Töne miteinander, in der Disharmonie aber nicht. Was heißt nun jenes „Verschmelzen"? Werden die Töne zu einem einzigen? Das gibt man nicht zu; wenn aber nicht, dann spricht man ja nur nicht von Verschmelzen.[22] In der Tat steht es aber auch ohne jede Analogie da, dass wir eine Vielheit von Qualitäten einer und derselben Gattung als Einheit, also ohne lokale Unterschiede wahrnehmen. Um dem zu entgehen, hat man gesagt, es handle sich bei einem Akkord allerdings um eine zeitliche Sukzession von Tönen, aber um eine so rasche, dass man die Vielheit gar nicht bemerkt, sondern | sie für eine Einheit annimmt. Möglich hingegen wäre es, dass auf einer direkten Verbindungslinie zweier Punkte der Tonspirale andere neue Töne liegen, ähnlich wie beim Farbenkörper. Ein einheitliches Verschmelzen liegt vor bei Geschmack und Geruch untereinander, ebenso bei Temperatur und Berührungsqualität. Bei Tönen und Farben ist dies jedoch nicht der Fall. Ja, sogar bei Temperatur, Geschmack und Geruch finden derartige Verschmelzungen statt. So schmeckt eine Speise kalt und warm gegessen verschieden; ebenso ein geschnittener und ein zerdrückter Erdapfel.

---

22 [*Vgl. Leisching Y 2/65:* „Werden sie zu einem? Das ist das, was ich meine. Nein, sie werden nicht zu einem, aber sie verschmelzen. Ich gestehe, dass ich gänzlich unfähig bin, das zu erkennen."]

XI. Vorlesung,
d. 10 Dezember 84

2. Intensität [ist ein zweites Element der Inhalte]. Sie wird in allen sinnlichen Vorstellungen gefunden. [Ewald] Hering bestreitet das; er meint, es gebe Vorstellungen ohne Intensität, und das wären Gesichtsvorstellungen; man findet keine Verwandtschaft, meint er, zwischen dem, was man beim Sehen, und dem, was man beim Hören, Intensität nennt; man kann etwas ebenso gut intensiv schwarz als intensiv weiß nennen. Marty, der dem hier entgegen streitet, macht geltend, dass doch unleugbar ein Intensitätsunterschied zwischen einer Wahrnehmung und dem ihr entsprechenden Phantasiebild bestehe, woraus folgt, dass Intensitäten vorhanden sein müssen.

Manche halten die Intensität für eine Größe, jedoch mit Unrecht. Herbart sagt, wo immer von einem Mehr oder Minder gesprochen werden kann, dort habe man es mit einer Größe zu tun; [Carl Friedrich] Gauß hingegen sagt, zur Größe gehöre noch etwas Anderes, nämlich dass sie gleiche Teile enthalte, und das ist richtig. Eine höhere Intensität ist nicht aus zwei gleichen niederen zusammengesetzt. Die Abstände zweier Intensitäten haben allerdings eine Größe, die Intensität aber hat keine, ähnlich wie Töne keine Größen sind, obwohl ihre Abstände es sind; dasselbe gilt von Farben, von Zeit- und Raumpunkten. Die Intensitäten lassen sich daher durch die *Punkte* einer Gerade symbolisieren, | nicht aber durch Strecken. Die Intensitäten sind also keine Größen, wohl aber Grade.

Sind Intensitäten aller sinnlichen Vorstellungen von einer Gattung? Ja, selbst Vorstellungen verschiedener Qualität können in Bezug auf die Intensität miteinander verglichen werden. So kann man von einem Geruch sagen, er sei intensiver als ein Ton.

3. Der Ort [ist ein drittes Element der Inhalte der sinnlichen Vorstellungen]. Es ist eine unrichtige Ansicht, dass der Ortsunterschied zweier Punkte nur durch das dazwischen Liegende ausgemacht wird; schon die Tatsache des blinden Flecks spricht dagegen; erst [Edme] Mariote hat die Existenz einer Lücke in unserem Sehfeld nachgewiesen, obwohl dieselbe bei jedem Menschen vorkommt; die Phantasie füllt eben diese Lücke aus.

Eine andere unrichtige Meinung ist die, dass der Ort nur aus Ortsverhältnissen bestehe (Leibniz hat diese Ansicht ausgesprochen); denn die örtlichen Relationen brauchen, wie überhaupt alle Relationen, Fundamente; sie ändern sich nur konkomitierend, während die Fundamente sich absolut ändern; irreführen kann allerdings die Tatsache, dass wir die Orte immer relativ bestimmen; aber derartigen Bestimmungen wenden wir auch in Gebieten an, wo es sich nicht um Relationen handelt, so wenn wir Farbennuancen bestimmen wollen, und doch ist die Farbe eine absolute Bestimmung. Bei einer einzigen Wahrnehmung sind unendlich viele örtliche Bestimmungen vorhanden, aber sie schließen sich in infinitesimalen Abständen aneinander. Deshalb ist jedes räumliche Bild ein Kontinuum; da nun eine Vielheit örtlicher Bestimmungen immer gegeben ist, so könnte man leicht zum Irrtum geführt werden, die Ortsbestimmungen bestehen nur in Relationen.

Man hat ferner bestritten, dass in den Wahrnehmungsvorstellungen Orte gegeben seien.[23] Orte, sagt man, seien nur in der Phantasie. Diese Ansicht ist falsch. (Vergleich darüber | Brentanos Vorlesung über ausgewählte Fragen aus der Psychologie [ws 1883], Kapitel „Empirizismus und Nativismus"[24]).

Es ist ferner gezweifelt worden, ob in allen Wahrnehmungsvorstellungen örtliche Bestimmungen gegeben seien, aber mit Unrecht. Selbst beim Hören sind sie gegeben.

Man könnte die Frage aufwerfen, ob der Ort bei den verschiedenen Sinnen von ein und derselben Gattung sei.

[William] Molyneux hat die Frage gestellt, ob ein Blindgeborener, der Kugel und Würfel durch den Tastsinn unterscheiden konnte, nach einer Operation dieselbe Unterscheidung mit dem Gesichtssinn machen könne. Locke antwortet: nein. Und zwar mit Recht; das Maß des Auges und das der Hand sind nicht dasselbe. Ja, selbst das Maß der Hand und der Körperhaut ist nicht dasselbe; so schätzen wir den Abstand zweier Zirkelspitzen an verschiedenen Körperstellen verschieden, wenn wir auch überall die Zeichen erkennen. Die Ortsbestimmung der verschiedenen Sinne sind nach Brentano von einer und derselben Gattung, aber allerdings spezifisch verschieden, so dass kein Gesichtsphänomen Ortsbestimmung zeigt, die denen gleich sind, die man beim Hören empfängt.

XII. Vorlesung,
13. Dezember 1884

Es handelt sich jetzt darum, ob wir nur Flächen oder auch Körper [empfinden]? Wenn wir nur Flächen empfinden, so empfinden wir gewiss gekrümmte Flächen, so wenn wir mit dem Finger um den Hals fahren und wieder an den Ausgangspunkt gelangen. Ferner ist sicher, dass wir in der Phantasie dreidimensionale Räume sehen. Die Phantasie vermag überhaupt die Räume zu erweitern

---

23   [*Vgl. unten, S. 237.*]
24   [*In Husserl Q 9 findet sich eine Gabelsberger Abschrift der Notizen Hillebrands zu diesem Kolleg.*]

und so neue Spezies zu bilden; dabei ist auch keine bestimmte Spezies anzugeben, obwohl die Phantasie den Raum nicht bis ins Unendliche erweitern kann; es bestehen individuelle Grenzen. Die Phantasie ist jedoch nicht imstande diesen drei Dimensionen eine vierte[25] Dimensionen hinzuzufügen. Vierdimensionale | Größen sind keine Absurdität, aber vierdimensionale Räume sind es. Ähnliches gilt vom Ausdruck „krummer Raum." Denken wir uns in einem vierdimensionalen Kontinuum einen dreidimensionalen Raum, der in Bezug auf die vier Dimensionen krumm ist, so haben wir einen Begriff vom „krummen Raum." Bei der Ortsspezies finden wir kein + und –, wie bei der Intensität. In keiner Wahrnehmungsvorstellung ein und desselben Sinnes erscheint derselbe Ort zweimal; eine Ausnahme wäre das Hören, wenn es wahr wäre, dass wir mehrere Töne zugleich wahrnehmen.

4. Die Zeit [müssen wir jetzt betrachten]. Über nichts ist so viel Unbetreffendes gesagt worden, während nichts verständlicher ist als Zeitbestimmung im gemeinen Leben. Zu Irrtümern kommt man, indem man etwas, was nur durch Hinweis auf Tatsachen erklärt werden dürfte, auf anderem Weg zu erklären [versucht]. Beispiele finden wir auf allen sinnlichen Gebieten der Phantasie; am besten entnehmen wir das Beispiel aus dem Gebiet der Töne. Denken wir uns zwei gleich intensive Töne von gleicher Qualität in einer Melodie; diese unterscheiden sich nur durch die Zeit. Eine irrige Meinung wäre nun, wenn man glauben dürfte, dass was den Unterschied ausmache, sei das, was dazwischen sei. Die bloße Pause widerlegt das. Ein anderer Irrtum: Die einzelne Zeitbestimmtheit besteht nur in einer Vielheit von Zeitverhältnissen des einen zeitlich Bestimmten zum anderen; die ganze Zeit wäre also nun eine Relation; zeitliche Relationen bestehen allerdings, aber sie bedürfen absoluter zeitlicher Bestimmungen zur Grundlage. Es bleibt auch Zeitbestimmtheit, wenn auch nur ein einziger punktueller Ton in der Phantasie vorkommen würde. Auch hier waren irreführend unsere steten relativen Zeitbestimmungen in unseren Zeitangaben. Aristoteles selbst fiel in diesen Irrtum. Auch bei der Zeit gibt es unendlich viele Spezies. Immerhin steht die Menge der Zeitarten hinter den Ortsarten zurück, als sie den Punkten einer einzigen geordneten Linie vergleichbar sind. | Ein einziger Punkt bedeutet die Gegenwart und scheidet Zukunft von Vergangenheit; sie ist eine äußere Grenze, keine innere; das heißt, sie gehört nicht zu den beiden aneinander grenzenden, sondern zu keinem von beiden: Die Gegenwart ist also ein *terminus extrinsecus*, wie die Scholastiker sagen.

---

25 [vierte *statt* dritte *im Ms.*]

Oft nennt man etwas, was zum Teil vergangen, zum Teil zukünftig ist, gegenwärtig: die gegenwärtige Stunde, der gegenwärtige Tag etc.

Folgender Zweifel wird erhoben: Kann die Gesamtheit der Zeitbestimmtheiten wirklich durch eine gerade Linie symbolisiert werden, oder vielmehr durch eine leicht gekrümmte Linie. Wäre das Letztere [der Fall], so würde ja die Zeit vielleicht in sich zurücklaufen. Wundt (kosmologisches Problem)[26] hat diese Hypothese in Betracht gezogen. Jedoch ist die Annahme absurd; nicht anders als, wenn einer bei der Intensität glauben würde, dass ihre Reihe eine krumme Linie sei, so dass die höchste Intensität mit dem Nullpunkt zusammen fiele; und genau so absurd ist die entsprechende Annahme in Bezug auf die Zeit. Die Gesamtheit der Zeitspezies ist einer endlosen und anfangslosen Gerade vergleichbar; dennoch ist dieses Kontinuum nicht sinnlich vorstellbar, so wenig als es ein unendlicher Raum ist oder eine unendliche Zahlenreihe. Es könnte nun aber einer sagen: Wir können doch nicht behaupten, dass die Zeitlinie endlos sei, wenn wir sie nicht endlos vorstellen können. Antwort: Man muss unterscheiden: die Frage, ob wirkliche Dinge anfangs- und endlos existieren, und[27] [die Frage], ob die Reihe der Zeitspezies nach beiden Seiten unendlich ist. Das ergibt sich aber aus dem Vergleich mit der geraden Linie. Von unzähligen Arten der Zeit sind jedes Mal unzählige in einer sinnlichen Vorstellung gegeben. Wenn wir etwas sinnlich vorstellen, | erweitert sich die Wahrnehmungsvorstellung immer durch eine dazu tretende Phantasievorstellung, und auch das ist mit ein Grund für die falsche Ansicht, dass die Zeit nur in Relationen bestehe. Noch ein anderer Umstand kommt dazu, der irreführt: nämlich, dass die Zeit, wenn sie auch wahr [bestimmt] ist, alle bis auf eine einzige Zeitspezies (Gegenwart) keine realen Bestimmungen sind, und von dieser einen (Gegenwart) ist es zweifelhaft, ob man sie eine absolute zeitliche Bestimmung nennen soll.

XIII. Vorlesung,
d. 17. Dezember 84

Es zeigt sich bisher die Zeit vielfach dem Orte verwandt; sie unterscheidet sich aber von allen früher betrachteten Elementen sehr; besonders dadurch, dass sie sich in ihren verschiedenen Spezies in keiner Wahrnehmungsvorstellung als solchen, sondern nur in der Phantasie findet. Durch eine besondere

---

26 [*Wundt 1877.*]
27 [*und* statt oder *im Ms.*]

Assoziation, nämlich durch eine ursprüngliche, treten die ersten Erscheinungen der Vergangenheit auf; man könnte diese Erscheinungen „Erscheinungen des momentanen Gedächtnisses" nennen; dieses Gedächtnis stellt aber nicht einen Zeitpunkt vor; eine nicht zu sehr langsame Bewegung wird merklich, ebenso ein wiederholter Wechsel, wie bei einer Melodie, von welcher man glaubt, man „höre sie," man glaubt, das unmittelbar Vorausgegangene werde gehört. Bei einer Hörensphantasie scheint dieses momentane Gedächtnis eine besondere Ausdehnung zu haben wie beim Gesichtssinn. Auf diesen Erscheinungen gestützt bildet dann die Phantasie die Vorstellung von Zukunft; der Prozess ist hier ähnlich wie da, wo sie zu neuen Tönen, Farben, Orten gelangt. Analog wie das Nächstvergangene zum Gegenwärtigen verhält, verhält sich das Gegenwärtige zum Zukünftigen. Dies haben wir z. B. bei der Erwartung. Man sieht hier klar, wie falsch die Ansicht ist, dass die Phantasie keine neue Momente bietet. Von welcher Bedeutung aber diese Abweichungen sind, das zeigt eine zweite Eigentümlichkeit, welche die vergangenen und zukünftigen Zeiten von allen früheren unterscheidet, nämlich dass sie die Elemente der sinnlichen Vorstellung nicht so wie diese einander determinieren, | sondern modifizieren: ein lautes C ist ein C, ein leises D ist ein D; ein hier oder dort seiendes Rot oder Blau ist ein Rot oder Blau; aber ein gewesener Ton C ist kein Ton C, ein zukünftiges Rot ist kein Rot, so wenig als ein gewesener König ein König ist, oder eine nächstjährige Ernte eine Ernte ist. Es determinieren also die vergangenen und zukünftigen zeitlichen Bestimmungen nicht das, womit sie sich verbinden, sondern sie alterieren es wesentlich; ähnlich wie bei den Vorstellungen „möglich" oder „vorgestellt"; ein bloß möglicher Taler ist kein Taler. Ebenso ist ein zukünftiger Taler kein Taler. Nur die Gegenwart macht eine Ausnahme, ein gegenwärtiger Kaiser ist wirklich Kaiser. Von ihr allein kann man nicht sagen, dass sie das, wozu sie komme, alteriere; man aber auch nicht sagen, dass sie es determiniere. Ein Kaiser ist dadurch, dass er gegenwärtiger Kaiser ist, nichts anderes als Kaiser. Es ist darum diese Zeitbestimmtheit, da sie weder determinierend noch alterierend eigentlich eine Null von Bestimmtheit zu nennen [ist], natürlich nur absolut genommen. In der Wahrnehmungsvorstellung kommt dadurch, dass sie etwas als Jetziges vorstellt, gar nichts Neues dazu. Die eigentlich nicht wirklich etwas Besonderes in die Vorstellungen bringenden zeitlichen Bestimmungen sind nicht so wohl determinierend, sondern vielmehr modifizierend. Hier ist die Stelle einer früheren Aussprache zu berichtigen. Wir haben nämlich gesagt, jede sinnliche Vorstellung enthalte Qualität, Intensität und Ort, sowohl die Wahrnehmungsvorstellung wie die Phantasievorstellung. Das ist nicht richtig. Die Phantasievorstellungen, die etwas als zukünftig oder vergangen vorstellen, tun das nicht. Sie enthalten keine örtliche Bestimmtheit, Qualitäten oder Intensitäten. Auch für die Ästhetik ergibt sich hier etwas Besonderes. Herbart hat alles Schöne in Verhältnissen von solchem gesehen, was in derselben Gattung liegt. Durch sein faktisches | Verfahren kommt er aber in Widerspruch mit seinen Prinzipien, nämlich bei seiner Idee der Freiheit. Nun sagten aber manche ([Friedrich Adolf] Trendelenburg und [Franz Karl] Lott), es gebe kein Verhältnis zwischen Wollen und Vorstellen nach Herbart, und dennoch soll in der Übereinstimmung beider das Wohlgefallen an der Freiheit liegen. Nun meinten manche Schüler Herbarts, man vergleiche nur das Wollen mit dem Vorstellen des Wollens. Aber das gedachte Wollen ist eben kein Wollen. Aber der Widerspruch ist viel gemeiner. In der Melodie gibt es Verhältnisse von einem gewesenen Ton und einem gegenwärtigen, und der gewesene Ton ist ja doch kein Ton. Ebenso kann ein Dichter zwischen dem, was er als bestehend und was er als zu erwarten vorführt, ästhetisch wirken.

Es ergeben sich nun einige Wahrheiten als Konsequenzen, vor allem, dass wir von allem Realen mit Sicherheit behaupten können, dass, wenn es überhaupt ist, es jetzt ist; denn durch das „Jetzt" wird gar kein Plus von Bestimmungen dazu gefügt. Ferner, da dieses Jetzt als Nullpunkt von jeder anderen zeitlichen Spezies einen bestimmten Abstand[28] hat, so folgt, dass alles zu allem in zeitlicher Beziehung steht. Weiter: Ebenso folgt, dass alles, was ist, in hundert Jahren ein gleichzeitig Gewesenes sein wird und vor hundert Jahren es ein gleichzeitig Zukünftiges.[29] Noch etwas ergibt sich aus dem Gesagten: Das Zukünftige erscheint dem Vergangenen entgegengesetzt. Nun schließen Gegensätze sich in demselben Subjekte aus. Dennoch kann etwas zugleich gewesen und zukünftig sein. Jeder Fall der Dauer ist dafür ein Beispiel, wo während der Dauer das Dauernde zu gleicher Zeit gewesen, zukünftig und gegenwärtig ist; das wird daraus klar, dass die vergangene und zukünftige Zeitbestimmtheit nicht determiniert, sondern modifiziert. Es ist ähnlich, wie wenn ich sagen würde, es komme einem Entgegengesetztes zu, wenn er zugleich geliebt und gehasst wird. Geliebt und Gehasst sind alterierende Bestimmungen. Wir haben nach dem Gesagten | an den Bestimmungen des Vergangenen und Zukünftigen höchst merkwürdige Eigentümlichkeiten bemerkt, aber wir haben noch hinzufügen [müssen], dass es keine reale Bestimmungen sind. Was ist gemeint, wenn wir sagen, gewisse Bestimmungen seien real? Wir wollen das durch Beispiele erklären. So das Vorgestellte, das Anerkannte, Gehasste,

---

28 [einen bestimmten Abstand *statt* einen bestimmten Anfang *im Ms.*

29 [*Vgl. Leisching* Y 2/94: „Da dieses Jetzt als Nullpunkt für die Lage der vergangenen wie zukünftigen Zeitbestimmungen von jeder Spezies einen bestimmten Abstand hat, so folgt, dass alles mit [*statt* von *im Ms.*] allem in zeitlicher Beziehung steht, dass alles, was ist, immer zukünftig gewesen ist und immer gewesen sein wird, und dass es, verglichen mit dem, was vor hundert Jahren bestand, ein hundert Jahre später Seiendes ist usw."]

Gemalte etc. sind keine realen Bestimmungen, ebenso die vergangenen und zukünftigen Zeiten. Diese Bestimmungen haben eine Ähnlichkeit, aber eine negative. Der Charakter des Nichtrealen verrät sich in einer Reihe von Eigentümlichkeiten. Wir finden die zeitlichen Bestimmtheiten in der Phantasie als Modifikationen von realen Elementen. Wir könnten sie auf anderes Reales übertragen. Wir können sie aber in derselben modifizierenden Weise zu Anderem und Nichtrealen hinzukommen lassen. Wir können von einer gewesenen Unmöglichkeit sprechen, von einer zukünftigen Unmöglichkeit. Dagegen kann ich von einer grünen oder blauen Unmöglichkeit [im Unterschied zu einer gewesenen oder zukünftigen] nicht sprechen, da Grün und Blau nicht [nicht]reale Bestimmungen sind.[30] Auch von einem Zentaur kann ich sagen, er sei als geglaubt gewesen; aber ich kann nicht sagen, er sei als geglaubt halb Mensch und halb Pferd gewesen, höchstens er sei ein geglaubtes halb Tier, halb Mensch gewesen. Ferner, wenn vergangene oder zukünftige Zeitbestimmtheiten zu realen Elementen hinzukommen, so modifizieren sie sie, aber so dass sie selbst zu Nichtrealen werden. Merkwürdig ist dabei nur das, dass diesen nichtrealen Zeitbestimmtheiten zu einer Reihe mit wirklich realer Zeitbestimmtheit gehören können und sich dann durch infinitesimale Differenzen an diese anschließen. Wie eine vergangene Zeit von einer anderen durch infinit[esimale] Unterschiede getrennt ist, so | der nichtreale Charakter zeigt sich auch darin, dass sie kein selbständiges Werden haben können. Sie werden und hören auf, ohne wirklich bewirkt oder zerstört zu werden. Jetzt gibt es einen vor[31] 1884 in Rom gelebt habenden Augustus. In hundert Jahren dagegen hat das aufgehört und es gibt einen vor 1984 gelebt habenden Augustus, und dennoch hat nichts auf den Augustus vor 1884 zerstörend eingewirkt, wie ja der gegenwärtige Augustus verschwinden kann. An jedes Entstehen und Vergehen, welches in der Gegenwart statthat, sind zeitliche Bestimmungen von aller Art als notwendige Folge geknüpft; denn von allem, was ist, ist es sicher, dass in Folge davon, dass es ist, es immer gewesen sein wird und immer in der Vergangenheit Zukünftiges ist. Diese Unselbständigkeit seines Werdens und Aufhörens hat es mit manchen anderen Nichtrealen gemein, so mit dem Vorgestellten, Geliebten, Gehassten; wenn das Vorstellen aufhört, dann hört das Vorgestellte auf, nicht etwa durch eine direkte Einwirkung. Wiederum begreift sich als Folge der Nichtrealität die klare Unmöglichkeit unmittelbarer Fernwirkung in der Zeit. Man hat es lange Zeit für lächerlich gehalten, dass etwas räumlich unmittelbar

---

30 [*Brentano* EL 72/12132: „Wir können z. B. von einer gewesenen oder zukünftigen Unmöglichkeit sprechen: Sie war, ist und wird sein. Dagegen von einer grünen oder blauen Unmöglichkeit u. dgl. nicht."]
31 [vor *statt* von *im Ms.*]

in die Ferne wirkt; absurd wäre diese Annahme nur dann, wenn es involviert, dass dasselbe an zwei verschiedenen Orten sein müsste. Das aber ist schwer zu erweisen. Bei der Zeit ist eine unmittelbare Fernwirkung nie anzunehmen, weil dann entweder Vergangenes, also Nichtreales als solches wirken oder ein Zukünftiges, also Nichtreales gewirkt werden müsste. So hat dann hier der gesunde Menschenverstand richtig gedacht. Auch vergangene und zukünftige Bewegungen und Veränderungen sind nicht real, aber auch eine gegenwärtige Bewegung ist es nur in der Weise, dass sie, solange sie gegenwärtig ist, allmählich verläuft, gewissen Teilen nach vergangen oder zukünftig ist. Ja, nur in einem einzigen Momente ist sie real. Das hat schon Aristoteles erkannt, | indem er sagt, die κίνησις sei eine ἐνέργεια ἀτελή [(unvollständige Wirklichkeit)].[32]

XIV. Vorlesung,
d. 20. Dezember 84

Wir haben schon früher die Frage aufgeworfen, ob den verschiedenen Bestimmtheiten ein + oder − zukomme. Tun wir dieselbe Frage in Betreff der Zeit. Hier ist von einem Grad nicht die Rede. Allerdings könnte etwas die Ansicht empfehlen. Die Gegenwart fügt keine neue Bestimmtheit zum gegenwärtig Genannten hinzu, während die vergangenen und zukünftigen zeitlichen Bestimmungen modifizieren. Dadurch könnte man sich veranlasst fühlen, die Gegenwart als Nullpunkt zu betrachten und die Bestimmungen der Vergangenheit und Zukunft als verschiedene Grade zu bezeichnen. Aber man kann nicht sagen, dass die erste infintessimale Zeit nach der Gegenwart eine Modifikation von geringerer Bedeutung wäre, da sie doch geradezu die Realität wegnimmt. Wollte man es doch zugestehen, dass man von Graden von Vergangenheit und Zukunft spreche, so müssten wir dagegen Einspruch erheben, dass einer eine einzige Zeitspezies als Größe annähme. Man vergesse nur nicht, dass weder die Vergangenheit noch die Zukunft als *eine* Spezies zu betrachten sind, sondern eine Unzahl von Spezies enthalten, die voneinander so verschieden sind wie sie selbst von der Gegenwart. Noch eine Frage.

Es könnte einer den Versuch machen, der momentanen Gedächtnisvorstellung die Zeitbestimmtheit abzusprechen und sie erst durch erworbene Assoziation hinzukommen lassen. Diejenigen, die hinsichtlich des Orts Empiristen sind, sehen sich immer genötigt, in den Wahrnehmungsvorstellungen gewisse Lokalzeichen anzunehmen. So würde man bei der Zeit von Temporalzeichen

---

32 [*Einfügung in eckigen Klammern nach Höfler E. 2. 1/74.*]

sprechen müssen. Doch wird man weder angeben können, worin diese Zeichen bestehen, noch woher die wahre Zeitbestimmtheit genommen oder wie sie von uns aus den gegebenen Elementen gemacht wird, um sie dann mit den Temporalzeichen zu assoziieren. Man könnte in Bezug auf die | erste Frage nur an Intensitätsunterschiede denken und diese als Wesen der Temporalzeichen ansehen. Wie sollen wir uns aber auskennen im Fall einer Abnahme des Reizes, der die Vorstellung hervorruft, so wenn einer descrescendo spielt, wo das Phantasiebild des vorigen Tones stärker ist als die darauf folgende Wahrnehmungsvorstellung; und dass das der Fall ist, kann nicht bezweifelt werden, da die Phantasie tatsächlich sehr stark ist. Aber woher soll man auch die Zeitvorstellung genommen haben, um sie zu assoziieren. Man könnte höchstens die Zeitbestimmtheit aus dem Urteil ableiten lassen, da man die Kopula zeitlich modifizieren kann. Doch davon muss bei der Lehre vom Urteil die Rede sein.

Relationen. Es gibt Relationen der Verschiedenheit. So ist Qualität verschieden vom Ort, Ton von Farbe. Ferner Relationen der Gleichheit: Wir haben zwei rote Punkte. Diese sind als rot einander gleich. Farbe und Ton sind als Qualitäten einander gleich; Farben, die zusammen wahrgenommen werden, sind als Farben von gleicher Zeitbestimmtheit einander gleich. Wir haben aber auch Relationen der Verbindung, sowohl Relationen des Verbundenen zum damit Verbundenen als auch Relationen von dem in der Verbindung Enthaltenen und dem die Verbindung Enthaltenden, also Teil und Ganzes. Die Tonqualität und Intensität sind Teile. Sie sind miteinander verbunden. Oder: Teile einer Farbe, die sich von einem Ort zum anderen erstreckt. Die beiden Beispiele zeigen aber, dass die Verbindungen sehr verschieden sind. So können wir mehrfache Verhältnisse von Teilen und Ganzen unterscheiden, hauptsächlich vier:

1. Die Verbindung zu einem Ganzen ist durch physische Zusammenhänge gegeben: ein Verhältnis von physischen Teilen und physischen Ganzen. Beispiel ist: die Teile einer Linie oder einer Zeitsrecke.

2. Das Verhältnis, wo die Verbindung statthat in der Weise, wie Eigenschaften miteinander verbunden sind: ein Verhältnis | von metaphysischen Teilen und metaphysischen Ganzen. Dazu gehören der Ort, die Zeitbestimmtheit, Qualität.

3. Die Teile sind miteinander verbunden wie Gattung und Differenz: ein Verhältnis von logischen Ganzen und logischen Teilen, oder logische Teile untereinander. Farbe verhält sich zur Röte wie ein logischer Teil zum logischen Ganzen. Jedes dieser drei Verhältnisse ist eine sehr innige Verbindung.

4. Eine weitere Verbindungsart besteht in jedem Fall der Zugehörigkeit zu einem gewissen von irgendwelcher Art von Relation verbindendem Komplex: Es sind die kollektiven Verbindungen. Ein besonders wichtiger Fall dieser vierten Arten ist der Fall, wo die Zusammengehörigkeit der Teile durch Relationen

der Gleichheit gegeben ist. Es ist dann das Verhältnis vom Teil zum Ganzen, das zwischen Einheit und Vielheit. Jede Einheit in der Vielheit ist der anderen gleich. Und die Vielheiten sind entweder endlich [oder unendlich. Wenn sie endlich sind,] dann ist das Ganze eine Zahl. Wenn [sie] unendlich [sind], dann ist es eine unzählige Menge, so die Punkte in einer Linie.

Jedes Verhältnis von Teil und Ganzem [ist in seiner Art von höchster Wichtigkeit für die ganze Logik und weit darüber hinaus].[33]

[Im Gegensatz zum kollektiven Verhältnis lässt] 2. das metaphysische Verhältnis von Ganzen und Teilen [sich in folgender Weise charakterisieren]: Jeder Teil eines Kollektivs trägt gleich viel zum Ganzen bei. Hier ist das nicht der Fall. Jedes der Elemente: Qualität, Intensität etc. Als das Vornehmste erscheint dem Menschen die Qualität. Wenn dieselben lokalen Verhältnisse gegeben bleiben mit anderen absoluten Ortsbestimmungen, so scheinen sie wenig geändert. Bedeutend[er] ist es schon, wenn eine Intensität [geändert wird].[34] So betrachtet man die Qualität als Hauptteil, als das Wesentliche. Dies zeigt sich auch in Vorliegendem. Es kann in unserer Gesichtsvorstellung, wenn wir einen roten Punkt vorstellen, eine Änderung eintreten, indem an einer Stelle die Qualität der Farbe sich ändert, die Intensität aber unverändert bleibt, oder | umgekehrt. So kann sich der Ort ändern,[35] [während die Intensität unverändet bleibt]. Im letzten Fall aber sagen wir nie, die Intensität habe den Ort geändert. Wir sagen nur, die Qualität habe sich geändert, oder das Phänomen habe sich seiner Qualität nach geändert.[36] So fasst man also die Qualität als das mit den anderen als Eigenschaften Behaftete, und dieses ist das Verhältnis, welches zwischen

---

33   [*Einfügungen in eckingen Klammern nach Brentano* EL *72/12149.*]
34   [*Einfügungen in eckingen Klammern nach Leisching* Y *2/109, wo der folgende Satz sofort danach geschrieben wird:* „Dennoch gilt auch eine Änderung des Grades der Intensität geringer als eine Änderung der Qualität."]
35   [der Ort ändern, *statt* der Ort ändern, Qualität und das Rot. *im Ms.*]
36   [*Brentano* EL *72/12150:* „Es kann in unserer Gesichtsvorstellung, wenn wir einen roten Punkt auf grauem matten Grund [sehen], eine Änderung eintreten, indem an einer Stelle die Qualität der Farbe sich ändert, die Intensität unverändert bleibt oder die Intensität sich ändert und die Qualität und die Ortsbestimmtheit bleibt, oder Intensität und Qualität bleibt, aber der Ort, wo auf dem matten Grund ein roter Punkt erscheint, ändert sich kontinuierlich. Im dritten Fall sagen wir: Die Qualität hat ihren Ort geändert. Im zweiten Fall: Die Qualität hat ihre Intensität geändert. Dagegen sagen wir im dritten Fall kaum, die Intensität habe ihren Ort geändert, oder im zweiten: Der Ort hat seine Intensität geändert. Im ersten Fall endlich: Wie drücken wir uns da aus? Auch da sagen wir nicht, die Intensität habe ihre Qualität geändert, oder gar, der Ort habe seine Qualität geändert, sondern nur, die Qualität habe gewechselt, habe sich geändert, oder auch, das Phänomen, d. h. das hier aus Qualität, Intensität und Ort bestehende metaphysische Ganze habe sich seiner Qualität nach geändert."]

Substanz und Akzidentien bestehen soll. Allerdings denkt man gewöhnlich unter Substanz keine sinnliche Qualität (so Aristoteles). Wir können aber die wenigen Schritten, die zu diesem Begriff führen, leicht verfolgen. Aristoteles glaubte an die Existenz sinnlicher Qualitäten in der Außenwelt. Er glaubte, Qualitäten verschiedener Sinne seien in der Wirklichkeit örtlich geeinigt und durchdringen sich; zwischen ihnen bestehe eine Zugehörigkeit zu demselben metaphysischen Ganzen. In diesem Ganzen aber war keine dieser Qualitäten der wesentlichere Teil zu nennen. So dachte nun Aristoteles einen anderen Träger vorhanden, und das war seine Substanz.[37]

[XV. Vorlesung,
d. 7. Januar 85][38]

[Über] 3. das Verhältnis der logischen Teile und des logischen Ganzen [können wir noch weiter sagen]: Dieses Verhältnis ist ein ganz besonders inniges. Das logische Ganze greift metaphysisch nie über einen einzelnen Teil hinaus und physisch nie weiter, als der logische Teil reicht. Zum Beispiel: „Die Röte" und „die Farbe" stehen in diesem Verhältnis. Farbe gehört demselben metaphysischen Teil an wie die Röte.[39] Das Beispiel „intensive Röte" und „Röte" hingegen wäre ein unrichtiges Beispiel, weil ein anderer metaphysische Teil dazu kommt,

---

37 [*Vgl. Brentano* EL 72/12151: „Aristoteles glaubte an die Existenz der sinnlichen Qualitäten und ihrer Intensitäten und Ortsbestimmungen und glaubte, Qualitäten verschiedener Sinne [seien] örtlich geeinigt und sich durchdringend. Da dachte er sich nun, zwischen ihnen bestände dann bei dieser wechselseitigen Durchdringung eine Zugehörigkeit zu dem metaphysischen Ganzen. In diesem Ganzen war aber keine von ihnen der wesentlichere Teil zu nennen, und so dachte er dann, in Analogie zu der Stellung der Qualität unseres Phänomens zu seinm Ort und seiner Intensität, einen anderen Träger vorhanden und dieser war ihm dann das eigentliche Wesen, an welchem alle Eigenschaften haften: die Substanz. Diese Betrachtung macht, richtg[?] gesagt, einer Fülle an Unklarheiten, an welchen die Logik und Metaphysik seit Jahrtausenden litten und noch leiten, ein Ende. Ganz ähnlichen Gewinn wird uns aber die genauere Betrachtung des Verhältnisses der logischen Teile bringen." Vgl. *auch Leisching* Y 2/III: „Diese Betrachtung macht einer Fülle von Unklarheit, an welcher die Logik und Metaphysik seit Jahrtausenden leidet, ein Ende. So wie Aristoteles sich die Sache dachte mit den Qualitäten behaftet, so kann die Sache nicht sein. Die Qualitäten existieren nicht wirklich, auch haften sie nicht daran. Ob aber mit Sicherheit behauptet werden darf, ob ein analoges Verhältnis, wie es in unserer Definition sich findet, sich auch wirklich findet, das ist eine andere Frage."]
38 [*Datum in eckingen Klammern nach Leisching* Y 2/III.]
39 [wie die Farbe *statt* wie die Röte *im Ms.*]

nämlich die Intensität. Dagegen richtig wäre das Beispiel „das Da und Dort" und „Ortsbestimmtheit," oder: „das irgendeinmal Seiende" ein logischer Teil von dem „dann und dann Seienden" oder: „dauerhaft" und „zeitlich." | Auch das ist bemerkenswert, dass das logische Ganze nur solches zum logischen Teil hinzufügt, was ohne ihn undenkbar ist, so dass die Ergänzung selbst nicht eigentlich als ein zweiter neuer Teil zu denken ist, sondern den ersten Teil einschließt. Zum Beispiel: Farbe ist ein logischer Teil von Röte. Damit aus Farbe Röte wird, was kommt hinzu? Das Rote. Liegt aber im Rot selbst die Farbe? Ja. Also ist die Teilung eine einseitige. Auch im „hier" liegt der Begriff der Ortsbestimmtheit. Die Teilung aber kann mehrfach wiederholt werden. Die Röte hat als logischen Teil die Farbe, dann aber auch die „Qualität." Den letzten logischen, nicht weiter teilbaren Teil hat Aristoteles, indem er den Ausdruck anders gebraucht als heute, „höchste Gattung" genannt. Eine Gattung und ihre Differenzen zusammen heißt „Art." Aber jede Differenz ist eigentlich mit der betreffenden Art selbst identisch. Die geordnete Zusammenstellung dieser logischen Teile von der höchsten Gattung bis zur letzten Differenz hat Aristoteles ὅρος – Definition genannt. Aristoteles hat also hier ein Verhältnis von Teil und Ganzem im Auge, welches vom Verhältnis der metaphysischen Teile sich wesentlich unterscheidet. Die ganze Kenntnis dieses besonderen Verhältnisses ist aber eigentlich verloren gegangen. So ist der Satz „Der Schimmel ist ein weißes Pferd" nach Aristoteles keine Definition, weil keine Wesenseinheit zwischen „Pferd" und „weiß" besteht. Ja, man könnte nach einer heutigen Ansicht von der Definition jede beliebige Zusammenstellung von Merkmalen mit einem Namen bezeichnen, und dennoch wäre keine Definition vorhanden. Man könnte dabei jedes beliebige Merkmal als Gattung annehmen. Ob man sagt „ein viereckiges Rot" oder „ein rotes Viereck," wäre gleichgültig. | Der eigentliche Begriff der Definition ist abhanden gekommen. Aristoteles nahm an, dass die Substanz logische Teile habe. Damit scheinen gewisse Beobachtungen gut zu stimmen. So bemerkt J. St. Mill:

> Die durch einen allgemeinen Namen bestimmten Gegenstand unterscheiden sich von den nicht darunter begriffenen oft nur in gewissen Einzelheiten, die man aufzählen kann, während sich andere in mehr Einzelheiten unterscheiden, als wir aufzählen könnten, oder jemals wissen zu können hoffen dürfen.[40]

---

40 [*Mill 1877, 1.7.§ 4:* „Die in manchen Classen eingeschlossenen Dinge unterscheiden sich von anderen Dingen nur in gewissen Einzelheiten, die man aufzählen kann, während sich andere in mehr Einzelheiten unterscheiden, als wir aufzählen können, oder sogar in mehr als wir jemals zu wissen erwarten dürfen."]

Etc. Ferner:

> Wenn sich aber jemand vornhemen wollte, die gemeinsamen Eigenschaften aller Dinge zu untersuchen, welche dieselbe Gestalt haben oder dieselbe Farbe oder dasselbe spezifische Gewicht [besitzen], so wäre das eine handgreifliche Absurdität, da ihnen keine anderen Eigenschaften gemeinsam sind als die in den Namen eingeschlossenen. Es ist daher nicht unpassend zu sagen, dass von diesen zwei Klassifikationen, die eine einer viel radikaleren Unterscheidung in den Dingen selbst entspricht.[41]

Was lag nun näher, als diese radikale Unterscheidung als Unterscheid in der Substanz zu begreifen, der als metaphysischer Teil nach [den] verschiedensten Richtungen bestimmend ist.[42] So scheinen diese Dinge in ganz besonderer Weise substantiell verwandt. Und da diese Klassenbegriffe teils allgemein, teils minder allgemein, so müsste man konsequent eine mehr generelle und mehr substantielle Verwandtschaft annehmen und dementsprechend verschiedene logische Teile statuieren. Zum Beispiel: Körper, lebendiger Körper, tierischer lebendiger Körper, Säugetier, fleischfressendes Säugetier, Katze, Löwe etc. Man hätte aber, selbst wenn man die Substanzhypothese gesichert glauben könnte, vorsichtiger sein müssen. Man hätte doch erwägen müssen, dass diese Unterschiede in verschiedener Weise auf Unterschiede der Substanz zurückgeführt werden müssen. Vielleicht liegt den Eigentümlichkeiten der Tiere, die die Erfahrung zeigt, keine Annahme der Substanz, sondern | ein System der Substanzen zugrunde, und es genügt, dass in diesem eine oder mehrere in verschiedener Weise verbundene eine Menge von Eigentümlichkeiten liefern würde. Indessen war man nicht so vorsichtig. Man tat noch mehr. Aristoteles selbst verfiel in Irrtümer. Er wollte nämlich nicht bloß keinen Zweifel an der Existenz solcher Qualitäten dulden, sondern er war sich darüber nicht klar, dass die von ihm zugrunde gelegte Substanz eine von ihm gebildete Hypothese sei. Er bildete sich vielmehr ein, die Anschauung selbst zeige ihm die Substanz in Verbindung mit den Eigenschaften. Er meinte nun weiter: Es muss möglich sein, die eigentlich logischen Teile der Substanz, ihre Gattung und höhere

---

41 [*Ibid.*: „Wenn sich aber Jemand vornehmen wollte, die gemeinsamen Eigenschaften aller Dinge zu untersuchen, welche dieselbe Gestalt, dieselbe Farbe oder dasselbe spezifische Gewicht besitzen, so wäre dies eine handgreifliche Absurdität. Wir haben keinen Grund zu glauben, dass irgend andere gemeinsame Eigenschaften zwischen ihnen existiren, als in der Voraussetzung selbst liegen oder durch ein Causalgesetz davon ableitbar sind." „Es ist nicht anpassend, zu sagen, dass von diesen zwei Classificationen die eine einer viel radikaleren Unterscheidung in den Dingen selbst entspricht."]
42 [bestimmend ist *statt* bestimmend sind *im Ms.*]

und niedere Differenzen anzugeben, statt sich zu bengügen in einem gewissen Komplex von Eigenschaften einen Hinweis auf sie zu erblicken. So glaubte er, Körper, Tier, Pflanze seien Begriffe von Substanzen, die durch Namen von Gattung und Differenz ebenso eigentlich definiert werden können, wie das „Rot" und „Blau." Er bemühte sich nun, den angeblichen Definitionen der Substanzen den Charakter jener wahren Definition zu geben, also besonders die Forderung zu erfüllen, dass die logischen Teile einseitige Teile sein müssen, und dass jede folgende Differenz die Differenz der nächst vorhergehenden sein soll. Man musste nun von Aristoteles abgehen. Dagegen hielt man die Ausdrücke Differenz, Definition, Art, Gattung fest und vergaß den ursprünglichen Sinn. Man redete von Gattung und Art bei jeder natürlichen Klassifikation, wo also bei einer fortschreitenden Einteilung von Gegenständen ein einheitlicher Zweck festgehalten war. Von irgendwelcher Beziehung zu logischen Teilen war gar nichts mehr übrig geblieben. Auch das Volk bildet Klassen und jeder allgemeine Name der Volkssprache ist der Ausdruck für eine Klasse. | Dabei ist aber von einem einheitlichen Zweck wie bei der naturgemäßen Klassifikation gar keine Rede, und es wäre nichts vorhanden, was die geringste Ähnlichkeit hätte mit Gattung und Differenz im Sinn des Aristoteles. So ließe man als Definition gelten, wenn einer sagte: Die Bürgschaft von Schiller ist ein Gedicht, welches Schiller zur Verherrlichung der Freundschaft in dem und dem Jahr gedichtet hat. Wir haben hier also eine Erklärung durch Angabe von Umständen, die ganz äußerlich zum Gegenstand gehören. So finden wir denn das Wort Definition häufig nicht mehr im Sinn irgendwelcher Begriffsanalyse, sondern einfach als Worterklärung gebraucht.[43] Auch wir werden uns in klarer Weise dieses Ausdrucks bedienen, aber das besonders wichtige Verhältnis von logischem Ganzen und logischen Teilen muss in seiner Eigentümlichkeit mit voller Klarheit festgehalten werden. Der logische Teil im Sinn des Aristoteles ist an und für sich unbestimmter als das logische Ganze. Aber auch im logischen Ganzen fehlt die volle Bestimmtheit. Die volle Bestimmtheit wird durch solches gegeben, was nicht im logischen Ganzen begriffen ist. Individualisiert wird ein „Rot" z. B. durch Angabe von „Ort" oder Zeit oder Intensität, also durch Bestimmungen, die nicht zu demselben metaphysischen Ganzen gehören. Über die physischen Teile sprechen wir besser nach den Relationen der Gleichheit und Verschiedenheit.

---

43 [EL 72/12162: „So finden wir heutzutage das Wort Definition sehr häufig nicht bloß nicht mehr im aristotelischen Sinn, der ganz verloren ist, sondern überhaupt nicht mehr im Sinn irgendwelcher Begriffsanalyse sondern gleich bedeutend mit Worterklärung."]

[XVI. Vorlesung,
d. 10. Januar 84][44]

Gleichheit und Verschiedenheit.
Sie sind mannigfach je nach dem, wodurch das Gleiche gleich und das Verschiedene verschieden ist.[45] Etwas kann der Qualität nach gleich sein, wie alles Rote, oder der Intensität nach oder dem Ort nach, oder der Zeit nach. Auch von dem, was der Qualität [nach] gleich ist, ist es nicht alles in derselben Weise. Das eine ist nur der Gattung nach qualitativ gleich. So ist das verschieden Farbige als farbig qualitativ gleich; anderes aber ist wieder der letzten spezifischen Differenz nach gleich. Und von einem, was nur der Gattung nach gleich ist, | ist eines der niederen, ein anderes der höheren Gattung nach gleich. Besonders zu beachten ist folgender Unterschied: der Unterschied zwischen Gleichheit im eigentlichen Sinn und einer wesentlichen anderen Übereinstimmung, [d. i.] die Quasigleichheit oder Gleiches mit μετάβασις εἰς γένος. Diese besteht z. B. zwischen einem Menschen und einem vorgestellten Menschen, der nichts Reales und nicht wahrhaft Mensch ist. Im Bereich dessen, was wir bisher analysierten, gilt es solche Fälle von Gleichheit, so zwischen einem gegenwärtigen und einem in der Gedächtnisvorstellung enthaltenen gewesenen Ton. So gibt es auch eine Quasi-Gattungsgleichheit oder quasispezifische Gleichheit. Die Verhältnisse der Unterschiede sind nicht minder mannigfaltig. Besondere Beachtung verdienen die Unterschiede der untersten logischen Differenzen (im Sinn des Aristoteles), bei Gleichheit der niedersten Gattung. Hat nämlich eine neiderste Gattung mehr als zwei Spezies, so sind ihre Unterschiede immer das, was man Abstand nennt. Das heißt, wenn man einen Unterschied zwischen zwei mit dem zwischen zwei anderen vergleicht, so findet man, dass der eine mit dem anderen gleich oder größer oder kleiner, als er ist. Die Unterschiede zwischen verschiedenen Zahlenspezies sind entweder gleich oder kleiner oder größer. Oder: Die Unterschiede zwischen Farben sind Abstände. Die Unterschiede der Töne sind ebenso Abstände. Die Unterschiede der Intensitäten sind ebenso Abstände. Ebenso bei den Orten, Zeiten. Bei den Zahlenspezies sind die größeren Unterschiede, bei den anderen Klassen sind alle Unterschiede Größen (im Sinn des Gauß, nach welchem die Einheit keine Größe ist, darum sind bei den Zahlen nur Größenunterschiede gemeint). Von anderen Unterschieden außer denen von verschiedenen Spezies der niedersten Gattung gilt nirgends

---

44 [*Datum nach Leisching Y 3/6.*]
45 [wodurch das Gleiche gleich und das Verschiedene verschieden ist *statt* wodurch das Gleiche = und das Verschiedene = ist *im Ms.*]

43 dasselbe: so ist der Unterschied von Zeit und Ort | und der Unterschied von Rot und Farbe weder gleich noch größer noch kleiner.

Sagt man, zwischen Qualität und Zeitbestimmtheit [sei] ein größerer Unterschied als zwischen Raum und Zeit, so meint man nur: Es bestehen mehr Unterschiede [zwischen Qualität und Zeitbestimtheit], da ja bei Zeit und Raum manche Ähnlichkeiten sich finden. Nur von den Spezies von quasigleicher Gattung machen manche eine Ausnahme und verhalten sich wie zwei Spezies derselben Gattung, nämlich immer dann, wo die alterierende Bestimmung, die eben die Quasigleichheit ausmacht, Abstände zeigt. So besteht ein Abstand zwischen einer jetzigen Farbe und einer Farbe vor einer Sekunde, da hier die Zeitbestimmung als alterierend hinzukommt und diesen Abstand zeigt. Wo es Abstände gibt, sind immer unendlich viele koordinierte Spezies und Quasispezies vorhanden. Von diesen Abständen ist manchmal einer der kleinsten möglich, so bei den Zahlenspezies die Einheit, manchmal aber nicht vielmehr sind kleinere Unterschiede denkbar in jedem rationalen und irrationalen Verhältnis, so bei den Orten, Farben. Bei diesen ist darum jeder spezifische Abstand eine Größe (nach Gauß genomen); kein Abstand aber ist hier unendlich klein oder groß; nur in der Gattung *Menge*, in welcher es einen kleinstmöglichen spezifischen Abstand gibt, nämlich die Einheit, gibt es einen spezifischen Abstand, den größtmöglichen, der von unendlicher Größe ist, nämlich der Abstand zwichen der Unzahl und jeder endlichen Zahlenspezies. Es ist ein Unterschied zwischen eigentlicher und uneigentlicher Unendlichkeit zu machen. Nehme ich die Reihe 1 + 1 + 1 + 1 + 1 etc. und lasse sie so wachsen. Zu welcher Größe wächst sie heran? Die Summe wird unendlich groß, aber im uneigentlichen Sinn. Sie übersteigt nämlich jede angebbare endliche Größe. Es gibt aber auch
44 eine Unendlichkeit im eigentlichen Sinn. Bespiel: | Die Menge der Punkte in einer Linie ist unendlich im eigentlichen Sinn. (?)[46] Die möglichen Zahlen sind eine Unzahl. Das hat Bolzano (*Paradoxien des Unendlichen*) richtig bemerkt. Folgendes ist merkwürdig: Wenn man zwei unendlichen Mengen hat, so kann man paarweise ein Glied der einen Menge einem Glied der anderen Menge zuordnen. Denken wir uns eine unendliche Zahlenreihe 1, 2, 3, 4, 5 etc. und die Reihe 2, 4, 6, 8, 10 etc., und zwar so, dass beiderseits kein Rest bleibt, indem man nämlich zu 1, 2, 3, 4, 5 wieder die Reihe 2, 4, 6, 8, 10 [setzt].[47] Man kann sie aber auch so einander zuordnen, dass beliebig auf der einen oder anderen Seite ein Rest bleibt. Man hat diese Unterschiede, die sich aus der Weise der Zuordnung ergeben, „Anzahl der unendlichen Menge" genannt (so G. Cantor).

---

46   [*Das Fragezeichen in runden Klammern ist eine Einfügung mit Rotstift.*]
47   [Reihe 2, 4, 6, 8, 10 *statt* Reihe 1, 2, 3, 4, 5 *im Ms.*]

So könnte einer fragen, ob es, wie es möglich, die Punkte einer größeren und kleinen Linie paarweise zuzuordnen, so dass ebenso gut hüben wie drüben ein Rest bleibt, es ebenso möglich ist, die Punktmenge einer Linie zuzuordnen der Punktmenge einer Fläche. Denken wir uns eine gerade Linie und das Quadrat über diese Linie.

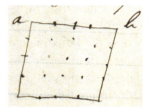

Halbiert man *a b* in infinitum allseitig und ebenso das ganze Quadrat, so haben wir in *a b* zunächst 3 Punkte, dann 9, dann 17. Also 3, 9, 17, 33, etc. Beim Quadrat bekommen[?] wir 9, 25, 81, etc. Nun ist es klar, dass die Punktmengen 3, 5, 9, 17, 33, etc. größer ist als die Menge 2, 4, 8, 16, 32. Die Reihe 9, 25, 81, etc. ist aber kleiner als die Reihe 16, 64, 256. Diese letzte Reihe könnte enthält Ziffern, die uns in der Reihe 2, 4, 8, 16, 32 vorkommen. | Also kann man die Punkte des Quadrats ähnlich paarweise in Beziehung setzen zu den Punkten der Linie.

[XVII. Vorlesung,
d. 14 Januar 1885][48]

Cantor hingegen glaubt, dass auch in diesen Unzahlen gewisse größere Unterschiede seien, die er Mächtigkeit nennt, indem manche sich so unterschieden, dass man sie nicht paarweise einander zuordnen könne. Brentano glaubt an diese Unterschiede nicht. Er meint, alle Unzahlen gehören einer Anzahlenspezies an. Eine Folge davon ist, dass die Möglichkeit besteht paarweise zwei unendliche Mengen Glied für Glied einander zuzuordnen. So die Punkte einer Linie, dann einer Fläche, eines Kubus – eines n-dimensionalen Gebildes. Auch die Zeitpunkte der Ewigkeit lassen sich dann einer Sekunde paarweise zuordnen. Nehmen wir einen Körper, der sich eine Sekunde lang gleichmäßig fortbewegende Strecke A – B zurücklegt. Jeder Punkt der Linie wird in einem anderen Punkt der Sekunde und umgekehrt erreicht. Es ist also leicht, die Punkte der Linie und der Sekunde eindeutig einander zuzuordnen. Denken wir

---

48   [*Datum nach Leisching Y 3/13.*]

nun einen anderen Körper, welcher dieselbe Strecke nicht mit gleichmäßiger Geschwindigkeit, sondern in allmählich langsamer werdenden Bewegung verläuft, so dass er in der ersten Sekunde [die erste] Hälfte, [dann] in der zweiten [Sekunde] das dritte Viertel, dann [in der dritten Sekunde] das siebte Achtel, [dann in der vierten Sekunde] das fünfzehnte Sechzehntel etc. [durchläuft]. Er kommt niemals zu Ende. Da er nun in seinem Lauf jeden Punkt vor B erreicht, so ist auch die ganze Punktmenge außer B eindeutig der Punktmenge der Ewigkeit zugeordnet. Es ist also klar, dass dasselbe bezüglich der Punktmenge der Sekunde geschehen kann. Weiter: Wir haben gesehen, dass die Punktmenge eines endlichen linearen Kontinuums zu paaren ist mit der Punktmenge eines endlichen Gebildes von n Dimensionen. Es ist also klar, [dass] sie sich [der Punktmenge] eines unbegrenzten Kontinuums von n Dimensionen zuordnen ließe. | Ja, selbst für eine Punktmenge von unendlichen Dimensionen gilt dasselbe. Es gilt also auch für ein Kontinuum von unbegrenzt vielen und unbegrenzten Dimensionen. Es scheint also von jeder Unzahl in Bezug auf jede andere unendliche Menge dasselbe zu gelten. Das Gegenteil aber haben manche Mathematiker behauptet, besonders Prof. Cantor in Halle. Derselbe stellt den Begriff der Mächtigkeit für unendliche und endliche Zahlen auf: Jeder wohl definierten Menge kommt eine bestimmte Mächtigkeit zu, wobei zwei spezifisch verschiedene Mengen dieselbe Mächtigkeit haben, wenn sie sich eindeutig einander zuordnen lassen. Jede endliche Zahlenspezies hat also eine andere Mächtigkeit, aber auch Unzahlen sollen nicht von derselben Mächtigkeit sein. Viele haben dieselbe Mächtigkeit, aber nicht alle. Cantor unterscheidet danach eine 2., 3., 4. Zahlenklasse, jede von einer höhere Mächtigkeit als die vorhergehende. Fragen wir nach einem Beispiel, so verweist er uns auf den Unterschied zwischen der unendlichen Menge der Glieder in der Reihen der ganzen Zahlen und der Punktmenge in einer Linie. Das allerdings soll richtig sein, dass die Menge der ganzen Zahlen gleichmächtig sei der Punktmenge der Linie, die man durch Teilung in allen rationalen Verhältnissen erlangt. Aber für irrationale Teilungsverhältnisse gilt das nicht. Diese sind unendlichmal mehr, meint er, ja unvergleichlich mehr, also weder durch Addition noch durch Multiplikation noch durch Potenzation noch durch Ultrapotenzation (z. B., $3^{3^{3}}$ ist Ultrapotenzation oder $\infty^{\infty^{\infty}}$) erreichbar. Es bestünde demnach unmöglich eine eindeutige Zuordnung. Indessen glaubt Brentano, | dass Cantor im Irrtum ist. Auch die genannten zwei unendlichen Mengen sind spezifisch gleich. Dann aber müssen sie auch gleichmächtig sein. Es soll zunächst der Beweis durch Anwendung einer Formel geführt werden: Zugegeben wird uns, dass die Menge der Zahlen gleichmächtig ist der Menge aller Punkte, die durch fortgesetzte Halbierung ins Unendliche erlangt werden. Zu diesen Punkten gehören natürlich nicht alle Punkte der Linie, so wird keiner der Drittelungspunkte erreicht.

Was gilt aber von jenen Punkten, die wir durch Halbierung erreicht haben würden, wenn die Gesamtheit der möglichen Halbierungen durchgeführt worden wäre? Cantor glaubt, es gelte dasselbe, denn auf einen unmöglichen Halbierungspunkt könnten wir nicht gestoßen sein, und die Menge der wirklichen Halbierungspunkte wäre = der Menge der möglichen. Wenn nun aber nicht jeder Punkt der Linie zu diesen Punkten gehören soll, wievielen nicht dazu gehörigen Punkten begegnet man, ausgehend vom Anfangspunkt der Linie bis hin zur ausgeführten ersten Linie des Halbierungsstammbaums? Eigentlich gar keinem. Denn der Punkt A ist die Grenze, der sich die erste Linie des Stammbaums ins Unendliche annähert. Das ist klar, dass der Abstand nicht so groß ist und sein kann wie irgendwelche gegebene Linie.

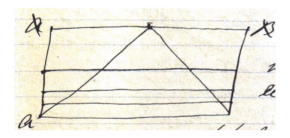

Somit könnten auch keine Punkte und [noch deutlicher] keine zwei Punkte dazu sein, und wenn auch nun das Letzte zugibt, so ist klar, dass die letzten Linien immer gleich weit auseinander sind, wenigstens die Hälfte der Punkte der Linie zu den Halbierungspunkten gehören müssen. Wenn N die Menge der ganzen Zahlen ist, so ist die Menge dieser Punkte gleich $(2 + 2N)^{-1}$ und somit wären die Punkte der Linie = $2 + 2 \cdot 2^{N-1}$, also $4 + N^2$. Nun ist aber 2^N gleichmächtig wie N, da es selbst gleichmächtig ist wie N^N. Also ist Cantors Behauptung falsch. Aber auch das Gegenteil hat einen Schein für sich. Die Drittelungspunkte scheinen allein nicht weniger zu sein als die Halbierungspunkte, die Fünftelungspunkte etc. und endlich die Punkte, die durch Punkte in irrationalen Verhältnissen erreicht werden. Wie stimmt nun dazu, dass die Halbierungspunkte jeden zweiten Punkt der Linie enthalten? Antwort: Die durchgeführte Halbierung würde alle Punkte der Linie enthalten. Im Endlichen fällt kein Halbierungspunkt mit einem Drittelungspunkt zusammen. Im Unendlichen hingegen müssen sie zusammenfallen, und dem gibt Cantor (p. 15) selbst Zeugnis, wenn er sagt, dass eine unendliche Menge ebenso gut eine gerade oder eine ungerade Zahl genannt werden könne. „Die Zahl ist gerade" heißt: „Sie kann durch Zwei geteilt werden." Dasselbe gilt aber auch von der Drittelung. Jede unendliche Zahl muss gedrittelt, gefünftelt werden können etc. Also muss sie in jedem rationalen Verhältnis teilbar sein, und ist dies erkannt, so kann dasselbe von jedem irrationalen Verhältnis gesagt werden, da die rationalen den irrationalen Verhältnissen im Unendlichen sich unendlich annähern. Somit muss die Gesamtheit der Halbierungspunkte mit der Gesamtheit der Teilungspunkte in allen rationalen und irrationalen Verhältnissen identisch sein. Wo es sich aber um verschiedene Linien handelt, werden sie wenigstens spezifisch gleich sein. Somit sind sie auch gleichmächtig, und der von Cantor angeführte Begriff der Mächtigkeit ist völlig gegenstandslos geworden.[49] Man wird durch solche Annahme zu Absurditäten geführt. Zum Beispiel: | Wenn es Größenunterschiede gibt zwischen unendlichen Mengen, so frage ich: Welche Summe ist größer, die der Reihe 1 + 2 + 3 + 4 + 5 + 6 + 7 etc. oder 2 + 4 + 6 + 8 + 10 + 12 + 14 etc.? Bolzano meint, die Summe der zweiten Reihe sei größer, weil ich sie bekomme, wenn ich die erste Reihe zu sich selbst addiere. Aber man kann ja auch durch Subtraktion gelangen, wenn man 1, 3, 5 etc. wegnimmt. Also müsste wieder die erste Reihe größer [sein]. B[olzano]: Es handelt sich nicht um wachsende Reihen, sondern um ausgewachsene, denn bei gleichen Zeiten würde die Zeitreihe als wachsend angenommen größer sein. Aber einer könnte sagen: Ist nicht oft eine unendliche Menge Teil einer anderen, also kleiner? So die Punktmenge der halben Linie und die der ganzen. Darauf ist zu antworten: Wer diesen Grundsatz hier anwendet, versteht den Sinn davon nicht. „Das Ganze ist größer als der Teil" gilt nicht von allen Verhältnissen, so z. B. nicht vom logischen Teil oder vom metaphysischen Ganzen und Teil. Nur eine gewisse Klasse von Ganzem und Teil ist es, für die dieser Satz gilt, nämlich jene, wo durch Hinzufügung und Wegnahme des anderen Teils vom Ganzen ohne weiteres eine spezifische Veränderung gesetzt wird. So allerdings bei den Mengen, bei den unendlichen ebenso wohl wie bei den endlichen. Während aber bei den endlichen, wo jeder Teil, der weggenommen wird oder zugefügt wird, eine andere Spezies zur Folge hat, das Ganze größer wird als der Teil, gilt beim unendlichen nur dasselbe bezüglich ihren endlichen Teilen, von welchen sie gleichmäßig einen unendlichen Abstand hat, nicht vom unendlichen Teil, von dem sie keinen spezifischen Unterschied hat. Ihre spezifische Differenz ist ihre Unermesslichkeit, und sie bleibt, wenn sie überhaupt da ist nach wie vor, wenn ich beliebig oft 1 wegnehme, ja wenn ich unendlich viele | Einheiten wegnehme, wenn nur unendlich viele bleiben, so dass die spezifische Differenz der Unermesslichkeit bleibt. Aber wird dann, wenn wir sagen: „Die Hälfte und das Ganze ist unendlich," dadurch nicht jede unendliche Menge unbestimmt, wenn sie sich nicht spezifisch unterscheiden und doch nicht dieselben

---

49 [Höfler E.2.1./54: „Der von Cantor eingeführte Begriff der Mächtigkeit ist gegenstandslos."]

sind? Viele leugneten darum das Unendliche. Allein auch die anderen Spezies sind alle unbestimmt. Das logische Ganze ist immer unbestimmt und wird erst durch die metaphysischen Teile individualisiert (siehe früher). Es genügt auch in unserem Fall, die vielen Bestimmtheiten zu geben, die die anderen metaphysischen Teile spezifizieren. Die unendliche Punktmenge einer Fläche ist nicht die Punktmenge einer anderen Fläche, wie die Röte einer Fläche nicht die Röte einer anderen ist.

[XVIII. Vorlesung,
d. 17 Januar 1885][50]

In welchem Sinn man von einer unendlichen Menge sagen kann, sie sei größer als eine andere.
In verschiedenem Sinn spricht man in uneigentlicher Weise von Ganzen.
1. Versteht man unter einem Ganzen etwas, das ein anderes in sich begreift und noch etwas dazu, so kann man auch bei unendlichen Mengen den Satz [für wahr] halten, dass der Teil größer sei als das Ganze. Wie uneigentlich dies gemeint ist, sieht man darin, dass manches Ganze größer ist, ohne groß zu sein. So das metaphysische Ganze, ebenso das logische. Obwohl Rot in sich Farbe und noch etwas dazu enthält, ist Rot dennoch keine Größe.[51] Ebenso sind 2 Punkte in uneigentlichem Sinn größer als 1 [Punkt], obwohl keiner von ihnen groß ist. Denn Größe ist das, was Teile unterscheiden lässt (Gauß).
2. Weiter: Eine unendliche Menge kann größer sein als eine andere, weil sie von größerer Fülle ist als die andere. So ist die Menge der Raumpunkte einer geraden Linie von 2 M größer als die Menge der Raumpunkte einer geraden von 1 M, aber nur weil die Punkte einen größeren Abstand füllen. Während für die Größe die Gattung der gezählten Objekte gleichgültig ist (3 Engel sind ebenso viele wie 3 Punkte), so ist sie für die hier bezeichnete uneigentliche Größe nicht gleichgültig, | denn verschiedenen Gattungen angehörige Dinge können nicht einen ebenso großen Abstand füllen. Oder: Nehmen wir einen Farbenabstand; gewisse Farbenspezies füllen den Abstand zweier gewisser Farben. Füllen nun Farbenpunkte auch einen räumlichen Abstand? Nein. Die massiven Übergänge von Rot zu Gelb lassen sich auf verschiedene Räume verteilt denken.

51

---

50 [*Datum nach Leisching Y 3/20.*]
51 [Obwohl Rot in sich Farbe und noch etwas dazu enthält, ist Rot dennoch keine Größe. *statt* obwohl Rot in sich enthält Farbe und noch etwas dazu und dennoch ist Rot selbst keine Größe. *im Ms.*]

3. Von einem Größer und Kleiner von unendlichen Mengen kann gesprochen werden, weil die eine unendliche Menge Abstand in einer größeren oder kleineren Zahl von Dimensionen füllt als die andere; so ist die Punktmenge in der Seite des Quadrats kleiner als die in der Fläche des Quadrats. Dieser Fall ist kein spezieller Fall des vorigen, was man vielleicht glauben könnte. So ist die Menge der Zeitpunkte in einer Stunde kleiner als die Menge der Raumpunkte in einem Kubikschuh.[52] Auch hier wird das Größer in einem uneigentlichen Sinn genommen. Man sieht, wie bedeutend der Gattungsbegriff des Aristoteles für die Logik ist. Trendelenburg sagt, die Logik seit Aristoteles hat nicht nur nicht einen Fortschritt gemacht (wie Kant meinte), sondern sogar Rückschritte. (Aber das ist nicht richtig.)[53]

Unter den Abständen zwischen Spezies jener Gattung[54] ist nicht einer der kleinstmögliche. Dies wäre keine Größe. Andere aber sind es. Von anderen Gattungen gilt es, dass von den Abständen der Spezies keiner der kleinstmögliche sei, dass vielmehr in jedem rationalen und irrationalen Verhältnis Abstand möglich sei. Qualität, Intensität, Ort, Zeit etc. sind Beispiele dafür. Die Qualitäten der Farben haben Abstand, aber es gibt hier Abstand in jedem rationalen und irrationalen Verhältnis. Die Abstände in verschiedenen Gattungen sind immer ganz unvergleichbar. Dagegen können Abstände in verschiedenen Gattungen einander proportional sein. Auch anderes ist den Gattungen gemeinsam. Obwohl die Abstände unendlich verschieden sind und bis ins Unendliche größer und kleiner sind, so ist doch keiner unendlich klein und keiner unendlich groß. Mathematiker glaubten oft an ein absolut unendliches Kleines und Großes. | So wenn sie sagen: Parallele Geraden sind solche, die sich in

---

52 [Kubikschu *nach Leisching Y 3/23 statt Zeichnung im Ms.*]
53 [*Dieser Satz in runden Klammern ist eine Einfügung mit Blaustift. Vgl. Brentano* EL 72/12192 (*nach weiteren Betrachtungen über Gattung und Spezies*): „Sie sehen von welcher Bedeutung der Aristotelische Gattungs- und Speziesbegriff [ist]! Wie ohne ihn die für die elementare Logik wesentlichsten Unterscheidungen nicht zu machen [sind]! Wie unermesslich die moderne Logik schon durch den einzigen Umstand, dass er ihr verloren [ist], zurückgesunken [ist]! Kant und Trendelenburg! Aber auch wie unmöglich auch nur die eresten Schritte zur Klärung sind, ohne Studium der empirisch gegebenen Vorstellungsinhalt, wie jede formale Logik ein Widersinn wird!" *Vgl. auch Leisching Y 3/23:* „Sie sehen, von welcher Bedeutung der Aristotelische Gattungs- und Speziesbegriff für die elementare Logik fort und fort wird, wie ohne ihn die wesentlichsten Unterscheidungen gar nicht zu machen sind, wie unermesslich die moderne Logik dadurch, dass dieser Unterschied verlorengegangen ist, hinter der antiken zurücksteht. Kant sagt einmal, die Logik seit Aristoteles keinen Fortschritt und keinen Rückschritt gemacht. Trendelenburg meint: Keinen Fortschritt, sondern nur Rückschritte. Ich glaube, Trendelenburg hat Unrecht. Ohne Studium des empirisch gegebenen Vorstellungsinhalts ist kein Fortschritt möglich."]
54 [*Es lässt sich nicht deutlich bestimmen, um welche Gattung es sich hier handelt.*]

unendlicher Entfernung schneiden. Hier ist also der Schneidungspunkt absolut unendlich entfernt. Cantor[55] ist auch in diesem Irrtum befangen. Er meint, es gebe Linien, die sich in gewisser Weise sich nähernd in der Unendlichkeit ein gewisses Verhältnis zueinander haben. Es gibt hingegen nur ein Wachsen in die Unendlichkeit, aber keine absolute Unendlichkeit ([Joseph-Louis] Lagrange). Nur bei Mengen und dem, was aus Mengen besteht, gibt es absolut unendliches Größes, aber eine unendliche kleine Menge gibt es auch hier nicht. Eine weitere Eigenheit ist auch, dass bei diesen Gattungen Kontinua möglich sind. Wenn in einer Gattung in allen rationalen und irrationalen Verhältnissen kleinere Abstände möglich sind, so sind auch Teilungen eines Abstandes in diesen Verhältnissen möglich. Zwischen zwei Spezies einer solchen Gattung ist also immer eine dritte möglich. Sie ist eine den Abstand vermittelnde Spezies. Solcher Spezies aber gibt es unendlich viele, und in jedem Abstandsverhältnis sind es möglich. Nehme ich nur einen Teil von ihnen als verwirklicht an, so bleiben Lücken. Nehmen wir dagegen an, sie seien alle verwirklicht, so wäre die Vermittlung eine lückenlose, eine vollkommene. Die Gesamtheit der Spezies zwischen den beiden vermittelnden Extremen wäre eine lückenlose und vollkommen vermittelnde Reihe. Aber das ist nicht der Begriff der Reihe im Sinn, der üblich ist. Man nennt auch solche Spezies einen Abstand vermittelnde, welche nur den beiden Elementen näher liegen als diese einander selbst.

Ja, selbst wenn sie ferner liegen, aber wenn sie nur einer Reihe angehören, von welchen je zwei aufeinander folgende Elemente einander näher liegen, als die beiden Extreme.

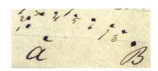

So wenn ich ein Rot habe und Schwarz. Hätte ich nur alle Nuancen von Rot und Weiß | und alle zwischen Weiß und Schwarz, so würden sie zusammen die voll-

---

55 [*Randbemerkung:*] Cf. Georg Cantor, *Grundlagen einer allgemeinen Mannigfaltiichkeitslehre* 1883 Teubner. [Cantor 1883a.] „Über unendliche lineare Pruntenmannigfaltigkeiten," *Mathematische Annalen*, Bd. XXI, p. 545 ff. [Cantor 1883, 545–586, auch in Cantor 1932, 165–204.]

kommene Vermittlung zwischen Rot und Schwarz bilden. Wo eine Lücke ist, da gibt es unter den vermittelnden Spezies zwei nächsten, für welche unendlich viele näherliegende angegeben werden könnte. Ich kann also die Reihe, ohne eine Spezies wegzulassen, in zwei Teile teilen, sodass keine Spezies beiden Teilen gemeinsam ist. Wenn dagegen in einer vermittelnden Reihe keine Lücke ist, so gibt es unter den vermittelnden Spezies nirgends zwei nächste Spezies (wenn auch nähere und fernere). Ich kann daher die Reihe nicht so in zwei Teile teilen, dass keine Spezies beiden Teilen gemeinsam ist. Vielmehr wird das Ende des einen Teils der Anfang des anderen Teils sein. Wo immer nun eine Reihe von vermittelnden Spezies diese Eigentümlichkeit hat, haben wir eine vollkommen vermittelnde Reihe vor uns. So ist die Reihe der Punkte in einem halben Kreis eine vollkommen vermittelnde Reihe. Es kann bei gewissen Gattungen mehrere solcher vermittelnden Reihen geben. Nur *eine* vermittelnde Reihe gibt es bei der Zeit, ebenso bei der Intensität. Mehrere aber sind möglich. Ja, sogar unzählige sind möglich, beim Ort, bei den Farben und wahrscheinlich bei allen solchen Qualitäten. Wo nur zwei solcher vermittelnden Reihen möglich sind, nennen wir sie zusammen eine geschlossene Reihe. Was wir hier erörtert haben, deckt sich nicht mehr mit dem Begriff des Kontinuums und der geschlossenen Figur.

[XIX. Vorlesung,
21 Januar 1885][56]

Unterschied zwischen der vollkommen vermittelnden Reihe und dem Kontinnum.
    Das ist leicht zu zeigen: Denken wir uns eine Ebene, welche farbig ist und über die hin die Farbe sich ändert von Rot bis Blau, ganz allmählich, dann von Blau bis Grün, dann bis Gelb, dann bis Rot. Würde man nun etwas Derartiges eine geschlossene Figur nennen? Nein. Dennoch eine geschlossene Farbenreihe. Es könnte einer sagen: mit dem Begriff der vollkommen vermittelnden Reihe ist er nicht dem Begriff des Kontinuums gleich? Nein. Es gibt vollkommen vermittelnde Reihen, die das nicht sind. | Es seien zwei Körper mit ebenen Oberflächen durch einen leeren Raum getrennt. Die eine Fläche des einen Körpers bildet kein Kontinuum mit einer Fläche des anderen. Nehmen wir nun an, eine Fläche enthalte alle Spezies von Rot bis zu einem gewissen Violett, die andere alle Spezies von Rot bis hin zu Blau. Bilden nun diese beiden farbigen Gegenständen ein Kontinuum? Nein. Aber doch ergänzen sie sich

---

56   [*Datum nach Leisching Y 3/28.*]

zu einer vollkommen vermittelnden Farbenreihe. Was ist nun aber ein Kontinuum? Man hat sich mehrfach um die Begriffsbestimmung bemüht, obwohl die Mathematiker es am wenigsten getan haben. Cantor (*Über die Grundlagen der allgemeinen Mannigfaltichkeitslehre*) gesteht dies ein. Er sagt: Man habe zwar unter Zugrundelegung einiger oder mehrerer kontiniuierlichen Größen den Begriff eines von ihnen ein- oder mehrdeutigen abhängigen Kontinuums ausgebildet. Aber das unabhängige Kontinuum ist von mathematischen Autoren nur in jener einfachsten Erscheinungsform vorausgesetzt und keiner eingehenden Betrachtung unterworfen worden. (Das Zitat ist nicht ganz genau.) Cantor sah sich nun bei Philosophen um, so bei Bolzano. Es könnte einer sagen: Wozu so viele Bemühungen? Genügt nicht der einfache Hinweis auf die Beispiele? So auf Zeit und Raum? Cantor lässt eine derartige Erklärung nicht als genügend gelten. Ja, er sagt, dass die Heranziehung an der Zeitanschauung bei der Erörterung des viel ursprünglicheren Begriffs des Kontinuums nicht in der Ordnung sei. Ebenso soll man mit der Anschauungsform des Raumes nichts anfangen können, da auch diese nur mit Hilfe eines bereits fertigen Kontinuums jenen Gehalt erlange, mit Hilfe dessen sie Gegenstand mathematischer Untersuchung werden können. In dieser Bemerkung Cantors ist Wahres und Falsches. Allgemeiner ist der Begriff des | Kontinuums als der des Raums und der Zeit. Ob aber deshalb der Begriff des Kontinuums ursprünglicher sei, ist eine andere Frage. Dass ferner der Raum seinen Gehalt erst durch den fertigen Begriff des Kontinuums erhalten könne, ist nicht richtig. Ob ferner deshalb, weil Raum und Zeit weniger allgemein sind, die Heranziehung von Raum und Zeit nicht in der Ordnung sei, ist auch noch sehr die Frage. Indessen ist es in unserem Fall so: der Begriff des Kontinuums ist kompliziert und fordert zu einer Analyse auf, und wir müssen uns dabei hüten, spezielle Eigentümlichkeiten gewisser Kontinua für allgemeine Eigentümlichkeiten zu halten. Deshalb werden wir aber doch auf diese Kontinua Rücksicht nehmen, wie es der Geometer tut in Bezug auf eine speziell gezeichnete Figur.

Unterschied zwischen der vollkommen vermittelnde Reihe und dem Kontinuum.

Hören wir nun die Begriffsbestimmung Bolzanos:

> Versuchen wir nämlich, uns den Begriff, den wir mit den Benennungen „eine stetige Ausdehnung oder ein Kontinuum" bezeichnen, zu einem deutlichen Bewusstsein zu bringen: so können wir nicht umhin zu erklären, dort, aber auch nur dort sei ein Kontinuum vorhanden, wo sich ein Inbegriff von einfachen Gegenständen (von Punkten in der Zeit oder im Raume oder auch von Substanzen) befindet, die so gelegen sind, dass jeder einzelne derselben für jede auch noch so kleine Entfernung wenigs-

tens einen Nachbar in diesem Inbegriff habe. Wenn dieses nicht der Fall ist, wenn sich z. B. unter einem gegebenen Inbegriffe von Punkten im Raume auch nur ein einziger befindet, der nicht so dicht umgeben ist von Nachbarn, dass sich für jede – nur klein genug genommene Entfernung ein Nachbar für ihn nachweisen lässt: so sagen wir, dass dieser Punkt *vereinzelt* (isoliert) dastehe, und dass jener Inbegriff eben deshalb kein vollkommenes Kontinuum darbiete. Gibt es dagegen nicht einen einzigen in diesem Sinne isoliert stehenden Punkt in einem vorliegenden Inbegriffe von Punkten, hat also jeder derselben für jede auch noch so kleine Entfernung wenigstens einen Nachbar: so erübrigt nichts mehr, was uns berechtigen könnte, diesem Inbegriffe die Benennung des Kontinuums abzusprechen.[57]

Cantor ist mit dieser Erklärung nicht zufrieden und bestimmt das Kontinuum also: „ein Kontinuum ist eine perfekt zusammenhängende Punktmenge." Dabei verallgemeinert er den Begriff des Punktes vom Räumlichen oder Zeitlichen zum „rein arithmetischen Punkt," ein Punkt eines | n-dimensionalen arithmetischen Raumes.

Ist eine von diesen Definitionen richtig? Die von Bolzano ist gewiss unrichtig. Sie ist zu weit. Denn auch in den Punkten von zwei getrennten Kontinuis ist bereits etwas gegeben, was nach Bolzano ein Kontinuum sein würde. Zudem, meint Cantor, gelte dasselbe auch von der Gesamtheit der möglichen Halbierungspunkte einer Linie. Diese Punkte liegen sich so nahe, dass man immer noch Halbierung dazu findet. Da aber der Drittelungspunkt nicht dazu gehört, so sind immer Lücken dazu. Was nun Cantor hier sagt, ist nicht richtig, wie bereits früher besprochen wurde. Man müsste ja dann den ersten und letzten Punkt wegnehmen können, dann aber hätte sie keinen Anfang und kein Ende, ohne unendlich zu sein. Cantor will das dann ein Semikontinuum nennen. Cantor begegnet sich hier mit den Scholastikern, so mit Suarez.[58] Was ist nun darüber zu halten? Die Lehre ist unrichtig. Man kann die Linie nicht festhalten, wenn man einen Punkt wegdenkt. Dagegen wäre es wohl möglich, den Punkt zu behalten, während die Linie wegfällt. Denken wir einen Verbindungspunkt zweier Linien. Er bleibt, wenn der erste Teil wegfällt, aber auch wenn der zweite wegfällt. Der Punkt besteht in der Linie nur als Grenze. Beim Raum mag es sogar geschehen, dass ein Punkt als Grenze von unendlich vielen Linien besteht. Es könnte noch einer sagen: Ist dann der Punkt abtrennbar?

---

57 Bolzano, *Paradoxien des Unendlichen* (Leipzig 1851), § 38, pp. 73–74.
58 Cf. Suarez, *Disputationes Metaphysicae* XL, sect. v, art. 41.

Die Gegenwart ist doch nur ein Zeitpunkt und dennoch ist sie abgetrennt, da sie weder zur Vergangenheit noch zur Zukunft gehört. Oder weiter könnte einer sagen: Denken wir zwei parallele Geraden und eine dritte schneidende.

Denken wir nun von a eine unendliche Linie schneidend. Dreht sich dieselbe nun, so schneidet sie die Parallelen immer in anderen Punkten, und schließlich fällt sie mit einer der parallelen Linien zusammen und schneidet die anderen nicht mehr. Nun entsprechen allen Richtungen | gewisse Punkte, nur der letzte nicht. Also hätten wir ein Kontinuum ohne Ende. Darauf ist zu antworten: Es kann nicht zugegeben werden, dass von dieser äußersten Grenze das Übrige abgelöst wäre. Stellt jemand die *ganze* Vergangenheit vor, so muss er die Gegenwart mitvorstellen. Man nimmt oft das Gewesene als nichtexistierend, aber das ist unrichtig. Wenn ich ferner im zweiten Fall alle Richtungen des Strahls[?] bis zur Parallelität nehme, alle in ihrer Gesamtheit, so kann ich nicht die letzte Stellung nicht wegdenken. Der letzte Vorwurf Cantors gegen Bolzano ist also unrichtig. Aber ein anderer Vorwurf könnte gemacht werden. Die Definition ist nämlich nach einer gewissen Seite zu eng. Wenn Bolzano sagt, es handle sich um einfache Gegenstände, soll das heißen: um Gegenstände, die keine Vielheit von Teilen haben? Dann ist kein Farbenpunkt ein einfacher Gegenstand. Er hat metaphysische und logische Teile. Meint nun Bolzano unausgedehnte Gegenstände, dann ist es seltsam die Ausdehnung zu definieren durch den Begriff des Unausgedehnten. Auch könnte man entgegnen: Wenn man es so[59] fasst, dann ist die Definition Bolzanos vielleicht nicht mehr zu eng, aber in besonderer Weise zu weit. Selbst die Reihenfolge der ganzen Zahlen wäre dann ein Kontinuum. In der Zahlenreihe gibt es eine kleinstmögliche Entfernung, nämlich die Einheit.

Ist aber die Begriffsbestimmung Cantors die richtige? Nein. Denn das, was er sagt, ist nicht mehr als das, was wir mit früher erklärten Worten bezeichnen würden als eine Menge, in welcher zwei Abstände durch Reihen vollkommen vermittelt wären. Diese Bestimmung aber deckt sich nicht mit dem Begriff

---

59 [es so *statt* so es *im Ms.*]

des Kontinuums. Diesem Fehler unterliegt aber auch die Definition Bolzanos. Die Definition Cantors trifft wesentlich mit unserer „vollkommen vermittelten Reihe" zusammen.

[XX. Vorlesung, d. 24. Januar 85][60]

58 Was ist denn die wahre Bestimmung des Begriffs des Kontinuums? | Wo ein Kontinuum ist, da haben wir immer vollkommen vermittelte spezifische Abstände. Stellen wir nun Beispiele von solchen, welche zu den Kontinuis gerechnet werden, und solche, die nicht dazu gerechnet werden, gegenüber, so wird die Eigentümlichkeit der ersteren klar werden. Eine farbige Ebene, die mit einer roten Linie beginnt, und mit einer gelben schließt, und dazu alle möglichen Nuancen von Orange durchläuft, ist ein Farbenkontinuum. Dagegen sind zwei durch einen leeren Raum getrennte Ebenen, von denen die eine von Rot bis Orange variiert, die andere mit dieser letzteren beginnt und zu Gelb führt, allerdings eine vollkommen vermittelte Farbenreihe, aber kein Kontinuum. Oder: eine zeitliche Sukzession der Farben, wenn sich eine Stelle aus einer roten in eine gelbe verwandelt. Hier haben wir ein Kontinuum von Farben oder, besser gesagt, Quasifarben. Dagegen wäre kein Kontinuum von Farben gegeben,[61] wenn, nachdem eine Fläche von Rot bis zu einer Nuance von Orange variiert hätte und dann aufhörte zu variieren, aber von da eine andere Nuance beginnen und zu Gelb führen würde. Wo liegt also der Unterschied zwischen dem Kontinuum und derselben zwischen denselben Abständen vollkommen vermittelnden Reihe von Spezies? Es ist klar, dass die Vermittlung eine verschiedene ist hier und dort, insofern bei der vollkommen vermittelnden Reihe, die ein Kontinuum ist, jedes vermittelnde Glied, das das Ende des einen Teiles an den Anfang des anderen Teiles der Reihe bindet, nicht bloß spezifisch gleich, sondern individuell dasselbe ist. Wo das Ende des einen Teiles dem Anfang des anderen nur spezifisch gleich ist, aber nicht individuell, da ist die Kontinuität gar nicht da. *Ein*[62] *Kontinuum ist eine unendliche Menge von Individuen,*
59 *die, der | untersten Gattung oder Quasigattung nach übereinstimmend, spezifische Unterschiede zeigen, aber so, dass in ihr jeder spezifische Abstand eines Individuums vom anderen vollkommen und mit individueller Einheit der Bindeglieder*

---

60   [*Datum nach Leisching Y 3/37.*]
61   [*Randbemerkung, Verweis auf einen unbekannten Text:*] Kein Farben- oder kein Raumkontinuum? Vergleich meine „Einwände gegen Brentano."
62   [*Von hier bis Ende des Satzes ist der Text mit Rotstift unterstrichen.*]

vermittelt wird.[63] Ob durch eine vollkommen vermittelte Reihe [von Farben] ein Kontinuum hingestellt wird, zeigen die anderen metaphysischen Teile, also Ort, Intensität etc. Bei einem Ortskontinuum also sind die Qualität und Intensität entscheidend; sind diese anderen metaphysischen Teile für je zwei einander folgende Teilmengen der Reihe sämtlich spezifisch gleich oder in ihren Abständen durch die Zwischenglieder ebenfalls vollkommen vermittelt, so ist die Reihe ein Kontinuum. Beispiel: ein Farbenkontinuum, von Rot bis Gelb; es könnte nun sein, dass die Intensität für dieses Hauptkontinuum die gleiche ist. Es könnte aber sein, dass die Intensität variiert. Auch dann wäre es ein Qualitätskontinuum. Oder [gibt es] eine Stelle, die zuerst rot erscheint und sich allmählich in Gelb verwandelt, aber so, dass die Intensität dieselbe bleibt, so haben wir ein Kontinuum von Quasifarben, aber auch wenn die Intensität wechselt. Dagegen wird das Kontinuum nicht mehr gegeben sein, wenn irgendwo ein unvermittelter Ortsabstand hin[zu]gedacht wird, oder ein unvermittelter Zeitabstand, oder ein unvermittelter Intensitätsabstand. Allerdings ist es zweifelhaft, ob nicht mancher etwas für ein Kontinuum halten würde, was wir nicht für ein solches halten. So wenn ich eine blaue und eine rote Fläche haben, die aneinander stoßen. Da könnte einer behaupten, es sei wenigstens ein Raumkontinuum, wenn auch kein Farbenkontinuum. Der Fehler liegt hier darin, dass der Betreffende glaubt, die Grenze zwischen den zwei Ebenen sei ein und dieselbe, während sie doch verschieden ist. Wir haben hier nicht eine Grenze, sondern zwei Grenzen, die nur miteinander koinzidieren. | Wir können das so beweisen: Eine Qualität ist nicht möglich, die nicht örtlich bestimmt wäre. Wir haben nun hier eine räumliche Linie, diese bestimmt nur als eine Bestimmtheit von dem Rot und dem Blau. Kann sie nun zugleich die Bestimmtheit von Rot und Blau sein, also individuell dasselbe sein? Nein. Man hat es hier vielmehr mit einer blauen Grenze zu tun, die blau ist als Grenze des Blau, und mit einer roten, die nur rot ist als Grenze des Rot. Es sind also zwei individuelle Elemente, die nur koinzidieren.[64] Was hier irreführt, das ist eine Eigentümlichkeit, nämlich die Undurchdringlichkeit von Qualitäten gleicher Gattung im Raum. Es kann nicht ein Raum mit Gelb und Blau erfüllt sein. Verschiedene Räume können zwar in derselben Fläche erscheinen, aber es können nicht viele Farben mit derselben räumlichen Bestimmtheit in einer gewissen Ausdehnung erscheinen. Farben, die einen spezifisch gleichen Ort erfüllen, erscheinen immer individuell einheitlich, und der Raum selbst ist individuell einheitlich. Aber dies gilt nicht für die örtlichen Grenzen, die für sich nichts sind, sondern

---

63 [*Randbemerkung mit Rotstift:*] Brentanos Definition des Kontinuums.
64 [*Randtitel mit Rotstift:*] Grenze zweier Flächen von verschiedener Qualität.

alles nur im Zusammenhang mit dem Begrenzten. Indem etwas von verschiedenen Richtungen her eine gewisse Ortsspezies als Grenze erreichen kann, kann auch spezifisch Verschiedenes zugleich diese Ortsgrenze erreichen, also von der einen Seite *eine* Farbe, von der anderen eine andere. Und dann wird die Grenze im Zusammenhang mit beiden Flächen[65] an beiden Spezies partizipieren. Dann aber haben wir individuell zwei örtliche Bestimmtheiten. So ist dann z. B. die der Farbe nach geschiedene blaue und gelbe Linie, die eine blaue und gelbe Ebene voneinander scheidet, ebenso wenig eine individuelle Linie als die dem Orte nach unterschiedene Nuance von Orange im früheren Beispiel von den | wechselnden Farben. Wo vier Quadraten, rot, grün, schwarz und weiß, zusammenstoßen, da haben wir nicht einen individuellen Mittelpunkt, sondern vier individuelle Punkte. Es könnten auch noch mehr solche Punkte koinzidieren, ja unendlich viele. Denken wir uns einen Kreis, sodass ein gewisser Radius in seiner Drehung die Variationen von Rot und Blau anzeigt, wo derselbe wieder in seine alte Lage zurückgeht, hätten wir zwei individuell verschiedene Linien. Im Mittelpunkt des Kreises aber hätten wir dann alle Stufen von Farben, also unendlich viele. Das Paradoxon Galileis gehört hierher. Er sagt: Der Mittelpunkt ist so groß wie der ganze Kreis. Wenn man da, wo eine gleiche Vielheit von Punkten gegeben ist, eine gleiche Größe statuiert, dann hat Galileo Recht.

Der richtige Ausdruck für unsere Beispiele von der roten und blauen Fläche ist nicht der, dass sie „zusammenhängen," sondern dass sie „aneinander stoßen," „aneinander rühren," „aneinander grenzen," nicht aber „zusammenhängen." Die Physiker scheiden Kohäsion und Adhäsion. Von der ersten sprechen sie, wenn eine spezifische Gleichheit herrscht. Wenn aber nicht, dann sprechen sie von Adhäsion. Sie denken dabei wenigstens an etwas wie wir selbst. In einem Fall ist eine individuelle Grenze [da], im anderen aber zwei solche. (Die Ähnlichkeit ist übrigens nur eine ganz rohe.) Man sollte den Ausdruck „anstoßen" verallgemeinern, und dann könnten wir sagen, dass, wenn wir eine Farbenfläche haben, die von Rot bis Orange variiert, dann eine, die von Orange bis Gelb wechselt,[66] sie aneinander stoßen, nicht räumlich, sondern der Farbe nach.

---

65 [*nach* mit beiden Flächen *irrtümlich geschrieben* wird die Grenze]
66 [*nach* bis Gelb wechselt, *irrtümlich im Ms.* sagen, dass]

[XXI. Vorlesung,
28 Januar 85][67]

Wir sagen, dass der Begriff des Kontinuums ein relativer Begriff ist, da er auf gewisse Relationen der Gleichheit und Verschiedenheit ruht. Dabei gehört er doch selbst ins Gebiet der Relationen der Verbindung physischer Teile (Teil mit Teil und Teil mit dem Ganzen). Jedes Kontinuum gehört entweder zu einem physischen Ganzen oder es ist selbst eines. Die sämtlichen zusammenhängenden, nicht mehr bloß zusammenstoßenden | Kontinua bilden ja immer ein Kontinuum. Die Vereinigung einer unendlichen Menge in einem solchen physischen Ganzen ist ohne Zweifel eine ganz andere und viel innigere als die gewisser Elemente zu einem kollektiven Ganzen. Die bloß kollektive Menge hat keine Einigung der Teile außer der, welche in der Übereinstimmung der Glieder in dem, was die Einheit bildet, gegeben ist. [Ich habe sechs Äpfel. Jeder ist ein Apfel.][68] Beim physischen Ganzen hingegen besteht eine Zusammengehörigkeit, die von der Art ist, dass jedes Individuum einer Spezies, das als Element darin enthalten ist, nichts für sich ist, und alles, was es ist, nur in Zusammenhang mit anderen ist. (So ist ein Punkt nichts für sich, sondern was er ist, ist er nur im Zusammenhang mit allen anderen Punkten.) Gar nicht allein von elementaren Bestandteilen gilt das, [sondern] auch von Kontinuis, die zu einem physischen Ganzen gehören. *Alles, was in dieser Weise nur im Zusammenhang mit einem Kontinuum etwas ist und sein kann, das nennen wir Grenze.* So sind Punkt, Linie, Fläche Grenzen. Bei dieser Abhängigkeit der Grenzen vom Begrenzten besteht aber oft eine relative Unabhängigkeit. So ist es bei jeder vermittelnden Grenze. Für sie gibt es einen mehrfachen Zusammenhang. Wo das eine Begrenzte aufgehoben, so bleibt sie in ihrem Zusammenhang mit dem anderen bestehen. Anderes gilt natürlich von einer *letzten Grenze*, wie vom ersten Zeitpunkt, wo etwas zu sein beginnt. Hier besteht nur ein einziger Zusammenhang. Würde dieser weggenommen, so würde der Punkt nicht bestehen bleiben können. Die Abhängigkeit der Grenze vom Begrenzten dürfen wir nicht auffassen als eine Teilnahme an der spezifischen Natur der anderen Grenzen, die mit zu einem Kontinuum gehören. Im Gegenteil hat sie mit der zunächst mit ihr verbundenen Grenze keine spezifische Gemeinsamkeit. Eine Grenze, die von einer Spezies ist (so eine rote Linie), begrenzt nicht spezifisch Verschiedenes und hat an keiner der Spezies des Begrenzten teil. Das Begrenzte

---

67 [*Datum nach Leisching Y 3/41.*]
68 [*Das Textstück in eckigen Klammern ist ein Beispiel der Übereinstimmung, die die Einheit eines kollektiven Ganzen bildet, aus Leisching Y 3/43.*]

selbst partizipiert an der Natur der Grenzen. Es besteht also die innigste Verwandtschaft, welche mit Ausschluss der Gleichheit möglich ist. | Ist die Grenze ein Kontinuum, so besteht sie selbst aus Grenzen. (So besteht eine Linie, die in Bezug auf eine Fläche eine Grenze ist, selbst aus Grenzen.) Und in letzter Instanz besteht jedes Kontinuum aus Grenzen, die selbst keine Kontinua sind. Es sind demnach die ersten Elemente eines Kontinuums nicht selbst Kontinua. Es klingt nun sehr paradox zu sagen, ein Kontinuum bestehe aus lauter Nichtkontinua, ein Ausgedehntes aus Unausgedehnten. Aber die Folgerung sei falsch, dass dasselbe Etwas aus Nichts bestehen muss. Vielmehr besteht es aus nichts Ausgedehntem, aber nicht aus Nichts. So setzt sich jede Zahl zusammen aus kleineren Zahlen und schließlich aus Einheiten. Es setzt sich also auch hier aus Nichtvielheiten die Vielheit zusammen.

Widerlegung[69] *des Einwandes, dass das Ausgedehnte aus Nichts bestände analog mit der Zahl.*

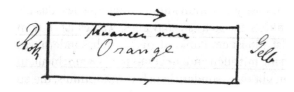

Denken wir uns hier einen kontinuierlichen Übergang von Rot durch alle Nuancen von Orange bis zu Gelb, so setzt sich diese Fläche aus lauter Farbenlinien zusammen. Diese sind in der Richtung des Übergangs allerdings nicht ausgedehnt, aber sie sind dennoch keineswegs Nichts. Diese nichtausgedehnten Grenzen sind in gewissem Sinn die letzten physischen Teile des Kontinuums. Dieses besteht demnach aus einer Vielheit nichtausgedehnter Grenzen. Eine solche Grenze nennen wir nun, das Wort im weitesten Sinn genommen, Punkt (Zeitpunkt, Raumpunkt, Farbenpunkt, Intensitätspunkt etc. etc.).

Bis jetzt sprachen wir nur immer von solchen Teilen des Kontinuums, welche Grenzen sind. Es gibt aber auch andere Teile, und an diese denkt man gewöhnlich, wenn man von physischen Teilen spricht, weil diese Teile von der Art sind, dass[70] sie ohne Widersprüche von allen übrigen Teilen des Kontinuums abgelöst werden können und dennoch das für sich sein würden, was sie im Zusammenhang mit den anderen waren. Von ihnen fügt sich einer an den anderen | als nächster Teil an, was bei zwei Grenzen in einem Kontinuum nicht

---

69 [*Dieser Satz ist als Randtitel mit Bleistift geschrieben.*]
70 [von der Art sind, dass *statt* von der Art sind, weil *im Ms.*]

der Fall ist. Selbst wenn Farbenpunkte räumlich koinzidieren, stehen sie voneinander ab und stehen entweder in keinem oder nur in einem mittelbaren physischen Zusammenhang. So wenn wir C uns rot denken und in seiner Bewegung alle möglichen Farbennuancen durchlaufen, haben wir im Zentrum eine räumliche Koinzidenz aller Farben. Aber spezifisch stehen sie voneinander ab.

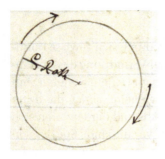

Beispiele für ablösbare Teile: *eine* Stunde. Die Hälfte eines Körpers ist das für sich, was sie vorher im Zusammenhang mit der anderen Hälfte gewesen war. Wenn nun jeder solche physische Teil ablösbar ist und dann für sich sein würde, was er im Zusammenhang mit dem Kontinuum war, wäre es dann nicht möglich ein solches Kontinuum in unendlich viele Kontinua aufzulösen? Nein. Warum nicht? Nur deshalb, weil es keinen unendlich kleinen Abstand gibt. Aus diesem Grunde sind auch unendlich viele abrupte Übergänge ohne Aufhebung der Kontinuität unmöglich. So wäre ein abrupter Übergang ein wirklicher.

Zeno argumentierte in der bekannten Weise gegen die Bewegung.

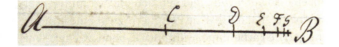

Ein Endpunkt, meinte er, könne nicht von A nach B gelangen, denn er müsste zuerst zu einem Halbierungspunkt C gelangen, dann aber nach D, E, F, G, etc. Er müsste also unendlich viele Punkte erreichen als den Punkt B, was auch unendlich viel Zeit beanspruchen würde. | Immer käme er in die Hälfte, nie an das Ziel. Darauf ist zu antworten:[71]

[Der ganze Grund, warum es unmöglich ist, [ans Ziel zu kommen,] liegt darin, weil ein unendlich kleiner Abstand unmöglich ist. Aristoteles sagt ganz

---

71 [*Im Ms. fehlt die Antwort auf Zeno.*]

richtig: Ein *infinitum* [*in*] *actu* sei unmöglich, aber ein *infinitum in potentia* sei möglich. *In potentia* sind unendlich viele Teile in einem Ganzen, aber [*in*] *actu* können sie nicht werden.]⁷²

[XXII. Vorlesung,
d. 31. Januar 85]⁷³

Es erübrigt nun nur noch das speziell darzulegen, wodurch sich gewisse Kontinua von anderen unterscheiden. Wir haben von einer Vermittlung des Abstandes zweier Spezies durch eine dritte in einem engeren und einem weiteren Sinn gesprochen. War die Vermittlung im engeren Sinn gemeint, so lag die dritte Spezies so zwischen den beiden anderen, dass der Abstand der letzteren sich zusammensetzte aus den beiden Abständen, die die vermittelnde Spezies von jedem der beiden Extreme hätte. Bei der Vermittlung im weiteren Sinn dürfte auch ein Umweg gemacht werden. Dieser Unterschied besteht nun auch bei Kontinuis, so bei einer geraden und ungeraden Linie: aber nicht allein bei Ortskontinuis, auch bei Qualitätskontinuis, so bei Farben oder bei Intensitätskontinuis. Auch hier kann die Vermittlung der beiden Extreme eine Vermittlung im engeren und im weiteren Sinn sein. Denken wir uns einen Kreis: Der sich drehende Radius gehe von Rot aus und mache alle Nuancen von Violett durch bis Blau. Denken wir uns dann einen anderen Kreis, dessen Radius mit Rot begänne und über Blau, Grün und Gelb wieder zu Rot zurückkehrte. Beim ersten Kreis haben wir im Mittelpunkt alle Farben von Rot bis Blau. Beim zweiten aber ist die Folge keine Gerade, weil schon der Umstand zeigt, dass wir wieder nach Rot zurückkehren. Wir könnten nun, wie wir von einer geraden und krummen Raumlinie sprechen, ebenso auch von einer geraden und krummen | Farbenlinie sprechen. So wäre beim ersten Kreis die Peripherie zwar eine krumme Raumlinie, aber doch eine gerade Farbenlinie, während sie beim zweiten Kreis auch eine krumme Farbenlinie wäre. Um jedoch Missverständnisse zu vermeiden, die durch die Anwendung des Ausdrucks „Linie" in nichträumlichem Sinn leicht entstehen könnten, wollen wir uns lieber eines Ausdrucks bedienen, den Pseudo-Aristoteles (*On the Universe*) und Theophrast angewendet haben, nämlich Grammoid oder Grammode und demnach von einem geraden Grammoid (Ortoid) und einem krummen Grammoid sprechen. So ist jede kontinuierliche Zeitreihe oder Intensitätsreihe ein gerades Grammoid.

---

72 [*Text in eckingen Klammern nach Leisching Y 3/50.*]
73 [*Datum nach Leisching Y 3/51.*]

Nehmen wir nun ein Zeitkontinuum zwischen zwei Zeitpunkten. Dieses erscheint als eine Größe, und zwar nicht bloß als eine unendliche Größe, sondern auch als endlich, insofern es einen endlichen Abstand füllt, da [es] aus gleichen Abständen sich zusammensetzt, so z. B. aus zwei halben.[74] In diesem Sinn ist das ganze Zeitkontinuum doppelt so groß als jeder Teil, während das im ersten Sinn (in Bezug auf die Menge der Punkte) nicht gesagt werden kann. Auch das ungerade Grammoid ist eine solche Größe und kann in dem Sinn, dass es einen gewissen Abstand erfüllt, mit einem geraden verglichen werden, wenn beide derselben untersten Gattung angehören. So ist die krumme Linie einer geraden gleich, die einen Abstand erfüllt, dem sich die krumme Linie durch Zerlegung in unendliche Teile ins Unendliche annähert. Ein Grammoid ist eine unendliche Menge von keiner Dimension und eine unendliche Größe von *einer* Dimension. Außer von Größe des Abstandes, in Bezug auf welche auch das vermittelnde Grammoid groß genannt werden kann, ist auch von einer Richtung des Abstandes zu sprechen. Der Abstand von A nach B ist in Bezug auf seine Richtung dem Abstand von B nach A entgegengesetzt. Die Abstände der Punkte eines geraden Grammoids (Ortoids) von A aus hat dieselbe Richtung, | die von B dagegen alle die entgegengesetzte Richtungen. Bei einem ungeraden Grammoid ist dies nicht durchwegs der Fall. (Selbstverständlich ist auch hier der Begriff „Richtung" vom Raum hingenommen und verallgemeinert.) Der Begriff der Richtung wird von Abständen auf das Grammoid, das Abstände vermittelt, übertragen oder ihm adaptiert. So sagen wir: Im geraden Grammoid haben alle Teile dieselbe Richtung, im ungeraden nicht (immer in Bezug auf ein und denselben Endpunkt). Auch sagen wir: Das ungerade Grammoid ändert seine Richtung. Diese Änderung kann innerhalb eines endlichen Grammoids endlich oft oder unendlich oft und überall vorkommen. Im ersten Fall ist diese Änderung eine plötzliche, abrupte. Eine solche unvermittelte, abrupte Änderung kann nie unendlich oft eintreten. Sie muss endlich sein. Ist die Änderung jedoch eine allmähliche und dann unendlich oft vorkommende, so haben wir es mit einem krümmen Grammoid zu tun. Krümmung ist nichts anderes als ein Kontinuum von Richtungen. Wenn ich zwei Punkte habe und sie mit Festhaltung der gleichen Entfernung verschiebe, so wechselt beständig die Richtung des Abstandes. Nehmen wir drei spezifisch verschiedene Punkte, die nicht in gleicher oder entgegengesetzter Richtung von einander abstehen und vermitteln die Abstände durch gerade Grammoide, so bekommen wir ein geschlossenes Grammoid. Denken wir nun die Gesamtheit der möglichen Punkte zwischen den Punkten dieses geschlossenen Grammoi-

---

74 [*Frage mit Bleistift am Rand:*] Was heißt Abstand?

des vermittelt, so haben wir eine von drei Grammoiden begrenzte geschlossene Ebene (im weitesten Sinn) ein sogenanntes begrenztes Planoid. Ein solches Planoid ist mit einem Grammoid nicht verglichen, nicht weil es Punkte von niederer Gattung enthielte, sondern weil die es erfüllenden Abstände nicht Abstände von Punkten, sondern Abstände von kontinuierlichen Punktereihen sind. Es ist eine kontinuierliche Reihe von Grammoiden. So haben wir ein Kontinuum von zwei Dimensionen. | In jedem Punkt innerhalb eines Planoides können Grammoide so einander schneiden, dass das scheinende Grammoid genau die mittlere Richtung hat zwischen den entgegengesetzten Teilen des geschnittenen Grammoids. Es ist nun der Fall denkbar, dass beide noch durch ein drittes Grammoid ebenso geschnitten werden, welches aber dann nicht zu demselben Planoid gehört; geschieht dies und verbindet man die Endpunkte dieser drei Grammoide durch andere Grammoide und die letzteren durch Planoide, verwirklicht man ferner alle zwischen den Planoiden möglichen Punkte, so kommt man zu einer dreidimensionalen Größe, welche durch andere geschlossene zweidimensionale Kontinua in kleinere dreidimensionale Kontinua zerlegt werden kann. Ein solches dreidimensionales Kontinuum ist z. B. eine geometrische Figur von drei Dimensionen oder auch der sogenannte Farbenkörper.[75] Wir können nun durchaus nicht leugnen, dass außerhalb unserer Erfahrung Kontinua möglich seien, für welche dreidimensionale Kontinua nur die Grenzen sind. Solche Kontinua wären dann vierdimensional. Ebenso sind 5, 6, 7, 8 etc.-dimenionsionale Kontinua von vornherein weder widersinning noch unmöglich. Nur soll man sich hüten, von einem mehre als dreidimensionalen *Raum* zu sprechen. Was ins Bereich unserer Vorstellungen fällt, zeigt überall höchstens drei Dimensionen und ist auch einer vierten Dimension nicht fähig. Ein Ortskontinuum hat nicht mehr als drei, ein Zeitkontinuum nicht mehr als *eine* Dimension. Diese können sich durchaus nicht zu vier Dimensionen zusammensetzen, da beide zu ganz verschiedenen Gattungen gehören. Wäre es doch leichter von einer Zeitdimension zu sagen, sie stünde auf einer Raumlinie. (Unpassend sind auch die Ausführungen Wundts in seiner *Physiologischen Psychologie.*) | (Wenn Fechner die Zeit als vierte Dimension einführt, so tut er es wohl nur scherzhaft als Dr. Mises.)

Auch die Begriffe des Winkels und der Gestalt sind nun auch leicht begrifflich zu machen. Es steht nichts im Wege auch sie zu verallgemeinern. Die Gestalt eines geschlossenen Gebildes ist der Gestalt eines anderen gleich, wenn die Abstände der Grenzen proportional sind (die Grenzen in demselben Rich-

---

75 [*Randbemerkung mit Rotstift:*] Vergleich Lotze, *Metaphysik,* Kapitel über „Deduktuion des Raumes."

tungsverhältnis genommen), wenn also die Größenverhältnisse der Abstände der Grenzpunkte in demselben Richtungsverhältnis einander gleich sind. Man hat es also bei der Gestalt mit Verhältnissen von Verhältnissen zu tun, ein Umstand, der es sogar erlauben dürfte (bei verallgemeinerten Begriffen von „Gestalt"), von der Gleichheit von Gestalt in ganz heterogenem Sinn zu sprechen. Denn man kann zwar nicht von gleichen Bestimmungen auf heterogenen Gebieten sprechen, aber doch von gleichen Verhältnissen solcher Bestimmungen. So könnten wir einen Intensitätswinkel einem Winkel im Raum gleichststellen. (Aristoteles hat gemeint, dass nicht bloß Ausdehnung, sondern auch Gestalt eine Art letzten, absoluten Elementes unserer sinnlichen Phänomene sei.)

[XXIII. Vorlesung,
d. 4. Februar 85][76]

Wir wollen nun heute von Verhältnissen sprechen, die aus den Beziehungen der Kontinua zu ihren metaphysischen Teilen entstehen. Von der unendlichen Menge von Spezies, die jedes Kontinuum enthält, ist jede in jedem Punkt durch die Spezies metaphysischer Teile individualisiert.

Das kann nur in dreifacher Weise geschehen. 1. Ein gewisser metaphysischer Teil kann für alle Punkte eines Kontinuums spezifisch gleich sein. 2. Er kann durchgängig ein Kontinuum sein. 3. Teils das eine, teils das andere kann der Fall sein. Ein 4. Fall ist undenkbar.

Beispiele:

1. Fall: Eine rote einheitliche Fläche ist ein Beispiel der ersten Klasse. Die Fläche ist ein Kontinuum im Raum. Mit örtlicher Bestimmtheit ist aber Rot gegeben und durchgängig gegeben als zweiter metaphysischer Teil. [70a] Oder: eine gleichmäßig intensive Fläche. Oder: eine in einem bestimmten Zeitpunkt gewisse einheitliche Fläche; die zeitliche Bestimmtheit ist für die ganze Fläche gleich. Oder: Ein eine Stunde lange dauernder einheitlicher örtlicher Punkt; hier haben wir ein Zeitkontinuum. Die Quasispezies des Orts aber ist dieselbe. Die Farbenräume im Mittelpunkt des Kreises (Paradox des Galileo), wo die örtliche Bestimmtheit spezifisch gleich ist.

2. Beispiel: Eine farbige Fläche. Hier haben wir ein Farben- und ein Ortskontinuum.

---

76 [*Datum nach Leisching Y 3/59.*]

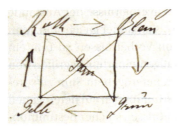

Oder: eine der Intensität nach in der Zeit kontinuierlich wechselnde kontinuierliche Einheit, so ein Punkt, der immer intensiver leuchtet.

3. Farbige Linie von folgender Beschaffenheit.

Diese Linie geht von Rot nach Blau, bleibt aber dann blau. Oder ein Quadrat wie [das folgende]:

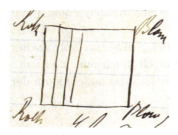

Horizontal besteht Kontinuität im Farbenwechsel; vertikal aber vollkommene Gleichheit; daneben ist es aber auch Ortskontinuum.

Betrachten wir den ersten der drei Fälle noch einmal: Das Ganze ist hier nur einem metaphysischem Teil nach ein Kontinuum. Die übrigen Teile werden nur uneigentlich so genannt. Eine vollkommen rote Fläche ist kein Farbenkontinuum. Nur als Raum betrachtet ist die Fläche Kontinuum. Die Farbe ist nur Kontinnuum *per accidens*, der Raum aber Kontinuum *per se*. Im zweiten Fall aber haben wir ein Doppelkontinuum *per se*. Im dritten Fall endlich hat man etwas, was zwischen einem Doppelkontinuum *per se* [70b] und einem Kontinuum *per accidens* in der Mitte steht. Es ist eine Art unvollkommenes Doppelkontinuum *per se*. Es gibt auch Doppelkontinua *per accidens*. Ein Doppelkontinuum *per se* ist ein bewegter Punkt (Änderung des Orts und der Zeit). Ein Doppelkontinuum *per accidens* ist ein ruhender Körper. Er ist ein Kontinuum im Raum und in der Zeit. Es ist mit ihm als einem ganzen Körper eine gewisse und zwar immer dieselbe zeitliche Bestimmung verbunden. Mit jedem Zeitmoment ist der ganze Körper verbunden. Ein geradlinnig bewegter Körper ohne Drehung wäre ein vollkommenes Doppelkontinuum *per se*. Auch das ist ein merkwürdiger Fall. Denken wir eine um ihr Zentrum sich drehende rote Halbkugel. Das wäre ein unvollkommenes Doppelkontinuum *per se*. (Brentano führt auch den Fall von einer dehnenden Kugel oder Scheibe, die sich dreht und dennoch keine örtliche Veränderung erleidet.) Bei einem Doppelkontinuum *per se* muss man nicht glauben, die zwei metaphysisch vereinigten Kontinua seien in dem Sinn gleich, als sie gleiche Abstände vermitteln, da es doch ganz heterogene Abstände vermitteln. Wenn man etwas Derartiges annähme, würde man in Widersprüche geraten. Denn ein Kontinuum, das einmal mit einem anderen nicht geeinigt ist, kann doch auch mit dessen qualitativ ein anderes Mal geeinigt sein. So bei einer langsamen und raschen Bewegung. Diese Unterschiede werden Verschiedenheiten der Dehnung oder Dichtigkeit genannt. Wenn aber die Abstände durchwegs ohne Gleichheit und Größer- oder Kleinersein sind, so können sie bei den beiden Kontinuis doch proportional sein, und dann sind die Kontinuis gleichmäßig gedehnt: so eine gleichmäßige Bewegung. Hier haben wir keine Gleichheit, aber eine Proportionalität zwischen Raum und Zeit. Die Dehnung kann aber auch ungleichmäßig sein, so bei einer beschleunigten Bewegung. Diese ungleichmäßige Dehnung kann in den mannigfaltigsten Verhältnissen stattfinden, die aber eine funktionelle | Wechselbestimmung[?] haben, anders aber ganz ohne solche sein [können].[77] Falsch wäre es, wollte man ein Kontinuum mit spezifischer Gleichheit eines anderen metaphysischen Teils als Doppelkontinuum fassen, dessen einer Teil bis ins Unendliche gedehnt ist. Bei unendlicher Dehnung (die etwas Unmögliches ist) würde die Spezies im ganzen Kontinuum individuell *eine* sein, während jetzt individuelle Vielheit besteht.

Obwohl kein Punkt des Kontinuums gedehnt sein kann, so ist er doch, was er ist, nur im Zusammenhang mit dem Kontinuum, und dieser Zusammenhang ist kein anderer, wenn das, womit er zusammenhängt, individuell ein anderes ist. Er hat also einen anderen Zusammenhang bei anderen Gliedern der Dehnung und so kommt jedem Punkt eines Doppelkontinuums, insofern er etwas begrenzt, ein Dehnungsmaß zu. Das ist, was die Mathematiker *Differenzialquotient* nennen und dies an sich also verständlich machen ohne Annahme von unendlich kleinen Abständen zwischen zwei Spezies.

---

77 [*Vgl. Leisching Y3/63:* „diese ungleichmäßige Dehnung kann in den mannigfaltigsten Verhältnissen stattfinden, die aber noch eine funtionelle Wechselbestimmung zulassen, die im ganzen ungleichmäßig sind."]

[XXIV. Vorlesung,
d. 7 Februar 85]⁷⁸

Es gibt nun Dehnungen in verschiedenem Sinn: So hätten wir eine Dehnung, wenn wir eine von Rot kontinuierlich nach Blau übergehende Fläche mit einem Vergrößerungsglas ansehen und dasselbe allmählich nähern oder entfernen. Auch würden wir nirgends eine Lücke haben. Bei der Dehnung in dem Sinn, in welchem wir hier von ihr sprechen, handelt es sich noch nicht um ein Auseinandertreten, sondern vielmehr um ein Auseinandersein. Wir haben von Dehnungen gesprochen, wo das Dehnungsmaß variiert, die Dehnung selbst also ungleichmäßig ist. In einem Kontinuum kommt jedem Punkt ein Dehnungsmaß zu, obwohl er selbst nicht gedehnt ist. Denn jeder Punkt is das, was er ist, nur im Zusammenhang mit dem Kontinuum. Und dieser ist ein anderer, wenn das, womit der Punkt zusammenhängt, individuell ein anderes ist. So kommt einem jeden Punkt eines Doppelkontinuums, insofern er begrenzt und so vielfach er begrenzt ist, ein Dehnungsmaß zu. Wir nennen es Differenttialquotient. |

Ein Dehnungsmaß kann unter Umständen unendlich kleiner sein als ein anderes. Denken wir uns die folgende Fläche von Rot nach Blau und wieder zurück nach Rot übergehend, so ist klar, dass das Dehnungsmaß eines gewissen Punktes in der Linie *am* ein anderes sein wird als das des entsprechenden Punktes in der Kreislinie *aym*.

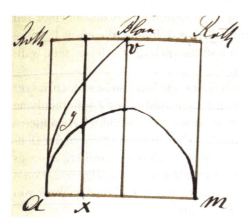

---

78 [*Datum nach Leisching Y 3/66. Diese Vorlesung ist die letzte, die in Leisching Y 2 and Leisching Y 3 mitgeschrieben ist.*]

Und zwar wird das Dehnungsmaß dieser letzteren Linie ein ungleichmäßiges sein. Es wird umso größer sein, je näher der gewählte Punkt dem Punkt a liegt. Wie groß ist es dann nun in a selbst? Unendlich groß. Es ist nämlich $a\,x = x\,y : m\,x$. Also $x\,y^2 = a\,x \cdot m\,x$. Je näher dem a der Punkt liegt, desto mehr nähert sich $m\,x$ dem Durchmesser d und desto mehr verschwindet $a\,x$. Unmittelbar vor dem Verschwinden wäre dann $a\,x$ unendlich klein, während $m\,x$ dem Durchmesser d unendlich näherte. Es wäre dann $x\,y^2 = a \cdot a\,x$.

Von einer unendlichen Dehnung, die gleichmäßig ist, innerhalb einer Linie zu sprechen, wäre unrichtig, wie bereits bewiesen wurde. Hier jedoch sprechen wir von dem Dehnungsmaß eines einzigen Punktes. Ja, wir können eine andere Linie nachweisen, in welcher das Dehnungsmaß noch größer ist als in der Linie, in welcher wir für einen Punkt das Dehnungsmaß als unendlich nachgewiesen haben. Das wäre z. B. die Kurve $a\,v$. Ja, es ließe sich eine Linie nachweisen, bei welcher das Dehnungsmaß des Punktes a unendlich mal größer ist als ihre Kreislinie $a\,y\,m$. Das wäre die *Zykloide*. Hierbei darf man aber nicht glauben, dass der unendlich kleine Bruch, der das Dehnungsmaß des Punktes a in der Zykloide ausdrückt, größer wäre als der entsprechende Bruch | bei der Kreislinie. Wir haben ja schon früher gesagt, dass in Folge der Gleichheit unendlicher Mengen jede mit jeder anderen Punkt für Punkt eindeutig in Beziehung gesetzt werden kann. Es könnte nun einer glauben, dass bei der Gattung, die eine metaphysische Vereinigung zulässt, je zwei Mengen vollkommen vermittelter Spezies zu einem Doppelkontinuum vereinigt werden können. Dennoch wäre das ein Irrtum. Eine solche Vereinigung ist nur bei unendlichen Mengen derselben Dimension möglich. Denn eine nichtgeschlossene Linie setzt jeden ihrer Punkte nur nach zwei Richtungen in Zusammenhang. Um sich aber mit einem zweidimensionalen Kontinuum metaphysisch zu decken, müsste sie jeden Punkt in unendlich vielen Richtungen in Zusammenhang bringen.[79]

Zu einer solchen Vereinigung fehlt demnach nicht die nötige Menge von Punkten, sondern die nötige Menge von Zusammenhängen. Wäre das nicht der Fall, so könnte ja auch eine unendliche Menge von Spezies, zwischen welchen endliche Abstände bestünden, also ein Nichtkontinuum, mit einem Kontinuum von einer Dimension metaphysisch zur Deckung gebracht werden. Denken wir uns eine Tonreihe, in welcher je zwei aufeinander folgende Töne

---

[79] [*Vgl. Leisching Y 3/69:* „Eine nicht geschlossene Linie setzt jeden ihrer Punkte nur nach zwei Richtungen hin lückenlos in Zusammenhang. Um aber mit einem zwei dimensionalen Kontinuum metaphysisch zusammenzufallen, müsste sie es in unendlich vielen Richtungen tun. Ähnlich setzt eine nirgends geschlossene Fläche jeder ihrer Linien nur in zweifachen Zusammenhang." *Hier endet Leisching Y 3. Es ist außerdem unmöglich, die Mitschrift von hier ab in datierte Vorlesungen zu teilen.*]

um einen ganzen Ton abstehen, so könnte die Reihe, da ja die Tonhöhe unbegrenzt ist, eine unendliche sein. Wenn nun ein Ohr so vollkommen wäre, dass es keine Grenze in der Höhe der Töne kannte, so würde dasselbe dennoch diese unendliche Reihe nicht als Kontinuum hören.

Dementsprechend sagten wir auch früher, eine unendliche Menge könne umso größer genannt werden als eine andere, insofern es mehr Dimensionen erfüllte. Es wurde aber auch betont, dass dieser Unterschied kein größerer Unterschied im eigentlichen Sinn sei.

Die Mehrzahl der Gattungen, welche uns unsere physischen Phänomene und die innere Phantasie zeigen, sind solche, | deren Spezies nicht bloß als Grenzen, sondern an und für sich bestehen können, und nicht zu einem Kontinuum gehören müssen. So kann die Farbe Rot in einem Kontinuum erscheinen, aber sie kann auch gleichmäßig und für sich erscheinen, so bei einer gleichmäßig gefärbten roten Fläche, die allerdings ein Raumkontinuum, aber kein Farbenkontinuum ist. Dasselbe gilt von Tönen, von der Intensität etc. etc. Vermöge dieser Eigentümlichkeit sind auch jene Semikontinua möglich, so eine Fläche, die von Blau zu Rot übergeht, aber nur nach der Weite.

Andere Gattungen zeigen hingegen, dass auch das Entgegengesetzte der Fall sein kann, dass also die Spezies derselben nie an und für sich, sondern immer nur als Grenzen bestehen. Daher gehören nun Raum und Zeit. Was zunächst den Raum anbelangt, so könnte einer fragen,[80] ob die Räume, die die Anschauung zeigt, uns zwei- oder dreidimensional erscheinen; das Letztere hält Hering für das Richtige und Brentano stimmt ihm bei.

Kann ein Kontinuum von Länge und Weite für sich erscheinen oder erscheint es als Grenze von einem dreidimensionalen Kontinuum? Früher glaubte man ausschließlich das Erstere. Man meinte, man sehe keine dritte Dimension. Doch mit Unrecht, aus folgenden Gründen.

1. Es ist nachweisbar, dass, wenn die Ortsspezies nur als Fläche erschienen, diese Fläche nicht eben könne. Beim Gefühl wird das durch den Rücklauf der Lokalisation, aber auch beim Gesichtssinn ist das der Fall. [Franciscus Cornelis] Donders nahm einen schwarzen Kisten und in diesem Kisten ließ er einen einen Punkt leuchten. Einen anderen Punkt ließ er entstehen durch einen elektrischen Funken bald vor, bald hinter dem Punkt. Wenn er mit *einem* Auge hineinsah, durfte er nie bestimmen, ob der elektrische | Funke vorn oder hinten gesprungen sei. Mit zwei Augen jedoch sehr leicht.[81]

---

80 [so könnte einer fragen *statt* so könnte einer zweifeln *im Ms.*]
81 [*Vgl. Stumpf 1873*, 228.]

Die Umkehrung des Reliefs kann nicht begreiflich werden, wenn wir annehmen, dass beide Flächen, die wir mit den beiden Augen sehen,[82] Ebene seien. Denn ich könnte nicht unterscheiden, ob im einen Auge der *eine* Punkt rechts liegt oder im anderen. Nehmen wir die beiden Flächen als gewölbt an, so wäre das nicht der Fall (Stumpf, *Ursprung der Raumvorstellung*).[83]

2. Eine dritte Dimension ist jedenfalls in der Phantasie nachweisbar. Wäre das nicht der Fall, so würden, wenn wir hinaussehen und dabei etwas phantasieren, beide Vorstellungen einander stören und zerstören. Wenn wir nun in der Phantasie den dreidimensionalen Raum haben, dann erscheint als Grenze dieser Raumerscheinung etwas Zweidimensionales. Und ganz so wie die Anhänger der Flächenhaftigkeit es sich denken, im Fall, wo wir einfach etwas sehen. Es erscheinen also nach ihnen ein und dasselbe bald als Grenze, bald nicht als Grenze. Als Grenze, nur wenn ich in der Phantasie die anderen Dimensionen dazu füge. Allein, was bald als Grenze, bald nicht erscheint, kann doch nicht so, wie es als Grenze erscheint, das andere Mal für sich erscheinen. Denn als Grenze erscheint es als etwas, was an und für sich nichts [ist]. Es muss also, um für sich zu erscheinen, anders erscheinen. Tatsächlich erscheint es aber in beiden Fällen gleich. Wir sehen uns also zu einem Widerspruch geführt durch die Annahme, dass wir nur zwei Dimensionen wahrnehmen. Die Kraft dieses Arguments wird noch größer, wenn wir bedenken, dass Widersprechendes und Absurdes, wie es nicht in Wahrheit bestehen | kann, auch nicht in einer einheitlichen Anschauung bestehen kann. Jeder erkennt nun, der bloß flächenhafte Raum nicht für sich in der Wirklichkeit bestehen könnte. So kann dann auch eine bloße Fläche für sich in der Anschauung nicht bestehen.

Woher kommt nun der Schein des Gegenteils? 1) Die Anschauung in der dritten Dimension ist gewiss eine sehr geringe, darum wird sie weniger beachtet. 2) Vielleicht ist sie konstant immer dieselbe, darum erreicht sie kein Interesse. 3) Sie ist bedeutungslos, deutet auf keinen Unterschied in den Dingen hin und wird darum kein Gegenstand der Aufmerksamkeit. Ja, die Unaufmerksamkeit wird zu einer unbesiegbaren Gewohnheit. Daher die Schwierigkeit perspektivisch richtig zu zeichnen. Hier kommt es auf die lokalen Unterschiede der Vorstellung an, nicht auf das, was sie bedeuten. Wir haben hier die Unmöglichkeit, auf andere Beziehungen als auf eine gewisse Acht zu geben. So steht es auch mit der dritten Dimension, die für uns gänzlich bedeutungslos ist.

Aus allem dem ergibt sich: *Was nur als Kontinuum sein kann, kann nur als Kontinuum von so vielen Dimensionen sein, als in den betreffenden Gattungen*

---

82 [beide Flächen, die wir mit den beiden Augen sehen *statt* beide Flächen der beiden Augen *im Ms.*]

83 [*Vgl. Stumpf 1873, 229ff.*]

möglich sind. Was aber sowohl als Punkt oder auch ohne Zugehörigkeit zu einem Kontinuum sein kann, das wird im letzteren Fall immer als Ersatz für die in so vielen Dimensionen Punkte eines Kontinuums per accidens sein, als das vollkommene Kontinuum, in welchem es als Punkt erscheinen würde, Dimensionen haben würde.

Wir wollen demnach zwei Klassen von Kontinua unterschieden: notwendige Kontinua und nichtnotwendige Kontinua.

Eine weitere Eigenheit, welche bei einer Gattung von notwendigen Kontinua vorkommen kann, ist, dass in ihr die Spezies einer gewissen anderen untersten Gattung, mit der es in | metaphysischer Verbindung steht, undurchdringlich sind. Das heißt, es können *weder* zwei Spezies *noch* auch durch lose Individualisation verschiedene Spezies dieser Gattung mit zwei zu ihr gehörigen spezifisch gleichen Kontinuis anders als Momente oder als Grenzen von verschiedenen Seiten hier gleichzeitig vereinigt werden. Beispiel: der Raum. Farben und andere Gattungen sinnlicher Qualitäten sind im Raum undurchdringlich.[84] Als Grenzen können allerdings zwei Farbenlinien konizidieren. Dasselbe gilt bei allen anderen sinnlichen Qualitäten. Bei den Tönen wird das zwar von manchen gleugnet. Doch haben wir uns für die entgegengesetzte Annahme entschieden. Es steht nichts im Wege anzunehmen, der Anlaß bestünde bei Dingen, die gar nicht Objekte unserer Erfahrung werden können. In Wahrheit wissen wir gar nicht, ob unser Raum wirkliche oder nur phänomenale Existenz hat. Das aber ist klar, dass ein Analogon unseres Raumes besteht und das scheint diesem Analogon mit unserem Raum gesichert zu sein, dass andere Gattungen, die mit ihm verbunden sind, undurchdringlich sind.

Eine andere Eigentümlichkeit kann ganz kurz erörtert werden, nämlich die Eigentümlichkeit der Zeit und aller durch die Zeit modifizierten Konintua, dass sie nicht mehr als *einem* Momente nach und somit nur immer in unvollständiger Weise real sind. Diese Zeit ist wie auch die Bewegung eine ἐνέργεια ἀτελή.[85]

Eine weitere Eigentümlichkeit ist die, dass gewisse Kontinua keinen unendlichen Zuwuchs gestatten, sondern dass es in ihnen ein größtmögliches Konti-

---

84 [*Vgl.* Brentano EL 72/12251–12252: „Eine merkwürdige Eigenheit, welche bei einer Gattung von notwendigen Kontinuis vorkommen kann, ist, dass in ihr die Spezies einer gewissen untersten Gattung, mit deren sie in metaphysischer Verbindung steht, undurchdringlich sind; d. h. es können *weder* zwei Spezies *noch* durch lose Individuation verschiedene Spezies dieser Gattung mit zwei zu ihr gehörigen spezifisch gleichen Kontinuis anders als etwa Momenten oder als Grenzen von verschiedenen Seiten her gleichzeitig vereinigt werden. Das einzige Beispiel einer solchen Gattung, die uns in dem Bereich unserer Phänomene vorliegt, ist der Raum. Farben, sowie andere Gattungen sinnlicher Qualitäten, sind in ihm undurchdringlich."]

85 [*Vgl.* oben, p. 172.]

nuum | gibt. Sie können nach jeder Richtung hin eine gewisse Grenzen nicht überschreiten. Beispiel: die Farbe. Wenn ich von Weiß durch Grau nach Schwarz gehe, so werde ich fertig. Ich kann nicht weiter. Ebenso von Rot nach Grün. Oder von Blau nach Gelb. Aber nicht bloß hier findet sich diese Eigenheit. Auch bei Geschmack und Geruch scheint etwas Ähnliches zu bestehen und es ist schwer diese Gebiete zu durchforschen, da wir nicht im Stande sind, Merkmale genau derselben Erscheinungen hervorzurufen. So zwischen Bitter und Süß, welches zwei Extreme sind, über die man nicht hinausgehen kann. Wenn wir sagen, es gebe einen größtmöglichen endlichen Abstand und ein größtmögliches endliches Kontinuum, bei Raum, Zeit, Intensität etc., sei das nicht der Fall, gibt uns das nicht das Recht zu sagen, bei diesen letzten Gattungen sei etwas Größeres möglich als bei den ersten Gattungen? Nein. Wir müssen sagen, dass wegen der Unvergleichbarkeit der Größen von verschiedener Gattungen nicht gesagt werden kann, es gebe eine größere Zeit, als es einen Abstand zweier Farben [gebe].

Noch eine Eigentümlichkeit. Physiker wollten gewisse Hypothesen machen, um die Endlichkeit des Raumes zu erweisen. Sie meinten, ohne eine solche Endlichkeit würde sich die Materie verflüchtigen. Sie suchten zu erweisen, gestützt auf die Annahme, der Raum sei krumm, was aber nur möglich ist, wenn der Raum eine bloße dreidimensionale Grenze eines vierdimensionalen Kontinuums sei. Das aber wäre undenkbar, dass der Raum eine Grenze sei und dennoch etwas für sich. Viel vernünftiger wäre der Hinweis auf die Weise, wie die Dimensionen der Farben endlich sind. Die Unendlichkeit ist nicht die einfache Folge der Geradheit, wie die Farben beweisen. Es wäre also vernünftiger zu sagen: Der Raum, wie wir ihn vorstellen, ist vielleicht nicht wirklich, vielleicht nur ein Analogon. Dieses Analogon könnte sich vielleicht vom Raum in einer [gewissen] Beziehung unterschieden und Ähnlichkeit | mit der Farbe haben. Damit sei keineswegs gesagt, dass eine derartige Hypothese wahrscheinlich sei. Sie stünde ja auch in Widerspruch mit der Physik, so mit dem Gesetz der Trägheit. Ja, die Annäherung an die Grenze müsste eigentlich eine Änderung in den Bewegungserscheinungen verursachen.

Hinsichtlich der früheren[?] Unterschiede ist hier noch Einiges zu ergänzen. Mit der Lehre von Kontinuis haben wir abgeschlossen.

Wir haben gesehen, dass es in gewissen untersten Gattungen in jeder möglichen Richtung einen größtmöglichen Abstand der Spezies gibt (so bei der Farbe). Auch die Gattung der Richtung gehört selbst hierher. Denn es gibt nicht bloß größere und kleinere Abstände von Richtungen, für welche der Winkel das Maß ist, sondern auch Abstände zweier Richtungen von einer dritten in verschiedener Richtung, vielleicht von gleicher Größe. Dabei ist *ein* Abstand der größtmögliche. So bei einem gestreckten Winkel. Spezies, die in solcher Weise voneinander verschieden sind, deren Abstand also der größtmögliche in einer gewissen Richtung ist, nennt man Gegensätze. Es sind aber drei Fälle solcher größtmöglichen Abstände zu unterscheiden.

1. Der Fall, in welchem der größtmögliche Abstand zweier Spezies in einer gewissen Richtung der einzige größtmögliche ist in der ganzen Gattung, so dass kein anderer ihm gleich käme. So bei Weiß und Schwarz. Das ist ein Gegensatz im engsten Sinn. Offenbar gibt es nicht in allen Gattungen solche größtmögliche Abstände. So bei Intensitäten, Tönen, etc. In unserer Erfahrung ist vielleicht die Farbe die einzige Gattung, in welcher es in diesem engen Sinn Gegensätze gibt.

2. Der Fall, in welchem der größtmögliche Abstand zweier Spezies in einer gewissen Richtung zwar der größtmögliche Abstand in der Gattung überhaupt ist, aber nicht so, dass kein anderer ihm gleich wäre. Nur ist keiner größer als er. So ist mit den Abständen zwischen zwei einander entgegengesetzten Richtungen.

So ist der Richtungsabstand von *ao* und *ob* ebenso groß wie der von *co* und *od*. | So kann es sein, dass jede Spezies einer Gattung ein Gegensatz ist. So gibt es keine Richtung, welche nicht eine entgegengesetzte hätte.

3. Der Fall, in welchem der größtmögliche Abstand zweier Spezies kleiner ist als andere mögliche Abstände in derselben Gattung, aber in anderer Richtung. So Rot und Grün, Blau von Gelb. Das ist Gegensatz im weitesten Sinn des Wortes. Rot und Grün werden oft als Gegensätze bezeichnet. Seltener dagegen werden eine gewisse Nuance von Violett und eine gewisse von Gelbgrün als Gegensätze bezeichnet. Diese Unregelmäßigkeit des Sprachgebrauchs kommt daher, dass man nicht weiß, dass man es im letzteren Fall mit einheitlichen Farben zu tun hat. Noch weniger dürfte es geschehen, dass Rot als Gegensatz zu Weiß oder Blau bezeichnet wird und doch sind auch diese Kontraste. Weil man zu Rot schon Grün und zu Weiß schon Schwarz als Gegensätze nennt, glaubt man, es gehe nicht an, dass noch etwas anderes als Gegensatz bezeichnet wird. Aber das war zwar bei den früher bezeichneten zwei Fällen unmöglich. In unserem dritten Fall aber ist es nicht unmöglich, dass Mehreres in Gegensatz zu *einem* steht. So ist sowohl Schwarz als Rot zu Weiß ein Gegensatz. Vielleicht sagt einer: Zum Kontrast gehört, dass eine Spezies zur anderen einen größeren Abstand habe als zu jeder anderen in dieser Gattung, darum bezeichne

man Grün und Weiß nicht als Gegensätze. Diese Vermutung wäre unrichtig, da Gelb weiter von Schwarz absteht als von Blau. Ebenso wenig haltbar wäre die Annahme einer konstanten Mitte als Durchgangspunkt, so z. B. Grau. Wahrscheinlich liegt zwischen Gelb und Blau und zwischen Rot und Grün nicht dasselbe Nuance von Grau in der Mitte.

Dazu kommt aber noch ein fünffacher anderer Gebrauch des Wortes „Gegensätze," von welchen die drei letzten wenigstens entschieden ein Missbrauch sind.

1. Manche nennen Gegensätze auch solche letzte Artunterschiede, die in der Gattung die einzig möglichen sind. Hier ist also weder größerer noch ein kleinerer Abstand. Dieser einzige Abstand aber ist gar keine Größe. Es ist der einzig mögliche, aber nicht der größtmögliche. Auf dem Gebiete der inneren Phänomene finden sich solche „Gegensätze," wie bei der „Bejahung und Verneinung," „Liebe und Haß." Manchen schwebt vielleicht als Drittes ein neutrale[r] Zustand vor. So könnte bei den Urteilen das Wahrscheinlichkeitsurteil als Mitte angesehen wird. Bei den Gemütsakten Liebe und Haß könnte man die mäßigen Akte von Liebe und Haß für die ausgeprägtesten Vermittlungen ansehen. Allein in beiden Fällen haben wir keinen eigentlichen Abstand. Die Wahrscheinlichkeitsurteile sind Urteile über ganz andere Gegenstände, nämlich über die Chancen. Wir können ferner von einer extremen Liebe und einem extremen Haß nicht sprechen, da die Intensität keine Grenze hat. Bei der Gleichgültigkeit und Liebe und Haß können wir nun von Gegensätzen der Intensität sprechen, aber nicht von Gegensätzen zwischen Liebe und Haß.

2. Manche haben Gegensätze auch solcher Klassen genannt, welche nicht letzte Arten, ja überhaupt nicht Arten sind, aber sich gegenseitig ausschließen und als Einteilungsglieder sich ergänzen. Das sind die negativen Gegensätze „Grün und Nichtgrün." Grün ist eine Art von Farbe, Nichtgrün ist gewiss keine Art von Farbe. Dieser Gebrauch von „Gegensatz" ist höchst uneigentlich, aber kaum zu beseitigen. (Aristoteles hat zwei Urteile, von denen ein Urteil das bejaht, was das andere verneint, nicht ἀναντία genannt, sondern ἀντικείμενον.[86])

3. Manche haben jeden Abstand einen Gegensatz genannt, auch wenn er weder schlechthin noch in einer gewissen Richtung der größtmögliche ist. Man nannte das positive Gegensätze. So wäre Violett ein Gegensatz zu Rot. Es hat aber gar keinen Grund, das Gegensatz zu nennen, da der Ausdruck „Abstand" vollkommen genügt. Der Fall wurde noch schlimmer dadurch, dass der Begriff

---

86 [Vgl. Brentano EL 72/12260: „Er unterschied andere ἀναντία, von welchen er glaubte, dass wahrhaft größte Abstände der Urteile (konträre, nicht bloß kontradiktorische) [bestände]."]

von Spezies und Gattung getrübt wurde, ja verloren ging. Ja, „Gegensatz," wie man sie vielfach nennt, war dann oft nicht einmal „Abstand," geschweige denn Gegensatz.

4. Der komparative Gegensatz. Von solchen Gegensätzen spricht man dort, wo irgendwelcher Unterschied angegeben wird, aber keineswegs ein extremer. So, wenn ich sage: „Etwas ist höher, ein anderes tiefer." Offenbar ist das [ein] Übertragen von dem Gegensatz der Richtung der Abstände. So bei Rechts und Links. Was rechts ist, liegt nach Rechts, also steht ab in einer gewissen Richtung. Nicht der Ort ist dem Ort entgegengesetzt, nicht die hellere Farbe der dunkleren sind entgegengesetzt, sondern die Richtungen.

5. Man bezeichnet oft alle Korrelativa als Gegensätze, wenn sie nicht gerade eine Übereinstimmung ausdrücken (wie gleich und gleich, klein und klein). So sagt man, das Ganze und der Teil seien Gegensätze, Ursache und Wirkung, Herr und Diener. Hier liegt in Wahrheit nichts vor als ein Unterschied in der Richtung der Beziehung. Das gibt keinen Grund von Gegensatz zu sprechen, denn ein solcher Unterschied der Richtungen liegt vor, sogar wenn ich sage: Dieses ist jenem gleich und jenes diesem, wo auch ein Gegensatz der Richtung vorhanden ist. Dieser Gebrauch ist jedenfalls ein Missbrauch. Uns gehen hier nur die drei ersten an, wo wir einen größtmöglichen Abstand haben, nicht aber die fünf letztgenannten Anwendungen des Wortes „Gegensatz."

Noch ein anderes Verhältnis bedarf einer gewissen Erläuterung: das Verhältnis der Ähnlichkeit. Der sprachliche Ursprung des Wortes ähnlich ist „angleich." Also nahezu gleich.

Man nennt also 1. ähnlich vor allem und im eigentlichsten Sinn das, wozu ein verschwindend kleinerer spezifischer Abstand besteht. So zwei Nuancen von Violett, Rot und Rötlich. Wo fängt die Ähnlichkeit an und hört sie auf? Eine bestimmte Grenze ist gar nicht anzugeben. | Eine Grenze nach einer Seite hin ist erst bei einem Extrem gegeben. So ist zwischen Rot und Blau alles dem Rot in gewisser Weise ähnlich, das Blau aber nicht, da es ein Extrem ist.

2. In einem zweiten Sinn gebraucht man das Wort [„ähnlich"] da, wo an Ungleichem eine Gleichheit von Verhältnissen sich knüpft. Diese Ähnlichkeit heißt Analogie. So steht zwischen Zeit und Raum eine Analogie. Zwischen einem Intensitäts- und Quantitätskontinuum besteht eine Analogie. Eine weitgehende Ähnlichkeit in jenem Sinn besteht besonders in jenen Fällen, die wir als Übereinstimmung mit μετάβασις εἰς ἄλλο γένος genannt haben, so 100 vorgestellte Taler und 100 wirkliche (contra Kant). Ein gewesener König und ein wirklicher König sind Analoga. Bei diesem letzten Beispiel haben wir sogar eine doppelte Ähnlichkeit. Es kommt nämlich zur Ähnlichkeit im Sinn der Analogie der Umstand, dass der zeitliche Abstand ein außerordentlich kleiner sein kann, so dass eine Ähnlichkeit im erst betrachteten Sinn noch dazu kommt.

Wenn die Mathematiker von Ähnlichkeit sprechen, so handelt es sich auch bei ihnen um Gleichheit von Verhältnissen. Und ihre Ähnlichkeit ist nichts anderes als Gleichheit der Gestalt, da die letztere nur in Verhältnissen liegt. In Wahrheit begünstigt die Gleichheit der Gestalt mehr als vieles andere die Verwechslung von Verschiedenem.

3. Es geschieht auch noch, dass wir etwas ähnlich nennen, wo weder im eigentlichen Sinn noch im Sinn der Analogie von einer Ähnlichkeit gesprochen werden kann, nämlich da, wo wir zwei Objekte haben, die aus einer Mehrheit von Teilen zusammengesetzt sind und die in gewissen Stücken gleich oder im eigentlichen Sinn ähnlich sind, in den anderen aber ungleich, wenn nur die ersteren Stücke in ihrer Bedeutung überwiegen. So sagen wir | oft: „Ein ähnlicher Fall ist mir schon vorgekommen." Man könnte geneigt sein zu glauben, dass diese Ähnlichkeit eine Ungleichheit in mehr als *einem* Stück fordere, und zwar solche, von denen nicht die eine in der anderen simuliert ist. Denn auch bei jeder Gleichheit im eigentlichen Sinn sei ja doch etwas gegeben, was einen Unterschied bildet. Wir hätten hier also Gleichheit. Indessen könnte man darauf antworten: Wenn ich etwas Rotes habe und noch etwas anderes Rotes, so sei diese Röte jener Röte gleich, dagegen dieses Rote jenem Roten ähnlich. So könnte man auch reden von einer bloßen Ähnlichkeit, wenn ich ein so und so intensives Rote habe da und dort, wo der Unterschied nur in Örtlichkeit liegt.

Was aber ist dann die Identität? Wie unterscheidet sie sich von der Ähnlichkeit? Das ist leicht, da die Identität mehr als Gleichheit ist. Von der Gleichheit unterscheidet sich die Identität dadurch, dass das Gleiche auch nur unterschieden ist durch den Zusammenhang mit anderen metaphysischen Teilen. Die Identität hingegen ist vollkommen unterschiedslos. Identisch ist dieses Rote mit diesem Roten. Aber auch „dieses Rote ist identisch mit diesem Runden," wenn ich eine rote Kugel habe.

Sind die Relationen real oder nicht?

Nicht real sind einmal gewisse, eben Relationen, die zwischen Nichtrealem bestehen. So wenn wir etwas Gewesenes mit einem Zukünftigen vergleichen. Das Gleiche wird aber da auch von gewissen anderen gelten, die ebenso wohl zwischen Nichtrealem als zwischen Realem gefunden werden. So die Verhältnisse von Gleichheit und Verschiedenheit. In der Tat findet sich diese ebenso gut zwischen Realem und Nichtrealem. Gleichheit und Verschiedenheit ändern an den Elementen nichts. Keine reale Bestimmung wird hinzugefügt durch die Gleichheit oder Verschiedenheit. Man nennt hier die beiden Elemente, | zwischen, denen eine Gleichheit oder Verschiedenheit besteht, Fundamente der Relation. Wenn wir diese Relationen betrachten, so haben sie ein direktes *fundamentum in re*. Es gibt aber Gleichheiten und Verschiedenheiten, die nur ein indirektes Fundament haben. So die Größenverhältnisse zweier Abstände. Die Größenverhältnisse sind in Abständen gegeben. Diese aber selbst nur in den abstehenden Elementen, die dann die indirekten Fundamente sind. Auch Ähnlichkeit und Identität sind nicht real. Dasselbe aber wird auch von den Zahlen unendlicher Mengen gelten, da diese Kollektive ganz auf der Gleichheit und Verschiedenheit beruhen. Ja, von allen Kollektiven ist dasselbe zu sagen, wenn es auch aus lauter realen Elementen besteht; es selbst ist als solches nicht real, es ist auch mit da, wenn die Teile da sind. Es bleiben nur noch die anderen Verbindungen von Teilen mit Teilen und in Verhältnis zum Ganzen zu erörtern übrig. So die metaphysischen, logischen und physischen Teile. Bei den metaphysischen Teilen haben wir einen wesentlichen anderen Fall vor uns. Nehmen wir an, wir hätten ein Blau mit einer örtlichen Bestimmtheit *a* und Rot mit der örtlichen Bestimmtheit *b*. Dieselben vier Elemente würden wir aber auch haben, wenn wir Blau mit der örtlichen Bestimmtheit *b* hätten und Rot mit *a*, und doch wären beide Fälle verschieden. Hier dürfte also die Relation als etwas Reales angesehen werden. Ähnliches von der Relation des logischen Ganzen zum logischen Teil gälte. Zur Farbe, die als Teil im logischen Ganzen „Blau" wirklich ist, steht das Rot nicht in derselben Beziehung, in welcher es zwar in dem Wirklichen [als] Farbe beseht. Dagegen könnte man vom physischen Ganzen, welches ja ganz auf Relationen spezifischer Unterschiede beruht, | mehr mit Recht sagen, dass seine Verhältnisse zu den physischen Teilen keine realen Relationen seien, da sie ganz auf Verhältnissen von Gleichheit und Verschiedenheit beruhen. Mit seinen drei Dritteln ist das Kontinuum sofort gegeben und fügt nichts mehr hinzu. Ebenso[?], wenn sämtlich Grenzen gegeben sind. Doch haben wir Grund, hier noch eine andere Art von Relation zu suchen. So haben wir dann: 1. nichtreale Relationen ohne reale Fundamente, 2. nichtreale Relationen mit realen Fundamenten. 3. reale Relationen. In den Kausalverhältnissen aber haben wir noch anderen realen Verhältnisse begegnet.

Die sinnlichen Vorstellungen sind Einzelvorstellungen und so bestimmt, dass es ausgeschlossen ist, dass ihnen, wenn überhaupt etwas, mehr als *eines* entspricht. Gilt dasselbe auch von jedem Elemente der sinnlichen Vorstellung? Man könnte glauben: nein. So könnte man an den logischen Teil denken. Aber mit Unrecht, denn auch sie sind in Zusammenhang mit anderen vorhanden und in diesem Zusammenhang sind sie individualisiert. Würden sie allein sein, so wären sie allerdings universell. [Die folgende unnummerierte Seite des Manuskriptes ist wegen schwieriger Lesbarkeit nicht transkribiert.]

[I. Anhang]

1. Begriff der Realität im Gegensatz zur Existenz. (J. St. Mills „possibilities of sensation" von vornherein ausgeschlossen.)
2. Besitzen wir nur überhaupt direkte Kenntnis von etwas Realem? Notwendig, sonst hätten wir nicht seinen Begriff.
3. Wir haben von nichts anderem direkte Kenntnis als von psychischen Phänomenen und ihren intentionalen Korrelativen.
4. Nur die ersteren sind real.
5. Darin ist involviert, dass auch nur sie wirken | und Wirkung empfangen können, nicht aber die intentionalen Korrelate.
6. Die Annahme, dass die psychischen Realitäten durchwegs wieder durch Realität gewirkt werden, ist von vornherein möglich (Idealismus).
7. Sie verträgt sich auch mit der Verschiedenheit dieser Realitäten in Hinsicht auf ihre Korrelate, hat sie aber nicht zur Folge.
8. Es besteht aber nicht bloß diese Verschiedenheit, sondern auch eine gewiss[e] Gesetzmäßigkeit der Sukzession und der Koexistenz. |
9. Worin besteht diese Gesetzmäßigkeit? A. Auf dem Gebiete der bloßen Vorstellungen. Hierher gehören alle jene konstanten Suksessionen, die ihren Ausdruck in den physikalischen Gesetzen finden, soweit sie in die Erscheinung fallen, so die Trägheit etc. |

[II. Anhang: Hörder der Vorlesungen zur Logik, 1884/85]

[Eduard] Leisching
Fuchs
[Josef] Kreibig
[Otto] Aron
[August] Eder
[Franz] Hillebrand
[Emil] Lemberger
Hanin
[Edmund] Husserl
[Adolf] Bauer
Herzog
Berger
[Georg] Fulda
Wimheruntz [?]
Hofer [?]

Pfann
[David] Feuchtwang
[Hans] Schmidkunz

CHAPTER 6

Franz Hillebrand, *Elementary Logic and the Reforms Necessary in It according to the Lectures of Dr. Franz Brentano* (Winter Semester 1884/85, Vienna)

Lecture I.
25 October, 84

Logic is defined in very diverse ways. Some call it an art, while others call it art and science. The former designate it either as an art of inferring or as an art of thinking. Hegel says:[1] Logic is the science of the pure idea, the scientific development of concepts from pure reason which are the basis of all thinking and being. Logic is the exposition of the truth as it is for itself, without any encasing, the exposition of God as he is in his eternal essence prior to the creation of the world and of a finite mind; it is the realm of shadows, which are, however, the simple essence free of all material, into whose diamond net the entire universe is constructed.[2]

What we must adhere to, above all else, is that logic is a *practical discipline*, and in this regard it is also defined by some as an art. Brentano defines it as the art of judging. It is to teach us the procedure that leads to the cognition of truth, i.e. to correct judgment.

It is not the art of correct inferring.

If one says that logic is the art of inferring, we must note the following: Everyone who infers judges, insofar as he infers, but not everyone who judges already draws a conclusion. Nonetheless, the difference between the two definitions is

---

[1] [*The remainder of the this paragraph is apparently an exposition rather than an exact quotation from a work by Hegel.*]

[2] [*Critique of this conception of logic in Brentano El 72/12008:* "Rejection of Hegel: Those are certainly lofty-ringing, sublime-sounding words. Nonetheless you will excuse [me] if I give them no further consideration. Aside from fundamental errors of his system with which the definition of logic given by him is connected, Hegel completely shifts the traditional meaning of the name by transferring it to certain metaphysical investigations. It would be an altogether unjustiable arbitrary move if were to follow his example in this way rather than understanding by logic what one has designated with this name generally and from ancient times."]

not so great, for though our judgment is often not an inference we can also say that the art of judging almost completely lies in the art of inferring. The correct inferences are for us mediating cognitions. The unmediated ones do not pose the same difficulty. Indeed, one might believe that the cognition of the immediately luminous truths leaves no room at all for an art, and thus the art of judging and the art of inferring would coincide. If this were true, the definition of logic as the art of inferring would deserve preference insofar as it would be clearer. Yet, the fact of the matter is different. It occurs that people accept what is *not* an immediate cognition, indeed something that is perhaps downright false, as an immediate cognition. Examples: the evidence of outer percpetion, of memory, of the statement: *effectus cognitio a cognitione causae dependent et eadem involvit*[3] (Spinoza, *Ethics*, 4th axiom),[4] or the statements: "Like causes like,"[5] "The cause must be nobler than the effect."[6] Here belong also many "axioms" of the philosophy of the French Enlightenment, such as the statement of inalienable rights, of the sovereignty of a people, etc.[7]

---

3 [*Spinoza 1994, 86:* "The knowledge of an effect depends on, and involves, the knowledge of its cause."]
4 [*Critique in Brentano* EL 72/12011: "The consequence [of this axiom] no less than: that all knowledge [is] deductive. God's existence [is however] immediately luminous [according to Spinoza]." *Cf. Leisching Y* 2/3: "This is put forward as an axiom, as [an] immediately luminous statement. Yet, this is certainly neither a luminous statement nor a true one. Its consequence would be that all cognition must be deductive, none [of it] inductive. And finally as an ultimate consequence: God's existence is immediately luminous if he is the cause of all things. Spinoza in fact cites the ontological argument – which is nothing but a common paralogism – as proof for the existence of God."]
5 [*Critique in Brentano* EL 72/12011: "Things that have nothing in common with each other cannot have an effect on each other (Body – mind.)" *Cf. Leisching Y* 2/3: "That is supposedly luminous! God can thus not have any effect on the world, nor body on the mind. If the statement is correct, it can only be based on experience, [but] it is not luminous."]
6 [*Critique in Leisching Y* 2/4: "From the egg the chicken develops. Is the egg nobler than the chicken?"]
7 [*Vgl. Leisching Y* 2/4: "For instance: 'Full-fledged personal freedom' is allegedly one. It was at once preached: elimination of monastaries, of marriage. Indeed, every contractual obligation is eliminated, for it restricts full-fledged personal freedom. So also the statement: 'All human beings are equal.' The equality of rights is attached to this. Then private property is thereby eliminated, but even if that was done all would not be equal. Example: Beethoven and his brother got into a fight while only exchanging letters with each other. The latter signed 'proprieter of land,' and the former answered this with the signature 'proprieter of brain.' As a consequence, the former could indeed be deprived of his land, but could the latter be devprived of his brain? Thus also the dogma of 'sovereignty of the people.' This is based on coarse confusions. One focuses the correct statement 'The highest goal of the state is the best

It also occurs conversely that that immediately luminous statements are not accepted as such. This happens with regard to inner perception and the law of non-contradiction, the evidence of which Epicurus and Hegel not only doubted, but even denied. For this group of cognitions as well, not only for the mediating ones, certain rules are therefore not without value. In this case, however, it is wrong to exclude these rules of logic, as the definition of logic as the art of inferring would do. Strictly speaking, the definition of logic as the art of judging or of cognition is therefore correct.

Nor is it the art of thinking.

Others define logic, as already mentioned, as the art of thinking. By thinking they include presenting. Logic must of course enter into a discussion of presentations, since judgment requires these. Though logic for this reason alone is concerned also with presentations, the definition is incorrect. This result will also arise from the following elucidation: Every practical discipline is defined by its goal. In the case of logic the goal is exclusively cognition and not presentations. Aesthetics, not logic, is the art of presentations and strives in this matter for perfection. As the definition of logic as the art of inferring is thus too narrow, [the definition of] logic as the art of thinking is too broad.

Lecture II.
30 October, 84

Nor is it a science.

Some define logic not as art, but also as science. It is to be the science as well as the art of inferring. Thus Ueberweg says, "Logic is the science of the regulative laws of human knowledge."[8] (Whately also holds this view.) Art and science are distinguished from each other. It is essential to *art* that a practical goal gives unity to the truths, to *science* that the complex makes up an intelligible genus. The Aristotelians already called those writings of their master concerned with logic *Organon*. In order to be an art in the proper sense, logic need not at all be a science. It can deal with completely heterogeneous phenomena. The goal of

---

of the people' with the statement 'The people are to be the highest governing body'." *Cf.* continuation of the critique in Brentano EL 72/12012: "Sad results: Brotherly love preached – guillotine; freedom preached: Caesarism and despotism, militarism and thus also whatever true in the thought of *equality* is turned into the opposite. The tyrant used all others only as tool for his purposes."]

8 [*Ueberweg 1871, 1.*]

logic is to lead to cognition, to be able to preserve us from errors. When it satisfies such goals by characterizing correct judgments in contrast to incorrect ones, we might also perhaps call it a science, for these regulative laws might be viewed as a group of related truths. However, logic cannot be kept within these limits. It must teach us, besides the canon of cognitive activity, still a good deal from other psychical realms to preserve us from temptations. Thus it must deal with the force of habit, with laws of association, and with the influence of the will. It also has to consider linguistic and grammatical matters. It must also borrow truths from metaphysics and likewise draw upon mathematics in the estimatation of probabilities. Logic also enters into relations of different special sciences, for everything cannot be regarded as a closed group of intrinsically related truths. Examples from works of significant logicians can show with what heterogeneous questions logicians are occupied. The first work of Aristotle concerns the categories, i.e. the highest genera of that which *is*. That belongs to metaphysics. The next work concerns grammatical matters. The *Posterior Analytics* concerns the four causes, and then the simultaeity of cause and effect, for instance. Equally diverse are the *Topics* and the *Sophistical Refutations*. All these writings diverge from one single intelligible genus. A mere glance into the table of contents of the logic by John Stuart Mill shows the same. Alexander Bain even considers the conservation of energy. We find something similar in the case of Jevons. Even Pascal, where he is concered with the art of persuasion, gives four rules concerned with definition among the eight that he formulates. Kant and Herbart of course wanted to formulate a formal science of logic. Albert Lange (*Logical Studies*), however, objects that what they in fact offer is anything but such a formal science. No logic has been able to be a formal logic, he says. Logic compels us to mix in other elements. It is therefore an art and not a science. If, however, we want to have a purely formal logic, what remains of it? Almost nothing, only a small piece of psychology. It is incomprehensible why this small piece ought to be declared as the science of logic. It is of practical interest indeed to pick out this small piece, but only to combine it with all that which the practical goal otherwise requires. A. Lange condemns this, but he could not avoid it in his own *Logical Studies*. For in its second part, which was not completed due to the author's death, shows in sketches that have been retained how Lange too wanted to treat completely heterogeneous matters. The smaller section of logic, which is taken from psychology and would therefore contain heterogeneous knowledge, might well be called "Concerning the General Character and the Manners of Correctly Made Judgments."

Lecture III.
5 November, 84

Like ethics, logic can be understood in a broader and in a narrower sense. The former teaches us to lead ourselves and others to knowledge. This was the view Thomas Aquinas who includes rhetoric and poetics in logic. Aristotle himself sometimes expands the boundaries of logic, as does Pascal ("The Art of Persuasion"). Arnauld also approaches this view by saying, "Logic is the art of conducting reason well in knowing things, as much to instruct ourselves about them as others."[9] Logic in the broadest sense includes two parts, individual logic for the sake of self-improvement in cognition, and logic which gives rules for leading others to the truth, communicative logic (which divides into didactic, dialectic, and rhetoric). Individual logic is the earlier part and can be treated independently. It divides into two parts, corresponding to the two situations wherein we confront a cognition to be acquired. Knowledge stands before us as either given or not given. In the first case we must be able to *assess* the given cognition with certainty. In the second case we must first be able to *discover* it. The first part deals with the *testing* of given cognitions, the second with *discovery*. Much of our knowledge is given to us without any need to discover. The first part of logic, testing, is the simpler and more independent one. For this reason it takes first place. We know immediately luminous truths without searching for them. Other people also teach us much. Hence, the part that is concerned with testing is the earlier one. For us and our time this is completely clear. Also in the case of the first thinkers, however, it was necessary that some knowledge had to be given to them in order for them to be able to aim at the discovery yet more. Also we are in the position to test earlier than to discover. Comte has expressed this [by saying]: "The living are governed more and more by the dead." That is to say, what is handed down keeps growing, and whoever adds more to it is becoming an increasingly smaller fraction. If someone even discovered more than he received from others, he would nonetheless often be in the situation of assessing rather than discovering, for the task of assessing is included in the task of discovering. Testing is also the simpler [task]. What the person who is testing does is also what the researcher must do, as he does something in addition. The rules for the discoverer are dependent on the rules of the one who tests. Also in the situation of discovery people will deal first with the discovery of proof and then only with finding the truth, and then concerning the correct question. The first part is often the only one called

---

9 [*Arnauld and Nicole 1996, 23.*]

logic, as it is by John Stuart Mill. If we expand logic further, the logic of testing is the relatively elementary part. The logic of discovery is the higher part. Our logic is therefore the logic of testing, elementary logic (program of the semester).

Value of logic.

What sort of value does this discipline have? Logic shares the fate of all of philosophy in its evaluation, but for a different reason. Other disciplines of philosophy are regarded as unreliable, but logic is regarded as worthless. Every art is all the more valuable the more significant the goal that it serves. And with the exception of ethics, no other art is comparable to logic as regards its goal. Whoever does not judge well is useless. Everywhere we must judge and infer, and it is not a matter of indifference whether we do it in an accomplished or unaccomplished way. Nonetheless, they regard logic as worthless. They say that knowledge is not worthless, and yet this instrument is despicable. This instrument is dispensable, perhaps not even beneficial. Nature and practice, not logic, make us acute thinkers. There are many great thinkers who have never occupied themselves with logic. Natural disposition is certainly not a matter of indifference, nor can it be replaced by logic. In the case of the investigation of truth it is also practice that makes us masters. Yet, logic is not for this reason superfluous. It is in fact true of every great and practiced mind that it is in fact not protected against all error by talent and practice alone. It is clear how all have erred. And if each science had an index, the works of the greatest men would be placed on it. It was logical errors that led one person or the other into error. In the case of mathematics at best, this claim might not be made. Also in practical life, however, we come across many such logical mistakes. Now since no one is out of danger of violating the laws of judgment, it is clear that anyone who knows the laws will, under conditions that are the same in other respects, will observe them more easily than someone else. Whoever knows the dangers avoids them more easily. For the clear facts do not always constitute a control for the correctness of conducting proofs. In the case of the highest sciences such a control is not given. With these [laws of judgment] the highest practical goals, such as politics and pedagogics, are connected. An exacting attentiveness, some will say, is directed towards finding mistakes. According to them, the special attention that follows the logical rules is not more effective than a repeated attention to argument. But this too is false, and experience refutes it. The greatest thinkers have in fact often failed to recognize fallacies, even when they were pointed out to them. Aristotle showed Plato the mistakes in his arguments, but Plato never did see these mistakes. Also with regard to the ontological argument it was like this. Gaunilo brought the error to the attention of Anselm of Caunterbury, and the latter never saw it. Nor did Descartes [see it]. Kant asserted that one must keep the law of causality strictly within the boundaries of possible experience, and yet he assumed a thing in itself that was efficacious. He never did see this mistake. The same goes for the antinomies. Here he put forward a good many paralogisms, and the fact of an antinomy could have already brought this to his attention. The same thing occurred in the case of Herbart. Indeed, there is often even dispute about what is proven or not. It is thus with regard to teleology and the theistic proofs based upon it, or with regard to the credibility of miracles (see D. Hume on miracles in his *Enquiry concerning Human Understanding*), or with regard to the proof of an empty space: some prove it by pointing out expansion by heat, while others say that in this way we could in fact also prove that it is impossible to accelerate a motion.

Lecture IV.
8 November, 84

Logic is also beneficial for the discovery of new truths. Thus Bacon of Verulam advanced natural science by formulating the correct method. Logic lies in method. At the beginning of each of his works Aristotle employs reflections concerning the method of the discipline in question. He therefore begins with a logical consideration. Bacon says: The part of philosophy that concerns logic is not suited to the taste of many and seems to be nothing but a snare of spinose subtlety; especially when we want to measure everything by its proper service, we must say that logical science is the key to the sciences: as the hand is the instrument of instruments, logic is the art of arts (*ars artium*). Thus Leibniz also placed logic very high. [Justus von] Liebig did so as well. Nowadays, however, logic does not give what it should, but it creates useless ballast as a by-product. Descartes complained about this, as did Pascal too. Logic, even elementary logic, also contains errors, although many believe that it is already a finished product [whereas] something else is still lacking. Bacon himself thinks that an intellectually weak person who is in possession of logic can outdo someone [intellectually] better who did not have it, as a child with a ruler can draw a better straight line than a good free-hand drawer can.

As far as the view that logic is an already perfected discipline is concerned, Leibniz already opposes it by saying, "There is nothing more imperfect than logic. The art of inferring from probable reasons is not yet developed."

Chapter One:
Necessity of Certain Preliminary Remarks concerning Psychical Phenomena and their Linguistic Expressions.

Aristotle says in his *Nicomachean Ethics*:

> Since happiness is an activity of soul in accordance with complete excellence, we must consider the nature of excellence; for perhaps we shall thus see better the nature of happiness. The true student of politics, too, is thought to have studied this above all things; for he wishes to make his fellow citizens good and obedient to the laws... But clearly the excellence we must study is human excellence; for the good we were seeking was human good and the happiness human happiness. By human excellence we mean not that of the body but that of the soul; and happiness also we call an activity of soul. But if this is so, clearly the student of politics must know somehow the facts about soul, as the man who is to heal the eyes must know about the whole body also; and all the more since politics is more prized and better than medicine; but even among doctors the best educated spend much labour on acquiring knowledge of the body. The student of politics, then, must study the soul, and must study it with these objects in view, and do so just to the extent which is sufficient for the questions we are discussing; for further precision is perhaps something more laborious than our purposes require.[10]

Something quite similar is true of logic. Whoever gives rules concerning cognition cannnot avoid the labor of some observations concerning psychical phenomena in general. Judgment belongs among the psychical phenomena, but other psychical phenomena as well are closely connected with judgment, especially presentations which are, after all, the basis of judgments. Some have often asserted and still frequently assert in our day that judgment consists in the affirmation or rejection of presentations. The remaining psychical phenomena, however, are related to judgments to a smaller extent.

Logicians usually employ considerations not only concerning psychical phenomena, however, but also concerning their linguistic expression. Aristotle discusses it in his own work regarding this subject matter (Περὶ Ἑρμηνείας). The Stoics followed his example. So did the scholastics, some of whom (the

---

10   [1102 a 5–15, translation by W.D. Ross.]

nominalists) fell into the danger of conceiving of logic as a whole as an investigation concerning language. John Locke dedicated the entire third book of his *Essay concerning Human Understanding* to a discussion about words. John Stuart Mill begins his logic with an investigation concerning names. Even the logicians who wanted to be purely formal have unintentionally fallen into linguistic investigation. This is what Friedrich Albert Lange (*Logical Studies*) did. How do we explain this? Language has the goal of communicating thoughts. Via the association of ideas, however, linguistic expression gets closely connected with thoughts and thereby acquires great influence on our thoughts. This influence is indeed on the whole a beneficial one. The closeness of this connection is indeed best shown by the expression: "He thinks in French." The traditionalists in fact think that we cannot at all think without speaking (cf. A. Marty "On the Origin of Language").[11] In some cases, however, language can also become detrimental to thinking. Let us briefly consider the advantages and disadvantages that language brings to thinking.

Lecture v.
11 November, 84

The advantages are as follows:
1. The associated word often prevents the confusion of concepts, especially for those which are grasped only by reflection on our own psychical activity, further however in the case of abstract concepts as well. This is seen especially in the case of numbers. 9 and 10 would be difficult to distinguish if they did not have different names. This is all the more so in the case of larger numbers.
2. Also as an aid for memory, language benefits thinking. The link of thoughts with signs is the principle of mnemonics. Thus it is hard for us to state the thoughts the Lord's Prayer in our own words without continually bringing to mind the actual wording of this prayer.
3. Language benefits thinking, however, also in the way in which the mathematician's sign benefits calculation when he replaces a simple sign, for instance, for a long one that he repeatedly needs in his calculation. The same is true of the names of large numbers. No one can present a million, for he if could do so he would have to be able to distinguish it from 10001, which is is not the case. He imagines only the name or the numeral. Something similar occurs again and again wherever a much too large complication arises.

---

11 [See *Rollinger 2010, 133–234*.]

4. In the acquisition of the mother tongue alone a wealth of communications is already made. Alexander Bain has especially appreciated this advantage.

The disadvantages of language are as follows: 1. For unequal thoughts there are often the same linguistic expressions. This circumstance is the cause of equivocation. This is of course not always equally dangerous. If concepts as such are distinguished by powerful sensory features, confusion is not to be feared. Confusion can easily come about, however, if the concepts that have the same linguistic expression are as such very similar. This is especially the case when the linguistic expression is used in reference to the same terminus (such as "imperial," which always has a relation to "emperor," but a relation that can be very different, as when we say "an imperial decree," "imperial purple," "the imperial prince," etc.). (See Franz Brentano, *Von der mannigfachen Bedeutung des Seienden*, Freiburg i. Br., 1862, pp. 96 ff.)[12] In the case of very abstract and especially complex concepts this danger is likewise very great, because the meaning of these words is as such very difficult to grasp. Mathematics is of course very abstract, but the simple technique of its words and written signs prevent the mistakes of equivocation. As soon as a mistake is made here, we avoid the equivocation with its great danger, such as [the one that occurs] when someone designates two different angles with the same concepts in a geometrical proof.

2. Yet, the converse case also frequently takes place. Different linguistic signs are often used for the same thoughts (synonymy). Here the difference of associated words prevents the discernment of the sameness of thoughts. This, however, happens especially where one of the expressions is used more in this phrase, the other more in that phrase. Or [it also happens] if the words themselves are equivocal, as in the case of the expressions "location," "place," and "local determination," etc., which are all in a certain way synonymous, though we nonetheless use them in different senses and thereby cause equivocations. Synonymy has had the effect of us often regarding identical judgments as different.

3. Some linguistic expressions are vague and often do not even have a uniform use, such as the word "formation."

4. There are also many gaps in the customary usage. Some concepts do not have a fully adequate expression.

5. The customary classification is often also incorrect (cf. Aristotle, *Posterior Analytics* II), as in the case of "chessnut," which puts wild and cultivated chessnuts together in a class.

---

12   [Brentano 1975, 65 ff.]

6. The following prejudice often makes language dangerous: Thinking reflects itself in language. The different languages have something in common and in this commonality the mirror image of thinking is to be discerned. The consideration of language, some often think, can replace that of thinking. This is altogether wrong. A certain commonality is explainable by the fact that the same is to be designated by the same instrument even if that this [commonality] in what we designate is so dissimilar that it [the instrument] cannot be regarded as an image of it [the designated]. Screaming in pain, for instance, is the same for people of the most diverse languages, and yet we do not want to assert that screaming has a similarity with pain. Many a mistake has also arisen from judging thought in accordance with linguistic expression. Thus some have believed that the subject of a statement is thought earlier than the predicate since the expression of former precedes that of the latter. This, however, is not true.

In order to avoid such mistakes, some have thus thought that we should introduce a more exact language in which these mistakes would be impossible. Leibniz occupied himself extensively with a universal written language via signs which would be intelligible for everyone receiving instruction, completely regardless of his nationality. He even expresses the hope of completing this language if he had 12 intelligent assistants. Such an endeavor would no doubt be very useful. We would have to start with the elementary concepts, however, and create very exact expressions for them. (Brentano thinks that this would also really be done.) Many logicians wanted to invent at least a new language of judgment for which the concepts, however, retain the old names. Hence they developed for judgments new algebraic signs (Lambert, Boole, Jevons).

Lecture VI.
22 November, 84

These attempts receive a certain justification, on the one hand, by the needless complication of those modes of expressions, synonymies of judgments, whereas the ambiguity of normal language in the expression of judgment [must not be overlooked]. One and the same form often expresses completely different judgments. (Quotation from Lange's *Logical Studies*.)[13] The language

---

13 [*Lange 1876, 146f.*: "Attempts have been made in two different ways to bring languages and logic into harmony. The first great attempt was made by logicians of the later middle ages with whom the direction taken by Ueberweg agrees in principle, according to the precedent of Becker and Trendelenburg. Here one tries to analyze everything logically in

that Jevons introduces makes it impossible to express all judgments. Jevons: All judgments are statements of identity and thus they can all be reduced to equations.[14] But that is incorrect, for certainly not all judgments are statements of identity. Example: "The good are the happy." Jevons would say: "The good = the happy (a = b)." Another example: "All human beings are mortal." Jevons: "The human beings are the human mortals." "Human being" = "mortal that is human." Or: "No stone is living." Jevons would say: "The stones = the non-living things that are stones." Or: "There is a tree." Jevons would say: "The tree N. N. is the existing thing that is the tree N. N." We see how complex the thought is; even if the two judgments are equivalent, they are still not the same; we cannot even translate some judgments as equivalents into Jevons' language. One must look as to whether in the manifold of ordinary language we do not perhaps encounter a form that is not unintelligible; that is better than the invention of a new form. Brentano has taken this path. Land (from Leiden) condemns Brentano's approach as unnatural. Natural and unnatural are in this case not even applicable; the language of the common people will not be designated as natural in opposition to scientific terms; natural classification is not the classification belonging to the people, but rather belonging to science.

Chapter Two:
On the Basic Classes of Psychical Phenomena

Phenomena are all that we perceive. One does not include appearances of the imagination among them.[15] When we perceive *colors*, we also perceive the *see-*

---

language and to find for every case, every mood, every form-word, etc. an exact formula with whose aid these modifications of speech can be adopted in the logical analysis. The other way is the one just described, which throws aside everything in language as useless and interfering which cannot be brought into an equation between subject and predicate. This second way has the advantage of thoroughness, whereas the like rejection of the nature of language is the basis for both. Through an exact language of signs the logician creates a new, purely intellectual medium for the expression of thought. It is lacking all the advantages of language for mental life, but is free of the disadvantages with respect to precise judging, free of all ambiguities. Its instruments are the small, flexible, strictly conventional spatial images of letters and the signs of operations. Through *taxis* and *thesis* of these in space, an unforeseeable wealth of strictly connected expressions is made possible, and it is a basic property of our cognition that every strictly consistent usage of such signs leads through all shifts of identity-expressions once again to strictly correct, directly or indirectly applicable forms."]

14 [See Jevons 1883, vol. 1.]
15 [Cf. Leisching Y 2/41: "What do we understand by a phenomenon? To make it clearly by a common expression, I say: We can call a phenomenon everything that we perceive,

ing of colors. Here the expression "perception" is even more appropriate. The color is perceived only as a phenomenon, whereas seeing is perceived as something really existing. It seems conceivable, however, that someone sees without perceiving this seeing. People have made this claim and similar ones. If this were the case, seeing would not exist as a phenomenon, but rather only in reality. But in such cases one has also called it by a modifying adjective "unconscious phenomenon" rather than a determining one. [Eduard von] Hartmann has made this claim. We shall not investigate the reasons, since they do not concern us. Some people just out-and-out deny that we ever perceive seeing. They claim that all such phenomena could be analyzed into tones, muscular feelings, colors, etc. (Reply to R. Wahle.[16]) All phenomena fall into the classes of the physical and the psychical. [The physical ones are phenomena of outer, the psychical ones however phenomena of inner perception.]

---

tones that we hear, colors that we see, heat and coldness that we feel. Something else holds for the tones and colors that we merely present in the imagination. We should not believe, however, that we do not include these fantasy-phenomena among the phenomena because nothing real corresponds to them. Also in the case of tones that we hear, etc., this is not so. It is not color that corresponds in reality to the phenomenon color. However, there are other perceptions for which the perceived does in fact exist at the same time in reality."]

16 [*Wahle 1884: 68:* "Who has perceived hearing – of course not separately, but rather together with the tone? No one can discover, in addition to the tone, also a conscious psychical phenomenon in connection with it; only tone and bodily movement and bodily sensation offer themselves." *Cf. EL* 72/12073: "This theory contradicts immediate experience. And when it requires an additional refution, the best means could be found in the consideration of the particular analyses that its advocates themselves have attempted." *Cf. the consideration in Leisching Y 2/43:* "What is willing if we dissolve it into color, tone, muscular sensation? There is a wishing present together with muscular sensation, muscular feeling. However, there is missing an exact description of what kinds of muscular feelings those are. And yet not any kind of muscular feeling could be corresponding. For it would otherwise be curious if every wishing is connected with a muscular feeling, and when I want to take a walk and go, I have a muscular feeling in my legs, etc. So what is wishing? A fantasy-presentation with muscular feelings. Now, if willing is already a wishing with muscular feelings, now [it must] therefore [be] muscular feelings to the second power! If someone at the same time has several fantasy-presentations, does he wish everything that he presents? Certainly not; from the case of choice, for instance, the contrary comes about. I wish one thing and the other [does] not. Hence it cannot be meant and one would have to express it more clearly, but would then wind up in greatest difficulties. If one finally asks also, 'What kinds of muscular feelings would someone have if he wished to have lived at the time of Alexander the Great?,' they say: Indeed, here there are no muscular feelings at all. This, however, did not lead them astray into believing that in general the fantasy-presentations are a wishing with muscle feelings. Here there is *only* a fantasy-presentation. They think that if a wish is directed at something impossible, it would be merely a fantasy-presentation. But let us take the case of someone saying, 'I wish

Lecture VII.
26 Nov. 84

The latter was designated as "inner perception," since it is itself included among the phenomena that are perceived. The physical phenomena have the common element that they appear spatially. In the case of the visual sense everyone will concede this point, whereas someone may doubt it in the case of hearing. Aristotle, however, points out that the phenomenon of hearing is localized. After immersing his head in water, [Ernst Heinrich] Weber could distinguish the direction from which a noise was coming. Even with respect to the visual sense, however, locality has been denied, but unjustifiably. The opposite is true of psychical phenomena. They do not appear spatially. Of course, one claims that pain is localized. This is true, but one must distinguish between the quality of the sense and the displeasure that is tied to it. The psychical phenomena, however, have another positive feature in common, namely the relation to an immanent object. And this relation belongs exclusively to the psychical phenomena. Nothing like it occurs among the physical phenomena. The relation to the immanent object is diversified, and according to differences in this relation one distinguishes three the main classes of the psychical phenomena: presenting, judging, states of emotion. There follows an explanation of these three classes of psychical phenomena. When an activity of the soul is not absent, each of these three classes is always represented in us, but they make up a single phenomenon that is not simple, but rather a plurality of phenomenal parts is distinguishable. The division of the three classes is not acknowledged. Usually one gives another division: thinking, feeling, willing. The claim is made [by Brentano] that in judgment a new fundamentally different relating to the immanent object exists and that these two classes [i.e. judgment and presentation] are just as distinct from each other as are thinking and willing in the old division, which I do not report here (cf. Brentano [1874], emp. psych., vol. I). The view that judgment consists in a separation or combination of presentations is combated [by Brentano]. As a proof against that view: The existential sentence "The tree is green" in comparison to "the green tree." Furthermore, in the act of memory we have an acceptance of something, or something in the past. Is memory a predication? Certainly not. The first perception is already inwardly perceived as evident without us predicating existence of it, for we do not have the concept of "existence" yet.

---

to come into the world once more,' and someone else says, 'I do not wish that,' then they both in fact present the same thing."]

Lecture VIII.
29 November 84

[Chapter Three:]
Relativity and Two-Sidedness of All Phenomena[17]

Jevons thinks that in every judgment we affirm something and deny something. "The good are the happy" means also "The non-good are not happy."

Bain formulates the following law: Every phenomenon of perception and every appearance of the imagination is, properly speaking, a relation, a connection between two positive opposites, hence two-sided. A top is not without a bottom. Heat not without cold. Also the act in which we present these phenomena is two-sided. Such a character also belongs to psychical acts. We apprehend only relations. We enjoy health and wealth only in contrast with sickness and poverty. Bain then also reaches the conclusion: The name of "being" must be devoid of all meaning, for no other opposite can be stated besides "nothing." This, however, is not a positive opposite, and thus "being" is a word without meaning since it would otherwise have to have a positive opposite. By what means does Bain justify the law? On the basis of psychologischen and psychophysical hypotheses, a decision is made about what would have to be shown to us by direct experience if it were correct. And thus he arrives at that objectionable conclusion which experience by no means confirms. Bain points out that no presenting is possible without any change, as is clear in the case of sensations. In the case of constantly persisting stimuli consciousness disappears, as it becomes stronger with a powerful change. Many transitions give powerful impressions. Every sensation must therefore be the sensation of the difference between positive opposites. As it is for sensation, it must also be similar for the other presentations. For imaginings, for example, [it must be so, according to Bain]. Hence, we cannot think of heat without presenting coldness in our thoughts. Without the thought of a straight line, that of a curved line is impossible.[18]

Critique of Bain's view: It is undeniable that we, as often as we present, have a diversified content of presentation. We always have psychical and physical phe-

---

17 [*Title of Chapter III according to Brentano 72/12002, 12083:* "Of the Presumptive Laws of Relativity and Two-Sidedness of all Phenomena"]
18 [*Vgl. Leisching Y 2/48–49:* "Thus we cannot think of heat unless we make the transition in thought from heat to coldness and from coldness to heat. Motion [is] not [conceivable] without relating it to rest. No top without a bottom even in our imagination. Accordingly, the two-sidedness and relativity seems to be a general fact for everything that we present."]

nomena. The diversified presentation is also always undergoing associations. Every single intuition exhibits a spatial adjancency of various parts. And thus [the observation of] the diversity of differences between those presentations is correct. Yet, this is no reason for us to believe that everything presented is a relation. The difference between red and blue is a relation. But even if we present both, each of them is for itself not a relation. They are the foundations. Bain's whole proof is based on change being necessary in senation. Is it proven that a change in sensation has taken place when the external stimulus changes? Is it not possible that through the increase of the external stimulus the increasing dullness of my sensation might be compensated, and thus the actual sensation remains the same? However, even if we grant this, [that the intensity changes,] can we not assume a mere change without change in quality? According to Bain, all positive determinations would constantly have to be subject to change. No red without blue. Indeed, Bain even claims that the presentation of change is not possible without a simultaneous presentation of[19] rest, whereas if everything were constantly changing there could not at all have occurred a positive presentation of rest. If, furthermore, Bain's proof did not have all these deficiencies, we might still say that what is presented is nonetheless not a relation.

Jevons and J. Stuart Mill do not accept this view of Bain. However, Mill acknowledges an echo of a truth. He also believes that every presentation is the presentation of two opposites, though only one of the opposites needs to be positive, the other negative. If I present "something" I must present "nothing." The distinction of an opposite from its contradictory opposite, according to Mill, is necessary for his consciousness, and likewise every judgment supposedly has a similar double reference to contradictory opposites. Besides the truth of being, the falsity of non-being is not something we infer, according to Mill, but rather both claims are essentially identical. For this reason, Mill thinks, no one can doubt the law of "non-contradiction." Even for phenomena of emotion, something similar exists. Whoever loves an object hates its contrary. Thus, the law of reference to contradictory opposites would be universally true.

Critique: If we hear the assertion that the denial of being is the acceptance of non-being and the hatred of being is the love of non-being, this is plausible, but "the acceptance of being is the rejection of non-being" is a harsher sounding assertion. Let us begin with an investigation of presentations: But

---

19 [*There is here an undecipherable word. Cf. the following passage in* EL 72: "And he goes so far as to fall into the coarse contradiction of claiming that the presentation of change is not possible without a simultaneous presentation of its positive opposite of rest, whereas if everything is constantly changing with respect to every positive determination a sensation and consequently a positive presentation of rest can obviously never have occurred."]

in the very domain of presentations the assumption of the law encounters an insurmountable obstacle. If it lies in the nature of psychical phenomena that there is connected with every positive presentation a presentation of its negative opposite, this must have already been so originally and in the case of the first sensation. If the first presentation was one of warmth, I must have had at that time the presentation of the non-existence of warmth. But that is impossible if what Mill says is true, that the concept of non-existence is obtained only through the reflection upon a negating judgment. The first presentation in life, however, cannot be obtained from a judgment that would have been made earlier. Being and non-being are obtained [as concepts] *only after* we make judgments. The first presentation was therefore not a presentation of an opposition, but in that case it is also incomprehensible why it is not also impossible for us later to have a presentation without conducting the negative opposition. Wherever we really and properly connect the two opposites, things are quite different. As the first presentation therefore exhibits no relation, neither does the first judgment and the first feeling exhibit a relation to a negative opposite. It is clear as a general matter that if the law is no longer tenable in the domain of presentation, there is no universal validity [of this law] in other domains, since the presentations are the basis of all other [psychical] phenomena.

Lecture IX.
3 December 84

[Chapter Four:]
Nature and Origin of our Presentations[20]

What our presenting is and how it differentiates itself from judgment and the phenomena of emotion has been shown. There is no presenting without something presented, the latter of which is often called "presentation." Belonging to the presentations are [1)] the presentations of outer perceptions (intuitions), [2)] the presentations of outer imagination, [3)] the presentations of inner perception and [4)] those of inner imagination. Included among them are also the abstract and the *a priori* presentations, which are not acceptable for everyone.

By abstract presentations one has in mind presentations that have been obtained by a kind of simplification from other ones, and we include these

---

20 [*Title of Chapter Four according to* EL 72/1203: "Of the Nature and Origin of our Presentations"]

among the presentations from experience, whereas the *a priori* presentations are independent of experience. They are either individual, and then they are *a priori* intuitions, or general, and then one calls them *a priori* concepts. One includes among *a priori* intuitions space (according to Kant), while the concept of cause belongs among the *a priori* concepts (according to Kant). The separation of the first two classes from the last two, i.e. [the separation] of the outer presentations [1) and 2)] from the inner ones [3) and 4)], is quite clear. The separation of inner perception from the presentation of inner imagination is equally clear to us. Not so clear, however, is the separation between the class of outer perception and that of imagination. We may indeed say that everything that is presented as past or future belongs to imagination. This has often been overlooked, as when one believes oneself to be actually perceiving motion or rest, likewise the presentations of change and endurance. If something is presented as present, it is however not for this reason alone a presentation. We have no criterion here. But one has tried to find such a criterion in intensity. The perceptual presentation is to have greater fullness and greater intensity. Yet, that is not true. The fantasy-presentations have different degrees of intensity. Where is now the limit by which we can tell that it is a presentation and no longer a fantasy? The fantasies of those sick with fever and dreaming belong here, also those of waking people sometimes, as [we see] from Goethe, also from Johannes Müller.

Some have said, however, that a perceptual presentation is wherever there is stimulation of the peripheral organ. If, however, the nerve in the midst of the traversed course is stimulated or right at the entry into the brain, would we still call it peripheral? We can no longer clearly distinguish. And this difference was surely known in earlier times when physiology was less known. Even before physiology one spoke of darkness before the eyes. Hence, no stimulation would exist here, and still this presentation belonged among the perceptions. Some have wanted to see the difference in psychical preconditions by saying that we have voluntary power over the fantasy-presentations. However, the will often has a very incomplete power over the fantasy-presentations. Some have furthermore said: A fantasy-presentation is always a repetition as an effect of an earlier impression. But this is also insufficient. The imagination shows something as past, whereas perception never shows it as past, and thus we have a different presentation. One might perhaps say that the fantasy-presentation is a result of an earlier psychical disposition as acquired through similar acts. Certain products are also neither pure sensory presentations nor pure fantasy-presenations. There is thus likewise a great affinity between the fantasy-presentations and the perceptual sensations. This distinction is thus important for psychology, but not for logic, since presentations of either kind do not have the advantage of reality. More important is a characterization of the *content* of this whole main genus [i.e. outer intuitions]. They are always complex presentations, for they contain [a series of elements]:

1. Sensory quality: They are of different genera, and according to their number one divides the number of senses and of the corresponding classes of outer fantasies.

Color.

a) Such a genus is color. Six colors are of particular importance: black, white, blue, yellow, red, green; all other colors are to be determined by extraction from these. The *color-body* follows. The distances of the particular corner-colors are not equal to each other. Thus blue is closer to black than yellow is. The method of finding the relative ratios of distance might be the "method of the just-noticeable differences" (as [Gustav] Fechner calls it). This [method], however, is not precise, for in the case of greater practice smaller and smaller differences are noticed. We see this more clearly in the case of tones, for in very high and very deep tones one no longer perceives differences that one perceives in the middle tonal range. In this range, however, one has the greatest practice.

Lecture x.
6 December, 84

Sound.

b) Sound [is a second genus of sensory quality]. There are countless kinds of sound. The most important are pure simple tones which make up the scale. This has often been compared with a straight ascending line, but very wrongly. The octave seems to be closer to the fundamental tone than is every other tone, and after this the fifth. The tonal ladder has thus been compared with a spiral. It is highly questionable, however, whether every sound lies in this. [Hermann von] Helmholtz does not believe so regarding certain noises, although we can distinguish also among these higher and lower ones. But doubts can also be raised with regard to the tones that are not pure and simple. Thus in the case of chords and tones that have a timbre in their entire unison. An attempt to explain this has been made by [appealing to] the overtones. It is nonetheless possible that some vibrations of various kinds exist outside. The question, however, is whether they arouse a unitary acoustic product or whether they are perceived as a plurality. When Helmholtz says that he selectively hears the overtones from the particular vowels, this would be proof if it were true. This is very doubtful, however, as it is likewise not true that we selectively see yellow and red from orange, as Goethe thought. If no true unitariness were given in a chord, we could not grasp why it is more difficult to distinguish its particular tones than when we hear them in temporal succession. Indeed, one should be able to hear them yet much more distinctly in the chord, since they are temporally much more condensed. There is further a curious circumstance in the case of certain chords in contrast with others. As regards harmonic multi-sounds, we apprehend the plurality with much greater difficulty than in regarding unharmonic ones. The latter are accompanied by an unpleasant feeling, by a feeling that never accompanies simple tones. Many people could thus, in their judgment of the plurality of sounds, arrive at this feeling and thus see it as the criterion of plurality. Some say that in harmony the tones fuse with each other, whereas in disharmony they do not. What does does this "fusing" mean? Do the tones become one single tone? One does not concede this. If not, however, one simply does not speak of fusing.[21] Yet, the fact is also there, without any analogy, that we perceive a plurality of qualities of one and the same genus as a unity, therefore without distinctions of location. In order to escape this, some have have said that in the case of a chord there is in fact a temporal succession of tones, but one that is so rapid that one does not at all notice the plurality, but rather accepts it as a unity. It might be possible, however, that on a direct line between two points of the tonal spiral there are other new tones, similar to the case of the color-body. A unitary fusing is before us in the case of taste and smell together, just as in the case of temperature and tactile quality [e.g. roughness and smoothness]. Thus some food tastes differently when eaten cold and warm, just like sliced or mashed potatoes.

Lecture XI.
10 December 84

2. Intensity [is a second element of contents]. It is found in all sensory presentations. [Ewald] Hering disputes this. He thinks that there are presentations without intensity, and these are visual presentations. No affinity, he thinks, is found between what we see and what we hear with regard to what we call intensity. We can call something "intensely black" just as we can call something "intensely white." Marty, who opposes this view, asserts that there is undeniably a difference in intensity between a perception and the corresponding fantasy-image, from which it follows that intensities must exist.

---

21 [*Cf. Leisching Y 2/65:* "Do they become one? That is what I think. No, they do not become one, but they fuse. I admit that I am completely unable to grasp this."]

Some regard intensity as a magnitude, though [they do so] wrongly. Herbart says that wherever we can speak of a "more or less" we are dealing with a magnitude. Gauß, by contrast, says that magnitude involves something more than this, namely that it contains equal parts, and this is correct. A higher intensity is not composed of two equal lower ones. The distances between two intensities do in fact have a magnitude, but intensity has none, just as tones are not magnitudes although their distances are. The same goes for colors and temporal and spatial points. The intensities can therefore be symbolized by the *points* of a straight line, but not by line-segments. The intensities are therefore not magnitudes, but in fact degrees.

Do intensities of all sensory presentations belong to one genus? Yes, for even presentations of different quality can be compared to each other with regard to their intensity. We can say of a smell that it is more intense than a tone.

3. Location [is, in addition to quality and intensity, also an element of sensory presentations]. It not true that only what lies between two points establishes the difference between them. Already the fact of the blind spot speaks against this. It was [Edme] Marriot who first demonstrated the existence of a gap in our visual field, although this occurs in the case of every human being. Imagination simply fills out this blind spot.

Another incorrect opinion is this: that the location consists only of local relations. (Leibniz spoke in favor of this view.) The local relations need foundations, as do all relations as such. They change only concomitantly, whereas the foundations change absolutely. We can, to be sure, be misled by the fact that we always determine the locations relatively. But we turn to such determinations also in domains where relations are not under consideration, as when we determine nuances of color, and yet color is an absolute determination. In the case of a single perception, infinitely many local determinations exist, but they are connected together in infinitesimal distances. For this reason every spatial image is a continuum. Since a plurality of local determinations is always given, we can easily fall prey to the error that the local determines consist only in relations.

Some have further opposed the view that locations are given in the perceptual presentations.[22] Locations, they say, are only in the imagination. This is

---

22 [*It was above all Hermann Lotze who disputed this and put forward his theory of local signs in opposition to it. This theory is for Brentano and many of his contemporaries an empiricist theory of the presentation and perception of space, whereas the view that locations are included in the contents of sensations was for them a nativist theory. Cf. Stumpf 1873, where the nativist theory receives support, although the author of that work was a student of Lotze as well as Brentano.*]

wrong. (Cf. Brentano's lectures on selected questions of psychology [winter semester 1883], chapter "Empiricism and Nativism"[23]).

It has further been doubted whether local determinations are given in all perceptual presentations, but wrongly. They are given even in the case of hearing.

We could also raise the question whether location is of one and the same genus for different senses.

[William] Molyneux posed the question whether someone born blind who could distinguish a sphere and a cube by means of the tactile sense can make the same distinction with the visual sense after an operation. Locke answers: no. And indeed correctly; the eye's sense of proportion and the hand's sense of proportion are not the same. Indeed, even the hand's sense of proportion and the skin's are not the same. Thus we estimate the distance between two points of a compass upon different places of the body, although we discern the signs everywhere. According to Brentano, the local determinations that we establish by different senses are of one and the same genus, but certainly different in species, such that no visual phenomenon shows a local determination that is equal to those which we receive in hearing.

Lecture XII.
13 December, 1884

The question is now whether we [have sensations of] only surfaces or also of bodies. If we have sensations of only surfaces, we certainly have sensations of curved surfaces, as when we run our finger around the throat and back to the starting point. It is furthermore assuredly true that we see three-dimensional spaces in our imagination. The imagination is able as such to expand the spaces and thus to form new species; nor is a definite species to be stated here, although the imagination cannot expand space infinitely; there are individual limits. The imagination cannot in any case insert a fourth dimension into these three dimensions. Four-dimensional magnitudes are not an absurdity, but four-dimensional spaces are so. The same is true of the expression "curved space." If, in a four-dimensional continuum, we think of a four-dimensional space that is curved with regard to the four dimensions, we have a concept of a "curved space." In the case of the species of the location we do find a + and −, as in the case of intensity. In no perceptual presentation of one and the same sense does

---

23   [*Hillebrand's notes from this lecture are copied in Husserl Q 9.*]

the same location appear twice; an exception would be hearing, if it were true that we perceive several tones at the same time.

4. Time [must still be considered]. Nothing has been the topic of so many incorrect claims, whereas nothing is more intelligible than temporal specification in common life. Some fall prey to errors by attempting to explain in another way something that might be explained only indicating facts. We find examples in all sensory domains of the imagination. We can best take the example from the domain of tones. Let imagine two equally intense tones of the same quality in a melody. These are differentiated only by time. It would be an erroneous opinion if one were to believe that what makes the difference is what lies between them. A mere pause refutes this. Another error: The particular temporal specification consists only in a plurality of temporal relations of something temporally determinate to something else. All of time would therefore be a relation. Temporal relations certainly do exist, but they require absolute temporal specifications as their basis. There also remains temporal specification whenever only one single punctual tone would occur in imagination. Here too our constatnt relative temporal specifications in our indications of time were misleading. Aristotle himself fell prey to this error. Also in the case of time, there are infinitely many species. However, the set of temporal kinds lags behind the local kinds, as they are comparable to the points of one single ordered line. One single point indicates the present and divides future from past. It is an external limit, not an internal one. That is to say, it does not belong to the two adjacent points, but rather to neither one of those two. The present is therefore a *terminus extensecus*, as the Scholastics say.

We often call something that is partly past and partly future "present": the present hour, the present day, etc.

The following doubt is raised: Can the totality of temporal specifications really be symbolized by a straight line, or rather be a slightly curved line. If the latter were so, time might well return into itself. Wundt (cosmological problem)[24] has taken this hypothesis into consideration. It is nonetheless absurd, no different if one were to believe in the case of intensity that its series is a curved line, such that the highest intensity would coincide with the zero-point. The corresponding hypothesis concerning time is exactly as absurd. The entirety of the temporal species is comparable to a straight line without beginning or end. Nonetheless, this continuum cannot be presented in a sensory way, just as an infinite space or an infinite series of numbers cannot. Someone might now say, however, that we cannot assert that the temporal line is endless if we

---

24   [*Wundt 1877.*]

cannot endlessly present it. Reply: One must distinguish the question whether real things exist without beginning and end or whether the series of temporal species is infinite in both directions. This, however, is the result of a comparison with a straight line. Of the countless kinds of time, countless ones are given every time in a sensory presentation. If we present something in a sensory manner, the perceptual presentation expands itself constantly through an added fantasy-presentation, and this is also a reason for the false view that time consists only in relations. There is yet an additional circumstance that misleads: namely that time, even if it is truly determined, consists of determinations none of which is real except one single temporal species (present), and it is doubtful whether we should call this (present) an absolute temporal specification.

Lecture XIII.
17. December 84

Time has thus far shown itself to be akin in many ways to location. However, it very much differentiates itself from all earlier considered elements, especially by the fact that in its various species it is found in no perceptual presentation as such, but rather only in the imagination. Through a special association, namely through an original one, the first appearances of the past arise. One could call these appearances "appearances of the momentary memory." This memory, however, does not present a temporal point. A motion that is not too slow becomes noticeable, just as a repeated change, as in the case of a melody of which one believes that one "hears it," one believes that what what has immediately occurred before is heard. In the case of an auditory fantasy this momentary memory seems to have a special extension as in the case of the visual sense. Supported by these appearances, the imagination then forms the presentation of the future. The process here is similar to those where it arrives at new tones, colors, locations. As the just-past relates to the present, the present by analogy relates to the future. We have this, for instance, when we are expecting. Here it is clear how wrong it is to think that the imagination offers no new moments. What the significance of this is, however, is shown by divergences, as shown by a second peculiarity which differentiates the past and future times from all earlier ones, namely that they do not determine the elements of the sensory presentation in way in which those elements determine each other, but rather they modify them. A loud C is a C, a soft D is a D. A red or blue that is here or there is a red or blue. But a past tone C is not a tone C, a future red is not a red, not any more than a past king is a king, next year's harvest is a harvest. The past and future temporal specifications therefore do not determine that with which they are connected, but rather alter them essentially. It is like the case of the presentations "possible" or "presented," a merely possible dollar is not a dollar. A future dollar is not a dollar. Only the present is an exception, for a present emperor is really an emperor. By the fact that an emperor is a present emperor, he is simply an emperor. This temporal specification can therefore be called a zero of specification, properly speaking, for it is neither determining nor altering, speaking of course only absolutely. In a perceptual presentation there is nothing at all added because it presents something as now. The temporal specifications which, properly speaking, do not really bring something special into our presentations are modifying rather than determinative. Here is the place for correcting an earlier statement. We have said that every sensory presentation contains quality, intensity, and location, both the perceptual presentation and the fantasy-presentation. That is incorrect. The fantasy-presentations that present something as future or past do not do so. They contain no local specification, qualities, or intensities. Also for aesthetics there is a special result here. Herbart saw everything beautiful in relations of what lies in the same genus. Through his actual procedure, however, he came into contradiction with his principles, namely in his idea of freedom. Some (Trendelenburg and [Franz Karl] Lott) have said that there is no relation between willing and presenting according to Herbart, and nonetheless the enjoyment of freedom is to lie in the correspondence of these two. Some of Herbart's students have thought that one only compares willing with the presentation of willing. But imagined willing is simply not willing. The contradiction, however, is more general. In the melody there are relations between a past tone and a present tone, and the past tone is in fact not a tone. A poet can likewise be aesthetically engaged between what he shows as existing and he shows as to be expected.

There arise as consequences some truths, above all, that we can claim of everything real with assurance that if it *is* it is *now*, for there is no "plus" of specifications added by the "now." Furthermore, since this now as a zero-point has a definite distance from every other temporal species, it follows that everything stands in a temporal relation to everything. Furthermore, it likewise follows that everything that is will be in a hundred years something simultaneously in the past and it was a hundred years ago something simultaneously in the future.[25] Something else results from what has been said: What is future appears [as] opposed to what is past. Opposites are mutually exclusive in the

---

25 [*Cf. Leisching Y* 2/94: "Since this now as a zero-point has a determinate distance from every species for the position of past and future temporal specifications, it follows that every-

same subject. Nonetheless, something can be past and future. Every case of duration is an example of this, where during the duration what endures is at the same time past, future, and present. This becomes clear from the fact that the past and future temporal specification does not determine, but rather modifies. It is like saying that opposites belong to someone when he is loved and hated at the same time. We have, on the basis of what has been said, noticed highly curious peculiarities of the specifications of past and future, but we still have to add that they are not real specifications. What is meant when we say that certain specifications are real? We shall explain this with examples. Just as the presented, the accepted, hated, painted, etc. are not real specificiations, past and future times are not so. These specifications have a similarity, but it is a negative one. The character of the non-real betrays itself in a series of peculiarities. We find the temporal specifications in the imagination as modifications of real elements. We could transfer them to other real things. We can, however, allow them to be added in the same modifying way to something else and to something non-real. We can speak of a past impossibility, of a future impossibility. However, I cannot speak of a green or blue impossibility, for green and blue [unlike past and future] are not [non-]real specifications.[26] I can also say of a centaur that it was believed-in, but I cannot say that it, as believed-in, was half man and half horse, at best that it was a believed-in [half] animal, half man. Furthermore, when past or future temporal specifications are added to real elements, they modify them, but such that these become non-reals themselves. The only curious thing here is that these non-real temporal specifications can belong to a series with actually real temporal specification and then connect with this through infinitesimal differences. How a past time is separated from another by infinitesimal distinctions is shown by the non-real character in that they can have no independent becoming. They become and cease to be without really being effected or destroyed. There is now an Augustus-having-lived-1884-years-ago-in-Rome. In a hundred years, however, this has ceased and there is an Augustus-having-lived-1984-years-ago, and yet nothing has destructively affected Augustus 1884 years ago, as indeed the present Augustus can disappear. Temporal specifications of all kinds are attached as a necessary consequence to all coming-about and passing-away that takes place in the present, for of

---

thing stands in a temporal relation with everything, that everything that is has always been in the future and will always be past, that it, compared with what existed a hundred years ago is something that is a hundred years later, etc."]

26 [*Brentano EL 72/12132:* "We can, for instance, speak of a past or future impossibility: It was, is, or will be. By contrast, [it is] not [permissible to speak] of a green or blue impossibility and the like."]

everything that *is* it is certain that, due to the fact that it *is*, it will always *have been* and always is *something-future in the past*. It has this independence of its becoming and ceasing in common with some other non-reals, hence with the presented, loved, hated. If presenting ceases, presenting ceases, the presented ceases, certainly not through a direct affecting. Once again, the clear impossibility of immediate action at a distance in time is understandable as a consequence of non-reality. One has for a long time considered it to be ridiculous that something has an immediate effect spatially into the distance. This hypothesis would be absurd only if it involved thinking that the same thing would have to be in two different locations. This, however, is difficult to demonstrate. In the case of time an immediate action at a distance is never acceptable, for in that case either something past, i.e. something non-real as such, would have to have an effect or something future, i.e. something non-real as such, would have to have been affected. In this case common sense has been correct. Also past and future motions and changes are not real, but also a present motion is so only in that it, as long as it is present, gradually runs its course and is past or future in certain parts. Indeed, it is real only in one single moment. Aristotle already knew this when he said that κινήσις is an ἐνέργεια ἀτελή [(incomplete actuality)].[27]

Lecture XIV.
20 December 84

We have already earlier raised the question whether a + or – belongs to various specifications. Let us ask this with regard to time. Here there is no question of a gradation. Of course the view might be recommended. The present does not add a new specification to what is called present, whereas the temporal specifications "past" and "future" modify. This might make us feel compelled to consider the present as a zero-point and to designate the specifications of past and future as different degrees. Yet, one cannot say that the first infinitesimal time after the present is a modification of smaller significance, for it does in fact remove reality. If indeed one were to concede that one speaks of degrees of past and future, we would have to object that someone takes one single temporal species as a magnitude. Just don't forget that neither past nor future are to be regarded as one species. Rather, they include a host of species that are as different from each other as they are from the present. Another question.

---

27 [*Insertion in square brackets according to Höfler E. 2. 1/74.*]

Someone might attempt to deny of the momentary memory-presentation the temporal specification and have this added only by acquired association. People who are empiricists with regard to location always feel compelled to assume certain local signs in the perceptual presentations. Thus, one would have to speak of temporal signs in the case of time. Yet, it is impossible to state in what these signs consist or from where the true temporal specification is taken or how it is made by us from the given elements for the sake of associating it with the temporal signs. As regards the first question, we might think only of differences in intensity and view these as the essence of temporal signs. How should we find our way in the case of a decrease of a stimulus that evokes our presentation, as when someone plays a decrescendo where the fantasy-image of the previous tone is stronger than the following perceptual presentation. There can be no doubt that this is the case, for the imagination is in fact very strong. From where, however, is one also to take the temporal presentation for the sake of associating it. One might at best derive the temporal specification from judgment, since one can temporally modify the copula. This, however, is something to be discussed in the theory of judgment.

Relations. There are relations of difference. Thus, quality is different from location, tone from color. Furthermore, relations of equality: We have two red points. These, as red, are equal to each other. Color and tone are equal to each other as qualities. Colors that are perceived together are equal to each other as colors of equal temporal specification. However, we also have relations of combination: relations of the combined to what is combined with it as well as relations between what is *contained* in the combination and what *contains* the combination, i.e. part and whole. The tonal quality and intensity are parts. They are connected with each other. Or: parts of a color that extends from one location to another. The two examples, however, show that the combinations are very different. Thus, we can distinguish various relations of parts and wholes, mainly four:

1. The combination with a whole is given through physical connections: a relation between physical parts and physical wholes. An example is: the parts of a line or of a temporal stretch.

2. The relation where the combination occurs in such a manner as properties are combined with each other: a relation of metaphysical parts and metaphysical wholes. These include location, temporal specification, quality.

3. The parts are combined with each other as genus and differentia are: a relation of logical wholes and logical parts, or logical parts among each other. Color relates to redness as a logical part to a logical whole. Each of these three relations is a very intimate combination.

4. An additional manner of combination consists in each case of belonging to a certain combining complex of some type of relation: These are collective combinations. An especially important case of this fourth kind is the case where the belonging of the parts is given by relations of equality. It is in this case the relation of part to whole, that between unit and plurality. Every unit in the plurality is equal to the other. And the pluralities are either finite [or infinite. If they are finite,] the whole is a number. [If they are] infinite, it is an innumerable set, e.g. the points in a line.

Every relation of part and whole [is, in its manner, of the highest importance for all logic and far beyond that].[28]

[In contrast with the collective relation,] 2. the metaphysical relation of wholes and parts [can be characterized as follows]: Each part of a collective contributes equally much to the whole: This is not the case here. Each of the elements [are] quality, intensity, etc. What appears as the most prominent to a human being is quality. If the same local relations remain given with other absolute local specifications, it seems to be little changed. It is indeed [more] significant, if an intensity [is changed].[29] Thus, one regards quality as the main part, as the essential one. This is also clear in the present discussion. A change can occur in our visual presentation when we present a red point and the quality of the color changes in one place, while the intensity remains unchanged, or vice-versa. Thus, the location can change, [while intensity remains unchanged]. In the latter case we never say that the intensity has changed the location. We only say that the quality has changed, or that the phenomenon has changed in its quality.[30] Thus we grasp the quality as that which is imbued with the others [i.e. intensity and location] as properties, and this is

---

28 [*Insertions in square brackets are made in this sentence in accordance with Brentano* EL 72/12148.]

29 [*The words added in brackets in this sentence are based on Leisching Y 2/109, in which the following sentence immediately follows:* "However, even a change of the degree of intensity is regarded as smaller than a change of quality."]

30 [*Brentano* EL 72/12150: "In our visual presentation, when we [see] a red point on a gray matted basis, there can ensue a change in that the quality of the color changes in the place, while the intensity remains unchanged, or the intensity changes and the quality and the local determination remains while the location where a red point appears on the matted basis changes continually. In the third case we say: The quality has changed its location. In the second case: The quality has changed its intensity. However, we hardly say in the third case that the intensity has changed its place, or in the second: The location has changed its intensity. In the first case, finally: How do we express ourselves? Here too we do not say that the intensity has changed its quality, or even that the location has changed its quality, but rather only that the quality has changed, or also the phenomenon, i.e. the metaphysical whole consisting of quality, intensity, and location, has changed in its quality."]

the relation which is to exist between substance and accidents. Of course, by "substance," we do not usually think of a sensory quality (according to Aristotle). We can, however, follow the few steps that lead to this concept. Aristotle believed in the existence of sensory qualities in the external world. He believed that qualities of various senses are locally unified in reality and interpenetrate each other. There is among them a belonging to the same metaphysical whole. In this whole, however, none of these qualities is to be called the more essential part. Aristotle thought of another bearer as existing, and that was his substance.[31]

[Lecture XV.
7 January, 85][32]

[Concerning] 3. the relation between the logical parts and the logical whole [we can further say:] The logical whole never reaches metaphysically beyond a single part and never [reaches] physically farther than the logical part reaches. For example: "Red" and "the color" stand in this relation. Color belongs to the same metaphysical part as red. The example "intense red" and "red," however, would be an incorrect example because another metaphysical part is added, namely intensity. However, the example "here and there" and "local specification" would be correct, or: "a being at a particular time" a logical part of the "a being at this or that time," or: "enduring" and "temporal." What is also noteworthy is that the logical whole adds to the logical part only what is incon-

---

31   [*Cf. EL* 72/12151: "Aristotle believed in the existence of sensory qualities and their intensities and local determinations and believed that qualities of different senses [are] locally unified and interpenetrating. Thus he imagined that between them there existed in this mutual interpenetration a belonging to the metaphysical whole. In this whole, however, none of the parts was to be called the more essential one, and thus he thought, by analogy to the position of the quality of the phenomenon to the location and its intensity, another bearer [as] existing, and this was for him thus the proper being to which all properties are attached: the substance. This consideration, correctly stated, puts an end to an abundance of unclarities from which logic and metaphysics have suffered for millenia and still do suffer. The more exact consideration of the relation of the logical parts, however, will yield for us a similar gain." *Cf. also Leisching Y 2/111:* "This consideration puts an end to an abundance of unclarities from which logic and metaphysics have suffered for millennia and still suffer. As Aristotle imagined the thing endowed with the qualities, the thing cannot be this way. The qualities do not exist really, nor are they attached to it. But whether it may be asserted with assurance whether we actually find an analogous relation, as found in our definition, this is another question."]

32   [*The date is taken from Leisching Y 2/111.*]

ceivable without it, such that the addition is itself not properly to be thought of as a second new part, but rather contains the first part. For example: Color is a logical part of red. In order for color to become red, what is added? Red. But does color lie in red itself? Yes. Thus, the division into parts is a one-sided one. Also in the "here" there lies the concept of local specification. The division into parts, however, can be repeated again and again. Red has color as its logical part, but then also "quality." The ultimate and no further divisible logical part was called the "highest genus" by Aristotele, insofar as his use of the term differed from today's. A genus and its differentiae together is called "species." But every differentia is, properly speaking, identical with the relevant species itself. The ordered arrangement of these logical parts, from the highest genus to the ultimate difference, was called called ὅρος – definition – by Aristotle. He therefore has in mind here a relation between part and whole that essentially differs from the relation of metaphysical parts. All the knowledge of this particular relation, however, has actually been lost. The the sentence "A stallion is a male horse," according to Aristotle, is not a definition because there is no essential unity between "horse" and "male." Indeed, according to a contemporary view of definition, one might designate any random arrangement of features by a name, and yet there would be no definition. One might in this case assume any random feature as a genus. It would be a matter of indifference whether one says "a rectangular red" or "a red rectangle." The proper concept of definition is lost. Aristotle assumed that the substance has logical parts. Certain observations seem to be in harmony with this. Thus, John Stuart Mill remarks:

> There are some classes, the things contained in which differ from other things only in certain particulars which may be numbered, while others differ in more than can be numbered, more even than we need ever expect to know.[33]

Etc. Further:

> While, if any one were to propose for investigation the common properties of all things which are of the same colour, the same shape, or the same specific gravity, the absurdity would be palpable. We have no ground to believe that any such common properties exist, except such as may be shown to be involved in the supposition itself, or to be derivable from it by

---

33   [*Mill*, A System of Logic, *I. 7. §4.*]

some law of causation... There is no impropriety in saying that, of these two classifications, the one answers to a much more radical distinction in the things themselves, than the other does.[34]

What would be better than to conceive of this radical distinction as a distinction in substance, a distinction which, as a metaphysical part, is determinative in the most diverse directions? Thus, these things seem substantially related in a very special manner. And since these class-concepts are sometimes more general, sometimes less general, one would have to accept, as a matter of consistency, a more general affinity and accordingly establish different logical parts. For example: body, living body, animal living body, mammal, carnivorous mammal, feline, lion, etc. We would however have to be more careful even if we believed the hypothesis of substance secured. We should indeed consider that these distinctions must be traced back in various ways to distinctions of substance. Perhaps the peculiarities of animals that are shown by experience is based on a system of substances rather than a hypothesis of substances, and it suffices that in this [system] one or several of them connected in different ways would provide a set of peculiarities. However, one was not so careful. More was done. Aristotle himself fell into errors. Not only did avoid doubts about the existence of such qualities, but he was not clear about the fact that the underlying substance for him was a hypothesis that he formed. Rather, he got it in his head that intuition itself shows him the substance in connection with the properties. In addition, he thought that it must be possible to state the properly logical parts of a substance, its genus and higher and lower differentiae, instead of being content to view in a certain complex of properties an indication of the substance. Thus, he believed that body, animal, plant are concepts of substances that can properly be defined by names of genus and differentia just as "red" and "blue." He endeavored to give the the presumptive definitions of substances the character of that true definition and thus especially to fufil the requirement that the logical parts must be one-sided parts, and that every following differentia is to be the differentia of the immediately preceding one. While it was necessary to diverge from Aristotle, people kept the terms "differentia," "definition," "species," "genus" and forgot their original meaning. They spoke of genus and species for every natural classification, where a unitary goal was thus maintained for every progressive division of objects. Nothing at all was left over of any relation to logical parts. Even the common people and every general name of their language is a term for a class. In this case, however, there

---

34   [*Ibid.*]

is no unitary prupose as there is in natural classification, and there could be nothing that had the slightest similarity with genus and differentia as understood by Aristotle. Thus, one would regard it as a definition if one were to say: "Die Bürgschaft" by Schiller is a poem that Schiller wrote in honor of friendship in this or that year. Here we have a explanation by means of a statement of circumstances that belong externally to the object. Hence, we find the word "definition" no longer used in the sense of any kind of conceptual analysis, but rather simply as "lexigraphical explanation."[35] We too shall clearly make use of this expression, but we must retain the especially important relation between logical whole and logical parts in its peculiarity with full clarity. The logical part as understood by Aristotle is in and of itself more unspecific than the logical whole. Also in the logical whole, however, full specificity is missing. Full specificity is given by what is not included in the logical whole. A "red," for instance, is individualized by the statement of "location" or time or intensity, hence by means specifications that do not belong to the same metaphysical whole. It is better for us to discuss the physical parts after the relations of equality and difference.

[Lecture XVI.
10 January 85][36]

Equality and difference.
They differ in each case depending on what makes equal things equal and different things different. They can be equal in quality, as all red things, or in intensity or in location or in time. Not all equals in quality are so in the same way. Some of them are so only as regards the genus. Differently colored things are thus qualitatively equal as colored. And of things equal only as regards the genus, some of them are equal as regards the lower genus, others as regards the higher genus. The following distinction is especially to be considered: the distinction between equality in the proper sense and an essentially different matching, [i.e.] quasi-equality or equals with μετάβασις εἰς γένος. For example, this obtains between a human being and a presented [or merely imagined] human being, which is nothing real and not truly a human being. In

---

35 [*EL 72/12162:* "Thus we find nowadays the word 'definition' very often being used not only no longer in the Aristotelian sense, which has been lost altogether, but rather not at all any longer in the sense of any conceptual analysis, but rather synonymous with 'lexigraphical explanation.'"]

36 [*The date is taken from Leisching Y 3/6.*]

the domain of what we have analyzed thus far, such a case of equality is that between a present tone and a past tone retained in our memory-presentation. There is also a quasi-generic equality and quasi-specific equality. The relations of difference are no less diverse. Special attention should be given to the differentiae between the lowest logical differences (as understood by Aristotle), whenever there is equality of the lowest genus. If a lowest genus has more than two species, their differences are always what we call "distance." That is to say, if we compare the difference between two with that between two others, we find that one of the differences is equal or greater or smaller with the other than it is. The differences between various species of number are either equal or smaller or greater. Or: The differences between colors are distances. The differences between tones are likewise distances. The differences between intensities are likewise distances. Likewise, with regard to locations, times. In the case of number-species the larger ones are differences, while in the case of other classes all differences are magnitudes (as understood by Gauß, according to whom the unit is not a magnitude, and thus in the case of numbers only differences in magnitude are meant). This is never true of other differences other than those of different species of the lowest genus. The difference between time and location and the difference between red and color is neither equal nor greater nor smaller.

If one says that [there is] a greater difference between quality and temporal specification than between space and time, one means only: There are more differences [between quality and temporal specification] since we find in the case of time and space some similarities. However, some of the species of quasi-equal genus are an exception and are like two species of the same genus, namely wherever the altering specification that simply makes up the quasi-equality shows differences. A distance thus obtains between a color now and a color a second ago, for here the temporal specification is added as altering and exhibits this distance. Wherever there are distances, there are always infinitely many coordinate species and quasi-species. Of these distances, a smallest one is sometimes possible, e.g. the unit in the case of the number-species, whereas smaller differences are sometimes not conceivable in every rational and irrational proportion, e.g. in the case of locations, colors. In these cases every distance is therefore a magnitude (as understood by Gauß), but no distance here is infinitely small or large. Only in the genus *set* in which there is a smallest possible specific distance, namely the unit, is there a specific distance, the largest possible which is of infinite magnitude, i.e. the distance between the uncountable and every finite species of number. There is a distinction to be made between proper and improper infinity. If I take the series $1 + 1 + 1 + 1 + 1$ etc. and allow it thus to keep growing, to what magnitude does it grow?

The sum becomes infinitely large, but in an improper sense. For it exceeds every specifiable finite magnitude. There is, however, also infinity in the proper sense. Example: The set of points in a line is infinite in the proper sense. (?)[37] The possible numbers are an uncountable number. Bolzano (*Paradoxien des Unendlichen*) correctly made this point. The following becomes curious: If one has two infinite sets, one can order a member of one set with a member of the other pairwise. Let us imagine an infinite series of numbers 1, 2, 3, 4, 5 etc. and the series 2, 4, 6, 8, 10 etc., such that in both cases no remainder is left over insofar as one coordinates the series 2, 4, 6, 8, 10 etc. to 1, 2, 3, 4, 5 etc. We can however also order them such that there is some random remainder left on one side or the other. One has called these distinctions that result from the manner of coordinating the "number of the infinite set" (G. Cantor). Thus someone might ask whether or how it is possible to order the points pairwise to a greater or smaller line such that there is a remainder on both sides and it is likewise possible to order the set of points of a line to the set of points of a surface. Let us imagine a straight line and the square beyond this line.

If we bisect the line *a b* and likewise the whole square *in infinitum*, we have in *a b* at first 3 points, then 9, then 17. Thus [we have] 3, 9, 17, 33 etc. In the square we get 9, 25, 81 etc. Now it is clear that the set of points 3, 5, 9, 17, 33 etc. is greater than the set 2, 4, 8, 16, 32. The series 9, 25, 81 etc., however, is smaller than the series 16, 64, 256. This last series contains digits that appear to us in the series 2, 4, 8, 16, 32. Therefore, one can similarly order the points of the square pairwise in relation to the points of the line.

[Lecture XVII.
14 January, 85][38]

Cantor, however, believes that also in these uncountables there are greater differences that he calls cardinality, for some of them differentiate themselves such that we cannot order them to each other pairwise. He thinks that all uncountables belong to a species of cardinal numbers. A consequence of this is that it is possible to order two infinite sets pairwise member by member. Hence, the points of a line, then of a surface, of a cube – of any n-dimensional figure. Even the temporal points of eternity can be ordered pairwise to a second. Take a body that uniformly traverses a progressing line segment A – B for a second.

---

37   [*The question mark in pathentheses is an insertion with red pencil.*]
38   [*The date is taken from Leisching Y 3/13.*]

Every point of the line is reached in another point of the second and vise-versa. It is thus easy to order the points of the line and those of the second univocally to each other. Let us now conceive of another body, which runs along the same line-segment, not with a uniform velocity, but rather in a gradually decelerating motion, such that it would [traverse the first] half in the first second, [then] third fourth in the the second [second], then the seventh eighth [in the third second], [then] the fifteenth sixteenth [in the fourth second] etc. It never reaches the end. Since in its course it reaches every point before B, the whole set of points outside of B are also univocally ordered to the set of points of eternity. It is therefore clear that the same can occur regarding the set of points of a second. Furthermore, we have seen that the set of points of a finite linear continuum is to be paired with the set of points of a finite figure of n dimensions. It is clear [that] it could be ordered to [a set of points] of an unbounded of n dimensions. Indeed, even for a set of points of infinite dimensions, this is true. It therefore also holds for a continuum of unboundedly many and unbounded dimensions. Hence, the the same thing seems to hold for every uncountable with regard to every other infinite set. Yet, some mathematicians, especially Prof. Cantor in Halle, have claimed the contrary. He formulates the concept of cardinality for infinite and finite numbers: There presumably belongs to every defined set a determinate cardinality, where two specifically different sets have the same cardinality when they can be univocally ordered to each other. Hence, every finite species of number has a different cardinality, but also uncountables are supposedly not of the same cardinality. Many have the same cardinality, but not all of them. Cantor therefore distinguishes a 2nd, 3rd, 4th class of numbers, each of a higher cardinality than the preceding one. If we ask for an example of this, he points out the difference between the infinite set of members in the series of whole numbers and the set of points of a line. It is of course correct that the set of whole numbers is equinumerous with the set of points of a line that we reach by dividing in all rational proportions. But this does not hold for the irrational proportions of division. These are infinitely more, he thinks, indeed incomparably more, and therefore attainable neither by addition nor by multiplication nor by exponentiation nor by ultra-exponentation (e.g., 3^{3^3} is ultra-exponentation or ∞^{∞^∞}). Accordingly, there would be no univocal ordering. Brentano, however, believes that Cantor is mistaken. Even the two mentioned infinite sets are specifically equal. In that case, however, they must be equinumerous. The proof is supposedly conducted by application of a formula. It is granted that the set of numbers is equinumerous with the set of all points that are attained by continued bisecting into infinity. Belonging to these points are of course not all points of the line, as none of the trisecting points are reached. But what holds for those points that would be reached through bisection if the entirety of possible bisections would be executed? Cantor believes that it is the same, for we could not have come into contact with an impossible bisecting point, and the set of the actual bisecting points would be equal to the set of possible ones. If, however, not every point of the line is to belong to these points, how many points not belonging to them are encountered, starting from the beginning point of the line of the family tree of bisection? None of them actually. For the point A is the limit which the first line of the family tree approaches into infinity. It is clear that the distance is not as great and cannot be so as any given line.[39] Consequently also no points and [yet more clearly] no two points could be [ordered][?], and even if one also concedes the latter, it is clear that the last lines are always equally far from each other, [and] at least half of the points of the line must belong to the bisecting points. If N is the set of whole numbers, the set of these points is equal to $2 + 2^{N-1}$ and therefore the points of the line $= 2 + (2 \cdot 2)^{N-1}$, also $4 + N^2$. However, 2^N is equinumerous with N, since it is itself equinumerous to N^N. Cantor's claim is therefore false. But also the contrary has a semblance of truth. The trisecting points seem alone to be no fewer than the bisecting points, the quintsecting points, etc. and finally the points that are reached through points in irrational proportions. How does this square with the fact that the bisecting points contain every second point of the line? Answer: The executed bisection would contain all points of the line. In the finite, no bisecting point coincides with a trisecting point, and Cantor (p. 15) testifies to this when he says that an infinite set can just as well be called an even or an odd number. "The number is even" means: It can be divided by two. The same, however, is also true of the trisection. Every infinite number must capable of being trisected, quintsected, etc. It must therefore be divisible in every rational proportion, and if this is grasped, the same can be said of every irrational proportion, since the rational proportions infinitely approach the irrational ones in infinity. Consequently the totality of bisecting points must be identical with the totality of dividing points in all rational and irrational propositions. Where there are, however, different lines under consideration, they are at least specifically equal. Consequality they are also equinumerous, the concept of cardinality, as cited by Cantor, has become completely irrelevant.[40] One will be led to absurdities by such assumptions. For instance, if there are differences in magnitude between infinite sets, I ask: Which sum is larger, that of the series $1 + 2 + 3 + 4 + 5 + 6 + 7$ etc. or $2 + 4 + 6 + 8 + 10 + 12 + 14$? Bolzano thinks that the sum of the second series is greater because I get it when I add the first series

---

39 [*See figure above, p. 183.*]
40 [*Höfler E.2.1./54:* "The concept of cardinality, as cited by Cantor, has become completely irrelevant."]

to itself. But one can indeed arrive [at it] through abstraction if one removes 1, 3, 5 ... Therefore the first series would again have to be greater. B[rentano][?]: Under consideration are not growing series, but rather full-grown series, for at the same time the temporal series, taken as growing, would be larger. But someone might say: Is not an infinite set often part of another one, therefore smaller? For instance, the set of points of the half line and those of the whole line. To this one should reply: Whoever applies this principle here does not understand its meaning. "The whole is greater than the part" is not true of relations between the parts of lines, e.g. not of the logical part or of the metaphysical whole and part. It is only a certain class of whole and part for which this statement is true: namely wherever via addition and omission of the other part of the whole there is posited without further ado a specific change of the whole. Hence, [this] of course [occurs] in the case of sets, both infinite and finite. In the case of finite ones, however, where every part that is omitted or added has another species as its consequence, the whole becomes larger than the part, whereas in the case of infinite this is true only with regard to those finite parts from which it uniformly has an infinite distance, not of the infinite from which it has no specific difference. Its specific differentia is its immeasurability, and when it is there it remains there as always if I take away any unit, indeed if I take away infinitely many units, if only infinitely many remain, such that the specific differentia of immeasurability remains. But when we say, "The half and the whole are infinite," does not every infinite set thereby become indeterminate when they do not differentiate themselves specifically and are still not the same ones. Many would for this reason deny the infinite. However, also the other species are all indeterminate. The logical whole is always indeterminate and becomes individualized only by the metaphysical parts (see earlier). It suffices also in our case to give the many determinations which specify the other metaphysical parts. The infinite set of the points of one surface is not the set of points of another surface, just as the redness of one surface is not the redness of another one.

[XVIII. Lecture.
d. 17 January 1885][41]

In what sense one can say of an infinite set that it is greater than another one.
　In various senses one speaks of wholes in an improper way.

41　[*The date is taken from Leisching Y 3/20.*]

1. If one understands by a whole something that includes something else and also in addition to this, one can regard the proposition [as true] also in the case infinite sets that the part is greater than the whole. How improperly this is meant, we see in the fact that many a whole is greater without being great. Hence [we see this regarding] the metaphysical whole, likewise the logical one. Although red contains color and also something in addition, red is nonetheless not a magnitude [size, largeness, or greatness]. Likewise, two points are greater than one [point] in an improper sense, although none of them is great. For greatness [size, largeness, or magnitude] is that which allows for the distinction of parts (Gauß).

2. Furthermore, an infinite set can be greater than another one because it is of greater fullness than the other. Thus the set of spatial points of a straight line of 2 M is greater than the set of spatial points of a straight line of 1 M, but only because the points fill a greater distance. While for magnitude the genus of the counted objects is indifferent (three angels just as many as three points), it is for the here designated improper magnitude not a matter of indifference, for things belonging to different genera do not fill an equally great distance. Or let us take a distance of color; certain color-species fill the distance of two certain colors. Do color-species also fill a spatial distance? No. The massive transitions from red to yellow are conceivable as distributed to different spaces.

3. It is possible to speak of a "greater and smaller" of infinite sets because the one infinite set fills distance in a greater or smaller number of dimension than the other other; thus the set of points in the side of the square is smaller than that in the surface of the square. This case is not a special case of the previous one, which one might perhaps believe. Thus the set of temporal points in an hour is smaller than the set of spatial points in a cubic yard. Here too the greater is taken in an improper sense. One says how significant Aristotle's concept of a *genus* is for logic. Trendelenburg [1870, 33 ff.] says that logic since Aristotle has not only made no progress (as Kant thought), but even regressions. (But that is not correct.)[42]

---

42 [*This sentence in parentheses is an insertion with blue pencil. Cf. Brentano* EL 72/12192 (*after further considerations of genus and species*): "You see of what importance the Aristotelian concept of genus and species [is]! How without it the most essential distinctions for elementary logic cannot be made! How immeasurably modern logic has sunken due to the single circumstance that it has lost this [concept]! Kant and Trendelenburg! But also how impossible merely the initial steps towards clarification are without studying the empirically given content of presentation, how formal logic becomes an absurdity!" *Cf. also Leisching Y 3/23:* "You see of what significance the Aristotelian concept of genus and species keeps becoming for elementary logic, how without it the most essential distinctions cannot be made, how immeasurably modern logic lags behind ancient logic due to

Among the distances between species of that genus,[43] one of them is not the smallest possible. Others, however, are so. Of other genera, it is true that none of the distances of species is the smallest possible, that rather distance is possible in every rational and irrational proportion. Quality, intensity, location, time, etc. are examples of this. The qualities of colors have distance, but there is distance here in every rational and irrational relation. The distances in different genera are always altogether incomparable. However, distances in different genera are proportional to each other. Also something else is common to the genera. Although the distances are infinitely different and are infinitely greater and smaller, none of them is infinitely small and none is infinitely large. Mathematicans often believed in absolutely infinitely large and small, as when I say, "Parallel straight lines are those which intersect in infinity." Here the intersecting point is therefore in the infinite distance. Cantor[44] is also under the spell of this error. He thinks that there are lines that have a certain relation in a cetain way as they approach infinity. There is, however, only a growth into infinity, but not an absolute infinity ([Joseph-Louis] Lagrange). Only in the cases of sets and what consists of sets is there is absolutely infinite magnitude [greatness or largeness], but here there is not also an infinitely small set. An additional peculiarity is also that in the case of these genera continua are possible. If in a genus smaller distances are possible in all rational and irrational relations, divisions of a distance are also possible in these relations. Between two species of such a genus, a third is therefore always possible. It is a species mediating the distance. There are however infinitely many of such species, and in every relation of distance they are possible. If I assume only a part of them as actualized, there would still be gaps. If, however, we assume that they are all actualized, the mediation would be an unbroken and complete one. The totality of the species between the two mediating extremes would be an unbroken and prefectly mediating series. But that is not the concept of the series in the sense that is usual. One also calls such species ones that mediate a distance, which lie only closer to the two elements than these to each other themselves.

---

the fact that this distinction is lost upon it. Kant says that logic since Aristotle has taken no step forward and no step backward. Trendelenburg thinks: no step forward, but rather steps backward. I believe that Trendelenburg is wrong. Without studying the empirically given content of presentation no step forward is possible."]

43 [*It cannot be determined which genus is under consideration here.*]
44 [*Marginal note:*] Cf. Georg Cantor, *Grundlagen einer allgemeinen Mannigfaltichkeitslehre* 1883 Teubner. "Uber unendliche lineare Pruntenmannigfaltigkeiten," *Mathematische Annalen*, Bd. XXI, p. 545 ff. [*Cantor 1883, 545–586, also in Cantor 1932, 165–204.*]

Indeed, even if they lie more distantly, but if they belong only to a series, every two successive elements of which lie closer to each other than the two extremes.

Thus if I have a red and black. If I would have only all nuances of red and white and all between white and black, they would together make up the perfect mediation between red and black. Where there is a gap, there are among the mediating species two closest ones for which infinitely many closer ones could be given. I can therefore divide the series into two parts without removing a species, such that no species is common to both parts. If, however, there is no gap in a mediating series, there is nowhere among the mediating species two closest species (albeit closer and farther ones). I therefore cannot divide the series into two parts in such a way that no species is common to both parts. Rather, the end of the one part is the beginning of the other part. Wherever a series of mediating species has this peculiarity, we have a perectly mediating series before us. Thus the series of points in a half circle is a perfectly mediating series. There can be in the case of certain genera several of such mediating species. There is only one mediating series in the case of time, likewise in the case of intensity. Several are possible, however. Indeed, even countless ones are possible, in the case of location, of colors and probably of all such qualities. Whever only two of such mediating series are possible, we call them together a closed series. What we have discussed here no longer coincides with the concept of the continuum and of the closed figure.

[Lecture XIX.
21 January 1885][45]

This is easy to show: Let us imagine a plane that is colored and across which the color changes from red to blue, very gradually, then from blue to green, then to yellow, then to red. Would one call something of this sort a closed figure? No. Yet, ⟨it is⟩ a closed series of colors. Somone might say: Along with the concept of the perfectly mediating series, is it not equal to the concept of the continuum? No. There are perfectly mediating series which are not that. Let two bodies with plane surfaces be separated by an empty space. The one surface of the one body does not form a continuum with another surface of the other. Let us now assume that a surface contains all species of red up to a certain violet, the other all species of red up to blue. Do these two colored objects make

---

45   [*This date is taken from Leisching Y 3/28.*]

up a continuum? No. But they do in fact complement each other in a perfectly mediating series of colors. So now what is a continuum? One has often troubled oneself about the definition, although the mathematicians have done so the least. Cantor (*Über die Grundlagen der allgemeinen Mannigfaltigkeitslehre*) admits this. He says: By establishing single or multiple continous magnitudes, one has developed the concept of a univocal or equivocal continuum dependent on them. But the independent continuum is presupposed by mathematical authors only in that form of the simplest appearances and not subjected to a thorough-going consideration. (The quotation is not altogether exact.) Cantor looked around for philosophers, thus Bolzano. Someone might say: Why so much effort? Does not the simple indication of examples suffice? Such as time and space? Cantor does not regard such an explanation as sufficient. Indeed, he says that drawing upon the intuition of time is not acceptable in the discussion of the much more original concept of the continuum. Likewise, nothing can be done with the intuitive form of space, since only with the aid of an already finished continuum does this also reach that content with whose aid they [i.e. space and time] can be the object of mathematical investigation. There is something true and something false in this remark from Cantor. The concept of the continuum is more general than that of space and time. Whether the concept of the continuum is therefore more original, however, is another question. It is not correct to say that space can further obtain its content only by means of the finished concept of the continuum. Furthermore, whether drawing on space and time is therefore not acceptable because space and time are less general is also very much a questionable matter. However, in our case it is thus: The concept of the continuum is complex and requires an analysis, and we must in this case be on guard against regarding *specific* peculiarities of certain continua as *general* peculiarities. We shall therefore take into account these continua as the geometer does with respect to an especially drawn figure.

Distinction between the perfectly mediating series and the continuum.

Let us now hear Bolzano's definition:

> If we attempt to gain a clear awareness [*Bewustsein*] of the concept which we designate by the expression a *continuous extension* or a *continuum* then we cannot help defining a continuum to exist where, and only where, a collection of simple objects (of points in time or space or even of substances) occurs which are so arranged that every single one of them has at least one neighbour in this collection at every distance however small. If this is not the case, for example, if among a given collection of points in space even only a single one occurs which is not so thickly surrounded by neighbours that for every distance, provided it is taken small enough,

a neighbor can be indicated, then we say that this point stands *single* (isolated) and that that collection accordingly does not present a perfect continuum. On the other hand, if there is not a single point that is isolated in this sense in the collection of points under consideration, therefore each of them has at least one neighbor for every distance however small, then there remains nothing which could justify us denying to this collection the name of continuum.[46]

Cantor is not satisfied with this explanation and defines the continuum thus: "a continuum is a perfectly cohesive set of points." He generalizes the concept of the point of the spatial or temporal to the "purely arithmetical point," a point of n-dimensional arithmetical space.

Is one of these definitions correct? Bolzano's is certainly incorrect. It is too broad. For also in the points of two separate continua there is indeed something given which would be a continuum from Bolzano's perspective. Moreover, Cantor thinks, the same also goes for the totality of possible bisecting points of a line. These points are so close to each other that one finds more and more bisection. Since the trisecting point, however, does not belong here, there are still gaps in it. What Cantor says here is incorrect, as already was discussed earlier. One would indeed have to be able to remove the first and last point, and then it would have no beginning and no end without being infinite. Cantor wants to call this a semicontinuum in such a case. Cantor here encounters the scholastics, thus Suarez.[47] What can be said about this? The doctrine is incorrect. One cannot retain the line if one imagines a point removed. It is indeed possible, however, to retain the point while the line vanishes. Let us imagine a connecting point between two lines. It remains when the first part vanishes, but also when the second one vanishes. The point exists in the line only as a boundary. In the case of space it can even occur that a point exists as a boundary of infinitely many lines. Someone might still say: Is the point separable in that case? The present is indeed only temporal point and nonetheless it is separate, since it belongs neither to the past nor to the future. Or again someone might say: Let us imagine two parallel straight lines and a third intersecting one. Let us now think of a intersecting an infinite line.[48] If it turns, it always intersects the parallels in other points, and ultimately it coincides with one of the parallel lines and no longer intersects the others. Now certain points correspond to

---

46 Bolzano, *Paradoxien des Unendlichen* (Leipzig, 1851), §38, pp. 73–74 [*as translated in* Bolzano 2004, 642–643].
47 Cf. Suarez, *Metaphysical Disputations* XL, sect. v, art. 41.
48 [*See figure above, p. 191.*]

all directions, but not the last point. We would thus have a continuum without end. We can reply: It is inadmissible that what is left over from this extreme boundary would be dissolved. If someone presents the *whole* past, he must co-present the present. One often takes what is gone as non-existent, but that is incorrect. If I further assume in the second case all directions of the ray[?] up to parallelity, all of them in their totality, I cannot imagine the final position as removed. Cantor's last reproach against Bolzano is therefore incorrect. But we could make another reproach. That is to say, the definition is too narrow from a certain perspective. If Bolzano says that this is a matter of simple objects, is this to mean: objects that have no plurality of parts? In that case no color-point is a simple object. It has metaphysical and logical parts. If Bolzano means unextended objects, it is odd to define extension by means of the concept of the unextended. One might also reply: If one conceives of it in this way, Bolzano's definition is perhaps no longer too narrow, but in a particular way [it is] too broad. Even the ordered series of the whole numbers would in that case be a continuum. In the series of numbers there is a smallest possible distance, namely the unit.

But is Cantor's definition the correct one? No. For what he says is no longer [the same] as what we would designate with previously explained words, as a set in which two distances would be perfectly mediated by series. This definition, however, does not coincide with the concept of the continuum. But Bolzano's definition is also subject to this error. Cantor's definition essentially coincides with our "perfectly mediated series."

[Lecture xx.
24 January, 85][49]

What is the true definition of the continuum? Where there is a continue we always have perfectly mediated specific distances. If we contrast examples of such [cases] that are included among the continua and such [cases] not included among them, the peculiarity of the former will be become clear. A colored plane that begins with a red line and ends with a yellow one, and also runs through all possible shades of orange is a color-continuum. However, if there are two plane surfaces that are separated by an empty space and one of them varies from red to orange, while the other begins with orange and goes to yellow, these plane surfaces are certainly a perfectly mediated color-series,

---

49 [*This date is taken from Leisching Y 3/37.*]

but not a continuum. Or [if we take the example of] a temporal series of colors where one place changes from a red one into a yellow one, here we have a continuum of colors or, to say this in a better way, quasi-colors. However, no continuum of colors[50] would be given if a surface would have varied from red to a shade of orange and then afterwards ceased to vary, but from there another shade would begin and lead to yellow. Where does the difference between the continuum and the same series of species mediating perfectly between distances? It is clear that the mediation is a different one in these cases insofar as in the perfectly mediating series that is a continuum every mediating member which connects the end of one part to the beginning of the other part of the series is not merely specifically equal, but individually the same. Wherever the end of one part is only specifically, but not individually equal to the beginning of the other, continuity is not at all there. *A continuum is an infinite set of individuals which, agreeing in the lowest genus or quasi-genus, exhibits specific differences, but in such a way that in it every specific distance of one individual from the other is perfectly mediated and with individual unity of the connecting members*. Whether a continuum is posited by a perfect series [of colors], this is something that the other metaphysical parts, hence location, intensity, etc., show. In the case of a continuum of location, the quality and intensity are therefore decisive; if these other metaphysical parts are all specifically equal for every two successive partial sets of the series or likewise perfectly mediated by the intermediate members in their distances, the series is a continuum. Example: a continuum of colors, from red to yellow. It might be [the case] that the intensity is the same for this main continuum. Yet, it might be [the case] that the intensity varies. Even then it would be a continuum of qualities. Or [if there is] a place that appears red at first and gradually transforms into yellow, but in such a way that the intensity remains the same, we have a continuum of quasi-colors, but also when the intensity changes. However, the continuum is no longer given if somewhere an unmediated local distance is added in thought, or an unmediated temporal distance, or an unmediated distance of intensity. It is of course doubtful whether many would not regard something as a continuum which we do not regard as one. Thus whenever I have a blue and a red surface which run into each other, someone might assert that it is at least a spatial continuum, though not a color-continuum. The mistake lies in this person believing that the boundary between the two planes is one and the same, whereas it is in fact different. What we have here is not a

---

50   [*Reference to an unknown Text:*] No continuum of colors or of space? See my "objections to Brentano."

boundary, but rather two boundaries that only coincide with each other. We can prove that in this way: A quality is not possible that would not be locally determined. We have here a spatial line, this determined only as a determinacy of red and blue. Can it at the same time be the determinacy of red and blue, thus individually the same? No. Here one is rather dealing with a blue boundary, which is blue as a boundary of blue, and with a red boundary which is red as a boundary of red. They are thus two individual elements that only coincide. What is misleading here is a peculiarity, namely the impenetrability of qualities of the same genus in space. A space cannot be filled with yellow and blue. Different spaces can, to be sure, appear in the same surface, but many colors with the same spatial determinacy cannot appear in a certain extension. Colors which fill a specifically equal location always appear individually unitary, and the space itself is individually unitary. But this is not true for the spatial boundaries which are nothing by themselves, but rather everything only in connection with what is bounded. When from different directions something can reach a certain species of location as a boundary, hence one color from the one side, something specifically different can also at the same time reach this spatial boundary, hence one color from one side, another color from the other side. And thus in the connection with both surfaces the boundary participates in both species. In that case, however, we have individually two spatial determinacies. Thus, the blue and yellow line, divided in color, which divides a blue and yellow plane from each other, is no more an individual line than the shade of orange, distinguished in location, in the earlier example of the changing colors. Wherever four squares, red, green, black, and white, come together, we do not have one indivudal central point, but rather four individual points. Yet more of such points, indeed infinitely many, might also coincide. If we imagine a circle, such that a certain radius indicates in its turning the variations of red and blue, where it goes back again to its old position, we would have two individually different lines. In the central point of the circle, however, we would then have all stages of colors, hence infinitely many. Galileo's paradox belongs here. He says: The central point is as great as the whole circle. If one establishes an equal magnitude where an equal plurality of points is given, Galileo is right.

The correct expression for our examples of the red and blue surface is not that they "cohere," but rather that they "collide with each other," "touch each other," "border upon each other," but not "cohere." The physicists distinguish cohesion and adhesion. Of the first they speak when a specific equality prevails. If not, however, they speak of adhesion. In that case they at least think of something as we ourselves do. In one case there is an individual boundary, but in the other case two of them. (The similarity, however, is only a very rough one.) One should generalize the expression "collide," and then, if we have a color-surface that varies from red to orange, then one that changes from orange to yellow, we might say that they collide into each other, not spatially, but with regard to color.

[Lecture XX.
28 January, 85][51]

We say that the concept of the continuum is a relative one since it is based on certain relations of equality and difference. In this case it in fact belongs in the domain of relations of connection of physical parts (part with part and part with the whole). Either every continuum belongs to a physical whole or it is itself one. All cohesive, no longer merely colliding continua always indeed form a continuum. The unification of an infinite set in such a physical whole is without a doubt an altogether different and much more intimate one than that of certain elements to collective whole. The merely collective set has no unification of parts except the one which is given in the matching of members in what makes up the unity. [I have six apples. Each one is an apple.][52] In the case of the physical whole, however, there is a belonging that is of such a kind that every individual of a species which is contained in it as an element is nothing by itself, and everything that it is is only in connection with others. (Thus a point is nothing by itself, but rather whatever it is, it is only in connection with other points.) This is not at all true only of elementary constituent parts, [but rather] also of continua which belong to a physical whole. *Everything that is and can be something in this way, only in connection with a continuum, we call "boundary."* Thus point, line, surface are boundaries. In this dependence of boundaries on the bounded, however, there is often a relative independence. This is true of every mediating boundary. For it [the mediating boundary] there is a multiple connection. If one bounded thing is eliminated, it [the mediating boundary] continues to exist in its connection with another [bounded thing]. The situation is of course different for an *ultimate boundary*, as for the first temporal point, wherever something begins to *be*. Here there is only a single connection. If this were removed, the point would not be able to exist. We may not conceive of the dependence of the boundary on the bounded as a participation

---

51 [*The date is taken from Leisching Y 3/41.*]
52 [*The passage in square brackets is an example of the matching that forms the unity of a collective whole, taken from Leisching Y 3/43.*]

in the specific nature of the other boundaries that also belong to a continuum. On the contrary, it has no specific commonality with the boundary that is first connected with it. A boundary that is of one species (e.g. a red line) does not bound specifically different [things] and does not participate in any of the species of the bounded [things]. The bounded itself participates in the nature of the boundaries. There is thus the most intimate affinity that is possible with the exclusion of equality. If the boundary is a continuum, it as such consists of boundaries. (Thus a line that is a boundary only with regard to a surface consists itself of boundaries.) And ultimately, every continuum consists of boundaries that are themselves not continua. Therefore, the first elements of a continuum are not themselves continua. It sounds very paradoxical to say that a continuum consists of nothing but non-continua, something extended out of unextended [elements]. But it is wrong to conclude that the same something must consist of nothing. Rather, it consists of nothing extended, not of nothing. Hence every number is composed of smaller numbers and finally of units. Here plurality is also composed of non-pluralities.

Refutation[53] of the objection that the extended consists of nothing, analogous with the number.

If we imagine a continuous transition from red through all shades of orange to yellow, this surface is composed of nothing but color-lines.[54] These are, to be sure, not extended in the direction of the transition, but they are nonetheless not simply nothing. These unextended boundaries are in a certain sense the ultimate physical parts of the continuum. This [continuum] accordingly consists of a plurality of unextended boundaries. We call such a boundary "point," the word used in the broadest sense (temporal point, spatial point, color-point, intensity-point, etc.).

Up to now we have spoken always of those parts of a continuum that are boundaries. There are, however, other parts, and one usually thinks of these whenever one speaks of physical parts because these parts are of such a kind that they can, without contradictions, be separated from all other parts of the continuum and would nonetheless be on their own what they were in connection with the others. One of them is added to the other as the adjacent part which is not the case regarding two boundaries in a continuum. Even if color-points spatially coincide, they are distant from each other and stand either in no connection or in a mediated physical connection. Thus whenever we think of C as red and run through all possible shades of color in its movement, we

---

53 [*This sentence is written as a marginal title in pencil.*]
54 [*See diagram above, p. 196: Roth = "red," Nuancen von Orange = "shades of orange," Gelb = "yellow."*]

have in the center a spatial coincidence of all colors.[55] Specifically, however, they are distant from each other.

Examples of separable parts: one hour. The half of a body on its own is what it had been previously in connection with the other half. If only each such physical part is separable and in that case would be on its own what it was in connection with the continuum, would it then not be possible to dissolve such a continuum in infinitely many continua? No. Why not? Simply because there is no infinitely small distance. For this reason also, infinitely many abrupt transitions without elimination of continuity are impossible. An abrupt transition would be a real one.

Zeno argued in a familiar way against motion.[56] An end-point, he thought, cannot go from A to B, for it would have to first arrive at the intersecting point C, but then at D, E, F, G, etc. It would therefore have to reach infinitely many points as B, which would also require an infinite amount of time. He would always be approaching half [of the distance towards the goal], never reaching the goal. The reply to this is:[57]

[The whole reason why it is imposible is because an infinitely small distance is impossible. Aristotle says with full justification: An *infinitum in actu* is impossible, but an *infinitum in potential* is possible. *In potentia* infinitely many parts in a whole, but in actu they cannot come about.][58]

[Lecture XXII,
d. 31 January, 85][59]

Now it remains for us to elaborate especially on what it is that differentiaes certain continua from others. We have spoken of a mediation of the distance of two species by means of a third one in a narrower and a broader sense. If the mediation meant in the narrower sense, the third species was situated between the two others in such a way that the distance of the latter was composed of the two distances that the mediating species would have from each of the two extremes. In the case of mediation in the broader sense a detour might also be taken. This difference exists also in continua, thus in a straight and unstraight line: but not only in spatial continua, also in qualitative continua, thus in con-

---

55   [*See diagram above, p. 197.*]
56   [*See diagram above, p. 197.*]
57   [*The reply to Zeno is missing in the manuscript.*]
58   [*The passage in square brackets is taken from Leisching Y 3/50.*]
59   [*The date is taken from Leisching Y 3/51.*]

tinua of colors and intensities. Also here the mediation of the two extremes can be a mediation in the narrower and in the broader sense. Let us imagine a circle: The turning radius goes from red and runs through all shades of violet to blue. Let us then imagine another circle whose radius would begin with red and would return to red through blue, green, and yellow. In the first circle we have in the central point all colors from red to blue. In the second the succession is not a straight line because already the circumstance shows that we return to red. As we speak of a straight and curved spatial line, we could also speak of a straight and curved line of colors. Thus in the first circle the periphery would indeed be a curved spatial line, but still a straight line of colors, whereas in the second circle it would also be a curved line of colors. In order to avoid misunderstandings that might easily arise through the application of the expression "line" in the non-spatial sense, however, we shall prefer to use an expression that the Pseudo-Aristotle (*De Mundo*) and Theophrastus have used, namely "grammoid" or "grammode" and accordingly speak of a straight grammoid (locusoid) and a curved grammoid. Thus every continuous temporal series or intensity-series is a straight grammoid.

Let us take a temporal continuum between two temporal points. This appears as a magnitude, and indeed not only as an infinite magnitude, but rather also as finite insofar as it fills a finite distance, since [it] is composed of distances, e.g. of two halves.[60] In this sense the entire temporal continuum is twice as large as each part, whereas this cannot be said in the first sense (with regard to the set of points). Also the unstraight grammoid is such a magnitude and is, in the sense that it fills a certain distant, comparable with a straight one if both belong to the same lowest genera. Thus the curved line is equal to a straight one that fills a distant which the curved line approaches through infinite dismemberment into infinite parts. A grammoid is an infinite set of no dimension and an infinite magnitude of one dimension. Besides the magnitude of the distance, with regard to which also the mediating grammoid can be called great, also a direction of the distance can be spoken of. The distance from A to B is opposed to the distance from B to A with respect to its distance. The distances of the points of a straight grammoid (locusoid) from A onward has the same direction, those from B by contrast all the opposite directions. In an unstraight grammoid this is not without exception true. (Obviously, here too the concept "direction" is taken and generalized from space.) The concept of the direction is transferred from distances to the grammoid which mediates distances or it is adapted to this. Thus we say: All parts have the same direc-

---

60   [*Question in pencil on the margin:*] What does distance mean?

tion in the straight gammoid, not in the unstraight one (always with respect to one and the same end-point). We also say: The unstraight grammoid changes its direction. This change can occur within a finite grammoid finitely often or infinitely often and everywhere. In the first case, this change is a sudden, abrupt one. Such an unmediated, abrupt change can never ensue infinitely often. It must be finite. If the change is however a gradual one and then occurring infinitely often, we are dealing with a curved grammoid. Curvature is nothing but a continuum of directions. If I have two points and move them while retaining the same distance, the direction of the distance constantly changes. If we take three specifically different points, which are not in an equal or opposite direction distant from each other, and we mediate the distances by means of straight grammoids, we get a closed grammoid. If we now imagine the totality of possible points mediated between the points of this closed grammoid, we have a closed plane (in the broadest sense) bounded by three grammoids, a so-called planoid. Such a planoid is not compared with a grammoid, not because it would contain points of a lower genus, but rather because the distances filling it are not distances of points, but rather distances of continuous series of points. It is a continuous series of grammoids. Thus we have a continuum of two dimensions. In every point within a planoid, grammoids can intersect each other in such a way that the intersecting grammoid has exactly the central direction between the opposing parts of the intersected grammoid. It is now conceivably true that both are still equally intersected by a third grammoid which however does not in that case belong to the same planeoid; if this is done and if one connects the end-points of these three grammoids by means of other grammoids and the latter by means of planoids, if one one further realizes all possible points between the planoids, one arrives at a three-dimensional magnitude which can be dismembered by means of other closed two-dimensional continua into smaller three-dimensional continua. Such a three-dimensional continuum is, for instance, a geometrical figure of three dimensions or also the so-called color-body.[61] Now we cannot at all deny that outside of our experience continua are possible for which three-dimensional continua are only the boundaries. Such continua would then be [at least] four-dimensional, as continua with five, six, seven, eight dimensions and more are in advance neither contradictory nor impossible. However, we should be on guard against speaking of a more than three-dimensional *space*. What is within reach of our presentations exhibits everywhere only three dimensions and is also not capable of a fourth dimension. A spatial continuum has no more than three, a temporal con-

---

61 [*Marginal note in red pencil:*] Cf. Lotze, *Metaphysik*, chapter on "deduction of space."

tinuum no more than one dimension. These cannot at all be put together into four dimensions, since both belong to very different genera. It would indeed be easier to say of a temporal dimension that it is on a spatial line. (Wundt's elaborations in his *Physiologische Psychologie* are also inept.) (When Fechner introduces time as a fourth dimension, he does so as Dr. Mises, presumably only joking.)

Also the concepts of an angle and of a shape are also easily made understandable. Nothing stands in the way of generalizing them. The shape of a closed figure is equal to the shape of another one if the distances of the boundaries are proportionate (the boundaries taken in the same ratio of directions), if the ratios of the distances of the boundary-points are therefore equal to each other in the same ratio of direction. In the case of shape one is therefore dealing with relations of relations, a circumstance that would even allow us (in the generalized concepts of "shape") to speak of equality of shape in an altogether heterogeneous sense. For one cannot speak of equal determinations in heterogeneous domains, but certainly of equal relations of such determinations. We might thus equate an angle of intensity to an angle in space. (Aristotle thought that not only extension, but also shape is a kind of ultimate, absolute element of our sensory phenomena.)

[XXIII. Lecture.
4 February 85][62]

Today we want to speak of relations that arise from the connections of continua to their metaphysical parts. Of the infinite set of species that every continuum contains, each one is individualized in each point via the species of metaphysical parts.

This can occur only in three ways. 1. A certain metaphysical part can be specifically equal for all points of a continuum. 2. It can be a continuum throughout. 3. Partly one of these and partly the other can be the case. A fourth case is inconceivable.

Examples:

First case: A red unitary surface is an example of the first class. The surface is a continuum in space. With spatial determinacy, however, red is given, and given throughout as a second metaphysical part. Or: an equally intense surface. Or: a certain unitary surface in a determinate temporal point; the temporal

---

62   [*The date is taken from Leisching Y 3/59.*]

determinacy is equal for the entire surface. Or: a unitary spatial point lasting an hour long; here we have a temporal continuum. The quasi-species of the location, however, is the same. The color-spaces in the central point of the circle (Galileo's paradox) where the spatial determinacy is specifically equal [are also instances of the first case].

Second example: A colored surface. Here we have a continuum of colors and locations.[63] Or: a continuous unity that continuously changes in time as regards its intensity. Thus a point that keeps become intensively brighter [is such an example].

Thirdly: Colored line with the following property.[64] This line goes from red to blue, but then remains blue. Or a square like [the one in the above figure].[65] Horizontally, continuity exists in the change of colors; vertically, however, perfect equality; it is however also a spatial continuum in addition.

Let us once again consider the first case of the three: Here the whole is a continuum only with respect to a metaphysical part. The remaining parts are called this only improperly. A perfectly red surface is not a color-continuum. Only as it is considered as space is the surface a continuum. The color is only *per accidens* a continuum, the space however *per se*. In the second case, however, we have a double continuum *per se*. In the third case one finally has something that is midway between a double continuum *per se* and a continuum *per accidens*. It is a kind of imperfect double continuum *per se*. There are also double continua *per accidens*. A double continuum *per se* is a point in motion (change of location and of time). A double continuum *per accidens* is a body at rest. It is a continuum in space and time. Connected with it, as a whole body, is a certain and indeed always the same temporal specification. The whole body is connected with every temporal moment. A body moving in a straight line without turning would be a perfect double continuum *per se*. This too is a curious case. Let us imagine a half sphere turning around its center. That would be an imperfect double continuum *per se*. (Brentano also presents the case of an expanding sphere or disk that turns and nonetheless undergoes no change in location.) Regarding a double continuum *per se* one does not have to believe that the two metaphysically unified continuua are equal in the sense in which they mediate equal distances, since it is in fact entirely heterogeneous distances that mediate. If one were to assume something like this, one would get ensnared in contradictions. For a continuum that is at one time not joined with another can also be joined with it qualitatively at another time. For example, a slow and

---

63 [*See figure above, p.* 202: Roth = "red," Blau = "blue," Gelb = "yellow," Grün = "green."]
64 [*See figure above, p.* 202.]
65 [*See figure above, p.* 202.]

rapid motion [is such a continuum]. These distinctions are called differences of expansion and density. If, however, the distinctions are altogether without equality and greater or smaller magnitude, they can still be proportionate in both continua, and in that case the continua are uniformally expanded: thus a uniform motion. Here we have no equality, but [we have] a proportionality between space and time. The expansion can however be non-uniform, as in the case of accelerated motion. This non-uniform expansion can occur in the most diverse relations which have a functional determination[?] of changing, [and can] otherwise be without this.[66] It would be wrong if one wanted to grasp a continuum with specific equality of another metaphysical part as a double continuum, one part of which is infinitely expanded. In the case of infinite expansion (which is something impossible) the species in the whole continuum would be individually one, whereas individual plurality exists currently.

Although no point of the continuum can be expanded, it is nonetheless what it is only in connection with the continuum, and this connection is not a different one if that with which it [the point] is connected is individually another one. It therefore has another connection in the case of other members of the expansion and thus a measure of the expansion belongs to every point of the double continuum insofar as it [the point] limits something. This is what the mathematicians call a *differential quotient* and thus make this as such intelligible without the assumption of infinitely small distances between two species.

[Lecture XXIV.
7 February, 85][67]

Now there are expansions in different senses: Thus we would have an expansion if we were to look with a magnifying glass, gradually closer and closer or farther and farther, at a surface that makes a transition continually from red to blue. We would also never have a gap anywhere. In the expansion in the sense in which we are speaking of it here it is not yet a coming-apart, but rather a being-apart under consideration. We have spoken of expansions where the measure of expansion varies [and] the expansion itself is therefore non-uniform. In a continuum a measure of the expansion belongs to every point, although it

---

66 [*Cf. Leisching Y 3/63:* "This non-uniform expansion can take place in the most diverse relations which, however, still allow for a function determination of change, which are on the whole non-uniform."]

67 [*The date is taken from Leisching Y 3/66. This lecture is the last one that is recorded in Leisching. Y 3.*]

itself is not expanded. For every point is what it is only in connection with the continuum. And this [point] is a different one if that with which the point is connected is individually another. Hence a measure of the expansion belongs to every point of a double continuum insofar as it limits and is thus diversely limited. We call it a differential quotient.

A measure of the expansion can sometimes be infinitely smaller than another one. If we imagine the following surface, from red to blue and then returning to red, it is clear that the measure of the expansion of a certain point in the line $a\,m$ is different one from that of the corresponding point in the circumference $a\,y\,m$.[68] And indeed the measure of the expansion of this latter line will be a non-uniform one. It will be all the greater, the closer the selected point is to the point a. In that case, how great is it in a itself? Infinitely great. It is in particular $a\,x = x\,y : m\,x$. Hence $x\,y^2 = a\,x \cdot m\,x$. The closer the point is to a, the more $m\,x$ approaches the diameter d and the more $a\,x$ vanishes. Immediately prior to vanishing, $a\,x$ would then be infinitely small, while $m\,x$ would approach the diameter d. In that case it would be $x\,y^2 = a \cdot a\,x$.

As it was already proved, it would be wrong to speak of an infinite expansion within a line that is uniform. Here, however, we speak of the measure of the expansion of a single point. Indeed, we can demonstrate another line in which the measure of the expansion is yet greater than in the line in which we have demonstrated the measure of the expansion as infinite for a point. That would be the curve $a\,v$, for instance. Indeed, a line could be demonstrated in which the measure of expansion of the point a is infinitely many times greater than its circumference $a\,y\,m$. That would be the *cycloid*. Here, however, we must not believe that the infinitely small fraction that expresses the measure of the expansion of the point a in the cycloid would be greater than the corresponding fraction in the case of the circumference. We have indeed said already earlier that due to the equality of infinite sets each one can be univocally put in a point-by-point relation with every other one. Someone might believe that in the case of the genus that admits a metaphysical union any two sets of perfectly mediated species can be unified into a double continuum. That, however, would be an error. Such a unification is possible only in the cases of infinite sets. For an unclosed line puts each of its points in connection only in two directions. In order to coincide metaphysically with a three-dimensional continuum, however, it would have to bring each point in connection in infinitely many directions.[69]

---

68   [See *diagram above, p. 204:* "Roth" = "red," "Blau" = "blue."]
69   [*Cf. Leisching Y 3/69:* "A non-closed line puts each of its points in connection without gaps

What is accordingly missing for such a unification is not the required set of points, but rather the required set of connections. If this were not the case, even an infinite set of species between which finite distances would exist, i.e. a non-contuum, could thus be metaphysically made to coincide with a continuum of one dimension. If we imagine a tonal series in which any two successive tones are distant from each other by a whole tone, the series could be an infinite one since the tonal pitch is indeed unlimited. If an ear would be so perfect that it knew no limit in the pitch of tones, it would however not hear this infinite series as a continuum.

Accordingly we said earlier also that an infinite set can be called all the greater than another one insofar as it would fill more dimensions. But we also emphasized that this difference is not a greater difference in the proper sense.

Most of the genera that our physical phenomena and inner imagination show us are ones whose species can exist not only as boundaries, but rather on their own and need not belong to a continuum. Thus the color red can appear in a continuum, but it can appear also uniformly and on its own, e.g. in the case of a uniformly colored red surface that is, to be sure, a spatial continuum, but not a color continuum. The same goes for tones, for intensity, etc. Because of this peculiarity, also those semicontinua are possible, hence a surface that goes from blue to red, but only with regard to its breadth.

Other genera, however, show that also the opposite can be the case, that the the species of them can thus never exist in themselves and on their own, but rather only as boundaries. Space and time belong here. As far as space is primarily concerned, someone might think whether the spaces that intuition shows appear to us in two or three dimensions. Hering regards the the latter [alternative, namely that intuitive spaces appear to us three-dimenstionally] at the correct one, and Brentano agrees with him.

Can a continuum of length and breadth appear on its own and does it appear as a boundary of a three-dimensional continuum? In previous times people believed the former [alternative, namely that intuitive spaces appear to us in two dimensions] to be the only one. They thought that they do not see a third dimension. But [they thought so] incorrectly, for the following reasons:

1. It is demonstrable that, if the species of location appear only as a surface, this surface cannot simply be a plane. By tracing back the localization in the case of feeling [i.e. tactile sensation], but also in the case of the visual sense,

---

only in two directions. In order for it to concide with a two-dimensional continuum metaphysically, it would have do it in infinitely many directions. Similarly a surface that is nowhere closed puts each of its lines only in a two-fold connection." *It is impossible to divide Hillebrand's notes from this point on into distinct lectures with dates.*]

this is true. [Franciscus Cornelis] Donders took a black box and had a point light up in this box. He had another point come about through an electrical spark now in front of, now in back of the [first] point. When he looked in with one eye, he could not determine whether the electrical spark arose in front or in back. But [he could do so] very easily with two eyes.[70]

The reversal of the relief cannot be understood if we assume that both surfaces that we see with both eyes are planes. For [in that case] I could not distinguish whether in one eye the point [under consideration] is to the right or [is so] in the other. If we assume both of the surfaces to be convex, this would not be case (Stumpf, *Ursprung der Raumvorstellung*).[71]

2. A third dimension is certainly demonstrable in the imagination. If this were not true, both presentations, whenever we look out and imagine something, would interrupt and destroy each other. If we have three-dimensional space in the imagination, something two-dimensional appears as a boundary of this spatial appearance. And this is exactly as the defenders of the flatness conceive of what occurs wherever we simply see something. One and the same thing appears to them now as a boundary, now as not a boundary. As a boundary only if I add the other dimensions in my imagination. However, what appears now as a boundary, now not [not as a boundary], cannot at another time appear on its own as it appears as a boundary. As a boundary, it appears as something that [is] nothing in and of itself. It must therefore appear differently in order to appear on its own. In fact, it appears in both cases [as] equal. We see ourselves therefore falling prey to a contradiction by assuming that we perceive only two dimensions. The force of this argument becomes yet greater if we consider that contradictory and absurd things cannot exist in a unitary intuition. Everyone knows that a merely flat space could not exist in reality on its own. Nor can mere flat surface thus exist on its own in intuition.

Whence does the appearance of the contrary arise? 1. The intuition in the third dimension is certainly a very slight one, [and] for that reason it is attended to less. 2. Perhaps it is constantly always the same, [and] for that reason it receives no interest. 3. It is insignificant, indicating no difference in the things and for this reason it does not become an object of attention. Indeed, unattentiveness becomes an insurmountable habit. Hence [there arises] the difficulty of drawing in a perspectivally correct way. Here the spatial differences of presentation are the concern, not what they signify. Here it is impossible for us to

---

70   [See Stumpf 1873, 228.]
71   [See Stumpf 1873, 229 ff.]

attend to other relations besides a certain one. This is how things are also with the third dimension which is for us altogether insignificant.

From all this, the result is: *Whatever can be only as a continuum can be only as a continuum of as many dimensions as are possible in the relevant genera. Whatever can be both as a point or also without belonging to a continuum will in the latter case always be as a replacement for the points of a continuum per accidens in as many dimensions as the perfect continuum, in which it would appear as a point, would have dimensions.*

We accordingly shall distinguish two classes of continua: necessary continua and non-necessary continua.

A further property that can occur in a genus of necessary continua is that in it the species of a certain other lowest genus with which it stands in a metaphysical connection are impenetrable. That is to say, *neither* two species of this [other] genus *nor* two species thereof that differ by loose individualization can be unified here simultaneously with two species belonging to it of equal continua in any other way but as moments or boundaries of different sides. Example: space. Colors and other genera of sensory qualities are unimpenetrable in space.[72] As boundaries, two color-lines can of course coincide. The same goes for all other sensory qualities. In the case of tones this will, to be sure, be denied by some. Yet, we have decided in favor of the contrary assumption. Nothing prevents us from assuming that the motive would exist in the case of things that cannot be objects of our experience. In truth, we do not at all know whether our space has real or only phenomenal existence. It is clear, however, that an analogue of our space exists, and it seems to be assured regarding this analogue with our space that other genera that are connected with it are impenetrable.

We can very briefly discuss yet another peculiarity, namely the peculiarity of time and of all continua modified by time: that they are real no longer than in one instant and consequently always only incompletely real. This time, as also motion, is an ἐνέργεια ἀτελή.[73]

---

72 [*Cf. Brentano* EL 72/12251–12252: "A noteworthy property that can occur in the case of a genus of necessary continua is that in it the species of a certain lowest genus with which it stands in metaphysical connection are impenetrable; that is to say, *neither* two species of this genus *nor* species thereof which differ through loose individuation can be simultaneously unified with two equal continua specifically belonging to it in any other way but as perhaps moments or as boundaries from different sides. The only example of such a genus that lies before us in the realm of phenomena is space. Colors and other genera of sensory qualities are unimpentrable."]

73 [*See above, p. 243.*]

An additional peculiarity is this: that certain continua do not allow for an infinite increase, but rather that there is in them a greatest possible continuum. They cannot exceed two particular boundaries in each direction. Example: color. When I go from white through grey to black, I am finished. I cannot go farther. Likewise from red to green. Or from blue to yellow. But not only does this property occur here. Also there seems to be something similar for taste and smell and it is difficult to research these domains, since we are unable to summon features of exactly the same phenomena. Thus between bitter and sweet, which are two extremes beyond which one cannot go. When we say that a greatest finite distance is possible and a greatest finite continuum is possible, [while] this is not the case for space, time, intensity, etc., does that not give us the right to say that for these last[-mentioned] genera something greater [e.g. the distance between two points in time] than for the former genera [e.g. the distance between white and black] is possible? No. We must say that, due to the impossibility of comparing the magnitudes of different genera, no one can say that there is a greater time than there is a distance between two colors.

One more peculiarity. Physicists have wanted to make certain hypotheses in order to demonstrate the finitude of space. They thought that without such a finitude matter would dissipate. They sought to demonstrate, by support of the assumption that space is curved, what is possible only if space is a mere three-dimensional boundary of a four-dimensional continuum. It would however be inconceivable that space is a boundary and nonetheless something on its own. It would be much more reasonable to point out the manner in which the dimensions of colors are finite. Infinity is not the simple consequence of straightness, as colors prove. It would therefore be more reasonable to say: Space, as we imagine it, is perhaps not real, perhaps only an analogue. This analogue might differentiate itself from space in a [certain] respect and have similarity with color. This is by no means to say that such a hypothesis is probable. It would indeed also be in contradiction with physics, hence with the law of inertia. Indeed, the approach towards the limit would actually have to cause a change in the phenomena of motions.

Regarding the earlier[?] differences, a few supplementary remarks are still in order here. We have finished the discussion of the theory of continua.

We have seen that there is in certain lowest genera in every possible direction a greatest possible distance of the species (hence in the case of color). Also the genus of direction itself belongs here. For there are not merely greater and smaller distances of directions for which the angle is the measure, but rather also distances of two directions of a third in different directions, perhaps of equal magnitude. One distance is here the greatest possible one. Thus in the case of an elongated triangle. Species that are different from each other in such a manner, whose distance is therefore the greatest possible one in a certain direction, we call opposites. There are however three cases of such greatest possible distances to be distinguished.

1. The case in which the greatest possible distance of two species in a certain direction is the only greatest possible one in the entire genus, such that no other would come to be its equal. Thus in the case of black and white. This is an opposition in the narrowest sense. There are obviously not such greatest possible distances in all genera. Hence in the case of intensities, tones, etc. In our experience color is perhaps the only genus in which there are opposites in this narrow sense.

2. The case in which the greatest possible distance of two species in a certain direction is the greatest possible distance in the genus as such, but not such that no other would be equal to it. Yet, no distance is greater than it. It is thus with the distances between two opposing directions.[74] The distance of direction of *a o* and *o b* is just as great as that of *c o* and *o d*. Thus it can be [the case] that every species of a genus is an opposite. Thus there is no direction that would not have an opposite direction.

3. The case in which the greatest possible distance between two species is smaller than other possible distances in the same genus, but in another direction. Thus red and green, blue from yellow. This is opposition in the broadest sense of the word. Red and green are often designated as opposites. Less frequently, however, are a certain shade of violet and a certain shade of yellow-green designated as opposites. This irregularity of the use of language arises because one does not know that unitary colors are under consideration in the latter case. Still less would it happen that red is designated as opposite to white or blue, although these are contrasts. Since green is already called opposite to red, as is black to white, one believes that it will not do to designate something else as an opposite. That was indeed impossible in the two cases that we have previously designated. In our third case, however, it is not impossible for several things to stand in opposition to one thing. Perhaps someone says: It belongs to the contrast that a species has a distance towards another one greater than [its distance] towards every other one in this genus, [and] for that reason one does not designate green and white opposites. This surmise would be incorrect since yellow is more distant from black than from blue. It would be no more acceptable to assume a constant center as a mediating point, e.g. grey. Probably the same shade of grey does not lie in the center between yellow and blue and between red and green.

---

74 [*See figure above, p. 210.*]

There are, however, yet five other uses of the word "opposites," of which the last three are decidedly misuses.

1. Some call opposites also those ultimate differences that are the only possible ones in the genus. Here there is thus neither a greater nor a smaller distance. This sole distance, however, is not at all a magnitude. It is the only possible one, but not the greatest possible one. In the domain of inner phenomena there are such "opposites," as in the case of "affirmation and negation," "love and hate." Some perhaps imagine a neutral state as a third item. Hence, in the case of judgments, the judgment of probability is regarded as something in the middle. In the case of the emotional acts, love and hate, one might regard the moderate acts as the most prominent intermediates. In both cases, however, we have no distance in the proper sense. The judgments of probability are judgments concerning very different objects, namely about the chances. Furthermore, we cannot speak of an extreme love and an extreme hate, as intensity has no boundary. In the case of indifference [on the one hand] and love and hate [on the other] we can speak of opposites of intensity, but not of opposites between love and hate.

2. Some have called opposites also such classes which are not ultimate kinds, indeed not kinds at all, but [which] exclude each other and complement each other as members of division. These are the negative opposites "green and non-green." Green is a kind of color, [whereas] non-green is certainly not a kind of color. This usage of "opposite" is most improper, but hardly dispensable. (Aristotle did not refer to two judgments, one of which affirms what the other negates, as ἀναντία, but rather [to each one] as ἀντικείμενον.[75])

3. Some have called every distance an opposition, even if it is neither absolutely nor in a certain direction the greatest possible one. One calls these positive oppositions. Hence violet would be opposite to red. There is however no reason to call this opposition, since the term "distance" is perfectly sufficient. The case became yet worse by the fact that the concept of species and genus was made obscure, indeed was lost. Indeed, "opposition," as one has often called them, was in that case often not even "distance," let alone opposition.

4. The comparative opposition. Of such opposites we speak wherever any distinction is stated, but by no means an extreme one. Thus when I say, "Something is higher, another is lower." Obviously this is taken from the opposition of the direction of distances. Hence [this pertains to] right and left. What is on the right lies [in the direction] towards the right, [and] is thus at a distance

---

75 [*Vgl. Brentano EL 72/12260:* "He distinguished other ἀναντία, of which he believed that truly greatest distances between judgments (contraries not merely contradictories) [existed]." *The* ἀντικείμενον *of a judgment is thus its negation.*]

in a certain direction. The location is not opposed to the location, nor [is] the brighter color opposed to the darker one, but rather the directions are.

5. One often designates all *correlativa* as opposites, if they do not express a match (like equal and equal, small and small). Hence one says that the whole and the part are opposites, cause and effect, master and servant. Here there is in truth nothing but a distinction in the direction of the relation. This gives [us] no reason to speak of opposition, for there is such a distinction even when I say, "This is equal to that, that to this," where also an opposition of direction is present. This usage is certainly a misuse. Only the first three are of interest to us, where we we have the greatest possible distance, not the five applications of the word "opposition."

Yet another relation requires elucidation to a certain extent: the relation of similarity. The linguistic usage of the word *ähnlich* is *angleich*.[76] Hence "almost equal."

One therefore calls 1. "similar" above all and in the most proper sense that to which an increasingly smaller specific distance obtains. Hence two shades of violet, red, and reddish. Where does the similarity begin and where does it end? A definite boundary cannot at all be stated. A boundary to one side is only given in the case of an extreme. Hence everything between red and blue is to a certain extent similar to red, but blue is not since it is an extreme.

2. In a second sense one uses the word ["similar"] wherever an equality of relations is tied to unequals. This similarity is called analogy. There is thus an analogy between time and space. There exists an analogy between a continuum of intensity and an intensity of quantity. A far-reaching similarity in that sense especially obtains in those cases which we have mentioned as a match by μετάβασις εἰς ἄλλο γένος, e.g. 100 imagined dollars and 100 real ones (*contra* Kant). A past king and a real king are analogues. In this last example we even have a double similarity. An additional aspect of a similarity in the sense of analogy is that the temporal distance can be an extraordinarily small one, such that a similarity in the first sense that we considered approximates it. If the mathematicians speak of similarity, it is for them too equality of relations. And their similarity is nothing but equality of shape [or form], for the latter lies only in relations. In truth, the equality of shape [or form] favors the shifting of different [elements] more than [is favored among] a great deal of other things.

3. It also occurs that we call something similar where there is no similarity in the proper sense or in the sense of analogy, namely wherever we have two

---

76   [*Since Brentano is concerned with a German etymology his terms are left in German here. The point, however, is that "similar" is "almost equal," as the following sentence indicates.*]

objects that are composed of a multiplicity of parts and are in certain respects equal or similar in the proper sense, in others however unequal if only the first respects prevail in their significance. Thus we often say, "A similar case has occurred to me." One might be inclined to believe that this similarity requires an inequality in more than one respect, and indeed inequalities of which the one is not simulated in the other. For even in every case of equality in the proper sense there is presumably still something given that constitutes a difference. Here we would thus have equality. However, one might reply: If I have something red and something else that is red, this redness is *equal* to that redness, but this red thing *similar* to that red thing. Thus one might also speak of a mere similarity if I have red things of such and such intensity here and there, the difference lying only in locality.

But what is identity in that case? How does it differ from similarity? That is easy, since identity is more than equality. Identity differs from equality in that the equal is distinguished only by the connection with other metaphysical parts. Identity, by contrast, is perfectly distinctionless. This red thing is identical with this red thing. But also "this red thing is identical with this round thing," if I have a red ball.

Are the relations real or not?

Certain relations are not real, plainly the ones between non-real things. Thus [we have a non-real relation] if we compare something in the past with something in the future. The same, however, will also hold for certain other [relations] which we likewise find between non-real and real. Thus the relations of equality and difference. We actually do find these just as well between real and non-real. Equality and difference change nothing in the elements. No real determination is added through equality or difference. Here we call the two elements between which an equality or difference exists "foundations of the relation." If we consider these relations, they have a direct *fundamentum in re*. There are however equalities and differences that have only an indirect foundation. Thus the relations of magnitude of two distances. The relations of magnitude are given in distances. These themselves, however, only in the distant elements which are in that case the indirect foundations. Also similarity and identity are not real. The same, however, will also be true of the numbers of infinite sets, since these collectives are based entirely on equality and difference. We can say the same of all collectives if they consist of nothing but real elements; it [the collective] as such is not real, and it exists also if the parts exist. There remain only the other connections of parts with parts and in relation to the whole to be discussed. Thus the metaphysical, logical, and physical parts. As regards the metaphysical parts, we have an essentially different case before us. Let us assume that we have a blue with a spatial determinacy a and red with the spatial determinacy *b*. We would also have the same four elements, however, if we had blue with the spatial determination *b* and red with *a*, and yet both cases would be different. Here the relation could be seen as something real. Something similar would be true of the relation of the logical whole to the logical part. To color, which is actually as part in the logical whole "blue," red is not in the same relation in which it exists in the actual thing [as] color. With more justification, however, one might say of the physical whole which is indeed completely based on relations, specific differences, that its relations to the physical parts are not real relations, since they are based entirely on relations of equality and difference. With its three dimensions, the continuum is at once given and adds nothing more, likewise[?] if all wholes are given. We in fact have reason to seek yet another kind of relation. Thus we have: 1. non-real relations without real foundations, 2. non-real relations with real foundations, 3. real relations. In the causal relations, however, we have encounted yet other relations.

The sensory presentations are particular presentations and so determined that it is ruled out that more than one thing, if anything at all, corresponds to them. Is the same also true of every element of the sensory presentation? One might believe: no. Thus one might think of the logical part. But without justification, for they too exist in connection with other ones and they are individualized in this connection. If they were alone, they would certainly be universal. [*Here begins a new unnumbered page of the manuscript which has not been transcribed or translated due to difficulties of legibility.*]

1. Appendix

1. Concept of reality in contrast with existence. (J.S. Mill's "possibilities of sensation" excluded from the outset.
2. Do we posses any direct acquaintance with something real? Necessarily, for otherwise we would not have a concept of it.
3. We have nothing but direct acquaintance with psychical phenomena and their intentional correlatives.
4. Only the former are real.
5. Involved in this is that also only they can affect and receive effect, but not the intentional correlates.
6. The assumption that the psychical realities are absolutely again affected by reality is possible in advance (idealism).
7. It is also compatible with the difference of these realities from their correlates, but it does not have this as a consequence.

8. Not only does this difference merely exist, but also a certain regularity of succession.
9. Wherein does this regularity consist? A. In the domain of mere presentations. Here belong all those constant successions that find their expression in the physical laws insofar as they fall into the appearance, hence inertia, etc.

11. Appendix [Auditors of the lectures on logic (1884/85)]

[Eduard] Leisching
Fuchs
[Josef] Kreibig
[Otto] Aron
[August] Eder
[Franz] Hillebrand
[Emil] Lemberger
Hanin
[Edmund] Husserl
[Adolf] Bauer
Herzog
Berger
[Georg] Fulda
Wimheruntz [?]
Hofer [?]
Pfann
[David] Feuchtwang
[Hans] Schmidkunz

CHAPTER 7

Hillebrand, *The New Theories of Categorical Inferences*

Introduction

§1   The tasks of the following investigation

When the philosopher from Königsberg uttered the familiar statement that since Aristotle logic has not been able to take a step backward, but not a step forward either, and therefore seems "closed and completed to all appearances,"[1] he might well have had in mind first and foremost the theory of inference. This is the most outstanding part of the whole discipline. Indeed, in this area the history of logic can record almost no progress even up to our time. The onslaughts that the edifice of Aristotelian teachings had to endure in the time of burgeoning nominalism, in the Renaissance, and at the beginning of the modern age had left that part of his teaching untouched. For the harsh blame that the syllogistic had to undergo at the time of rebirth did not pertain to it as such, but rather to the developments that its one-sided and exclusive business necessarily had as a consequence. Even the Cartesian school and many later thinkers, who match it in this regard, forgo the Aristotelian syllogistic, not because they regard it as false, but rather because they have doubts about its indispensability for progress in knowledge.

It was reserved for the modern age to become active with reforms here, partly because the ultimate principles from which the inferential procedure gets its justification were sought somewhere other than where they had been sought thus far, partly because the methods by means of which the particular inferential forms are derived were thoroughly transformed. In the former respect it was Friedrich Albert Lange who – in considering spatial intuition as the necessary precondition – saw the principles of all reasoning and inferring in synthetic judgments *a priori* upon which he wanted to build logic, similarly to the way in which Kant wanted to build geometry. In the latter respect, under the influence of Sir William Hamilton in Britain, aspirations made themselves felt for identifying, on the basis of new conceptions of the phenomenon of

---

1   [Kant, *Kritik der reinen Vernunft*, B VIII.]

judgment, the methods of deduction with those of algebra and proceeding in inference just as the mathematician does when he calculates from a numerical equation a number of unknowns. This method was developed by [George] Boole and [Augustus] De Morgan, but taken to such a degree of completion by [William] Stanley Jevons that it was supposedly ready for effortless calculation of any deductive work, however complicated. If the method that Jevons so devised with such refinement was really to prove itself to be free of error, this meant a collapse of the whole syllogistic tradition.

However, not only in Britain, also on German soil has a fundamental reform of syllogistic logic been started which is likewise tied together with looking at the essence of judgment in a way that completely differs from the traditional one. Franz Brentano has thoroughly exposed and justified a new conception of the essence of judgment and indicated briefly how, on this foundation, he conceives of a new shaping of the theory of inference.[2]

Neither the attempts of the British at a reform nor that of Brentano, however, have undergone a decisive critique. Indeed, with regard to the latter, it is not without astonishment that we can state that no specialist has up to the present day endeavored actually to take the path to which he pointed, to pursue to its consequences what he indicated sketchily. Yet, this would have been the first condition for an appropriate critical evaluation.[3]

The dominant position that the traditional syllogistic logic still occupies in relation to all attempts at reform is something that it therefore owes less to its internal advantages (which are in fact not at all established) than to the weight that a more than two thousand year-old tradition lends to it.

In view of this fact, it seems to be the time to subject the traditional syllogistic logic to a renewed examination, to investigate the correctness or incorrectness of the reasons that have prompted modern logicians to break with the tradition, and finally to investigate the new theories that should replace the old one according to the opinion of those logicians. As far as the reform initiated by Brentano is concerned, there is other work to be done in advance. It must first be developed from psychological laws concerning judgment and systematically worked out in its consequences.

---

2   *Psychologie vom empirischen Standpunkte* (Leipzig, 1874), Book II, Chapters VI and VII.
3   Windelband, "Beiträge zur Lehre vom negativen Urtheil" in *Strassburger Abhandlungen zur Philosophie*, pp. 165–195 [Windelband 2019] does, to be sure, think that the manner in which that reform would be conceivable is "not all too difficult to discern", but at the same time declares it to be "something very mysterious" and ultimately forgoes "the treatment of such an obscure proclamation". I shall leave open the question whether this procedure is in the interest of scientific progress.

This is essentially a characterization of the task that we have set for ourselves in the present essay. Not even half of it is occupied with the treatment of syllogisms, whereas the larger part is dedicated to the theory of judgment. This will not be alarming to any reader who knows that this theory is the actual support of the treatment of syllogisms. The syllogistic logic can thus be viewed as a corollary, so to speak, of the theory of judgment (a point we shall discuss later).

Chapter One:
The Psychological Features of the Inferential Process

§ 2 *By inference in the broadest sense one understands a motivated judgment. Difference between motivation and causation*

The Aristotelian definition of the syllogism as "λόγος ἐν ᾧ τεθέντων τινῶν ἕτερόν τι τῶν κειμένων ἐξ ἀνάγκης συμβαίνει τῷ ταῦτα εἶναι [a discourse in which, certain things being stated, something other than what is stated follows of necessity from their being so],"[4] we find accepted by almost all logicians insofar as they have not, like Hegel, adopted metaphysical viewpoints in their discipline. However, it requires a yet clearer interpretation and an essential supplementation.

The psychical act that we call inferring belongs without question among the judgments, and more particularly inferring is drawing a conclusion. The only question is what the distinction is between making a certain judgment (S is P) as a *conclusion* and making the same judgment (i.e. the same in matter and form) without its functioning as a conclusion, i.e. making it because it is without any motivation or in blind faith in the authority of others or in some other way.

There is without a doubt a difference between that judgment being produced by another judging and its not being produced in this way. Now, the causation by other judgments (or by another judgment) is, to be sure, a necessary condition, but by no means a sufficient one for the existence of an act of inference, for also those blind generalizations, occurring hundreds of times in daily life, and also the habitual "expectation of the similar under similar circumstances," which in fact also belongs to the animals, share this feature with what we call inferences in the proper sense. Here [e.g. in the case of animals] no psychologically educated person, however, will want to speak of a process of inferring.

---

4 *Prior Analytics* I.1, 24 b 18 and similarly *Topics* I.1, 100 a 25 and *Sophistical Refutations* 1, 165 a 1.

Rather, in order for us to be able to say of a judgment that it is inferred from others, it is necessary that we make it *due to that other one (or ones)*, i.e. that we are *conscious* of making a certain judgment only *because* we make another judgment (or several others). This "because" does not as such mean a *ground for knowledge*, but rather only a *conscious real ground*. In other words, a judgment is caused by another one (several others) and this causation is accessible within the domain of our inner perception. We are conscious of it. We can designate such a judgment as a *motivated* one, insofar as we understand by *motivation* in the broadest sense a *conscious causation* (not causation, simply speaking).

§ 3   *In order for an inference to be logically justified, its law must be given concretely as an evident and apodictic judgment in consciousness. Concept of evidence and apodicticity*

In the concept of motivation it is not implied that it is also *logically justified*. That is to say, we should not in advance assert that a judgment cannot be false if another one is true (for this is the meaning of "logical justification") *simply because* it is caused by that other one consciously. In the case of some paralogisms the moment of motivation does in fact also seem to be given, though of course without any logical justification.[5] We should therefore ask: What must be given besides that motivation in order for the reasoning to be a logically justified one?

In the concept of logical justification, the concept of *evidence* and that of *apodicticity* are no doubt contained. In order to make this clear, it will be necessary first to define both of these concepts and delimit them over against each other

A judgment is *evident* when it is correct and discerned as correct (characterized as correct) such that it is neither capable of nor in need of a proof. The

---

5   Not in the case of *all* paralogisms is this true. Very often it occurs that one premise gets replaced by another, very similar to it, without the inferring person noticing the shift. With respect to that new premise that has crept into the place of the original one, the act of inferring is a completely legitimate one and yet the conclusion can be false. Such "fallacies of confusion" (as John Stuart Mill [*System of Logic*, v.vii] calls them in connection with [Jeremy] Bentham) therefore do not prove that a judgment can be motivated by another one without following from it with logical justification. It is however questionable, first of all, whether *every* fallacy is of this sort (which I would not assert as definite), and secondly, even if this were true, it would still not be an argument against the *conceptual* separation of simple motivation from logically justified motivation. It would only prove that every motivation is *de facto* at the same time a logically motivated one, but not that this is already implied in the *concept* of motivation itself.

axioms are of this nature, but also the judgments of inner perception, for not only is it correct and discernible in itself as correct that the whole, for instance, is greater than the part, but rather it is also correct and discernible in itself as correct that I present, feel, will, doubt such and such, etc., as Descartes has rightly made a judgment of inner perception (*cogito*), as excluding all doubt, to be the foundation of his philosophy.

There is however an important difference between the axioms and the judgments of inner perception, even though they are both evident. The judgments of inner perception are not necessary truths. For even if it is *evident* that I am now presenting X, it would not involve any contradiction if I did *not* present it, in which case the truth expressed in the above-stated judgment would not obtain. If, however, we have an axiom, the judgment is made not only with evidence, but also with *apodicticity*. That is to say, we judge not only that something *is* so, but rather that it *must be* so, and indeed in our case because the opposite involves a contradiction.

An apodictic judgment need not be necessarily *evident*. "There cannot be antipodes" is [meant as] an apodictic (negative) judgment, which has been made often enough in its time, but certainly not with evidence, since it is not even true. On the other hand, we have seen from the judgments of inner perception that there can be evidence even without apodicticity.

In some manner, the moment of evidence and that of apodicticity must be given in the justified act of inference. The former, because a simple syllogistic step, if any guarantee for its correctness is given, can bear this guarantee only in itself; if it were to require a proof, we would again have to seek a warranty for the stringency of that, and so on into infinity. Yet, apodicticity must also exist in the justified act of inference, for it is essential to it that the acceptance of the premises and the denial of the conclusion involve a contradiction.

One might at first glance think of ascribing to the conclusion itself the character of evidence and apodicticity. Yet, it is at once clear that this would be completely wrong. The judgment "Caius is mortal" is by no means discernible as correct in itself, even if it is concluded with full justification from the judgments "All human beings are mortal" and "Caius is a human being." Nor is it apodictic, for it does not involve a contradiction to judge that Caius is not mortal.[6]

---

6 We might be deceived here by the following version of the conclusion: "Therefore Caius *must* be mortal." This "must" means only that the *hypothetical* judgment "If those premises are true, Caius is mortal," not that the conclusion as such is an apodictic judgment. If the premises themselves are evident and apodictic judgments, this will also have to be true of the conclusion. This, however, is only a special case and does not at all belong to the essence of the process of inference.

However, the objection might be made that there belongs to the conclusion, as *detached from the premises*, neither evidence nor apodicticity, but insofar as it arises as a motivated judgment it can nonetheless somehow share in the character of evidence and apodicticity. It is clear, however, that this standpoint is likewise unacceptable. For obviously also the conclusions of *materially* false inferences would have to bear that character as soon as they are only *formally* correct. That would however mean nothing but regarding judgments as evident which are false in spite of their evidence: a contradiction in terms.

An apparently obvious and at first sight highly plausible way out would be to say: Not the conclusion, but rather the *connection* between the conclusion and the premises is an evident and apodictic one.

Expressed in this form, this is, strictly speaking, an absurdity. Evidence and apodicticity are determinations which can, by their very nature, only belong to a *judgment*. A connection, i.e. a *relation* between judgments, cannot be evident or apodictic.

Something true nonetheless lies in this view. Not the connection itself, but a *judgment* that produces this connection can of course be evident and apodictic. And so it is as a matter of fact. The *law of the inference* must be co-thought and – since it is judgment – co-judged in an evident and apodictic manner, not abstractly and generally, but rather concretely, if the inference is to bear the warranty of its correctness. We say that the *concrete* law must be given in consciousness, and not the *general* one, for the requirement of the consciousness of a general law would lead to an infinite regress, as this can easily be shown. For an additional law would obviously be necessary which produces the connection between the general law of the inference and the particular inference that we simply make, and so on into infinity. This is not the case if the concrete law of the inference is present in consciousness, for here an additional judgment is no longer needed which would perhaps subordinate the particular act of inference to a higher law.

An example may serve to elucidate this point. "There are bodies, and thus there is something spatial."[7] Here the concrete law of the inference is "There cannot be bodies unless there is something spatial." This simultaneously made judgment, belonging to the motivating part of the whole process, is the concrete law of the above-stated inference and gives us a guarantee for logical justification due to its evidence and apodicticity.

---

7 A truly immediate inference, as we shall see in § 45.

(There is hardly any need to add that what we are saying holds only for simple inferences. The law of a complex inference[8] will not immediately come to light, but will require being traced back to ones that immediately come to light.)

It remains of course an issue of convenience, whether one wants to call a judgment that is motivated by another one an inference even if there is no evident law of inference, as this seems to be the case for many paralogisms (cf. above, p. 284).[9]

§ 4   *The so-called unconscious inferences. Helmholtz, Exner*

The conditions that must be fulfilled if a certain judgment is to be an act of inference have frequently not been fully discerned by psychologists and logicians. A mistake that we repeatedly encounter lies in confusing motivation with mere causal determination. It is thus understandable that some natural scientists, e.g. Helmholtz, speak of *unconscious inferences*. What this researcher calls "unconscious inferences" is, to be precise, nothing but a habitual judging. What it has in common with the genuine inferring is only that a certain judgment is *produced* by another one (or by the disposition that another judgment has left behind). This is clarified most of all by the fact that Helmholtz regards every judgment of so-called outer perception as an unconscious inference. Thus unconscious inferences are for him all "psychical activities by which we arrive at the judgment that a particular object of a particular nature is present to us at a particular place outside of ourselves."[10] Whenever we become convinced at some point that a certain psychical phenomenon arises in ourselves as soon as a particular event takes place in the external world, we "infer" the latter when the former is given to us, and we "infer" this in fact "unconsciously" insofar as the premises are not even really present to us. Of course it can also occur that a judgment that prompts another one under *ordinary* circumstances does so also under divergent, extraordinary circumstances, and thus leads us to make a false (but always *unconscious*) inference as it had previously led to a correct one. In fact, Helmholtz has made this circumstance a fruitful explana-

---

8   And here belong also the other categorical modes of the school-logic, as we shall see.
9   Sigwart, for example, separates the two cases, for "wherever our belief in the truth of a judgment is not immediately determined by the presentations of subject and predicate linked in it, but rather by the belief in the truth of one or several judgments" he finds that there is given "an inferring in the *psychological* sense," whereas he restricts inferring in the *logical* sense to those instances in which the inference is justified by an evident law. Cf. *Logik*, 2nd ed., vol. I, p. 423 and "Logische Fragen," *Vierteljahrsschrift für wissenschaftliche Philosophie* (1881), pp. 119 ff.
10   *Handbuch der physiologischen Optik*, 1st ed., p. 430.

tory principle for optical illusions. It is irrelevant here whether this is in all cases done successfully, or whether we have to accept with Hering in many cases genuine alterations in the content of sensation; it indeed remains true that countless illusions and errors are traceable to such processes, as Helmholtz tries to characterize them in the stated manner. However, there can be no *inferring* here, since the feature of motivation, understood in the above-indicated sense, is missing, and it must indeed be missing if the premises are not at all in consciousness. In *this* lies the essential feature for the act of inference. When Helmholtz, quite well discerning a difference between habitual associations and properly so-called inferences, nonetheless gives to the former processes also the name "inferences" because they have a "*similarity of results,*" he fails to see that the character of the act of inference lies in a judgment being made on the basis of other judgments, i.e. being caused (= motivated) consciously. The "similarity of results" does not at all justify the use of the term "inference." The habitual expectation of similar things under similar circumstances can lead someone to make the same judgment to which another person is led by a proper induction that is supported by the principles of probability calculus, and yet in one case there is a process of inferring, but not in the other case – although the "similarity of results" exists without any doubt.

I must also oppose Sigmund Exner for similar reasons when he denies a sharp boundary between habitual association, indeed mere instinctual action, and logically justified inferences and designates errors which have come about from habit as "mistakes in thinking." Between the behavior of a brood hen as she takes the position necessary for brooding, in spite of being deprived of her eggs, and the paralogisms of Zeno Exner in fact sees a "continuous chain of mistakes in thinking."[11] Whoever discerns in the above-cited manner which features are necessary for an act of inference must also discern that those features are either existing in their entirety or altogether missing. A judgment is motivated or not motivated. Transitions and intermediate stages are ruled out.

An inference in the broadest sense (i.e. a judgment that is *motivated* by one or more judgments) is therefore not given wherever a judgment is evoked by (unconscious) dispositions, even if these have been produced by earlier judgments, or wherever the causally efficient judgments are present in consciousness, but not perceived as causally efficient, in other words: wherever no motivation takes place.

---

11   "Über allgemeine Denkfehler," a lecture held at the 61st conference of German natural scientists and doctors in Cologne on 22nd September 1888. Published in *Deutsche Rundschau* 4 (1889), pp. 54–67.

§ 5 *The different conditions for the actual coming-about of a logically justified inference. Only those belong in the domain of syllogistic which are concerned with the descriptive features of judgments.*

If, however, motivation is given, it does not follow, as we have seen, that the inference is a logically correct one. For several cases are, once again, possible here. The law of the inference can be missing, or it can be wrong, or it can indeed be right, but without being grasped as right, or finally it can be grasped with evidence. Only in this last case does the inference bear in itself the guarantee for its correctness.

If an act of inference is perceptive in this manner, this is the only case in which there is a *syllogism* in the narrower sense.

Of the multitude of conditions which must be fulfilled if we are to arrive at a syllogism, some of them do not belong within the scope of logic's interests, for they are only an object of psychological or psycho-physical investigations. Consider especially the case of two people making judgments that are alike in all respects (except their individualization of course), where these judgments, as experience often shows, become one person's motive for making an additional judgment, whereas nothing arises from them for the other person, such that they become in the latter case neither a cause nor a motive for making an additional judgment. This indicates that besides the particular nature of the existing judgments yet other conditions must be given which concern not the state of consciousness at the time, but rather mental and physiological dispositions. The examination of these conditions belongs to the domain of genetic or physiological psychology. Even if they exist, however, and due to them there arises a motivated judgment, it still does not follow, as we have seen, that this motivated judgment comes about with evidence, i.e. according to an evident law. Even less does it follow that such an evident law must really be given in consciousness. This depends in part also on (unconscious) dispositions, but in part assuredly on the particularities of the motivating and the motivated judgment. This becomes clear from the following consideration. The law of an inference, we have said, must be an evident and apodictic judgment. In order for a judgment to possess both of these properties, it is required that its matter is of such a nature that the denial of it – provided that the judgment is affirmative – or the acceptance of it – provided that the judgment is negative – involves a contradiction, but then, even when the matter of the previous condition is met, there are mental dispositions required which must be in place in order to enable the emergence of an evident judgment. The examination of these dispositions is a task for genetic psychology and as such not realizable at present (but it never will be) in an exact way. The former investigation, i.e. the one concerning the nature of the matter that makes an evident judgment possible is an eminently logical one and realizable by means of the mere analysis of the matter. Hence we can say, for instance, that when a categorical judgment of a negative quality is to be made with evidence and apodicticity the matter must contain necessarily contradictory determinations. However, dispositional conditions must still be fulfilled in order for such a judgment really to come about. These cannot be specified, however, whereas the conditions given in the particularity of the matter [*Materie*] can be stated with precision.

It is similar with regard to that judgment which represents the law of an inference. It can obviously be evident and apodictic only if the premises and conclusion stand in relation to each other in determinate respects, conditioned by the particularity of matter and quality.

§ 6 *A theory of syllogisms must begin with a description and classification of judgments.*

A theory of syllogisms has to investigate which properties the motivating judgment (or judgments) and the motivated judgment must have in order that the law underlying the inference can be evident and apodictic.

To this end, a correct description of judgments in their essential features and a classification of them on this basis are especially required. For of course, if we are not clear in each single case about what the true matter and the true quality of the judgments under consideration are, we cannot at all expect a correct decision as to whether the law of an inference is evident or not. We shall repeatedly have in what follows an opportunity to see how differences in opinion about the question whether there follows from one given judgment (or more of them) another one are simply traceable to the different views concerning the meaning of these judgments. An example of this will suffice. The immediate inference by subalternation is characterized as valid by almost all logicians: "What is true of all is also true of some" is a proposition that seems immediately evident. In recent times Brentano has declared the inference by subalternation to be invalid in his assertion that the I-judgment may not be concluded from A and that the O-judgment may not be concluded from E.[12] To the superficially judging person, this might seem to be a case of the immediate evidence of one person being opposed by a denial that someone else takes to be equally evident. Yet, nothing is farther from the truth. In the so-called universal affirmative judgment "All S are P" (if it is truly simple) Brentano sees

---

12   *Psychologie vom empirischen Standpunkte*, vol. I, p. 305.

nothing but the denial of the matter "S which is not P," from which the affirmation of an S which is P cannot at all be concluded, since the former judgment ["There is no S which is not P"] is also true if there is no S. Almost all other logicians[13] beginning with Aristotle believe the existence of the subject's matter to be asserted in the universal affirmative judgment; and if they are right in this belief, the I-judgment can of course be concluded from A with immediate evidence.

We shall therefore begin our discussions with an investigation of the true essence of judgment.

§ 7   *From this vantage point, the theory of syllogisms has the task of investigating the laws under which the immediate inferences fall and finally to show how the mediated inferences are traceable to immediate ones.*

From this vantage point we will have to show what those laws are under which every correct inference must fall. In this manner we shall only arrive at an overview of those inferences whose laws are *immediately* evident.

This already indicates the third task, namely the task of expositing how laws of inferences that do *not immediately* come to light are traceable to ones coming to light *immediately*. We shall thus deductively arrive at a full-fledged overview of the valid categorical moods. For none of the categorical moods of the school-logic, as we may note here at the outset, come to light *immediately*; their laws must first be obtained through deduction from simpler and immediately evident inferences.

§ 8   *Note on the possibility of a dispute concerning the evidence of a law of inference. Lack of evidence and merely presumptive evidence*

We have indicated above that, regarding inferences that do not allow themselves to be traced back further, a dispute concerning validity can only be based on a difference in the *analysis of judgments*. If the law of such an inference is evident (which it must indeed be if the inference is correct), the question about an additional basis for its correctness is of course meaningless, as is every attempt to support it by means of proofs; an absolutely simple syllogistic step must of course bear in itself its justification, as proving cannot ever go on into infinity.

---

13   Exceptions here – as we shall see later – are De Morgan, Herbart, Trendelenburg, and Lange. Yet, not one of these have drawn from this the consequence for inference by subalternation.

It is of course possible that someone is missing the evidence for a law which might be evident in terms of its meaning. This deficiency, however, concerns the cognitive ability (hence the mental dispositions) of the person in question, not the law, and cannot justifiably give rise to a dispute in opinions, just as it is not any proof against the correctness of a geometrical theorem that an uneducated person does not understand its deduction [from axioms].

Also it can and in fact does occur that someone not only fails to grasp an evident truth with evidence, but even denies it. The history of philosophy also gives examples of this. Hegel denied the law of non-contradiction, and Trendelenburg restricted its validty (which moreover entails the full-fledged denial of it).

This seems to have the gravest epistemological consequences, particularly for the theory of syllogisms. If the waranty for the correctness of a syllogism lies in the immediate evidence of its law, and if we have no assurance against illusions even with regard to immediate evidence, it seems questionable whether we ever possess an indubitable guarantee for the correctness of an inference. For wherever there is anything immediately coming to light, it is impossible to inquire into further *criteria*. In this way we are seemingly pushed towards the precipice of absolute skepticism.

Only seemingly, however, for if someone says that we deceive ourselves in the concern with evidence, this is a vague and ill-conceived manner of expression. Above all, we need not concern ourselves further with those cases in which we are *missing* this evidence for truths which could be grasped in their nature with evidence. For the only thing that follows from this is that the sphere of our knowledge is more restricted than it could be with respect to the nature of the knowable. We are as a result lacking the truth, but are not subject to positive errors.

The threat of greater danger comes from those cases in which non-evident and downright false things are regarded as evident. Here it is of no use to say that the evidence is only presumptive and is not at all given in reality, for the question will at once arise: How do I know that a judgment is evident in truth and not merely presumptively evident? We have already stressed, however, that there cannot be criteria of evidence and consequently the above-stated question remains unanswered.

The difficulty is solved by distinguishing between *immediate* and *mediated* evidence (the latter as based on the former).

1. If something is wrongly held to be evident by mediation (i.e. if one believes oneself to be able to trace its truth back to something immediately evident), it is possible to discover the mistake by exhibiting a leap in the chain of proof and rendering it harmless. It does not matter whether what is held to be evident

by mediation is opposed to something evident by mediation or to something immediately evident. The latter was the case for Hegel. The denial of the law of non-contradiction did not seem immediately evident to him. Nor did it seem so to anyone else, for otherwise one would not have found it necessary to adduce proofs for this denial. From this perspective the possibility of knowledge is therefore not in the least endangered.

2. If something is (wrongly) held to be immediately evident, while its opposite is evident by mediation and can thus be *proven*, we will in fact not be able to show a deficiency in the proof to the *mistaken person*, as in the previous case, for such a person simply disregards proving, as he fancies himself to be in possession of *immediate* evidence. Yet, we can take up the proof of the opposite as evident through mediation and thus convince the opponent (or ourselves when we set about testing our own conviction) that the immediate evidence was only presumptive. It is therefore not to be feared here that it is impossible to uncover and exclude error.

3. The last possible case, however, namely that something is held to be *immediately evident* while the *opposite is immediately evident* has *never* been realized and seems inconsistent with the nature of the human capacity of judgment. One will in vain run through the history of philosophy which exceeds every other domain of knowledge in the abundance and variety of skeptical statements, as one will never find a case of presumptive immediate evidence of a proposition whose opposite is immediately evident. If this *were* at all possible for a mental entity that is in possession of the concept of evidence, I would be altogether unable to envision any protective floodgate against absolute skepticism. For cases 1 and 2 ultimately recur on the basis of the impossibility of presumptive immediate evidence where the opposite is immediately evident.

Chapter II:
On the Nature of Judgment

§ 9 *The definition of judgment as a combination of presentations has been seen to be insufficient from various perspectives. Arguments from J. St. Mill, Lotze, and Wundt*

The definition of judgment as a connection of presentations (more precisely, contents of presentation), as Wolff, for instance, still gives it, has for long time been regarded as insufficient. At first it became obvious that we can combine contents randomly without saying anything about the existence of the connected contents, as I can combine the elements "gold" and "mountain" into the presentation "golden mountain" without believing in the existence of a golden mountain (J. St. Mill).

It was furthermore clear that the combination of two contents must proceed in the very same way whether we accept the existence of the whole or whether we deny it. Since there are obviously in the two cases very different judgments, the moment of judgment could not lie in that connecting, which is in fact given in the same manner in both cases.[14]

Lotze offered another consideration that led to regarding the old definition of judgment as insufficient. If we consider, says Lotze in speaking of the particular judgment, that P cannot be stated of S in general, but rather only of that S which is indeed P, every judgment is represented as a case of the identity-judgment SP = SP. But since such a statement of identity does not in any way expand our knowledge whereas the judgment "S is P" does enrich our knowledge, one must assume that such judgments assert "no mutual relation between the single constituent parts of their content, but only that this content as a composite whole is a more or less extended truth [*Geltung*] in reality," just as this is so in the case of the existential judgment.[15]

Wundt puts forward an additional argument against the traditional doctrine. If the combination of two presentations would be a judgment, we cannot see why the combination of more than two presentations would not constitute more than one judgment. This, however, is obviously not always the case, for a lot of presentations can come together without more than one judgment emerging. Hence judgment cannot be defined as a mere combination of two presentations.[16]

§10 *Attempts to supplement the above-stated definition. Ueberweg, Sigwart*

Motivated by these and similar arguments, modern logicians have sought to correct the old definition. The moment of the combination of presentations was indeed still regarded as essential, since one considered the two-memberedness as a necessary property of judgment. However, one nonetheless believed, in accordance with Lotze's procedure, that the correct supplement was found in the moment of *objective validity*.

---

14   Cf. J. St. Mill, *A System of Logic*, I.v.§1.
15   Lotze, *Logik*, [§58], p. 83. What Lotze asserts here of the particular judgment must obviously also be true of the universal one "because the universal judgment ... admits of being formed by summing the singular and particular ones, and must therefore be perfectly homogeneous with them" [§38].
16   Wundt, *Logik*, vol. I (Stuttgart), p. 137.

Ueberweg defines judgment as follows:

> ... the consciousness of the objective validity [*Giltigkeit*] of a subjective union of presentations ..., i.e. the consciousness whether or not the analogous combination exists between the corresponding objective elements.
>
> ...
>
> Single concepts are never judgments, not even *relational concepts*; only the supervenient conviction of the occurrence or nonoccurrence of what is thought makes up the judgment.[17]

In a similar manner, Sigwart says the following:

> The unification of different presentations does not exhaust the essence of judgment; every complete judgment as such includes also the *consciousness of the objective validity of this unification*.

Then he says:

> All those definitions of judgment which limit it to the merely subjective connection of presentations or concepts overlook the fact that the meaning of an assertion is never merely to establish this subjective fact that I am making such a connection at this instant. On the contrary, a judgment via its form claims that this connection concerns the matter in reality, and for this very reason it [the connection] must be accepted by everyone. It is this which distinguishes judgment from the merely subjective combinations of ingenious and witty comparisons which assume the external form of a statement, but do not aim, as a judgment does, at formulating an objectively valid assertion. In the same way a judgment differs from mere conjectures, opinions, and probabilities.[18]

§ 11 *Critique of these attempts*

Upon the combination of presentations or – as Sigwart says – upon the unification of presentations there must still supervene the *consciousness of objective validity* if a judgment is to be reached. If at first we leave aside the fact that objective validity itself is defined by Sigwart differently (i.e. not as "agreement

---

17 *System der Logik*, 5th edition, [§ 67], p. 189.
18 *Logik*, 2nd edition, vol. I [§ 14], p. 98.

of the combination of presentations with an objective combination") from the way in which Ueberweg defines it, a *consciousness* of this objective validity is in fact required by both of them. We therefore ask at first what is meant by that "consciousness." A psychical act obviously. Is this act a presenting or a judgment? No doubt the latter: Only *cognition* (hence a *judgment*) that a subjectively executed combination is objectively valid can supplement the combination of presentations to form judgment. If now we in turn apply to that judgment about objective validity the definition which is to pertain to every judgment, according to Ueberweg and Sigwart, no alternative is left but to add to the combination of presentations (S P) together with the concept "objectively valid" (X) yet a further consciousness of objective validity and so on into infinity. What we mean can be quite well clarified as follows. The mere combination of S with P does not yield a judgment, as Sigwart teaches most correctly; it must first be cognized (hence *judged*): "S P is objectively valid." This latter psychical act, if it is to be in truth a judgment, may not be a mere combination of presentations, and consequently it may not at all be a combination of the elements S, P, and X (where X means "objectively valid"[19]). Obviously, there must therefore supervene in turn, as a supplementary moment, the conviction (i.e. a judgment) of the objective validity of the combination of the concepts S P X. It is clear, however, that even this conviction cannot be the mere combination of S, P, X, and Y, as a further judgment must again be added. If we are now to avoid an infinite regress, we must accept at some point a psychical act that is not again dissolved in the manner indicated by Sigwart. Yet, in that case we do not understand why such a primitive act of judgment is not at at once established for the matter S P itself.

Yet other doubts arise in opposition to Ueberweg's and Sigwart's views. If we have already seen that the concept of the *consciousness* of objective validity leads to insoluable difficulties, this is equally the case with regard to the concept of *objective validity* itself. We must discuss the views of both researchers separately, for they do not mean the same thing by "objective validity."

For Ueberweg, who sees it in an agreement of the objective combination with the combination of presentations, the concept of *existence* is certainly contained in it. Ueberweg's theory, however, fails to give any account of the provenance of this concept. It is certainly not contained in so-called outer perception. The presentations of outer perception offer us qualities, degrees of

---

19 This would indeed yield nothing but the *presentation* "objectively valid SP," which I can obviously also form when I am convinced that SP does not exist.

intensity, local determinations, but not existence. It is absurd to assert that a color, for instance, consists of its qualities and its existence.

Nor is the concept of existence obtained from presenting in the case of inner perception. It is indeed clear that we cannot say that whatever is presented is existent, for when we deny that an object exists we must present it simply in order to deny it. The concept of existence cannot be derived from feelings, wishes, striving either. Of the psychical phenomena there thus remains only the judgment from which it could be taken.[20] According to Ueberweg's theory, however, the concept of existence – insofar as it is contained in the concept of objective validity – is already presupposed in order for a judgment to come about. Hence, this theory must forgo an explanation of the provenance of this concept.

Sigwart defines the concept of objective validity differently.[21] According to him, it "is not immediately based upon the fact that the subjective connection corresponds to relations between the corresponding existing things, but rather upon the necessity of the unification" (i.e. of the presentations that make up the subject and predicate),[22] as this necessity may be a "sentiently given" one (e.g. in the judgment "Here is the letter A") or it may be grounded in the relation of concepts (e.g. in the judgment "An absolutely indivisible atom can have no extension").

"Objective validity then reduces itself to this: that both the process of forming the intuition and the act of judgment take place in a way which is universally valid," says Sigwart, where he speaks of the "simplest, merely denominative judgments," such as "This is snow."[23]

Perhaps Sigwart's notion is not very easy to grasp when exposited in this abstract manner. Thus I will cite those two examples, already indicated above, in his own words:

> If I say, "Here is the letter A," perception forces me to regard this judgment as valid, as its truth is based on the sentiently given necessity of positing this letter in this place in space. If I say, "An absolutely indivisible atom

---

20   In one of his articles "Über subjectlose Sätze und das Verhältnis der Grammatik zur Logik und Psychologie" Marty has convincingly shown that this is so. Cf. *Vierteljahrsschrift für wissenschaftliche Philosophie* (1884), pp. 171 ff., and also Brentano, *Vom Ursprung sittlicher Erkenntnis*, p. 76.
21   Concerning the analyses that Sigwart gives of the concept of existence, cf. Brentano's accurate critique in *Vom Ursprung sittlicher Erkenntnis*, p. 61 ff.
22   *Logik*, 2nd edition, vol. I [§ 14], p. 98; *Die Impersonalien*, p. 59 ff.
23   *Logik*, p. 101.

cannot have any extension," the relation between the concepts of extension and divisibility compel me to this proposition which is true whether I believe in the reality of such atoms or not.[24]

In this manner Sigwart defines the concept of objective validity. If we consider the above-stated examples, it will be easy to demonstrate that this way of supplementing the combination of presentations to form a judgment is also unsatisfactory. Granting that the perception (though better sensation!) forces me to make the judgment "Here is the letter A," and granting that in the second case the relation between the concepts of extension and divisibility compel me to make the judgment "An absolutely indivisible atom cannot have extension," this compelling or forcing is still not itself the judgment, but rather only perhaps its cause. If it should only come down to a determining cause, all combinations of presentations, hence even that "subjective combination of ingenious and witty comparison," would in truth have to be judgments simply because of the universal validity of the law of causality. Forcing, compelling supposedly mean more here, however, namely the (discerned) impossibility of getting free from a presentation or combination of presentations under certain circumstances. Nonetheless, this would only be a particular instance of causal determination and we would have to repeat what we said earlier: This forcing does not constitute a (phenomenal) feature of the *act of judgment*, but rather only perhaps a particular aspect of its *cause*. (I shall altogether leave aside the fact that a *discerned* compelling already presupposes a discerning, hence a judgment.) And when Sigwart repeatedly gives assurance that in the case of the "simplest and immediate judgments," as in the case of perceptual judgments, the corresponding presentations might "not at all be put into a relation without there occurring a concsciousness of necessity and validity (are these again not the different things?) of their belonging-together,"[25] that both are given "with one stroke," so to speak, I can only see this as a proof that certain presentations (e.g. those of so-called outer perception) *cause*, with an unchanging regularity, an affirmative judgment in ourselves with regard to their contents, that this judgment, hence without any reflection, is formed as a result of an instinctive urge,[26] but not "that the consciousness of validity cannot at all be separated from the thought of predication," provided that we understand separation here to mean a *conceptual* one and not merely a *temporal* one. (Sigwart

---

24 *Die Impersonalien*, p. 60.
25 *Die Impersonalien*, p. 60. [*The question in parentheses is Hillebrand's insertion.*]
26 Only in this sense is Sigwart right when he says, "I can in fact not *ask* if coal is black or snow is white, whether this table is rectangular or that ball is round." Ibid.

must be thinking of a conceptual separation since he does, after all, declare objective validity to be a necessity of the unification and thus regards the two as conceptually identical.)

The consciousness of objective validity, no matter if it be understood in Ueberweg's meaning or in Sigwart's, cannot therefore be what in truth supplements the presentation or combination of presentations in order to form a judgment, although both researchers are right in thinking that these require a supplement of some sort.

§ 12 *On the attempt to define judgment as subsumption of one concept under another one*

Yet another widespread theory, according to which judgment consists in a subsumption of concepts ([Friedrich Eduard] Beneke, [August] Twesten, [Hermann] Ulrici),[27] finds its refutation in a certain way already by means of earlier arguments. If by subsumption a judgment concerning the relation between extensions of concepts is understood, this is obviously not an answer to the question concerning the essence of judgment. The mere combination of presentations "extension of S" and "contained in the extension of P" does not yield a judgment, since in fact – as even Sigwart remarks – the moment of the combination of presentations does not fully exhaust the essence of judgment. If we describe the function of judgment in the *correct* way (leaving aside at first: which way?), the view might be justified in advance that the object of judgment is always a relation between extensions of concepts, but then the subsumption-theory would not be a theory of the *function* of judgment, but would rather concern only the *matter* of judgments. Regarding the theory of subsumption in this latter sense, we shall investigate it more thoroughly later.[28] Here it is not under consideration.

§ 13 *Attempts at a definition from J. St. Mill, Bain, and Herbart*

Of other attempts to supplement the definition of judgment as a combination of presentations, the one that J. St. Mill makes is worth considering, as is A. Bain's definition that is in full agreement with Mill's. Mill stresses that in a judgment there must supervene upon the combination of concepts an act of belief[29] and in agreement with this Bain says, "... apart from all belief, the

---

27 [*See Beneke 1832; Twesten 1834; Ulrici 1852.*]
28 See §§ 61 and 62 below.
29 *A System of Logic*, I.v.§ 1.

proposition has no meaning, no existence."[30] However, for both Mill and Bain it remains altogether unclarified what is to be understood by "belief." Neither one plainly states that it is a primitive psychical act that differs from presenting. Indeed, we do not find any single implication drawn from such a view (as we will find this in the theory of existential sentences). Thus their standpoint does, to be sure, deserve respect as a valuable testimony to the untenability of the old theory of judgment, but we cannot speak of it as its replacement by means a positive analysis of the phenomenon of judgment.

We must also say something similar concerning Herbart's definition of judgment as a decision about the connectability of given concepts.[31] Quite clearly, by "decision" the connection of concepts itself is not to be understood. The genus of psychical phenomena to which it belongs, however, is not something that Herbart clarifies for us. He, just like Hume and Mill, might well have come close to the knowledge that judgment is a primitive psychical act. Had he believed in a further analysis, it would not be good to assume of such an exact thinker that he would have not at least attempted it.

No matter how much the previously mentioned researchers in Germany and Britain diverge from the traditional theory of judgment, they all regard the moment of the combination of presentations as essential to judgment. Only Brentano has pointed out that this moment does not only fail to constitute a sufficient feature of judgment, but is not even a necessary one. The consideration of the existential sentence ("A is") guides us towards this latter thesis.

Here we might at best be inclined to accept a combination of the content A with the concept "existent" and maybe thus to rescue the traditional theory of the necessity of a *combination* of presentations. However, Brentano especially stresses that the concept "existence" is obtainable only through reflection on an already present act of judgment, whereas the disputed theory must presuppose it already as being there prior to any judgment, as we have already pointed this out on the occasion of investigating the concept of objective validity.[32]

§ 14 *The moment of combining presentations is neither sufficient nor necessary as a feature of judgment.*

For those who might be inclined to derive the concept of existence from another source (as this is done by Sigwart in particular in recent times), I would especially point out another argument which – quite independently of the question concerning the provenace of the concept of existence – much more immedi-

---

30 *Logic*, vol. I, p. 80.
31 *Lehrbuch zur Einleitung in die Philosophie*, § 52.
32 *Psychologie vom empirischen Standpunkte*, vol. I, p. 279, and Marty op. cit.

ately comes to light in its capacity of proving [Brentano's view on the relevant issue], though curiously almost never at all considered by our opponents.

Every affirmative judgment implicitly affirms every part of its matter. The judgment "A is X" cannot be true unless A is and X is, for this is implied in it. If now the existential judgment "There is an A" is as good as the combination of A with the concept "existent" (= X), both A and X would obviously have to be affirmed (accepted) according to the just-stated rule. But what is the point of the combination with X (= existent) if A is already accepted with it? As Brentano concludes from this, we thus "do not get past an inclusive simple acceptance of A." He continues by saying the following:

> What, however, would differentiate this simple acceptance of A from the acceptance of the combination of A with the feature "existence," as this combination is supposedly expressed in the sentence "A is"? Obviously nothing at all. Consequently, we see that the acceptance of A is rather the true and full-fledged sense of the sentence and therefore nothing but A is the object of the judgment.[33]

In a similar way it is clear also with regard to the negative existential sentence "A is not" that it cannot be conceived of as a denial of the combination of A with the feature "existence" (= X). We may simply consider that the denial of a complex absolutely does *not* involve the denial of its parts. Whoever denies the matter SP is not at all asserting that there is no S and no P. If accordingly the existential sentence "A is not" is conceived of as a denial of A with the concept "existence" (= X), this would involve neither the denial of A nor that of X. It therefore follows that whoever makes the judgment "A is not" has, in doing so, not denied A, but this is obviously absurd.[34]

Accordingly, even aside from the analysis of the concept of existence, it comes to light that the existential sentence cannot be regarded as a combination (or separation) of a content of presentation with (or of) the feature "existent."

§15 *Results of the investigation thus far concerning the essence of judgment*

The results of our investigation thus far are: 1) Judgment is not a mere combination of contents of presentation. 2) The supplement that this analysis has received through bringing into play the consciousness of objective validity

---

33   Ibid., pp. 276f.
34   Brentano has also already used this argument (see *Psychologie*, vol. I, p. 277).

proves to be unacceptable in two cases [namely those of Ueberweg and Sigwart]. 3) The moment of *combining* presentations is neither a sufficient feature nor a necessary one of the phenomenon of judgment.

§ 16 *Brentano's view concerning the nature of judgment: the idiogenetic theory in contrast with the allogenetic one*

The result up to now is a purely negative one. We have found ourselves compelled to reject three theses, at least one of which was contained in each of the theories that have thus far been formulated. I must regard only the view that Brentano advocates regarding the nature of judgment as exempt. Since I regard it as the correct view and must accordingly also consider it as the true foundation of the entire syllogistic (as I shall develop this in what follows), it is a requirement to exposit it first of all in its basic outlines and to defend it against the objections that have been raised against it. What it implies for the theory of inferences, as these are made either immediately or through mediation, will then easily come to light.

As the psychical phenomena (e.g. presenting, feeling, expecting, etc.) differ from the physical ones insofar as the relation to an immanent object (the presented, the felt, the expected, etc.) [die Beziehung zu einem immanenten Objekt (dem Vorgestellten, dem Gefühlten, dem Erwarteten etc.)] is essential to the former, the *different manner* of this intentional relation is decisive for the general differentiation of the psychical phenomena among themselves. In accordance with the three kinds of this relation, Brentano divides the psychical phenomena into *acts of presenting*, *acts of judging*, and *acts of emotion* (loving, hating, desiring, loathing, etc.). What interests us here is only the second class and its differentiation from the first class. The essence of judgment lies in a special intentional relation to the immanent object, as we can make this relation understandable only by indicating it in inner experience. While psychology has thus far endeavored to trace the act of judgment back to simpler mental elements, the analysis, on Brentano's view, must stop here as it stands before a primitive phenomenon.

Since the distinguishing characteristic of his theory consists in seeing a special genus (ἴδιον γένος) in judging, whereas all other theories see only a certain composite of psychical elements of another genus (ἄλλο γένος), we may call the first of these the *idiogenetic* theory of judgment and all others *allogenetic*, in order to have suitable names for such fundamental distinctions.

We have already familiarized ourselves with the arguments against the attempts at a further analysis of judgment. Yet two important implications remain to be drawn from the idiogenetic theory.

§17 *The concept of existence*

We have reproached the advocates of the opposing view by pointing out that they must use the concept of existence for constructing judgment, though without being able to show where they get this concept. The theory that we accept – the idiogenetic theory – naturally does not need this concept for the constitution of judgment, as it is by contrast able to show whence that concept of existence which we simply possess originates. We call something "existent" when the judgment in which it is accepted is true. Marty rightly remarks that the concept of existence is obtained in the following way:

> ... by reflection on a particular class of psychical phenomena, namely judgment. If we never had made an affirmative judgment, we would not possess the concept, for it designates only *the relation of some object* (by which we mean everything presented) to a *possible judgment that accepts it and is true or correct*.[35]

The idiogenetic theory therefore proceeds in the very reverse order in which the allogenetic theories do. An intentional relation, which is called judging, to an object is for the former theory the source of the concept of existence, whereas the latter theories derive judgment from the concept of existence. Which of these two standpoints is the correct one becomes clear from our earlier discussions. Yet, we can point out here that even the acceptance of the apriority of this concept (against which a good deal could be said) offers no means of getting past a function of judgment that in all cases differs from presenting. For if we assume that being is an *a priori* root-concept, given prior to all experience, the combination of it with some content X would nonetheless lead only to the *presentation* "existing X." Whoever has the presentation "existing golden mountain," however, does not for this reason *believe* in the existence of a golden mountain any more than a person who has the concept "non-existent house" therefore *believes* that there are no houses.

§18 *On the division of judgments into one-membered and two-memembered*

A further and no less important implication of the idiogenetic theory is that there is no specific distinction between one-membered judgments ("existen-

---

[35] "Über subjectlose Sätze," 2nd article, *Vierteljahrsschrift für wissenschaftliche Philosophie* (1884), pp. 172 f.

tial" or "thetic" in traditional logic) and two-membered judgments ("categorical" in traditional logic). As the existential sentence "S is" expresses nothing but the simple acceptance of S, the so-called categorical sentence "S is P" expresses the simple acceptance of the matter SP. Likewise, in the sentence "S is not P" the matter SP is rejected and there is obviously no reason to make a greater or smaller complexity of the matter [*Materie*] a principle for dividing judgments.[36] Accordingly, what is called "existential judgment" is only a particular form of the *statement*, i.e. the linguistic expression, and this form can be given to every truly simple judgment, whether it is a categorial judgment or an existential (thetic) judgment in accordance with traditional terminology.

(As the four kinds of judgment (A, E, I, O) which logicians have distinguished are to be expressed in extential form, this will receive attention in the critique of theory of the quantity of judgment as it has thus far been formulated. For what is worth knowing about this, see Brentano's *Psychologie*, vol. I, pp. 283.)

This is in its essentials the idiogenetic theory of judgment, as formulated by Brentano and defended by Marty.[37] This is the basis for what we shall say in the following regarding the theory of the immediate inferences and the categorical syllogisms.

However, since highly respected researchers have raised objections against this theory, it is our duty to deal with these.

Objections against the Idiogenetic Theory

§19 *First objection (Windelband) and its refutation*

Windelband has asserted that one is "to exhibit in a 'judgment', besides the function of presenting and combining presentations, the other function of (approving or disapproving) assessment,"[38] but for him it is not possible to infer from this the establishment of a special "class" of psychical phenomena. Rather, for Windelband (and also for [Julius] Bergmann, who holds the same view) the function of judgment is to be coordinated with the functions of desiring and

---

36 Provided that it expresses a truly *simple judgment* and not a complex or double judgment, which is something that we shall discuss later.

37 Cf. the Chapter VII of Brentano's *Psychologie* and Marty's articles "Über subjectlose Sätze," *Vierteljahrsschrift für wissenschaftliche Philosophie* (1884).

38 "Beiträge zur Lehre vom negativen Urtheil" in *Strassburger Abhandlungen zur Philosophie*, pp. 165–195 [see Windelband 1884, 172; Windelband 2019, 134].

willing, as he maintains that all of these are ascribable to "the practical side of the life of the soul." This perspective arises from the notion (as we gather it from his *Präludien*) that affirming or negating are *value-judgments* which decide whether a particular relation between presentations serves the expansion of knowledge as its *goal*. Since truth – just like goodness – has only to do with fitness for a certain goal, there is for him a merging of true and false, good and evil, pleasant and unpleasant into a single category, and consequently judging and desiring, as correlates of those concepts, cannot be specifically different activities of the soul, but rather must be assigned to one and the same – *practical* – part of psychical life.

By affirming and denying, we assess a single combination of presentations in terms the general *goal* of truth, but this fact – as Sigwart[39] correctly remarks against view under consideration – does not at all entail that affirming and denying are *themselves* a *practical conduct*. Approving and disapproving in the sense of *pratical* conduct[40] is a *consequence* of judging and not judging itself. Sigwart likewise points this out, quite correctly, as follows:

> We disapprove of the false because it is false, but it is not false because we disapprove of it. Our feeling must be grounded upon the theoretical knowldge that a judgment is true or false, just as we must know that the means will lead to our end before we choose them.[41]

> Consciousness of validity is not a form of willing, for it is the *fulfillment* of a striving and willing, just as the pleasant feeling of being satisfied is not a practical conduct since it is the object of striving for the person who eats.[42]

Moreover, *this* objection from Windelband has no significance for the present investigation, insofar as it does not deal with the specific difference between presenting and judging. The assertion that judging and desiring are simply the same is not one that Windelband makes either. He only disputes that there is

---

39   *Logik*, 2nd edition, vol. I, p. 157.
40   The terms "approve" and "disapprove" are, just like the terms "accept" and "reject," not free of the danger of ambiguity. "Rejecting a view" means *assessing* it as incorrect, whereas "rejecting an action" means *loathing* it as bad. The identity of names no doubt played a role in causing Windelband and Bergmann to overlook the specific distinction between judgment and emotion.
41   *Logik*, 2nd edition, vol. I, [Appendix A] p. 159. Cf. Brentano, *Vom Ursprung sittlicher Erkenntnis*, p. 56.
42   "Logische Fragen," *Vierteljahrsschrift für wissenschaftliche Philosophie* (1881), p. 101.

not the same fundamental distinction between judging and desiring as there is between judging and presenting. Even if this were correct (which we must decidedly reject, just as Sigwart does), it would leave the further implications for the theory of inference fully intact.

§ 20 *Second objection (Windelband) and its refutation*

The same is not true with regard to a further objection that Windelband raises against the idiogenetic theory of judgment. Concerning immediately certain perceptions, he thinks that it will not do to distinguish between *two* psychical acts, that of the presentation and that of the affirmation, "between which perhaps only an unnoticeable time passes," as such an assumption is in his own words:

> ... senseless, for the motive of this subsequent assessment can always be sought only again in the immediate evidence with which the presentation must have already asserted itself if it is later to be accepted as true.[43]

This objection obviously directs itself against the distinction between presenting and judging in the simple act of perception.

Above all, a *temporal succession* of these two acts is not necessary and is in a certain sense not even possible, since what is assessed [or judged] while it is being assessed [or judged] must also in fact be an object of presenting (if it can also be presented without being judged [or judged]).[44] Besides, it is not understandable how the mere *presentation* is to assert itself with *evidence* if evidence is a property of judgment and we can quite well speak of evident judgments, but not of evident presentations. The concept of evidence includes in itself that of truth, and truth belongs only to judgment. If Windelband cites propositions such as "This rose is red" as examples of such immediately evident perceptions – propositions which are by no means evident in the sense of the word as it has thus far been understood – we must assume that for him *evidence* is nothing but a *compulsion to judge*. If, however, this were correct, evidence would simply be a property of the presentation that becomes the *motive*

---

43 [*Windelband 1884, 176; Windelband 2019, 135. The translation of the word "Beurteilung" here was chosen to accommodate Windelband's thought. The term "judgment" in Windelband 2019 was reserved for "Urteil," whereas the two terms are often used as synonyms in the school of Brentano.*]

44 [*The term "beurteilt" is translated in Windelband 2019 as "assessed," whereas the alternative translation as "judged" must be kept in mind to bring across Hillebrand's point.*]

of the judgment. In this case, it would not be "senseless" to make a distinction between the motive and what is motivated, but not only this. It would be an out-and-out requirement.

§ 21 *Third objection (Windelband) and its refutation*

There still remains a third objection from this particular researcher.

If every (simple) judgment can be represented in an existential form, indeed if this very form most suitably expresses the psychical occurrence since it alone sharply sorts out the two parts of the judgment, matter and form, and thus reveals the distinction between categorical and so-called existential judgments as a merely linguistic one which does not concern the function of judgment, then obviously the sign for affirmation or negation must be a univocal one. That is to say, it should not be equivocal. Yet, the opposite seems to be the case [as Windelband elaborates in the following passage]:

> If we say, for instance, "Freedom is," we will indeed have to concede that we ascribe to it a different kind of "being" from the kind we ascribe to divinity in the sentence "God is." Yet, the two propositions have in common that this "being" under consideration means in both cases a "being actual" or "being real," although a substance "is" in a sense different from a property or activity. If, however, we change the proposition "Lightning is the cause of thunder" into the existential "The causal relation between lightning and thunder is," we can be very much in doubt about whether this "is" can be interpreted in the sense of "actuality," "reality." If we come to an existential proposition like "The subsumption of the rose under the concept of a flower is" – for this is the only way to transform the proposition "The rose is a flower" into an existential proposition – we would wind up in a hyperrealism, which not only hypostasized universals, but also their relations, if we interpreted this "being" also as "absolute actuality."[45]

Without a doubt, a harsh reproach against the disputed [idiogenetic] theory!

First of all, we should remark in passing that the proposition "The rose is a flower," expressed in the extistential form, would not be "The subsumption of the rose under the concept of a flower *is*," as Windelband thinks. (This will arise from later considerations.) But since it is possible to make the judgment

---

45   "Beiträge zur Lehre vom negativen Urtheil," p. 183 f. [*Windelband 2019, 139*].

"The subsumption of the rose under the concept of a flower *is*" (even though it is not identical with the judgment "The rose is a flower"), Windelband may nonetheless use it as an example for his argument.

Above all, it is incorrect to say that "being" means the same as "being actual," "being real." It has repeatedly been stressed recently, especially by Marty,[46] that we can say of a lack, an impossibility, and the like that they *are*, though without the least intention to assert that a lack and an impossibility are *realities*. Hence, if one says, "The subsumption of the rose under the concept of a flower *is*," the relation that one thus expresses between universals is by no means "hypostasized," as the sentence only means that this subsumption is to be accepted. We of course concede to Windelband that in the proposition "God is" a reality is accepted, whereas this is not the case in a proposition such as "There exists the impossibility that such and such is." But this is not to be understood as if the distinction would lie in "is" meaning the same as "is real" in the first case, but not in the second. In both cases "is" means the same thing, but since I understand by "God" a reality, it is of course a reality that I accept when I accept God. And since it belongs to the concept of a lack, of an impossibility, and the like, that they are not realities, no reality is accepted whenever a lack, for instance, is accepted. It is thus a distinction in the *matter* under consideration here, and not a distinction in the function of judgment which would reveal the sign "is" as an ambiguous term [*Homonymon*].

The standpoint that Windelband represents here would lead to the most egregious implications. For as soon as moments belonging to the *matter* of judgment are put into the *function of judgment*, any unitary explanation of the latter ceases from the outset. The differences between "being real" and that being [*Sein*] which belongs also to a lack and an impossibility are indeed not at all the only ones that we would have to acknowledge from this standpoint. If, for instance, God is to be understood as an intrinsically necessary and matter as a contingent entity, "is" in the propositions "God is" and "matter is" would already have to be an ambiguous term [*Homonymon*] since it would have in one case the meaning "being necessary due to itself," in the other case that of "being contingent." In fact, Windelband himself allows for "is" even in propositions such as "God is" and "freedom is" to be used only equivocally, although it is in both cases a reality under consideration, on his view. What differences Windelband is thinking of in this example is not clear. Very many of them, however, could be found as soon as one analyzes the concepts of God and freedom, but

---

46 "Über subjectlose Sätze," 2nd article, *Vierteljahrsschrift für wissenschaftliche Philosophie* (1884), pp. 172 ff.

any difference between them simply lies in the concepts themselves and not in the function of judgment.

Note. Sigwart, whose objections against the here advocated theory of judgment we shall soon discuss, seems to hold the view, similar to Windelband's, that the act of judgment as such participates in the peculiarities of the assessed [or judged] object. After he asserts that the consciousness of "objective validity" must supervene upon the "subjective combination of presentations" if any judgment at all is to come about, he continues as follows:

> The meaning of validity, however, differs depending on the character of the presentations. If our judging is concerned with objects which we, on the basis of perception, presuppose as actually existent, validity means the actual occurrence of what we assert within the world. If it is concerned with mere concepts, the validity of the judgment means a necessity lying in the presented content itself to assert a determinate predicate of it.[47]

Here we essentially see the same confusion that we have encountered in the case of Windelband. If "is" would mean the same as "is real" in some judgments, this meaning could certainly not hold for all judgments.[48] As already remarked, however, this is not the case, as "is" does not have this meaning in any judgment at all. If A is a reality, the proposition which says that A *is* asserts implicitly that a reality *is*, and indeed that reality which simply has the properties of A as such, but it does not ascribe reality to an A which would not be real by itself.

When Sigwart[49] asks those who regard propositions such as "It is snowing," "It is raining," as existential judgments to consider that "the actuality of what is asserted" is already included in them, "that the subject is presented as actually existing," and that there is thus no reason "to assert this existing," he is reproaching them for a view that they do not at all advocate, for the only ones who could

---

47 *Die Impersonalien*, pp. 59 f.
48 Sigwart correctly discerns this. However, the example that he cites for his assertion is not well chosen. The proposition "An absolutely indivisible atom cannot have extension" is true, as he correctly remarks, "whether or not I believe in the reality of such atoms." Yet, the just-cited proposition – in truth a *negative* one – does not even express an existence. Its meaning is fully exhausted by the denial of individisible, extended atoms. Propositions such as "A lack is," "An impossibility is" and the like serve much better to show the difference between being and reality, for these propositions *assert* an existence without a reality, whereas in Sigwart's example neither of these is asserted.
49 *Die Impersonalien*, pp. 54.

justly be targeted by the above-cited words would be those who believe that in propositions such as "It is snowing" reality is being asserted. In the assertion that the proposition "It is snowing" means the same as "Snowing *is*" this is however not at all involved. It is therefore a mistake on Sigwart's part and not the theory under his attack when he at once confuses "being" with "being real" and in this manner gives the opposing view a shape in which it is of couse vulnerable.

§ 22 *Fourth objection (Sigwart) and its refutation*

Aside from the objection conveyed above, yet other considerations have prompted Sigwart to fight against the idiogenetic theory of judgment.

In "acceptance" or "rejection," as Sigwart absolutely concedes, "there lies another function besides the merely subjective connecting of two presentations to each other." However, he disputes that this function "belongs to another domain of the soul [i.e. another class of psychical acts] than presenting does, and has a greater affinity with love and hate than with the thinking and presenting of particular objects."[50] We must concede at once that what Sigwart remarks regarding the [closer] relationship with emotions. What I cannot understand, however, is how he could make this remark *in opposition to* Brentano's theory. The division of psychical phenomena in accordance with the three fundamentally different relations to the immanent object simply does not exclude any closer relationship of one of the three classes with any of the others.[51]

§ 23 *Fifth objection (Sigwart) and its refutation*

Sigwart makes an additional argument in opposition to the establishment of *one-membered* judgments and thus implicitly in opposition to the idiogenetic theory of judgment as such. His argument is *implicitly* opposed to the whole theory, as I say, for it is irrelevant, according to this theory, whether the simple matter A or the complex matter SP is accepted (or rejected) since in both cases it only comes down to the peculiarity of the intentional relation. Whoever therefore regards it as wrong to posit a special intentional relation for a

---

50 *Die Impersonalien*, p. 59.
51 Steinthal too is guilty of the same misunderstanding (*Zeitschrift für Völkerpsychologie* 18, p. 175). The [critical] remarks from both [Sigwart and Steinthal] are much more applicable to the views of Windelband (op. cit.) and Bergmann (*Reine Logik*, pp. 46 ff.). Cf. Brentano, *Vom Ursprung sittlicher Erkenntnis*, p. 56.

"one-membered" judgment must consequently do so also with respect to the "two-membered" (so-called categorical) judgment, and thus with respect to any judgment at all.

With this preliminary consideration in mind, we turn at once to the above-mentioned counter-argument that Sigwart makes in the following passage:

> When I present an "object" A, I am at first conscious of it as something presented or thought of; its primary relation to me is that of being the object of my presenting. I cannot reject it, insofar as I actually present it, and if I wanted to accept it, then I simply could accept only that I actually present it. This "acceptance," however, would not be the assertion that it exists, for the issue at hand, besides the fact that I present it, is whether it has the additional significance of forming a part of the actual world surrounding me, whether it can be perceived by me and can have effects on me and other things. I must attach this latter notion to the mere presentation if I want to assert its existence.[52]

And along the same lines he says in *Die Impersonalien*:

> The concept as such requires no acceptance or positing. As soon as it is actually thought, all is done that is possible with respect to it as this single concept. The concern is not at all what it is to which the acceptance refers, or how, if the concept is actually thought, it can be refused and in which sense it could be rejected. The concern is not what it means for me to accept the concept of a circle or reject the concept of a square.[53]

And right after this, he says of a single intuition, e.g. a visual image, that there is no conceivable sense in which anyone could say that I accept or reject it. "It simply exists, the object of my consciousness, whether I want it to exist or not."[54] To be an object of acceptance or rejection is described as follows:

> [It can only be] the reference that it (the content of the concept), aside from being thought by me at present, can otherwise have, especially the notion that *another* object, given to me in intuition, corresponds to or

---

52 *Logik* [2nd edition, vol. I], p. 89 f. [Sigwart 1895, vol. I, 72].
53 *Die Impersonalien*, p. 62.
54 Ibid., p. 63.

is identical with the concept, but then the relation in which the concepts stands, not the concept itself, is the object of acceptance or rejection.[55]

Whoever knows the idiogenetic theory of judgment in the form that Brentano gives it must see at once that Sigwart has misunderstood it by being guilty of two confusions: first of all, between act of presentation and content of presentation, and secondly – in connection with this – between object and presented object.

First of all, we should make a remark in explanation of these terms. They are, to be sure, understood by everyone when each term is taken by itself, but as soon as they are all jointly brought into the domain of our considerations, simply due to ambiguity of expression, they fall prey to the confusion so readily that even thinkers such as Sigwart could be led astray into misunderstandings and errors.

Everyone knows what it means to say, "I am thinking of a dollar" (as I may represent it in my imagination or "perceive" it). What remains the same in species, no matter if I present a dollar, a horse, or a triangle is called the *act of presentation*. That which differentiates these three cases from each other is generally designated as *content* or *object* of presentation. (The word "presentation" is equivocally applied to act and content.) In our first example the object of presentation is therefore: *dollar*. It is not: *presented dollar*. The act of presentation is specified by the content and forms together with it a single mental reality. This mental reality can in turn be an object (content) of a presenting activity, as we do also inwardly perceive our presenting together with its content. I am therefore presenting that I have the presentation of a dollar. The object of this second act of presentation is thus no longer the dollar, but rather the presented dollar. In order to avoid any confusion between the two acts of presentation, we shall call the one the primary and the other the seconday act of presentation. We can accordingly say: The object of the primary act of presentation is the dollar, while the object of the secondary act of presentation is the presented dollar.

As the dollar itself (not the presented one!) can at one time be the object of a merely presenting conduct, the same dollar (and again not the presented one!) can at another time be the object of a judging conduct, i.e. of an affirmation or rejection, which is expressed in the sentence "There is a dollar" or "There is not a dollar."

---

55   Ibid., p. 62.

As we have previously noted that primary presenting can be the object of a secondary presenting, so can primary presenting and judgment in turn be an object of a secondary presenting and of a secondary judging (inner perception). (Indeed, psychological investigations, which are not our concern at present, show that this must be necessarily so.) Analogously to to our discussions above, we can also say: The dollar is an object of a primary judging, the presented dollar the object of our secondary judging. The primary judging can of course very well be negative since it has another object, whereas the secondary judging is affirmative. It indeed comes to light that I can be convinced simultaneously that there is not a real dollar, but that there a presented one. For the latter exists as often as I present it. And I must present it if I am to deny it.

In view of this distinction, let us now consider what Sigwart had ultimately adduced in opposition to the idiogenetic theory.

He says: "When I present an 'object' A, I am at first conscious of it as something presented or thought of; its primary relation to me is that of being the object of my presenting. Since I actually present it, I cannot to this extent reject it ..." And so forth. But *which* one is it that I cannot reject? Is it the presented object or the object itself? Obviously the former! For the secondary act of judgment, as an act of inner perception, must be affirmative, and indeed an evident affirmation. When Sigwart says that the object A exists for my *consciousness* as a presented one, as thought-of, the only thing that can be meant by "consciousness" here is the secondary act of judgment. By continuing with the statement "Its primary relation to me is that of being the object of my presenting," what was "the object as presented, as thought-of" has for him turned into the object itself, i.e. the object of the primary presenting, by sleight of hand. And this unnoticed shift of the subject is the cause of the whole misunderstanding. For when Sigwart immediately afterwards says, "I cannot reject it, insofar as I actually present it," this very well fits the "object as presented, as thought-of," but not the object itself which had been meant in the immediately preceding sentence ("its primary relation to me is that of being the object of my presenting"). Sigwart fails to get clear that when he continually speaks of the "object" it is only *seemingly* one and the same thing spoken of.

The same confusion also underlies the cited passage from *Die Impersonalien*: "The concern is not at all what it is to which the acceptance refers, or how, if the concept is actually thought, it can be refused and in which sense it could be rejected." The intuition "simply exists, the object of my consciousness, whether I want it to or not." I ask once again: *What* simply exists and cannot be rejected? Certainly not the object itself, for I can say of it, perhaps with conviction, that it does not exist, and yet I must present it in order to have this very conviction. What "simply exists and cannot be rejected" is the presented object.[56]

This takes care of the last and most important objection from Sigwart. It is important because the underlying confusions are concerned with difficult differences which are extraordinarily significant for psychology.

We see that not a single one of all the adduced arguments is effective as a proof and thus we regard ourselves as justified in persisting in our standpoint of the idiogenetic theory of judgment and drawing from it the further implications for the coming formulation of the theory of inference.

Before doing this, however, we must investigate what influence the new theory has on the doctrine of the *quantity* of judgments. Relations of quantity are indeed what traditional logic has made the basis of syllogistic procedure.

Of the Quantity of Judgments

§ 24 *The idiogenetic theory does not allow for a division of judgments in accordance with quantity in the traditional sense*

If judgment is actually nothing but a particular relation to the immanent object, as we can clarify this relation only by referring to experience, and if this relation can occur in two ways: as acceptance and rejection, the division of judgments into affirmatives and negatives immediately arises as the most fundamental, so to speak.

The school-logic has placed alongside this division an additional one: the division according to quantity. From the intersection of these two divisions we get the well-known four kinds of judgment, as these are designated by the letters A, E, I, and O.

The question is now whether the division according to *quantity* retains its significance once we no longer regard the so-called categorical judgment as a species alongside the existential judgment, but rather we regard these two as differing only due to linguistic expression, but as homogeneous phenomena, psychologically considered. This is the view involved in the idiogenetic theory.

What principle of division did the old logic use when it divided judgments into universal and particular ones?

If we at first disregard Sigwart's partly very accurate remarks in opposition to the theory of the quantity of judgments, as it has been formulated thus

---

56 I cannot imagine what Sigwart means when he says that even *acceptance* is meaningless here. Would it be senseless to make the assertion: "I am now thinking of a castle," by which the presented castle is obviously accepted as presented?

far, we find the view constantly expressed that the "the range in which the predicate is ascribed to or denied of the extension of the subject-concept"[57] provides the reason for dividing judgments into universal, particular, and singular. Since the predicate "mortal" is ascribed to the concept "human being" in its entire extension, the judgment "All human beings are mortal" was called universal. By contrast, the judgment "Some human beings are sick" was called particular, since being-sick is ascribed to only a part of those individuals which fall under the concept "human being." Under the same perspective the singular judgment ("Hannibal was a general") was usually assigned to the universal.

Now it is at once clear, however, that when we put the four kinds of judgment (A, E, I, O) into the existential form, such that a predicate P is therefore not ascribed to or denied of a subject S, but rather the complex object SP is accepted or denied, there is no indicatation in the formation of the *matter* SP as to whether P is connected with S in its entire extension or only in part of its extension. Nor can the moment of the universal or the particular lie in the *function* of judgment, for SP can only be either accepted or denied. There are thus only two judgments in the case of the same matter: SP is, SP is not.

§ 25 *On Jevons' attempt to put the quantity into the matter*

W. St. Jevons has nonetheless attempted to put the moment of quantity into the matter. For him the matter of the universal judgment is "All SP," that of the particular "Some SP."[58] Against this attempt, however, we should say that the presumptive expression for the universality of the matter "All SP" has by itself no meaning at all and accordingly this presumptive object cannot become the content of a judgment. What would the sentence "All mortal human beings – *are*" mean? Sigwart and Brentano correctly point out that "all" includes a double negation.[59] If so, however, then one of the two negations must belong to the *function* of judgment. If both were concerned with the matter, they would eliminate each other and would simply not be there for all practical purposes. Jevons' attempt is consequently unacceptable.

---

57 The words are Ueberweg's in his System der Logik [§ 70], p. 215. Similar formulations occur in the following: Bergmann, *Reine Logik*, pp. 189 ff.; J. St. Mill, *A System of Logic*, I.iv.§ 4; Alexander Bain, *Logic*, vol. I, p. 82. Of the older philosophers, see Kant and already before him the Cartesian logic (cf. *Logique de Port-Royal*, Part II, Chapter 3) and many others.
58 See *Substitution of Similars* (London, 1869), p. 33 and in many other passages.
59 *Logik*, vol. I, pp. 210 ff. and Brentano, *Psychologie vom empirischen Standpunkte*, vol. I, p. 283.

§ 26 *Matter and quality of the four kinds of judgment from the school-logic*

The reduction of the four kinds of judgment, as assumed by the school-logic, to the existential form as the most adequate expression of judgment as such will bring light into the investigation.

Regarding the *particular affirmative* and the *universal negative* judgment (I and E) there can be no doubt that they should be as follows in existential form: (I) There is SP. (E) There is not SP.

These propositions are obviously identical with the propositions "Some S is P" (or as most logicians say, "Some S are P"), or "No S is P."

We encounter greater difficulties already in the analysis of the so-called universal affirmative judgment. Here, as the school-logic teaches, the predicate is ascribed to the subject in its whole extension. This can only mean that the predicate is ascribed to every single individual falling within the extension of the subject. One has often conceived of this as if the "universal affirmative" judgment is a summarizing expression for a plurality of singular judgments. "All human beings are mortal" would in that case mean the same as "Peter is mortal, Paul is mortal, John is mortal, etc." One indeed had to concede that these single judgments are not actually made, and thus we find the view frequently advocated that in such propositions a certain property (e.g. mortality) is ascribed to the abstract and general concept (e.g. human being), and thereby implicitly to every single individual that falls under this concept. Accordingly the universal affirmative judgment would at least be an equivalent for a plurality of singular judgments. What is unsatisfactory in this analysis is nonetheless best shown by the fact that in the same sense the particular judgment too can be conceived of as an equivalent for several singular judgments and consequently the difference between universal and particular would disappear altogether.

The true sense of propositions such as "All S are P," as Brentano and Sigwart emphasize, lies in the *denial of exclusion*, hence in a double negation, one of which belongs to the matter, the other to the function of the judgment. The proposition "All S are P" denies that there are S which are not P. The quality of the judgment that is designated by the school-logic as "universal affirmative" is therefore in truth *negative*.[60]

As assuredly as the denial of the matter "S which is not P" belongs to the essence of this judgment, it may nonetheless be doubted whether it fully

---

60 This is true also of that judgment which one has designated as the principle of identity. "Every A is A" means "There is no A which is not A." The so-called law of identity is accordingly simply identical with the law of non-contradiction. Traditional logic is wrong when it places both laws alongside each other as different principles.

exhausts the sense of it. According to the school-logic, there is contained in "All S are P" also that there are S, whereas in the denial of the matter "S which is not P" the acceptance of S is not at all involved and thus the opinion might arise that this denial is, to be sure, essential to the "universal affirmative" judgment, but not the *only* thing essential to it. It is of course assuredly true that whoever expresses the proposition "All S are P" is very often making two judgments: first of all, that there is no S which is not P, but secondly that there is S. Somone who says, "All apostles were Jews" not only *denies* that there have been apostles of non-Jewish origin, but also *asserts* that apostles exist.

This would however only prove that the *sentence* "All S are P" is a *linguistic expression* for a double *judgment*. However, not even this is true in *all* cases. Among the logicians, doubts have arisen for quite a long time as to whether the acceptance of S is a necessary constituent part of the judgment "All S are P." Already Trendelenburg notes that in the judgment "The right triangle has the property that is stated in the Pythagorean theorem" nothing is said about whether a triangle is a right one or not.[61] And similarly, also Fr. Alb. Lange asserts that the propositions of stereometry or analytic geometry are true, "no matter whether corresponding bodies and surfaces or lines occur in nature or not."[62]

This is without a doubt correct. Sentences of the form "All S are P" therefore always express the denial of the matter "S which is not P," whereas at times *in addition* they express the acceptance of S. Since establishing a classification of *sentences* was – justly – not the concern of traditional logic, but rather its concern was to establish a classification of *judgments*, it would have supposedly not stopped short with those cases in which a complexity of judgments finds its expression by means of a simple sentence. If, however, *simple judgments* are under consideration, the erstwhile "universal judgment" will have to be characterized in truth as a negative judgment with partly negative matter.[63]

Note. Regarding those cases in which sentences of the form "All S are P" mean, besides the denial of the matter "S which is not P," also the acceptance of S, we can ask the question whether there is special mental interweaving of these judgments, or whether they are independently made alongside each other, so

---

61 *Logische Untersuchungen*, 3rd edition, vol. II, p. 272.
62 *Logische Studien*, p. 18.
63 Trendelenburg and Lange have not drawn this necessary implication of their own above-cited theories. De Morgan guarantees us of his merit in having discerned the negative qualities of these judgments. The judgments "All X are y" and "No X is Y" (where y means the contradictory opposite of Y) he declares as identical. Cf. A. Bain, *Logic*, Part I, p. 90.

to speak. We shall leave this question aside for the time being. Later we shall discuss it more thoroughly.[64] If we therefore assert that the sentence "All S are P" frequently expresses a double judgment, we are by no means creating a prejudice in favor of one of the two possible standpoints.

In the majority of cases sentences of the form "All S are P" express a double judgment, as we can easily explain. There is obviously more motivation to form the judgment "There is no S which is not P" when S exists than there is when it does not exist. We can quite simply say that whenever the judgment "All S are P" (in the sense of a simple, i.e. negative judgment) is obtained inductively, the assertion of the existence of S belongs together with it, that there are thus two judgments to which language gives expression through the simple formula "All S are P." We may consider further that people have obtained such general judgments more often inductively[65] than deductively, that they have without a doubt made judgments such as "All dogs are four-footed," "All stones sink in water," earlier than the judgments of geometry. Also in the history of language it is plausible to assume that for the formula "All S are P" the above-discussed double judgment was the *more original* meaning.

Sigwart probably had this in mind in the following statement:

> The "all" with which the subject of the so-called *universal judgments* ("All A are B") is bound together originally signifies a *definite number*, and a judgment beginning with "all" presupposes a limited number of countable single objects. Thus, according to its original meaning, "All A are B" can only be expressed in reference to *definite single* items.[66]

The usually (originally even totally) complex character of the judgments under consideration has not escaped Sigwart's attention, as he says the following:

> It is implied by the plural that there are many A, as it is also implicitly stated that there are A which are B; but the question to be dealt with and to be answered by the judgment is whether the A to which B belongs are all [of them], whether there is no exception.[67]

---

64 See below, § 67.
65 Or we should rather say "pseudo-inductively," insofar as they were not obtained through proper – logically justified – induction, but they are rather habitual generalizations which we cannot properly designate as inductive inferences.
66 *Logik*, vol. 1 [§ 27], p. 209.
67 Ibid., p. 211.

He likewise grasps that there are again cases in which "the actual existence of the subjects is not directly spoken of." Instead of inferring that one and the same form of statement sometimes means only a negative judgment, at other times *in addition to this* also an affirmative judgment, and that only in the former case there are grounds for establishing a special class of simple judgments, he looks for the distinction in a *twofold sense of generality*, in a *double meaning* of the word "all."[68]

According to him, "all" can introduce a judgment of "empirical generality," but also an "unconditionally general judgment." The former is the case when we obtain it "by means of considering single cases," the latter "by means of analysis of the subject-presentation." The judgment "All planets move from west to east around the sun" can be obtained by investigating the motion of the single planets. In that case it is a judgment of empirical generality. But it can also be deduced from the Kant-Laplace hypothesis. In this case, since the motion from west to east is adopted in the meaning of the word "planet," it is an analytic judgment in Kant's sense and as such no longer a judgment of empirical generality, but rather one of unconditional generality. The notion of generality is in the latter case secondary, insofar as it follows from the (primary) notion of necessity. In the case of judgments of empirical generality the existence of the subject is implied in the judgment, but not in the case of judgments of unconditional generality (such as the judgments of geometry).

Let us now ask *what* is under consideration in Sigwart's distinction. Is it the judgment itself or the manner of its production, or the justification with which it is made?

If someone on the basis of geometrical considerations arrives at the result that the sum of the angles of a triangle cannot be more or less than 180°, he has without a doubt obtained this judgment in a way different from that in which someone does who measures many triangles and makes the result of his measurements the basis of an inference by means of induction, whose conclusion is of course also "Every triangle has 180° as the sum of its angles." I do not understand, however, how one person is thereby asserting something different from what the other is asserting. Both deny that there are triangles with different sums of their angles. The only question is whether they are equally justified in doing so. Perhaps the person who proceeds inductively may only assert a probability of the proposition (however great this probability may be). But he is either aware of this or not. If he is aware of it, the *matter* of the judgment changes, as he no longer asserts the relation of the angles, but rather only

---

[68] Ibid., p. 213.

the probability thereof. If, however, he is unaware of this restriction, his judgment was logically unjustified, but it nonetheless remained the same judgment, whether or not it is justified. Indeed, nothing would change in its meaning even if it were made without any proof, altogether blindly. The manner in which the judgment is produced and the justification with which it is made are thus the moments that are affected by Sigwart's distinction. A *descriptive* difference has not been indicated by him. The difference lying in the phenomenon of judgment itself (and not in possible antecedents), hence the descriptive difference which Sigwart continually senses, consists in what we have noted above: that the negative judgment with partly negative matter, as we have discerned the essential characteristic in the co-called universal affirmative statement, sometimes (indeed, perhaps in the majority of cases) has an added affirmative judgment in reference to the matter of the subject. Sigwart has quite correctly characterized the mental antecedents which sometimes lead to a simple (negative) judgment, sometimes to a complexity of judgments (hence the *genetic* differences), whereas the *descriptive* differences have escaped him, and thus, in spite of many accurate remarks, he remained essentially oriented in the wrong standpoint which traditional logic had occupied in the doctrine of the so-called universal affirmative judgment.[69]

The difficulties that the investigation of the judgment called "particular negative" (some S is not P) by the old logic encounters are smaller. If this judgment is truly *simple*, if it therefore has one *quality*, this cannot be negative. The judgment would in that case simply *reject*, whereas the proposition "Some human beings are not healthy" or "Some human being is not healthy" involves without a doubt the assertion that there is a human being. In truth, as Brentano has demonstrated,[70] the negation in such judgments belongs to the *matter* and not to the *function of judgment*. The particular judgment which is wrongly called *negative* therefore in truth accepts the matter "S which is not P."

Note. The incorrect theory according to which the O-judgments are negative does not go entirely undisputed in logic thus far. Hamilton gives the minor premise of the mode Baroco the form "Some non-M are S," the conclusion

---

69 In order to prevent misunderstandings, I mention that differences in the *apodictic* or *assertoric* passing of judgments (differences that concern the *function* of judgment) must of course be discerned, but they have nothing to do with the above-mentioned ones. For the judgment "All S are P" can be made also in the sense of a truly simple (therefore negative) judgment sometimes apodictically, sometimes assertorically.
70 *Psychologie vom empirischen Standpunkte*, vol. I, p. 283.

"Some non-P are S," from which he seeks to demonstrate the reducibility of this mode to Darii.[71] De Morgan quite distinctly discerned the affirmative character of O.[72] Jevons has followed him in doing so.[73] Lotze too doubts the tradition on this point. He finds some of the disadvantages in the theory of the conversion of the "particular negative" judgment avoidable "by joining the negation to the predicate, and then converting the proposition 'Some S are non-P,' like a particular affirmative, into 'Some non-P are S.'"[74]

§ 27 *Of the true distinctions that correspond to the terms "universal" and "particular" in the customary sense*

Let us now return to our investigation concerning the quantity of judgment. We have already seen that the concepts of universal and particular in the sense of traditional logic have an application only to *two-membered* judgments. Since we have furthermore seen that two-memberedness does not at all belong to the necessary features of judgment, we concluded that the division of the old logic is not based on any of the moments that flow from the psychological analysis of judgment as such and do not at all hold universally. Now the question arises: What do the terms "universal" and "particular" (in the sense of the school-logic) properly mean under the supposition of the idiogentic theory?

The school-logic called the judgment "No S is P" (= "SP is not") universal because P is denied of S in its *whole* extension. But this means only that the judgment ("No S is P") rules out that there are S which are P. This is of course correct, but we must bear in mind that the property of that judgment called "universal" in this sense is based on a *relation*. Such "properties" (if we want to call them this) do not – like quality – concern the psychological nature of the phenomenon. Everyone quite well notices the difference when I say at one time, "It is a property of sinopia to be red," and when I say at another time, "It is a property of sinopia to have a color different from the viola." Likewise, the property of A, which is to consist in P being ascribed to S in its whole extension (a "property" due to which the judgment is simply called universal), can be traced back to a mere relation. For if the matter "S which is not P" is denied –

---

71 *Lectures on Metaphysics and Logic*, vol. III, p. 438. Of course the value of the above-stated remark becomes doubtful when we see Hamilton in another passage (ibid., p. 253) asserting, just as Hobbes does, that every *negative* proposition can be represented affirmatively. See the accurate refutation in J. St. *Mill's System of Logic*, I.iv.§ 2.
72 See the report in Alexander Bain, *Logic*, vol. I, p. 91.
73 See, for instance, *Substitution of Similars*, p. 39.
74 *Logik* [§ 81], 2nd edition, p. 166.

and this is indeed the meaning of the judgment A – this denial rules out that there is an S which is not P.

The situation is quite similar regarding the concept of particular in the usual sense. Logic calls the judgment "Some S is P" (= "There is an SP") particular and wants to say thereby that it does not rule out that there are also S which are *not* P. This therefore means nothing but: The judgment "There is an SP" is particular because it is compatible with the judgment "There is an S which is not P" and does not contradict this. Something analogous could then also be said of the O-judgment.

Universal and *particular* (in the traditional sense) are therefore *relational properties* of *two-membered judgments*. The corresponding principle of division is not applicable to the class of judgments in general.

§ 28 *Relations between the quality of judgment and the extension of the judged matter. "Universal" and "particular" in one of the senses diverging from the tradition*

In a certain way, but one which considerably diverges from the traditional sense, we can certainly divide judgments into universal and particular ones. In this case, however, the *whole of the judgment's matter* is taken into account (in a way to be explained soon). For as soon as the matter has any extension at all, i.e. as soon as a multiplicity of individuals can correspond to it, it is assured that due to the *rejection* of the matter all individuals that can correspond to it are rejected. However, the *acceptance* of such a general matter does not involve the acceptance of all individuals that can possibly correspond to it. The judgment "There is no A" denies all individuals that are A, hence AB, AC, etc. The judgment "There is A," however, does not accept AB, AC, etc. In this sense we can say that the rejecting judgments reject the whole extension of the underlying concept (the matter), whereas the accepting judgments do not accept the whole extension of the general matter. If one now wants to speak of universal or particular judgments depending on whether the whole extension is judged [*beurteilt*] or not, this would yield the law that (under the presupposition of a *general* matter, i.e. if we can at all speak of an extension) the negative judgments must be universal, the affirmative judgments particular. I hardly need to point out again that the words "universal" and "particular" in *this* sense are not identical with the homonymous designations in the school-logic, since we are *now* concerned with the extension of the whole matter of the judgment and not with a relation between the extensions of the subject and the predicate.[75]

---

75   As already noted, the division of judgments into universal and particular ones – in the

Under this aspect, every negative judgment is therefore universal, every affirmative judgment particular, and indeed the former is universal *because* it is negative, the latter particular *because* it is affirmative. Universal and particular are thus implied features of quality.

§ 29 *Retrospective*

If we summarize the foregoing [§§ 24–28], we may assert: *First of all*, of the two foundations for division, according to the old logic, only that of *quality* can be maintained insofar as the division is concerned with the phenomenon of judgment itself. *Secondly*, with regard quality, A and E are judgments designated as negative, I and O as affirmative. *Thirdly*, the differences of quantity in the traditional sense are concerned only with relational properties of certain judgments (i.e. two-membered ones) and are not fundamental. *Fourthly*, affirmation does not extend to the whole extension of the matter, whereas negation does so, and *in this this sense* the particular character is an implied property of the affirmative quality, the universal character an implied property of the negative quality.

Finally, what has been said is true only if the matter of the judgment is not individual.

Judgments with Universal and with Singular Matter

§ 30 Concept of the universal and individual matter. Difference between "individual" and "concrete"

The restriction that we had to make at the closing of the previous section leads us to the question: Wherein lies the difference between judgments with singular matter and with universal matter?

---

sense of the *old* logic – is applicable only to two-membered judgments, but not to all judgments. Nevertheless, a certain connection between the "particular" in the old and new senses cannot be dismissed. We have called the judgment "M is" (in the sense diverging from tradition) particular because it does not affirm the matter M in its whole extension, i.e. because it is true even if only one M exists. If, however, the matter becomes two-membered, we must again say: The judgment "AB is" is particular because it is true even if only one AB exists. If we translate this, so to speak, into the language of extensional relations, we can say: The judgment "AB is" is particular because it is true only if the extensions of A and B do not completely exclude each other. The feature "particular" in the *old* sense therefore flows from that in the *new* sense when the condition of two-memberedness is introduced.

With respect to terminology, we must initially mention that it is not recommendable to designate judgments with singular matter[76] as universal (or general) judgments, since this name, as used by logicians, already has another meaning. It stands in contrast with "particular," while both the universal and particular judgments of the old logic are judgments with universal matter. Such equivocations must of course be avoided.

A judgment is singular if its matter is individual, i.e. if only one individual can correspond to it. If several individuals correspond to the matter, it is general. What we are to understand by "matter," however, is not the object itself, but rather the judged object as judged (of course also presented).

It depends on the nature of the latter whether the object itself is only a single one or whether several of them can exist. If the matter is a concretum, for instance, it contains – as this is implied in the concept of something concrete – all determinations needed for individualization and only one object can correspond to it. If it is a physical phenomenon, for instance, the matter is fully individualized by the determinacy of the sensory quality, the intensity, the spatial position, extension, and shape, and only one object can correspond to it. If, however, one of these determinations is missing under otherwise like circumstances, the matter is not individualized and the relevant affirmation leaves it undetermined, however many objects correspond to the matter.

A concrete matter is always individualized and the relevant judgment is therefore always a singular one. However, not every singular judgment has a concrete matter, for also an abstractum can be individual and therefore become the foundation of a singular judgment. "Red," "Spherical shape," etc. is an abstractum and at the same time non-individualized, whereas "this red," "this spherical shape," are, to be sure, also abstract, but individualized since the demonstratives indicate that what corresponds to the concept "red," "spherical shape," etc. is completed in only one way into a concretum.

If there is missing individualization, it is possible for one object, but also *several* (of course always concrete and consequently individual) objects, to correspond to the matter. Purality here is just as possible and just as non-necessary as unity. The possibility of a plurality of objects is therefore a *consequence* of the lack of individualization in the matter.

A misunderstanding regarding the nature of the singular judgment is still to be ruled out here.

In many logic textbooks we find the requirement that the subject in a singular judgment should be an individual concept. This is incorrect, for it is not

---

76   [*Here the phrase "mit universeller Materie" is a misprint.*]

a question of the individualization of the *subject*, but rather that of the *whole matter*. The predicate can often be added to an intrinsically non-individualized subject those very determinations which individualize it. The judgment is then, in spite of the non-individualized subject, nonetheless singular. In the case of predicates such as "is here," "is there" this is obviously the case (cf. below, § 33).

§ 31   *Note*. Incorrecntess of the usual coordination of the singular with the particular and universal judgment. Consequences of this mistake

Two different principles of division are therefore made decisive when we distinguish judgments on the one hand into singular and non-singular ones, on the other hand into universal and particular ones. The principle of the first division is the individualization and non-individualization of the matter. The judgments with non-individualized matter, seen from the standpoint of *quality*, divide into affirmatives and negatives. The former are particular, the latter universal, both in the sense of the school-logic and under the aspect of the extension of the whole matter (cf. pp. 321 f. above). Many logicians have followed Kant by coordinating universal, particular, and singular judgments, because they overlooked that there are *two* divisions under consideration here. The resulting difficulties become quite distinct in the treatment of the singular judgment. It was initially clear that when one divided judgments into universal and particular ones, depending on whether the predicate is ascribed to or denied of the subject in its whole extension or in only a part of its extension, there was no more room for a third species. This consideration had to lead to the attempt to fit the singular judgments somehow into that dichotomous classification. Thus some logicians have attempted to insert them entirely into the class of universal judgments, whereas others allow them to fall into two classes, one of which belongs to the universal, the other to the particular judgments. The advocates of the former view set out from the consideration that in each singular judgment the extension of the subject is exhausted with one individual and consequently the predicate is actually ascribed to or denied of the subject in its whole extension. The advocates of the latter view assert this at least with respect to a certain class of singular judgments. Obviously, however, one had in this manner only seemingly got rid of that uncomfortable counter-example against the traditional principle of division. For how can one speak of a "whole extension" which, however, can by its nature have no parts at all? Is there in opposition to the "whole extension of the concept of Socrates" perhaps a "partial extension"? What could be conceived of under that partial extension? Just try applying the definition of the concept "extension" – the totality of kinds or individuals which the marks of a given concept has in itself – to the "extension of the concept of Socrates." Is it "the totality of the individuals which are Socrates"? This is indeed meaningless, for it lies in the concept of Socrates that there is not such a totality. Hence one must say, "Socrates makes up the extension of the concept of Socrates." And yet the *whole* extension where it is intrinsically absurd to speak of a *part*! Drobisch indeed correctly grasped this in his statement: "Not without jarring is it possible to say that an individual represents its entire extension, for it rather has no extension because it has no kinds."[77] Similarly Kant already stressed that in the singular judgment "a concept which has no sphere at all is consequently included as a part under the sphere of another concept,"[78] and accordingly he placed the singular judgment as a peculiar species alongside the universal and the particular.

As already noted, other logicians (such as Herbart and Ueberweg) had subsumed singular judgment only of a determinate kind under the universal ones, namely judgments "with a determinate subject," hence with a subject to which there corresponds a proper name or a linguistically equivalent term. Singular judgments whose validity is restricted by the indefinite article to a single case, which is not to be specified further, are included by such logicians among the particular judgments.[79]

As far as the latter judgments are concerned, they are either purely particular, as when I say, "A human being is sick," in the sense of "Some human being is sick," which does not rule out that more than one human being is sick – or, if the sense of the sentence rules out thinking of a plurality, they are of the same kind as those judgments whose subject is a proper name. The sentences "Fust was the inventer of art of printing books" and "A German was the inventer of the art of printing books," according to Herbart and Ueberweg, would have been included in different classes, while a single object in fact corresponds to the subject of both judgments, as Hamilton (who uses this example) correctly remarks.[80] Who does not see that things are separated here which by their nature belong together?

It is therefore clear that we cannot regard as an acceptable standpoint to subsume the singular judgments under the universal ones or to include some of them among the universal judgments and others among the particular judgments.

---

77 *Neue Darstellung der Logik*, 3rd edition, p. 49.
78 *Logik* (ed. Hartenstein), "I. Allgemeine Elementarlehre," § 21, p. 432.
79 See Herbart, *Lehrbuch zur Einleitung in die Philosophie*, § 62, Ueberweg, *System der Logik*, p. 215.
80 *Lectures on Metaphysics and Logic*, vol. III, p. 247.

J. St. Mill assuredly comes closer to the truth when he designates those judgments as singular whose subject is a singular name.[81] This definition, however, is not quite satisfactory, for the subject is not the name, but rather what is designated by the name. There thus remains the question concerning the nature of the *matter*, due to which the *name* (hence something altogether external to the judgment) is called singular.

§ 32 Double division of judgments: in accordance with quality and determinacy of the matter. Relation to the customary fourfold division

If we now look back at what we have said [in § 30], the result is that we too must accept a double division of judgments: one in accordance with quality, another in accordance with the aspect of the individualization of the matter.

From the intersection of both divisions the result is a partitioning of judgments according to four classes: 1) affirmative judgments with individual matter, 2) negative judgments with individual matter, 3) affirmative judgment with non-individual matter, 4) negative judgments with non-individual matter.

We see at once that not a single one of the four classes which the old logic had formulated coincides with one of our classes of judgments. The school-logic had regarded classes 1) and 2) as a kind of annex to the judgments A or E without duly appreciating the significant differences which in truth exist. Class 3) includes the I-judgments and O-judgments, while class 4) includes the A-judgments and E-judgments – according to the terminology of traditional logic.

§ 33 Some remarks concerning the linguistic expression of the four kinds of judgment

Yet a few words regarding the linguistic expression of the four classes of judgments remain to be said, insofar as it is prone to hide the true nature of the relevant judgment and indeed to cause downright wrong opinions about their quality and matter.

With respect to singular judgments (i.e. the judgments with individual matter), it has already been mentioned that the subject need not at all always be the bearer of the moment of individuality. It will thus not at all be necessary that in the linguistic expression of the singular judgment a proper name or

---

81   *A System of Logic*, I.iv.§ 4.

even just a singular name occupies the position of the subject, and this need not be the case for the predicate either.[82] Especially susceptible to concealing the singular character is the connection of the subject with the indefinite article, for this is usually applied in the case of the non-singular judgment. The individualization of the matter, as noted earlier, can occur by means of parts of the sentence other than the grammatical subject as such, e.g. by means of the predicate. It is moreover very frequently adverbial determinations of the location and the time which individualize the matter. If a physicist, while pointing to a particular place of the spectrum, tells his audience, "Here is a Frauenhofer line," he has thereby expressed a singular judgment – in spite of the indefinite article. Temporal determinations achieve something similar, as revealed either by special adverbial expressions or by the mere tense of the verb. In particular, we should point out here that a temporal determination is not necessarily attached to the present tense of the verb (or the copula). The signs "is," "are" and the like are in overwhelmingly many cases mere signs of the *function* of judgment, such that, whenever the matter is not temporally determined in some other way, the present tense of the copula or of the verb does not contain such determinacy in general. This is especially clear with regard to negative judgments: "No triangle *has* a greater sum of its angles than 2 R" does not restrict the validity of the familiar theorem to present triangles. Those cases in which the present tense contains a temporal moment must be decidable by the circumstances under which the sentence is uttered, particularly by the context of speech. It is different when the copula or verb arises in another tense besides the present. In that case they always join the expression for the function of judgment with a temporal determination that belongs to the matter, and this can sometimes make an otherwise indeterminate matter into a determinate one and thus make the judgment a singular one.

Even the expression of the judgments 3) and 4) has given rise to multiple errors. With respect to quality, we may note that the word "not" together with the copula or the verb is by no means always a sign of the negative quality, but rather frequently means a negation lying in the matter. As we have already remarked, Brentano has shown that this is the case for those judgments which the old logic has wrongly designated as particular *negative* ones.[83]

Traditional logic, as we know, has made distinctions of quantity by designating the judgments under 3) as particular (I and O), those under 4) as universal (A and E). We have already stated our views concerning the justification of a

---

82   See p. 325.
83   *Psychologie vom empirischen Standpunkte*, vol. I, pp. 283 ff.

psychological division in accordance with the aspect of quantity. Here only a few things are left for us to add about the linguistic expression of so-called particular judgments (i.e. the affirmative judgments with non-individualized matter). The formula "Some [*Einige*] S are P" or "Some [*Einige*] S are not P," which figures in the logical compendia almost always as an expression for the particular judgments, is altogether inaccurate. It has come about only due to an erroneous view concerning the psychological character of the judgments under consideration and has for its part contributed in turn to the failure to see it, even on the part of clever analysts.

First and foremost, [the plural] "some" [*"Einige"*] according to general linguistic usage excludes "all." Conforming to this usage, we do not say that *some* metals belong to the domain of minerals, but rather we say that *all* of them do. Secondly, "some" designates a plurality (although indeterminate in its number) and therefore excludes unity. We do not say that *some* metals are liquid in the case of room temperature, but rather only *one* (mercury) is. None of the two restrictions applies for the particular judgments of the old logic, i.e. for the affirmative judgments with non-individual matter. Traditional logic has [not] correctly grasped this point,[84] for in its theory of relations among judgments it does not oppose I to A or O to E. It also explicitly teaches that by "some S" perhaps only one S can be understood, as this is implied by the [allegedly] true characterization of these judgments. Such an alteration of linguistic usage would in itself not be highly objectionable if only one were constantly aware of it and consistently retained the new usage of the word "some." However, as people are driven by the power of habit, they have involuntarily fallen prey to the old linguistic usage and with respect to the particular judgments made assertions which could hold only under the presupposition of that old and generally common usage.

A quick look at the doctrine of the *conversion* of judgments will convince us of this.

It was an undisputed doctrine of traditional logic that the so-called particular affirmative judgments (I) are simply convertible. Only Trendelenburg began to doubt whether this conversion is permissible in all cases.[85] On his view, it is meaningless to convert the judgment "Some parallelograms are squares" into "Some squares are parallelograms," since all squares are in fact parallelograms.[86] He therefore restricts the simple conversion of I to those cases in

---

84 [*There seems to be a misprint here: "hat dies richtig erkannt."*]
85 *Logische Untersuchungen*, vol. II, pp. 333 ff.
86 Lotze also says something similar. See his *Logik*, p. 105.

which the predicate of the judgment to be converted expresses a mere accident and not a substantial kind of the subject. Also Friedrich Albert Lange finds such conversions troublesome.[87] In fact, we can find difficulties in the simple conversion of those particular affirmative judgments that have themselves come about through conversion by accident from general affirmative judgments. According to the rules of the old logic, the judgment "All triangles are polygons" is convertible into "Some polygons are triangles." The old logic, however, converts this judgment once again simply into "Some triangles are polygons" and thus arrives at an "obviously incorrect proposition" if Lange is right. If Trendelenburg and Lange would have clearly held to the view that the formula "Some S are P" is an adequate expression for its particular affirmative judgment when one – abandoning the old usage of language – sees in the word "some" no opposition to "all," they would have hardly taken exception to the above-mentioned, truly correct conversions.

But this is not the only concern. We rather believe that the application of the word "some" [in the plural] (just like that of the word *Etliche*, which Wolff uses for the particular judgments), even if one remains aloof in the indicated way from general linguistic usage, does not convey the true meaning of those judgments which the old logic has designated as particular (even though not very successfully). For however one may modify the meaning of the word, one will have to allow for it the concept of an *indeterminate plurality* in all cases. Herein, however, already lies a moment that does not belong to the judgments of our third class (i.e. the affirmative ones with non-individual matter). What characterizes these judgments, as noted earlier, is – besides the affirmative quality – the indeterminacy of the matter, but not the indeterminate plurality. If the matter is not individualized, the affirmation says nothing about whether the content occurs individualized in *one* way or in several ways, though plurality is to this extent possible, not necessary. However, even this mere possibility of a plurality can at best be viewed as a kind of secondary feature of the subclass in question, insofar as it arises from the non-individualized matter and the affirmative quality, as from the primary features of such judgments.

In both the categorial and the existential manner of expression, we prefer the word [to use] "some" [with a singular noun] ([as a synonym of] *irgendein*, *quelque*), for this word designates the very incomplete determinacy of the matter, hence exactly what distinguishes the judgments under consideration here. It does not rule out plurality either.

---

87   *Logische Studien*, p. 59.

Note. The application of the word "some" [with a plural noun] is better restricted to those cases in which the matter of the judgment is actually an indeterminate collective. Since an indeterminate collective is certainly not an individualized matter, such judgments, for which the formula "Some S are P" in fact fits, also to the "particular" judgments (to the judgments under 3). However, they make up only a part of these.

Concerning the judgments under 4), i.e. the negative judgments with non-individual matter, we have already pointed out that, provided that the matter of the predicate is negative, the judgment can be expressed in the form "All S are P," a form which is very prone to disguise the negative quality. To a considerable extent, however, this is the case in yet two additional manners of making statements: the formulas "The S is a P" and "An S is a P," e.g. when I say, "The human being is a mortal entity," "A square is a rectangle with equal sides and equal angles." Both judgments are negative in their quality and partly negative in their matter. The first judgment denies the matter "non-mortal human being," while the second denies the matter "square which is not a rectangle with equal sides and equal angles." In the form "An S is a P" the analytic definitions usually come to the fore. Statements in which the subject is connected with the indefinite article come into consideration for us here for the third time. They can designate singular judgments, also affirmative judgments and (as we have just seen) negative judgments with indeterminate matter.

These remarks, albeit not nearly exhaustive, may serve for the clarification of the most important cases in which the true sense of a judgment is obscured by the linguistic expression.

Chapter Three:
Of the Inferences from One Single Premise, the so-called Immediate Reasonings

§ 34 Preliminary remarks. Different questions that can be raised regarding the so-called immediate reasonings

From the discussions thus far the idiogenetic theory of judgment is, we believe, defended against the most essential objections, as we have also outlined the immediate implications that it has for the psychological description and – in this connection – for the classification of judgments. We have thus fulfilled the conditions that enable us to enter into an investigation concerning the so-called immediate reasonings.

We shall preface this investigation by considering the categorical syllogisms. We do so, first of all, because the school-logic since Aristotle sees the principle of categorical syllogisms in the so-called "maxim of all and none" [*dictum de omni et nullo*] which is in fact nothing but a single kind of immediate reasoning, namely the so-called inference to subalternates,[88] but secondly because we too need certain immediate reasonings, albeit different ones, for the sake of categorical syllogisms.

Perhaps it is desirable at this juncture to engage in a preliminary investigation concerning whether "immediate reasonings' are really reasonings, hence advancements in knowledge, or perhaps mere changes in linguistic expression. Here too the opinions of logicians are in fact divided. Alexander Bain, for instance, regards them only as "a transition from one wording to another wording of the same fact."[89] Ueberweg seeks to preserve the tradition when he stresses that there is not an instance of immediacy insofar as "no activity of thought is required to reach the derived judgment."[90]

This, however, is not yet the place for this question. It is, first of all, not established that *all* those processes which logic designates as immediate reasonings are one or the other: advancements in the activity of thought or only changes in expressions. The decision might turn out to be different for different kinds of those reasonings, and only the consideration of each kind in and of itself would in that case inform us about the truth of the situation. Secondly, however, it is questionable whether the immediate reasonings of the school-logic are all correct. If there are incorrect ones among these, they are the very ones that will make it look as if there is occurring advancement in knowledge. Also under this aspect an investigation of the single kinds must initially be conducted.

Let us therefore ask at first how far the rules for the immediate inferences that traditional logic gives can be upheld from the standpoint of the new theory of judgment. Brentano has already indicated the most important of the relevant implications in his *Psychologie*.[91] The only thing left for us to do here is to remind the reader of his remarks and – with a few supplementary words – produce their necessary connection with the fundamental theories concerning the nature of judgment.

---

88   The two propositions which make up the maxim of all and none are, as is well known: "Whatever is valid of all is valid of some and of each one [*quiquid valet de omnibus, valet etiam de quibus et singulis*]" and "Whatever is valid of none is not valid of some and of any single one [*quidquid valet de nullo, neque valet de quibusdam neque de singulis*]."
89   *Logic*, vol. I, p. 108.
90   *System der Logic* [§ 74], p. 225.
91   *Psychologie vom empirischen Standpunkte*, vol. I, p. 304 ff.

§ 35 Simple conversion

Let us begin with so-called *conversion*. If in the case of the simple categorical statement the division of the matter into subject and predicate is only something pertaining to linguistic expression, the question remains: What does conversion signify from now on?

Obviously, to the same unitary content that is expressed by the formula SP there also corresponds the formula PS. Hence, the judgment that accepts or rejects the object SP is no doubt identical (and not merely equivalent) with the judgment that accepts or rejects PS. The categorical statement "S is (not) P" and the categorical statement "P is (not) S" represent nothing but the acceptance (rejection) of the object SP or PS – which is indeed the same. Every simple categorical statement is therefore *simply convertible*, and it furthermore follows that this conversion in no way concerns the *judgment*, but only its *linguistic expression*.

Simple conversion was restricted by the school-logic exclusively to E and I. This was done because one overlooked the true matter of judgments. If the judgment "All S are P," simply converted, would be "All P are S," traditional logic would be right in declaring such a conversion to be impermissible.[92] In truth the judgment "All S are P" is the same as "No S is not-P," and this latter can without further ado be converted into "No not-P is S." If we furthermore see that the O-judgments ("Some S are not-P") affirm a partly negative matter – namely the matter "S which is not-P" – one will find nothing objectionable here in simple conversion. "Some S is not-P" is then converted into "Some not-P is S." Lotze saw this correctly,[93] whereas almost all other logicians do not regard the O-judgments as convertible, but rather only as capable of so-called contraposition. From the above-stated remarks, however, one sees that they diffentiate themselves from the I-judgments only through the matter. This can obviously have no influence on the conversion.

Hence all four kinds of judgment which the old logic had formulated are indeed capable of simple conversion. The principle of this is none other than that obvious law that Jevons designates as the "law of communicativeness,"[94] namely the law that AB and BA are two terms for one and the same object. The only rule of the conversion is that which prescribes discerning the true

---

92   The matter of the former judgment is, after all, "S which is not-P," while that of the latter is "P which is not-S." The rejection of one of the matters does not at all involve the rejection of the other.
93   *Logik*, p. 106.
94   [*Jevons 1883, 35.*]

matter of the subject and of the predicate and to switch around the two corresponding terms.

§ 36 *Note.* Are there psychological differences between the convertible and the converted judgments? Settling some objections against the views expounded in § 35 concerning simple conversion

I. The view that conversion concerns only the linguistic expression, that it therefore does not represent reasoning in the proper sense, seems to be opposed to the fact that the converted judgment is connected with the original one frequently through particles such as "thus," "consequently," "accordingly," etc. These are particles which are also applied in the case of the syllogism. "No human being is four-footed," and *therefore, accordingly, consequently* no four-footed entity is a human being. In their external form such phrases look exactly like actual reasonings. However, those particles express only the logical incompatibility of the opposite. With the judgment "No human being is four-footed" the judgment "There are four-footed entities which are human beings" is incompatible. This need not be an instance of reasoning. One can indeed quite well say, "A is identical with B, and *accordingly* B is also identical with A." No one, however, will assert that here we have two different judgments.

II. It is another question whether the converted statement is the expression of judgment that is *identical* or merely *equivalent* with the original judgment. First a few words to explain that contrast. It is above all required for the identity of two judgments that they have the same quality and the same matter. If this is not so, they can nonetheless be equivalent, provided that they are to be equated in their cognitive value because the same situation [*Sachlage*] corresponds to the one and to the other, such that from the one nothing more and nothing less can be inferred than what can be inferred from the other, as when I say: "4 + 6 = 10" and "It is true that 4 + 6 = 10." There is not a psychological identity, but certainly a logical equivalence. For two reasons one might be inclined to regard the original judgment and the converted one merely as equivalent.

1) The psychological formation is for such judgments frequently a different one and this seems not to be compatible with their identity. The two propositions "Some metal floats" and "Something that floats is metal", to be sure, both accept the same object: "floating metal," but in certain cases one will utter only the former, in other cases only the latter. Should this not indicate a psychological difference? This is indeed the case, but it is not so in such a way that it contradicts our earlier assertion. The psychological differences

are of two kinds here. A) One of them refers to those processes which precede the formation of the judgment. If we retain our focus on the above-given example, it is possible for someone, in order to decide the question whether metals float, to test the metals one-by-one with respect to this property, but he can also test even the most diverse floating bodies to see if they are metals. With the discovery of natrium, he will say in the first case, "Some metal floats," while in the latter case he will say, "One of the floating bodies is a metal."[95] These differences, as already noted, concern only the process preceding the judgment and consequently do not justify psychological distinctions regarding the two judgments themselves. B) *Another* difference that is connected with the previous one concerns the manner in which the *presentation* whose object constitutes the matter of the judgment under consideration is formed. The presentation of a thing that floats and is a metal can often be formed successively (not simultaneously). It is in that case not irrelevant for the kind of formation whether the initially arising presentation is that of metal or that of the floating body. Let us assume that the presentation of metal is initially formed. If the presentation is also abstract, there must also be an underlying individual, concrete content. The spatial position of this content is changed by the determination which only comes afterwards: "floating on water". That is to say, this determination replaces the original one (perhaps "lying on the table before me"). If, however, the presentation of a floating body is initially formed, there corresponds to it as concretum perhaps a particular piece of wood, and this is only afterwards replaced by the concept of metal, and the content "floating metal" is in this manner synthetically constructed. Here there is thus a difference in the *formation of the presentation*. The motives for such distinctions can be diverse. The manner in which the question concerning the existence of floating metals is investigated (see the above-specified difference in the antecedents of the judgment) can be decisive for one or the other formation of the presentation. Above all, however, the spoken or written word is influential here. Speech runs its course temporally and causes in the person who hears it a successive formation of concepts that will diversely run its course in the above-indicated manner, depending on whether A is the subject and B is the predicate or A is the predicate and A is the subject of the communicated sentence. However, in what manner the *presentation* of a determinate object comes about can have no influence on the *judgment* regarding the same object. A *judgment* cannot be characterized

---

95   See Brentano's review of Miklosich's "Subjectlose Sätze," reprinted in *Vom Ursprung sittlicher Erkenntnis*, pp. 118 ff.

insofar as the *presentation* of its object is formed in this or that manner. In the whole mental state there are accordingly differences, but they do not concern the judgment as such. They therefore do not prove that the the judgments "S is P" and "P is S" are not identical, and consequently we have no reason to doubt that conversion concerns merely the linguistic expression of the judgment.

2) The same error also underlies another argument which is directed against the identity between the original judgment and the converted one. Someone might be tempted to raise the objection: There are without any doubt categorical judgments in which the subject is again contained in matter of the predicate, as when we say that some horse is a stallion.[96] Here the subject is again presented in the predicate. The simple conversion would yield the judgment: Some stallion is a horse. Since the matter "horse" is implicitly accepted, the *special* acceptance of this seems altogether superfluous and the sense of the converted proposition seems only to be: There is a stallion. Yet, one will find it objectionable to posit this judgment as identical with the original "Some horse is a stallion." Accordingly the conversion, at least in this case, has had a change of judgment as a result and does not merely concern its linguistic expression. Cases of this kind stumped Lange in the conversion of "particular affirmatives."

Here too, however, there is nothing but a difference in the construction of the content of the presentation. What is *judged* is "male horse," and indeed in both cases, whereas what is *presented* is in one case "horse which is a male horse," in the other "male horse which is a horse." In both instances horse is therefore presented twice, and this is correct only because it would suffice for judging the content "male horse" if simply nothing else but "male horse" were presented and "horse" were not the object of a double presenting. It would not change anything if the matter "horse" were *judged* twice (which we leave aside), for this would occur in the original judgment as well as in the converted one.

As in the cases treated under 1), we arrive at such double presenting of a part of the matter of the judgment only if there are special causes for a *successive* formation of the presentation, as there are when a judgment comes about in succession of an oral or written communication from someone else.

III. An additional objection against the identity of the original judgment with the converted one could be supported by saying that in certain cases the former is true while the latter is without any doubt false. For example, in the judgments "Some human being is dead" and "Some dead thing is a human being." However, here we are concerned with determination which do not

---

96 [*The example "Ein Pferd ist ein Schimmel" is changed here to one that works better in English.*]

enrich the content, but rather alter or modify it. "Learned" enriches the content "human being," whereas "dead" modifies it.[97] The content "dead human being" is not at all divisible into "dead" and "human being," for the features of a human being (to which also being animate, for instance, belongs) are not added to the marks of the concept "dead" and do not in this way form the concept "dead human being." If, however, here and in all cases where such *modifying* determinations occur, a division of the matter is not at all possible, there cannot be any conversion at all. This restriction therefore holds also for Jevons' "law of communicativeness."

In the foregoing arguments we therefore can see no reason to abandon our view that the original judgment and the converted one are as such identical. We say with emphasis "judgment as such," for in the whole mental state of the person who judges, as in either the current state or the preceding one, in which other phenomena – particularly presenting – play a role, there are also still possible diverse distinctions.

The view that we advocate here concerning the essence of the simple conversion will first be seen in its full-fledged significance when we discuss the division of syllogisms according to the four figures.

§ 37 Conversion by accident

Concerning the so-called conversion by accident of A-judgments and E-judgments, there is no need here to discuss them in particular. It stands or falls with the justification of the inferences by subalternation, to be discussed later. The results of the latter (i.e. the I-judgments or O-judgments) in fact only need to be converted simply, and thus one obtains the same judgments which the conversion by accident produces from the A-judgments and E-judgments.

§ 38 Contraposition

The rules of contraposition, as the school-logic formulates them, are likewise only partially correct. The inference from "No S is P" to "Some non-P is S" could be correct only if the inference by subalternation from E to O were correct, for in fact the result of the latter – "Some S is not-P" – is only the simple conversion of the contraposed judgment – "Some not-P is S." We hope to show later that the inference by subalternation is wrong. The contraposition from E will therefore lead to an incorrect result.

---

97   See *Psychologie vom empirischen Standpunkte*, vol. I, pp. 286 ff. n.

The school-logic furthermore contraposes the judgment "All S are P" into "No not-P is S." This is correct. If, however, we consider that the meaning of the first judgment is nothing but "No S is not-P," one will see in that contraposition only the correct simple conversion of the judgment in question.

The same goes for the contraposition of the judgment "Some S is not-P" into "Some not-P is S." The truly affirmative character of the former judgment and the belonging of negation to the matter (and not to the function) show at once that we are concerned here only with a simple conversion.

The school-logic does not know further contrapositions besides the three just specified.

§ 39 Inferences by subalternation

We have already repeatedly had to point out the incorrectness of the inferences by subalternation. The proof of this point is easily adduced only if we correctly discern the matter and quality of the relevant judgments. If the judgment "No S is P" is actually simple, its meaning is exhausted by the denial the matter SP. From this denial we cannot infer that there is an S which is not-P, as O asserts this, for the former judgment is also true if there is no S, for which case the judgment "Some S is not-P" is obviously incorrect.

Earlier discussions have also yielded the result that the A-judgment, insofar as it is simple, consists only in the denial of the matter "S which is not-P." From this the acceptance of an S which is P (i.e. the meaning of the I-judgment) *cannot* be inferred, as is clear from the consideration that the former judgment is indeed true even if there is not an S, in which case the I-judgment naturally does not hold.

The two inferences by subalternation are therefore incorrect. This is of the utmost significance for syllogistic, for the principle of the inferences by subalternation is what makes up the content of the so-called maxim of all and none, and the latter has in turn been regarded by the great majority of logicians since Aristotle as the foundation upon which the whole edifice of the categorical syllogistic must be erected.

Note. We shall later discuss the point that the sentences "All S are P" and "No S is P" can also express double judgments, in which case the I-judgment can of course be inferred from the former and the O-judgment from the latter. This, however, is irrelevant to the theory of *simple* inferences, i.e. consisting of simple judgments.

From a historical perspective we may point out only that all those logicians who have held the view that in an A-judgment the existence of the matter of the subject is not implied, while they also refuse to dismiss the correctness of reasoning from A to I, do so only because of an inconsistency.

§ 40 Inferences to contradictories

As regards the inferences by *opposition*, it is clear from the principle of non-contradiction that judgments with the same matter, but opposite quality, can be neither true nor false at the same time, that from the truth of the one we can therefore infer the falsehood of the other and vice-versa. The same matter SP is accepted in the I-judgment and rejected in the E-judgment. Furthermore, the matter "S which is not-P" is rejected in the A-judgment and accepted in the O-judgment. Accordingly E is contradictorily opposed to I, as is A to O. The rules of the school-logic concerning the inferences by contradictory opposetion therefore remain effective.

§ 41 The inference to contraries

It is different regarding the so-called contrary opposition. The A-judgments and the E-judgments are negative and different in their matter. A denies the object "S which is not-P," while E rejects the object "S which is P." These judgments can both be false at the same time, as the school-logic correctly teaches, but they can also both be true at the same time. For if S does not exist, it is true that there is no S which is P and also that there is no S which is not-P. Consequently, if we are dealing with truly simple judgments, an inference from the truth or falsity of A cannot be made to the falsity or truth of E, and vice-versa.

§ 42 The inference from subcontraries

As regards the inference from subcontraries, it is equally easy to demonstrate that the doctrine of the old logic is wrong. The I-judgments and O-judgments cannot be false at the same, according to this logic. However, if there is no S, the judgment "Some S is P" and also the judgment "Some S is not P" are obviously false and thus an inference from the falsity of the one to the truth of the other is impermissible.

§ 43 Are the correct inferences of opposition truly reasonings?

Of traditional logic's inferences by opposition the only ones that are left over are therefore special cases of the law of non-contradiction, i.e. inferences to contradictories.

The two judgments of such an inference are, as is clear, *not identical*. Since the one is fact motivated by the other, there is here truly an instance of reasoning and not a mere difference in the linguistic expression, as there is perhaps in the case of simple conversion. The judgments are also indeed *equivalent*. If one wants to refuse to give the process of thinking the name "reasoning" because this is an instance of equivalence, this is merely a preference of linguistic usage and of no concern for psychological analysis.

§ 44 The inferences by equipollence

Not a single one of the so-called inferences by equipollence is a genuine instance of reasoning. The school-logic declares the judgments "All S are P" and "No S is a not-P" to be equipollent, whereas in truth the second proposition is different from the first only insofar as the *double negation* is expressed in one case by "all," in the other by "no" and "not."

Also the judgments "No S is P" and "All S are not-P" are regarded as equipollent. If, however, we dissolve the "all" into its two negations, one of which belongs to the matter of the predicate "not-P" and consequently gives P in conjunction with itself, whereas the other belongs to the function of judgment, we immediately get "No S is P." The two "equipollent" judgments are therefore identical.

The same goes for the judgments "Some S are P" and "Some S are not not-P." As earlier discussions have shown regarding the so-called particular negative judgment, the first "not" belongs to the matter of the predicate and not to the function. It is therefore eliminated with the second "not," such that P is left over as the matter of the predicate as it is in the first judgment.

Some, e.g. Ueberweg, also regard the judgments "Some S are not P" and "Some S are not-P" as equipollent. The latter judgment obviously asserts the existence of S which are not-P. If now the former is to have the same sense as this (as it indeed belongs to the concept of equipollence), the existence of S which are not-P is nonetheless involved in it. In this case the divergent expression, whether spoken or written, which makes it look as if the negation belongs to the copula, is to be decidedly rejected. If there is no reasoning, but a mere translation in the previous three cases, it is a bad translation.

Thus, of all the immediate reasonings that were ever formulated by logicians, only the inferences to contradictories truly deserve this name.

§ 45 Immediate inferences from the affirmation of the whole to the the affirmation of the part, from the negation of a part to the negation of a whole

We now face the question whether there are, besides these, perhaps other ones which the school-logic has *not* considered.

This is assuredly the case. Logic had thus far spoken of immediate reasonings only when judgments with equal (or at least presumably equal) matter, but with different quality or quantity were under consideration. The only actual changes of the matter had consisted in the predicate sometimes being switched into its contradictory opposite. Without any doubt two judgments can come into the relation of logical sequence when the matter of one makes up *part* of the matter of the other, a case that the school-logic has overlooked. If a complex matter is affirmed, each part is at least implicitly affirmed.[98] Therefore, from such a judgment other judgments can be inferred which affirm the single parts *explicitly*. As to what kind of relation that is, whether it is spatial, logical, etc., is irrelevant. From the judgment "Some human being is sick" we can infer "There is a human being," "There is something sick," but also "There is an living entity," for this makes up part of the concept of a human being, just as we can infer "There is an animal" from the judgment "There is a predator," or from "Some square is rectangular" we can infer not only "There is a square," but also "There is a figure," "There is something spatial," from the judgment "There are twelve apostles" the judgment "There are six apostles," and so forth. As some of the examples before us show, the parts of the matter are often not presented and judged one-by-one or explicitly, as one says, but rather only insofar as they are contained in the whole. This is the case when someone accepts the object "horse," for instance, without joining in a special act those elements of it which together make the content "animal" and then combining them in a predicative manner with the peculiarities of the content "horse." We say in this case that we have only implicitly co-judged the content "animal." An affirmative judgment regarding this will nonetheless be equivalent to another in which the parts of the matter are explicitly judged, and since from the latter we can without a doubt infer the acceptance of every single part this will also be the case with regard to the former. From the judgment "There is a horse" the judgment "There is an animal" can be inferred without any mediation.

Conversely, it is clear that if a determinate matter A is denied also every other matter must be denied in which A occurs as a part, a proposition that can be

---

98 See *Psychologie vom empirischen Standpunkte*, vol. I, p. 276.

traced back to the previously stated principle. For if the complex matter ABC is accepted, the affirmation of each of its parts, hence also of part A, would follow from this according to the earlier principle, whereas this [acceptance of A] contradicts the presupposition [of the denial of A]. Examples arise at once. From the judgment "There is nothing spatial" there immediately follows "There is no figure," "There is no triangle," "no equilateral triangle," "no red equilateral triangle," etc. Here too there is of course the case that the one matter is only implicitly contained in the other.

The laws of these two immediate reasonings are briefly stated in the following formulations:

I. Every affirmative judgment remains true when one omits any of the parts of its matter.

II. Every negative judgment remains true when one enriches its matter with determinations, however many these may be.

These two laws, as we shall later see, make up an important means for developing the categorical syllogisms.

Chapter IV:
The Inferences from Two Premises

§ 46 Preliminary remarks concerning the expression of judgments by means of written signs

The reasonings that have been developed thus far do not yet by themselves allow us to derive the inferences familiar under the name of categorical syllogisms. For this we require certain simpler forms of inference with two premises which, like the above-mentioned reasonings, immediately come to light because they represent special cases of the law of the excluded middle.

Just as we shall proceed later in displaying the so-called categorical syllogisms, we shall express the single judgments here in existential form, since this is the most adequate expression of a simple judgment. For they do not separate matter and function of judgment externally. Thus they keep us from being indecisive in each single case as to whether a negation belongs to the matter or to the function. As we have seen from many examples, the categorical form of statements lacks this advantage.

For the sake of brevity and clarity, it will furthermore be recommendable to establish a certain system of signs for the expression of judgments. The quality of judgment is to be expressed by the signs + and −, such that + is to be read as "is" ("there is" and formulas with the same meaning as this), and the sign − is to be read as "is not" ("there is not" and the like).

Moreover, I shall proceed as Jevons does by designating the negative concepts with small Latin letters, such that when S, for instance, means a positive content s is to mean its contradictory opposite (= Not-S).

Corresponding to the A-judgment, "All S are P," is thus the formula "Sp –," i.e. "S which is not-P is not," while there corresponds to I, "Some S is P," the formula "SP +," i.e. "There is an S which is P." To the judgment E, "No S is P," there corresponds the formula "SP –," i.e. "There is no S which is P," and finally there corresponds to O, "Some S is not-P," the formular "Sp +," i.e. "There is an S which is not-P." Moreover, for reasons of expedience, in the simplest inferences to be discussed we shall use the letters A and B (or a and b) for designating the matter.

§ 47 Inferences that immediately come to light from two premises; they have three terms, two of which are contradictorily opposed to each other.

With these preliminaries in mind, we first disply those inferences which come to light without any deduction, i.e. immediately. These are inferences with three terms, two of which are contradictory to each other, namely the following (to be called α):

$$\frac{\begin{array}{l} A\,B\,- \\ A\,+ \end{array}}{A\,b\,+}$$

This requires no proof: If there is an A and if there is not an AB, there must be an A which is not-B (= b). This comes to light from the principle of the excluded middle. It of course changes nothing in the inference if B in the first premise is replaced by b and if b in the conclusion is replaced by B, such that the inference takes on the form:

$$\frac{\begin{array}{l} A\,b\,- \\ A\,+ \end{array}}{A\,B\,+}$$

A further inference that likewise immediately comes to light (but can be obtained indirect from α) is the following (to be called β):

$$\frac{\begin{array}{l} A\,B\,- \\ A\,b\,- \end{array}}{A\,-}$$

It is indeed evident that if A existed there would have to be either B or not-B (= b); according to the premises, however, neither the one nor the other is the case: Therefore A does not exist.[99]

Note. I. If two of the three terms did not stand in the relation of contradictory opposition (e.g. if b were replaced by C), this would obviously yield no conclusion, or at least not one which would follow from one of the two premises by itself. If, however, two terms are contradictorily opposed to each other, it is easy to show that the inferences α and β are the only possible ones. It is at first assuredly true that both premises cannot be affirmative, for in this case one of them would be involved involved in the other (e.g. "AB +" and "A +") and therefore already one premise would suffice for obtaining the conclusion, *or* both premises would be of such a kind that the principle of the excluded middle would not be applicable to them (e.g. "AB +" and "Ab +"). If the two premises are negative, those combinations must again be excluded in which one is involved in the other (e.g. "A –" and "AB –," where the former immediately follows from the latter), and likewise those to which the law of the excluded middle does not apply (such in the case of the premises "Ab –" and "aB –"). Given differing quality of the premises, finally, those combinations are simply to be ruled out in which the one premise contradicts the other (e.g. "AB +" and "A –"). The reader, if he tests all combinations under these aspects, will easily see for himself that α and β are the only possible inferences.

If there is accordingly to be only two inferences with three terms, it is readily unacceptable that the 19 moods of the old logic are also inferences with three terms. The refutation will only later arise where we hope to show that all valid moods of the old logic are contained in the syllogisms with four terms, as these will be developed.

II. As far as the school-logic is concerned, it cannot come to the inference β, for the two premises of this inference could not be true at the same time in its conception, according to which they would stand in contrary opposition, as we have discussed this in detail (p. 339 above).

For the inference α, the school-logic possesses a substitute, wrongly described from a psychological perspective, in the form of conclusions of sub-

---

99 We see, moreover, that the school-logic is wrong to identify the immediate reasonings without further ado with the inferences from one premise. The above-stated inferences distinctly show this, as they possess two premises and come to light nonetheless without any deduction.

alternation, for it concludes from "AB −" at once "Ab +," from "Ab −" however "AB +." These reasonings are permissible under the presupposition of the existence of A, but this presupposition must be be expressed in a special premise, since it is not involved in the judgments "AB −" and "Ab −" insofar as these are simple.

§ 48 Concerning the position of the terms in a syllogism

We are from this point on able to deduce a system of syllogisms which contains all inferences of the old logic, insofar as these are valid, and a large number of inferential forms that have not been considered thus far.

Before this, however, a word should be said regarding the position of the terms. As we have done previously, we shall represent the single judgments in the form most adequate to them, i.e. in the existential form. According to the indication given above (p. 343), this will not give rise to difficulties in translating them into the usual categorical form. The existential form causes the distinction between subject and predicate to vanish, as we have reduced it to the distinctions in the antecedents of the judgment and in the formation of the underlying presentation, thus irrelevant to the essence of the simple judgment. We therefore omit that moment that grounded the division of the inferences according to the *four figures*. Given the same matter and the same quality of the premises, we can thus express a determinate syllogism in the form of each figure.[100] Which figure one chooses is totally irrelevant to the logical process. The arrangement of the terms in the form of the first figure is:

$$\frac{\begin{array}{c} M\ P \\ S\ M \end{array}}{S\ P}$$

This is completely arbitrary, as we could have just well used the scheme of the second, third, fourth figures as our basis.

---

100 Therefore also modes such as Darii and Datisi, or Disamis and Dimatis, and the like fall together into a single inferential form, as we shall see.

Deduction of the Categorical Syllogisms with Four Terms

A. Those with an Affirmative Conclusion

§ 49 Method of deduction

By means of the two laws that we have conveyed above (p. 342), we can derive the syllogisms with four terms from the already-discussed inferences:

I. AB −
    A +
    ─────
    A b +[101]

II. AB −
    Ab −
    ─────
    A −

1. Let us first investigate which syllogisms can be derived from the first of the two inferences.

a) The first step of the deduction consists in this: that A is replaced with a complex matter, as this is obviously permitted. If we assume that A is replaced with SM, for instance, and for the sake of tradition we write P in place of B, we initially get the following syllogism:

SMP −
SM +
─────
SMp +

(As usual, p expresses the contradictory opposite of P.)

b) The same inference would obviously have to arise also when the first premise would only be "MP −," for according to the second rule, as stated on p. 342, the content of a negative judgment may be enriched in whatever way and still be true. "MP −" therefore entails "SMP −." In accordance with this change, the above-indicated syllogism is from now on the following:

---

101 Or:
Ab −
A +
─────
AB +

This comes down to the same thing, since it is indeed irrelevant if the positive content B occurs in the premises or if the negative b occurs in the conclusion or vice-versa. It is essential only that B and b are contradictorily opposed to each other.

MP −
SM +
―――
SMp +

c) If now the judgment "SMp +" is true, any part of its matter can be omitted according to the rule stated on p. 342, and the judgment must remain true. If we omit the part M, we get the judgment "Sp +," which is obviously entailed in the judgment "SMp +."

According to this second change our syllogism is thus:

1) MP −
    SM +
    ―――
    Sp +

§ 50 Deduction of the single moods of inference

This syllogism has four terms (S, M, P, and p), two of which are contradictorily opposed to each other. If we express the premises and conclusion in the categorial rather than the existential form, we recognize at once the mood of Ferio of the school-logic:

MP −, categorically: No M is P
SM +, categorically: Some S is M
――――――――――――――――――
Sp +, categorically: Some S is not P

At the same time the above-stated inference corresponds to the old moods of Festino, Ferison, and Fresison.[102]

―――――――
102 The simpler inference is:
AB −
A +
――
Ab +

Instead of deducing these modes from this inference, as we do here, we could of course proceed in the reversed order, by regarding them as given and testing them with respect to their correctness. For instance, let Ferio be given:
MP −
SM +
――
Sp +

If, in accordance with the second rule stated on p. 342, we increase the matter of the first premise by adding the determination S, we get the premises:
(SM)P −
(SM) +

The method of deduction, as we have exposited it in detail under a), b), and c), remains the same one for all those syllogisms which are derived from the first of the two simple inferences:

AB –
A +
―――
Ab +

We therefore need not repeat the deduction for each and every one of these.

In order to find the remaining syllogisms which can be derived from the just-mentioned simple inference, it is only necessary to insert in the positions of B and A different matters (always complex ones of course for A), and the deduction obviously remains the same.

If we replace in this manner B no longer with P, but rather with p, there arises the syllogism:

2)   Mp –
     SM +
     ――――
     SP +

In this syllogism we see at once the mood of Darii or – by reversing the terms in the second premise – the mood Datisi.

There will of course be no change in the correctness of 1) and 2) if the negative content s is placed in the position of S. In this way we get the two syllogisms:

3)   MP –
     sM +
     ――――
     sp +

4)   Mp –
     sM +
     ――――
     sP +

We may replace (SM) with A, but replace P with B, and then the premises are:
AB –
A +
From these we get Ab + at once. If we once again insert the value SM for A, but p for b, the conclusion is: SMp +. From this an element, e.g. M, may be omitted in accordance with p. 342. In that case we in fact get the conclusion: Sp +.

If we put in the place of A in the simple syllogism no longer SM (or sM), but rather MP (or Mp), there must occur by analogy four additional syllogisms:

5) MP +
    SM −
    ———
    sP +

This syllogism is turned into 1), as soon as we replace S with P and P with S. Furthermore:

6) MP +
    sM −
    ———
    SP +

This inference would be obtained directly from 2) as soon as replace S with P and p with s. The just-mentioned syllogism, given the relevant placing of the terms, corresponds to the traditional moods of Disamis and Dimatis, as is easily seen.

If in 5) we replace p with P, we get:

7) Mp +
    SM −
    ———
    sp +

The same change, adopted in 6), leads to the syllogism:

8) Mp +
    sM −
    ———
    Sp +

This inference, given the relevant placing of the terms, corresponds to the old mood of Bocardo.

§ 51 Moods of inferences which are identical in their essence and different only in the categorical form of expression

We easily see, however, that the four syllogisms that we have last specified are not essentially different from the first four. One would have to deduce the former, as we have noted, just like the latter, only that one replaces the A of the simple inference not with SM (or sM), but rather with PM (pM). This can make a difference only when one designates the subject and predicate of the conclusion with S and P and by these one understands essentially differently characterized parts of the judgment. We have seen, however, that they are not at all so in the case of simple judgments, but must rather be regarded as coordinated parts of the matter of judgment, insofar as we are of course concerned only with the judgment itself and not with its antecedents or the formation of the corresponding presentation.

One might furthermore with the same justification allow those syllogisms to collapse into one, which differentiate themselves only by replacing P with p and by replacing S with s. Such questions in fact are only dependent on the convenience of the formation of classes.

If one wants always to speak of a new *syllogistic* mode whenever a negative concept replaces a positive one, there must be, besides the eight that have been named, yet an additional eight which are distinguished by the fact that M (= m) designates a negative concept. And in fact, if we make this change in the syllogism cited under 1), the following inference would arise:

$$\frac{\begin{array}{l}mP-\\ Sm+\end{array}}{Sp+}$$

The old logic formulated a special mode for this under the name Baroco.

It is to be noted, however, that for moods which must in such a manner be regarded as essentially identical certain linguistic expressions are often applied which are prone to conceal that identity, and that it is therefore not useless to display the schemata corresponding to them separately. This is above all true when the categorical way of making statements rather than the existential one is chosen.

The following examples may serve for elucidation, the syllogisms 5) and 6):

$$\frac{\begin{array}{l}MP+\\ SM-\end{array}}{sP+} \qquad \frac{\begin{array}{l}MP+\\ sM-\end{array}}{SP+}$$

These are essentially identical since indeed S can signify any content at all, consequently also not-S (= s). The second premise of the first of these two syllogisms would be, translated into categorical form "No S is M." The second premise of the second syllogism, however, can be expressed by "All M are S"

(= M s−). These two manners of expression, however, reveal at once that we have here judgments with the same quality which differ only by their matter and should therefore not in principle be separated. No less differently can the conclusions in the case before us be expressed, that of the second inference by "Some S is P," that of the first by "Some P is not S." Thus, for someone who allows himself to be deceived by linguistic forms concerning the true quality of judgments, it is important to separate both syllogisms in order to avoid the illusion that the table of inferences is incomplete.

Another example is this: We have said there are, in addition to the eight syllogisms which we have cited, eight more when we replace in each of the former the M with m. It is clear that no properly new syllogisms thereby emerge. Nonetheless, here too linguistic differences can conceal the essential equality, as we see this in the case of syllogism 2):

Mp −
SM +
―――
SP +

From this arises:

mp −
Sm +
―――
SP +

Categorically these inferences could be expressed thus:

All M are P.	All not-P are M.
Some S is M.	Some S is not M.
Some S is P.	Some S is P.

For someone who still adheres to the old division of judgments (A, E, I, and O) different moods (and therefore also labels) would have to correspond to these two syllogisms.

Such examples, which could still be multiplied, should sufficiently justify us in often separating identical syllogisms from each other only on the basis of − inessential − differences in the matter and thus reaching 16 moods with affirmative conclusions.[103]

---

103   A testing of the modes before us yields the correctness of the law, formulated by Brentano

B. Those with a Negative Conclusion

§ 52 Method of deduction

11. We now turn to those syllogisms which can be deduced from the simpler syllogism:

$$\frac{\begin{array}{l}AB-\\ Ab-\end{array}}{A-}$$

Here too we shall exposit the deduction extensively for only one syllogism. The method of deduction indeed remains one and the same for all the rest.

a) For this sake we replace A with the complex matter SP and write, for the sake of tradition, M for B. Thus we arrive at the inference:

$$\frac{\begin{array}{l}SPM-\\ SPm-\end{array}}{SP-}$$

b) According to the above-stated law, according to which a negative judgment remains correct, however much one enriches its matter, the first of the two premises would at once follow if the judgment "MP –" is true, the second premise likewise if the judgment "Sm –" is true. If the judgment "SP –" follows from the judgments "SPM –" and "SPm –," this conclusion must also follow from the premises "MP –" and "Sm –," since from them the two above-stated premises ["SPM –" and "SPm –"] can be obtained.

§ 53 Deduction of the particular moods of inference

Consequently we get the the following:

17) $\quad\dfrac{\begin{array}{l}MP-\\ Sm-\end{array}}{SP-}$

(*Psychologie vom empirischen Standpunkte*, vol. I, p. 303), that in the case of an affirmative conclusion one premise must have the same quality and one of the same terms [as that of the conclusion], the other premise the opposite quality and one opposite term.

This syllogism[104] corresponds to the moods of Celarent or Cesare of the old logic.[105]

If M becomes negative and m therefore becomes positive, we get the following syllogism:

18) mP –
    SM –
    ──────
    SP –

Given the relevant placing of the terms, this corresponds to the moods of Camestres and Calemes.

If P furthermore becomes negative (hence = p), we get from 17) the following syllogism:

19) Mp –
    Sm –
    ──────
    Sp –

As is clear, this is none other than the mood of Barbara in which a negative conclusion is thus drawn from negative premises.

The same change with 18) yields the following syllogism:

20) mp –
    SM –
    ──────
    Sp –

Finally, the four syllogisms which have just been specified, whenever the negative matter s replaces S, yield the following inferences:

---

104   We designate it as the 17th syllogism, as we bear in mind those additional 8 syllogisms that can be obtained from the first 8 when we replace M with m.

105   Here too one could take the reverse path by considering Celarant, for instance, as given and then testing it with respect to its correctness. One can increase the matter of the first premise (MP) by adding S while one can increase that of the second premise (Sm) by adding P, as this is indeed permitted because of the negative quality. The premises are then: "MPS –" and "PSm –."

    If we replace (PS) with A and replace M with B (or m with b), we get "AB –" and "Ab –," from which we can infer "A –" or, by replacing A again with SP: "SP –," the conclusion of Celarent.

21) MP –
    sm –
    ―――
    sP –

22) mP –
    sM –
    ―――
    sP –

23) Mp –
    sm –
    ―――
    sp –

24) mp –
    SM –
    ―――
    sp –[106]

§ 54 Moods whose identity is concealed by the categorical form of expression

Here we can also ask whether certain inferences are essentially identical with others. This is really so in the case of the last four in relation to the first four. Nonetheless, we have believed it necessary to make a division since that essential identity does not always clearly come to light, for it is concealed by categorical forms of expression. This is the case for inferences 18) and 22), for instance:

   mP –   mP –
   SM –   sM –
   ―――   ―――
   SP –   SP –

These exhibit only the inessential distinction of S signifying in the first case a positive concept, in the second case a negative concept (= s).

The essential identity can be veiled here through certain forms of expression for the second premises and the conclusions, thus when one expresses the second premise of 18) with "No S is M," that of 22) with "All M are S," the conclusion of 18) with "No S is P," that of 22) with "All P are S." We are certainly guarded in this manner against the reproach of incompleteness, but also against that of unconscious pleonasms.

---

106   Brentano (op. cit.) states the law that in the case of a negative conclusion each premise must have the quality and one term in common with the conclusion. This yields a test for the last 8 syllogisms.

§ 55 Retrospective on the highest laws which underlie the syllogisms with four terms. Erroneous views of Bain and Lange

This may be the place to remember that all deduction of syllogisms is supported 1) on the two propositions stating that the affirmation of a matter includes the affirmation of each of its parts, and that the negation of a matter is included in the negation of each of its parts (see p. 340), 2) on the two inferences:

$$
\begin{array}{ll}
\text{I.} \ AB- & \text{II.} \ AB- \\
\underline{A+} & \underline{Ab-} \\
Ab+ & A-
\end{array}
$$

The first two propositions immediately follow from the *principle of non-contradiction*, the latter two inferences from the *law of the excluded middle*.

These two immediately evident propositions are accordingly the only true sources from which all syllogisms flow.

Herein already lies the complete refutation of all those theories which involve the attempt to base the justification of deductive inferences on experience (as Alexander Bain does, for instance), but also the refutation of those theories which see the laws of syllogisms in synthetic knowledge *a priori* (as Friedrich Albert Lange does). We should thus avoid all arguments of this sort: In *experience* there can be no guarantee for the correctness of inferential laws since it would indeed have to be demonstrated beforehand what the source is from which the trust in experience receives its justification. Similarly we should avoid arguments (in opposition to the apriorist orientation) against the existence of synthetic knowledge *a priori*: The fact that the laws of inferences *can* be obtained from those *analytic* principles proves that their source is not to be sought elsewhere. The law of non-contradiction and of the excluded middle must indeed count as principles of knowledge for both the advocates of the empirical orientation and those of the apriorist orientation. If we are satisfied with these principles, we are guarded by methodological reasons against the preference of those who require, *besides* these principles, also other sources for the derivation of the laws of inference.

§ 56 The moods of Darapti, Felapton, Bamalip and Fesapo

In the above-stated table of categorical syllogisms, all the moods of the old logic are contained except four: Darapti [AAI in the third figure], Felapton [EAO in the third figure], Bamalip [AAI in the fourth figure], and Fesapo

[AAO in the fourth figure]. These four moods are in fact fallacious, as we shall now show.

As far as Bamalip is concerned, we find the premises of this mode in syllogism 22), though the conclusion is an essentially different one. For if there is no P which is not M, and no M which is not S, from this we can only reason that there is no P which is not S, but not that there are S which are P (as indeed the school-logic reasons). For both premises are true even if there is neither a P, nor an M, nor an S. In this case, however, it is obviously wrong to draw the conclusion "Some S is P."[107]

A similar mistake is also made in the mood of Darapti. Here both premises can also be true without there being an S, M, or P, whereas the conclusion decidedly involves the existence of S and P. Here and in the previous case, as we cannot emphasize often enough, it is presupposed that the premises are *simple* judgments. For if the proposition "All M are P" contains, besides the rejection of the matter Mp, also in addition the acceptance of M, then of course the conclusion of the old logic would be justified. We would in this case have a syllogism containing a premise that represents an equivalent for *two simple* judgments.

The two essentially identical moods of Falapton and Fesapo are false because their premises are true even if the object corresponding to the middle concept does not exist, for which case there is decidedly nothing in the premises about the existence or non-existence of S. It would therefore be compatible with the premises to judge that S does not exist. In this case, however, the affirmative conclusion "Some S is not P" is obviously false. Here too it is obviously presupposed that the premises are simple judgments.

Whoever sees in the judgment the expression of an extensional relation and accordingly – like almost all logical compendia – deduces from extensions all categorical inferences, but also as the adherent to the theory of quantification does,[108] is compelled with immutable necessity also to accept the four moods that we have just discussed. Their incorrectness would therefore simply demonstrate the unacceptability of those theories on which they are based.

---

107   Of course it is likewise wrong to conclude: "Some S is not P," i.e. Bamalo in which indeed the existence of S is also entailed. [*Bamolop would have the mood of AAO, although its figure is unidentifiable because it is not one of the types of syllogisms that have traditionally been regarded as valid. Just like Brentano, Hillebrand regards fifteen types of syllogism as valid and the four treated in this section as invalid. He only considers the total of nineteen types, just as Brentano does* [EL 13049ff.], *whereas tradition in some cases offers five additional ones which also violate Brentano's rules for syllogistic inference. See above, pp. 34ff.*]

108   See below, pp. 364ff.

§ 57 The fallacy of four terms

If the above-conveyed theory of categorical syllogisms is correct, it shows at once the invalidity of certain rules to which, according to the school-logic, every correct inference must submit.

The strictly proscribed fallacy of four terms has, above all, gained the status of a general law.[109] The correct moods of the school-logic, just like all others that are added to them, contain four terms, and only the false views concerning the quality and matter of single judgments could ignore the fact that in one of the premises of every syllogism there is contained a concept whose contradictory opposite occurs in the other premise or in the conclusion. We can take the stricture against four terms in the sense that a syllogism cannot contain four concepts if none of them is opposed to any of the others, for surely from the concepts M, S, P, Q we cannot form any inference.[110]

§ 58 On the presumptive law: "Nothing follows from negatives alone"

Furthermore, the old law that nothing follows from negatives alone is unacceptable. The syllogisms 17)–24) are nothing but counter-examples against it. But not only this, for the proposition "Nothing follows from affirmatives alone" is true. Proof of it is already the circumstance that all categorical syllogisms from the two simpler inferences, as conveyed in § 47, can be obtained only by changes in the matter, but the first of these contains an affirmative premise and a negative one, the second only negative ones.

Note. With respect to history, we point out here that the proposition that nothing follows from negatives alone does not belong to the undisputed laws of logic. De Morgan, when he correctly represents the judgments A in *negative* form, already cites examples of inferences in which both premises are neg-

---

109 See Brentano, *Psychologie vom empirischen Standpunkte*, vol. I, p. 303.
110 Boole already saw that there are inferences with four terms. He cites the example:
　　All Ys are Xs
　　All not-Ys are Zs
　　All not-Xs are Zs
　　If we replace X, Y, not-Y, Z with the signs S, M, m, P and express the judgments in existential form, we get the syllogism:
　　Ms –
　　mp –
　　sp –
　　It is the same as the one that have cited under 24). Concerning Boole's theory, see Alexander Bain, *Logic*, vol. I, p. 205.

ative. Indeed, even the "most frequent"[111] mode – Barbara – serves him for this purpose.[112] Jevons, who bases his opposition against the traditional law likewise upon the negative character of the judgments A, follows Boole by citing the example:

> Whatever is not metallic is not capable of powerful magnetic influence.
> Carbon is not metallic.
> Therefore carbon is not capable of powerful magnetic influence.[113]

§ 59 The traditional division of syllogisms according to four figures

Finally, concerning the question whether the division of syllogisms according to the four figures retains its significance, we have already stated our view. Our earlier discussions concerning the essence of simple conversion have shown that between the converting judgment and the converted one as judgments there is no difference, that as far as the judgments as such are concerned a division of the inferences according to the terms is therefore meaningless. If, by contrast, one is concerned with the antecedents of the judgment and, in connection with this, the formation of the underlying complex of presentations, that division remains – and the inferences are quadrupled in number. *Logic*, however, need not bother with such distinctions.

The Traditional Deduction of Syllogisms

§ 60 Derivation of syllogisms from extensional relations

The widely held view of the necessary two-memberedness of judgment had the result of logicians from time immemorial aspiring to subsume the possible relations of the two concepts that belong to a judgment under general laws. The relations of contents [or comprehensions] and extensions of those concepts were subjected to a careful investigation, and at least regarding the extensions they succeeded in tracing the existing diversity of to a limited number of general types and making the results which were obtained in this way the foundation for a deduction of all reasonings and inferences.

Indeed, the nature and number of the possible relations between the extensions of two concepts is analytically determinable, as is consequently a guaran-

---

111   [See *De Morgan 1847*, 257.]
112   See Alexander Bain's report in his *Logic*, vol. I, p. 164.
113   *Principles of Science*, p. 63.

tee for the completeness of classification. Two extensions, A and B, can only be identical (joined in a union), or inclusive, or intersecting, or finally altogether exclusive. Any other relation is *a priori* impossible, and experience only needed to be invoked in the question as to whether each of these relations is actualized in psychical life, something that was easy to decide in a positive way.

The significance that this statement of extensional relations has acquired for the development of syllogisms is known everywhere. The pictorial representation of them by means of spheres was invented by the rector of Zittau [Christian Weise] and made popular by [Leonhard] Euler, as the deduction of the inferences that is based on it has found its way into almost all textbooks on logic and has remained prominent in them to this very day. Indeed, Friedrich Albert Lange claims for it not only the function of sensory depiction of abstract and hardly intuitable material, but he regards spatial intuition for the essential moment of logical cognition and believes it possible from this viewpoint to demonstrate that the propositions of formal logic are synthetic judgments *a priori*, for he agrees with Kant in regarding space as an *a priori* intuition. However, this view has long been seen as erroneous and is nowadays hardly advocated by anyone.[114]

Here we cannot agree with the standpoint of the school-logic, as this already becomes clear at once from the fact that we have demonstrated as invalid certain moods of inference which arise with necessity from that viewpoint, and we have deduced a number of other moods that the school-logic had not been able to derive. On this point, however, where there is a doctrine that is supported by many authorities and by a long-standing tradition, it will be appropriate to exhibit the principle mistake from which it suffers.

§ 61   The judgments which the school-logic posits in place of the actual ones are not *identical* with these.

That conception by no means contradicts the idiogenetic theory of judgment as such, for it would from the outset be possible that the object towards which the judging conduct directs itself is an extensional relation. This might at least be asserted of the two-membered judgments.[115] We therefore raise the question: *Is the object of every judgment with complex matter a relation between the extensions of the subject and of the predicate?* Is the sentence "All S are P" the expression of a psychical act which accepts the inclusion of the extension of S in the extension of P? Is the proposition "No S is P" the expression of the exclusion

---

114   See Alfred von Berger, *Raumanschauung und formale Logik* (Vienna, 1886).
115   Cf. p. 299.

of the extension S from the extension of P? Is the sentence "Some S are P" the expression of a partial overlap? And so forth.

Above all, the theory that the matter of a judgment is an extensional relation involves a very inaccurate description of the psychical process. On this point J. St. Mill already says the following:

> When I say that snow is white, I may and ought to be thinking of snow as a class, because I am asserting a proposition as true of all snow: but I am certainly not thinking of white objects as a class; I am thinking of no white object whatever except snow, but only of that, and of the sensation of white which it gives me. When, indeed, I have judged, or assented to the propositions, that snow is white, and that several other things are also white, I gradually begin to think of white objects as a class, including snow and those other things. But this is a conception which followed, not preceded, those judgments, and therefore cannot be given as an explanation of them.[116]

Mill therefore rejects such an explanation as a hysteron-proteron.

Indeed, it is hardly possible to find a good description of the psychical process in that doctrine. Indeed, we may go farther still than Mill: Not only does one not think of the whole extension of the predicate, for even the extension of the subject is not actually contained in the object of the judgment. Aside from the singular judgments for which it is altogether doubtful whether one can speak of an *extension* of the subject, we cannot assert that the subject of each judgment is a collective concept. And this would have to be the case if judgment really consisted in putting the extension of the subject into a particular relation to the extension of the predicate.

§ 62 They are not even equivalent to them.

Even if there is here no correct description of the judging process, it would nonetheless be possible that every judgment might be replaced with another one which is equivalent to it and which for its part is a judgment concerning an extensional relation. For this case we would then be justified, as always, in basing the whole syllogistic procedure on the consideration of extensional relations. We would then have to translate in each syllogism the premises, so to speak, into the language of extensional relations. Similarly the physicist too in

---

116 *A System of Logic*, I.v.§ 3.

fact goes about his business when he solves a problem along the mathematical path by putting the given conditions into the form of equations. Then he may transform that result which he first acquires only in the form of an equation into a judgment that has a duly fashioned functional relation and not the simple equation as its object.

As we have already noted, however, this presupposes that for every judgment with complex matter it is possible to find an equivalent judgment whose object is the relation of extensions between those concepts which make up the matter of the original judgment. We shall now investigate whether this presupposition is accurate.

Obviously, if the extensional relation is to be a determinate one, the judgment about this must be affirmative, for the mere denial of a certain extensional relation (perhaps inclusion) would leave it undecided in which relation the two extensions actually stand (e.g. in that of intersection or total exclusion). Representing the E-judgment by means of two circles in separation means actually removing negation from the *function* of judgment and importing it into the matter, for the E-judgment is conceived of not as denial of inclusion, but rather as acceptance of the exclusion of the two extensions. And even if the school-logic keeps speaking of the negative quality of the judgments, it has nonetheless abandoned it in practice. The representation of judgment by means of comparing spheres is therefore far from providing us with a mere sensory depiction of the deduction of syllogisms – a tool for "training stupid minds," as Prantl expresses himself with his usual bluntness.[117] It rather involves the Hobbesian standpoint, according to which every negative judgment can be regarded as affirmative with negative matter. If this standpoint were acceptable, the tool would be an excellent one which even "non-stupid minds" would use with success.

Yet, we must ask whether the meaning of a negative judgment is correctly stated when one says that it asserts the mutual exclusion of the extensions of concepts? By no means is it so. We should consider that the acceptance of a relation always involves also the acceptance of its foundations. If the exclusion of the extensions of S and P is asserted, there lies in this assertion 1) that there is a multiplicity of S, 2) that there is a multiplicity of P, 3) that neither one of those two multiplicities is contained in the other – neither in its totality or in one of its parts. Now, however, it is clear that the first two of these three assertions are certainly not contained in the judgment "No S is P," as the matter SP is denied, while no decision is made as to whether S or P exists.

---

117   *Geschichte der Logik*, vol. I, p. 363.

In fact the judgment "No S is P" remains true even if there is neither S nor P. The judgment "The extension of S totally excludes the extension of P" is consequently not at all an equivalent of the judgment "No S is P." We have already earlier seen the inference by subalternation from E to O to be incorrect. Now we distinctly see the source of that mistake.

Nor can the judgment A be regarded as an assertion of the inclusion of the extension S in the extension P. For this judgment too, in truth a negative one, says nothing about whether there is S or P. Indeed, as we refer to previous discussions, it is correct if S and P do not exist. And for that reason the inference by subalternation from A to I is false, just as the moods of Darapti and Bamalip are. They are both inferences that the theory of spheres sanctions.

Here too traditional logic had not merely committed the error of a false psychological description of taking into consideration mere equivalents of different kinds of judgment (Mill), but rather the judgments that fit into its description are not even equivalent to those judgments that it was attempting to describe.

§ 63 *Note.* Concerning the sources from which the error of the school-logic could have arisen

It is of course correct to say that there are judgments concerning extensional relations. "A part of the vertebrates are mammals," "Among the inhabitants of America there are ones with brown colored skin," etc. are without any doubt judgments of this kind. An error occurs only when one asserts of *all* judgments that their object is an extensional relation.

There are lots of motives that could lead to this unjustified generalization. 1) Above all, it is clear that every judgment which inserts the extension of S into that of P gives justification for the additional judgment that all S are P. Likewise, the judgment which the mutual exclusion of the extensions of S and P provides justification for the additional judgment "No S is P." It was possible to fall into the error of reversing that relation and assuming that, *wherever* the judgment "All S is P" holds, also that other judgment holds which asserts the insertion of the extension of S into the extension of P, and likewise, *wherever* the proposition "No S is P" holds, also the other propostion holds which asserts the mutual exclusion of the extensions of S and P. This mistake was all the more readily made as indeed the investigation of extensional relations is frequently the way in which judgments such as "All S are P" and "No S is P" are obtained. 2) An additional misleading circumstance which is closely connected with the previously stated one lies in overlooking the difference between simple judgments and double judgments. If the proposition "No S is P" means, besides the denial of the matter SP, also the acceptance of S, then that double judgment certainly justifies us in making the judgment which asserts the mutual exclusion of the extensions of S and P. Propositions of the form "No S is P" in the overwhelming number of cases mean such double judgments. It is therefore no wonder that one saw that co-assertion of the existence of S as essential to the negative judgment and drew from this the implications which lose their validity as soon as we are concerned with simple judgments. Something analogous holds also for the sentences "All S are P" which, whenever they mean double judgments, contain besides the denial of the matter Sp also the acceptance of the matter S. 3) With regard to the particular judgment, the unsuitable expression "Some S are P" especially seems to me to support the error that here too the object of judgment is an extensional relation. This formula, properly understood, supposedly applies only to affirmative judgments concerning an extensional relation, and indeed only to that of the total inclusion of P in S. This alone is the true usage of language. Whoever asserts that part of the population of Europe are Catholics expresses this correctly by means of the sentence "Some Europeans are Catholics." He is in fact making a relational judgment, and this judgment, if one were to illustrate it by means of spheres, could not be represented by means of the intersection (as is usual), but rather by means of the inclusion of the sphere P in the sphere S. For the concern is the classification of Europeans, while there is no thought at all about Asian or American Catholics. The Catholics therefore make up a part of the sphere of Europeans, and nothing is said as to whether or not there are Catholics who belong to another sphere.

This, however, is only a side-remark. Whether it is an intersection or an inclusion, the assertion of an extensional relation without any doubt lies in the meaning of the formula "Some S are P" in accordance with the general use of language. Due to Kant, however, this formula became typical for the so-called particular judgment for which it does not at all fit, as we have seen earlier. Since the old use of language arbitrarily asserted its rights, one believed it necessary to see in every particular judgment a judgment about an extensional relation. If one now saw in the universal judgment a compilation from particular ones (as this has often been done, e.g. by Lotze), it was only a short step to regarding also the universal ones and consequently all judgments in general as judgments about extensional relations.

The Theory of Quantification

§ 64 The quantification of the predicate

Yet another attempt to represent all judgments as judgments about a relation must be mentioned here since it aims at a full-fledged reformation of the categorical syllogistic.

If the aforementioned doctrine sees in every judgment the assertion of an extensional relation, the theory under consideration now assumes that the object of every judgment is an identity.[118]

In the case of those "universal affirmative" judgments for which there is not an inclusion, but rather a union of the extensions of S and P it is clear that the meaning of the judgment is that S and P are identical. This holds for every correct definition, for instance, as the *definiendum* is identical with the *definitum*, hence "square" identical with "rectangle with equal sides and right angles." The sense of the judgment "All squares are rectangles with equal sides and right angles" is: "Square is identical with rectangle with equal sides and right angles." Such judgments would correspond to the form: "S = P."

Also regarding judgments in which the subject is included in the extension of the predicate, however, we find the assertion of total identity according the view of those logicians: namely identity between the subject and a certain *part* of the predicate. We only need to *quantify* the predicate, i.e. restrict its extension to a certain part, and then there is a mere identity wherever the whole extension of predicate contains more than the extension of the subject. An example will make this clear. The proposition "All metals are elements" does not correspond to the formula S = P, for there are also elements that are not metals. But it does correspond to the formula: "S = vP," where v means the same as "some," i.e. restricts the extension of P. Boole had already asserted this. Jevons goes yet a step farther. That part of P which can be posited as identical with S is not to be understood indeterminately, but rather as those very P which have the feature of being S. Therefore Jevons applies to the quantification of the predicate not the indeterminate letter v (= some, undecided which ones), but rather simply once again S. The above-stated sentences therefore corresponds to the formula "S = SP," e.g. "Metals are identical (not with "some," but rather simply)

---

[118] The beginnings of the theory are to found in the work of Sir William Hamilton. It was expanded and applied to the theory of syllogisms by Boole and De Morgan. In a fully systematic development, executed most strictly in its implications, we find it in the work of Jevons, whose version is the foundation of our exposition here. See *Principles of Science* and *The Substitution of Similars*.

with elements which are metals." This is to be the true meaning of every universal affirmative judgment insofar as a union of the extensions does not occur, as it does in the case of definitions, for which there is no need for quantification since the formula "S = P" already suffices without further ado.

The same equation "S = SP" also holds for the particular affirmative judgment, where S only has the meaning of "some S."[119]

The negative judgment "No S is P," according to Jevons, asserts the identity of S with a part of not-P, and indeed once again simply with that part which has the feature of being S. If we designate the contradictory opposite of a concept with the corresponding small letter of the alphabet, as Jevons does, such that p, for instance, means non-P, the general formula for the universal negative judgment (E) is "S = Sp," i.e. "S is identical with not-P which is identical with S": "No prime number is a square number" then means "Prime numbers are identical with non-square numbers which are identical with prime numbers." The particular negative judgment has the same formula: "S = Sp," only that S here means the same as "some S."[120]

§ 65 Rejection of this for the theory of the inferences

This is briefly the theory of the so-called *quantification of the predicate*. The advantages which this theory offers for the development of deductive and inductive logic, if we may believe Jevons, are extraordinary. It makes all the rules of the old logic concerning conversion, contraposition, equipollence – in short, everything that one calls immediate reasonings – superfluous by reducing them to the two rules: 1) that the parts of a matter may be switched around in whatever way (AB = BA, i.e. the law of *communicativeness*), 2) that every equation is reversible (if A = B, then B = A). It also makes the syllogism into an instance of pure calculation that anyone familiar with the axioms of mathematics can execute. Thus it frees the logician from the ponderous study of those numerous rules that the Aristotelian syllogism demands. From that point on, calculations are made with concepts as Algebra calculates with general numbers. And since the syllogistic operations correspond only to the very simplest algebraic operations, nothing stands in the way of also constructing a thinking machine, similar to calculating machines, whose task is mechanically to

---

119 Jevons leaves open the option of expressing "some" especially (perhaps with Q) and thus of using for the particular affirmative judgment the equation QS = QSP. See, *Principles*, p. 56. This is actually irrelevant.
120 Here too "some" could be expressed by the special symbol (Q). In that case the formula would be: "QS = QSp."

develop all those equations that are compatible with a given number of conditional equations (the premises). In fact, Jevons has constructed such a syllogistic machine in a highly clever manner (as he calls it a "logical abacus") on the basis of earlier developed theorems and described it in detail in the *Principles*.[121]

§ 66 Critique of the theory of quantification

In our transition to the critique, let us ask: Does every judgment assert an identity?

Here we must raise the same objection that we have already made against the subsumption-theory: namely that such a conception can never do justice to the *negative* judgments, since the assertion of identity always involves the acceptance of that which is posited as identical, but this assertion is not at all contained in the negative judgments. The proposition "No S is P" does not say that there are S and that these are perhaps identical with Sp. It obviously holds if there is no S at all. Similary, the proposition "No S is not-P" (= "All S are P"), to which the equation "S = SP" corresponds according to Jevons, says nothing about the existence of S, although it would have to do so if it were to assert the identity of S with SP. We accordingly see that all the mistakes which the old logic committed regarding subalternation and opposition recur also for Jevons since they came from the same source. Also the four false moods are justified from his standpoint just as they were from that of the subsumption-theory.

It hardly requires pointing out that the psychological description of the different kinds of judgment is altogether wrong, as almost no one will in fact agree with the view that whoever makes the judgment "All metals are elements" actually wanted to assert that metals are elements which are identical with metals. Another psychological inconvenience lies before us which should put the unacceptability of the theory under discussion in the glaring spotlight. All judgments are for Jevons affirmative without the slightest doubt. In the case of the seemingly negative ones, the negation on his view lies in parts of the matter. He had to assume this if he wanted to see in every judgment the assertion

---

121 In order to show Jevons' method by means of an example, we shall deduce the mode of Barbara. The premises "All M are P" and "All S are M" are represented, according to the quantification of the predicates, by means of the following equations: "M = MP" and "S = SM." If we substitute for M of the second equation the value given by the first MP, we get the equation "S = SMP" in which the conclusion of Barbara "All S are P" is contained, only that we see more precisely *which* P are the ones with which S are identical, i.e. those P which are S and M.

of an identity. If there are no negative *judgments*, however, from what source does Jevons obtain the negative concepts which he in fact requires needs? No answer to this question is possible, and consequently the theory turns out to be a fiction.

Jevons' view is fraught with such difficulties even if we restrict its application to the two-membered judgments. If, however, we apply it to the negative existential sentences, its unacceptability becomes clearer, if that is at all possible. The sentence "There is no dragon," if we designate a dragon with S, that which *is* with P (and thus that which is *not* with p), corresponds with equation "S = Sp." Now just try to intepret this formula! "A dragon is identical with a dragon which is *not*"? This is a contradiction. Or perhaps: "A dragon is identical with that non-being which is a dragon"? This is likewise clearly an absurdity.

This much is therefore established: From the theory of quantification a corrective reform of syllogistic is not to be expected.

Chapter v:
Complex or Double Judgment

§ 67 Concept of double judgment

We have based all discussions thus far on the presupposition that the judgments corresponding to the different statements are truly *simple*. This already pointed to the existence of *complex* judgments. Although we do not want to enter into an exhaustive psychological analysis here, we must at least explain what we actually mean by the expression "complex judgment." Otherwise it would hardly be possible to understand the concept "simple judgment" in such a way that allows us to rule out every misinterpretation.

What we understand by complex judgments are not combinations of judgments which are often called *conjunctive* judgments, and for which we simply have a plurality of subjects and predicates. Here the linguistic expression is only an abbreviation for a plurality of statements, to which a simple judgment therefore corresponds for each one. The sentence "Peter, Paul, Jacob, John, etc. were apostles" is merely a compilation of the sentences "Peter was an apostle," "Paul was an apostle," etc. If, due to such sentences, we were to adopt a division of judgments into simple and complex ones, we would indeed not be proceeding any more rationally than someone who – to use Mill's words – would classify horses into single horses and teams of horses.[122]

---

122   *A System of Logic*, I.iv.§ 3.

It is however other cases that we have in mind here.

That is to say, it is clear that there are judgments which represent themselves neither as a simple acceptance or rejection of a certain object nor as dissolvable into simple acceptances or rejections of several objects (as this is the case for "conjunctive" judgments). This holds for those cases in which an object S is accepted, while at the same time a P is ascribed to or denied of it. "This person is a criminal," "That plant is not poisonous," etc. The demonstrative already shows that the matter of the subject is accepted, in the second example therefore a plant located here or there, with such and such properties. The acceptance of a non-poisonous plant is also involved in the judgment. But it is at once understandable that these two judgments together still do not make up what is contained in the judgment "This plant is not poisonous." One cannot substract from it the acceptance already lying in the word "this" such that the remainder would not contain that acceptance, for this remainder simply does not contain the acceptance of *some* non-poisonous plant. The expression "this plant," however, includes already in and of itself an acceptance (i.e. a judgment). Between the parts of the cited judgment we therefore do not have a mutual detachability, but rather we only have a *one-sided detachability*. Brentano, who was the first to draw attention to the existence of such double judgments,[123] therefore rightly compares the relation that obtains between its two parts with the relation between the generic concept and the specific concept in the strictly Aristotelian sense, e.g. redness and color. If one wants to dissect the concept of redness into genus and specific difference, there is clearly in this case too a merely one-sided detachability, for the difference that must be added to the generic concept of color, in order to yield together with it the concept of redness, is none other than red. The difference includes the generic concept in itself.

In the domain of judgment there is, as already noted, an analogous one-sided interweaving wherever any determination is ascribed to or denied of a content which is accepted (hence already judged) as existing. This occurs extraordinarily often in psychical life. If we examine a thing in its familiar properties or in its relations to other things, the results of such investigations are always such double judgments.

§ 68 Remarks on the linguistic expression of double judgments

In very many cases we cannot see from the linguistic expression whether a psychologically simple or double judgment corresponds to it. As already said

---

[123] *Vom Ursprung sittlicher Erkenntnis*, p. 57.

earlier, the sentence "All S are P" signifies at one time the mere rejection of the matter Sp (in which case it says nothing about the existence of S), whereas at another time it also involves the acceptance of S and consequently has the meaning "There are S and none of these S is a not-P." The circumstances under which the sentence is uttered, namely the context of speech, will have to decide here as they often do elsewhere. In other cases, however, there are linguistic signs which at once reveal the existence of a double judgment. This holds in three cases: 1) When the subject of a sentence contains a personal pronoun or a possessive pronoun. In sentences such as "I am sick," "You are not in your right mind," but also "My house is dilapidated," and the like, the subject obviously already involves the acceptance of a personal entity or of a thing that stands in such a relation. 2) When the subject is a demonstrative expression, either a demonstrative itself or a substantive in combination with a demonstrative pronoun, or with a demonstrative adverb (here, there, etc.). 3) When the subject is a proper noun or an equivalent expression. In the sentence "Aristotle was the founder of logic" the subject already contains the acceptance of a man who lived in Greece, devoted himself to philosophical research, etc.[124]

§ 69 Quality of double judgments

Since one part of a double judgment always consists in a certain content being accepted, the other part in something being ascribed to or denied of this accepted content, it follows that the quality of such a judgment is either double-affirmative or affirmative-negative.

§ 70 Which modifications does the theory of the syllogisms undergo when there are double judgments among the premises?

The question now is what syllogistic must undergo if double judgments take the place of simple judgments.

I. Let us assume that the double judgment is double affirmative in quality. What we have said in general about double judgments holds for this case: It cannot be dissected into two simple and independent, i.e. mutually detachable judgments. This is not an obstacle, however, to our being able to find simple

---

124 This case of a double judgment is also given when the proper name is a *suppositio* – as the scholastics say – for something named as named. In this sense it is possible for someone not to believe in Poseidon and nonetheless make the judgment "Poseidon was the god of the sea." But of course we must consider that the true subject of the sentence is "something called Poseidon," for which the name Poseidon is a *suppositio*.

judgments which are logically *equivalent*, though not psychologically *identical* to it. If now a double judgment is double-affirmative in quality, there is equivalent to it a single simple affirmative judgment whose matter contains the subject and predicate of the double judgment. The judgment "Socrates is a Greek philosopher" is thus, to be sure, a double judgment, but clearly there is equivalent to it a simple judgment which accepts the matter "Greek philosopher Socrates," for also in the simple affirmative judgment every part of the matter is implicitly accepted. Though the double judgment accepts certain parts explicitly, this does, to be sure, make a difference in the *psychological* characterization of the phenomenon. However, it changes nothing with respect to its equivalence with the other judgment. Due to this logical equivalence, such a double judgment, whenever it arises as a premise, will lead to the very same conclusion as the simple judgment equivalent to it. From the perspective of double judgments with a double-affirmative quality, the syllogistic rules therefore do not have to undergo any change at all.

11. Things are different with respect to double judgments with affirmative-negative quality. For them a logical equivalent is possible only in the form of *two* simple judgments. The double judgment "All S are P" has its equivalent in the two simple judgments: "There are S" and "There is no S which is not P."

A syllogism, one premise of which is the judgment "All M are P" as a double judgment, is thus to be treated as if in the place of this judgment the two simple judgments "M +" and "Mp −" would stand. We shall elucidate this point by means of an example. There are given as premises: "All M are P" and "All M are S." If these are simple, we get no conclusion according to earlier arguments (invalidity of the mood of Darapti). If, however, the first premise is a double judgment, since it entails the existence of M, the two simple judgments can be placed as premises: "M p −" and "M +" which as such already lead to the conclusion: "MP +." This latter judgment, placed as a premise and united with "M s −," yields the syllogism 6) as specified above:

MP +
sM −
―――――
SP + (Some S is P).

Thus an inference which takes the name of Darapti in the school-logic is justified, and which we have discerned as false under the presupposition of the simplicity of premises. In a similar way we could show that also the moods of Felapton, Bamalip, and Fesapo, which we had to reject as incorrect, become valid as soon as even only one of the premises is a double judgment with affirmative-negative quality.

This of course does not excuse the procedure of traditional logic, for either it wanted to draw those inferences into the sphere of its consideration whose premises are truly simple – in which case those four moods are false, or it wants to understand every judgment in the sense of a double judgment – in which case it wrongly does not bother with the great number of those inferences which simple judgments yield.

The table of syllogisms, if one considers also the double judgments in the indicated manner, would undergo a great expansion. Yet, it is superfluous here to cite in particular all those inferences that would still be added among the earlier developed ones. Inferences with double judgments are indeed always testable, as noted, by dissolving the double judgments into those simple judgments which represent their logical equivalent and then applying the syllogistic rules as they hold under the presupposition of simple judgments.

If further the statements "All S are P" and "No S is P" represent double judgments, due to the acceptance of S to the denial of Sp or respectively of SP, also the inferences by subalternation to I or to O are justified. As soon as we dissolve the double judgments of the form A and E into the corresponding pair of equivalent judgments, we at once get the inferences:

$$\frac{\begin{array}{c}Sp -\\ S +\end{array}}{SP +} \qquad \frac{\begin{array}{c}SP -\\ S +\end{array}}{Sp +}$$

We have already considered these inferences under § 47. Under the presupposition of the simplicity of those judgments from which one reasons, the inferences by subalternation are of course false.

IV. In the case of double judgments the position of the terms is no longer irrelevant as it is in the case of simple judgments. Rather, the division of matter into subject and predicate (and the position of the corresponding to this division) first gets its justification in the double judgment. What we have to regard as the subject of double judgments is that part of the matter whose acceptance is detachable, as an independent part, from the double judgment. In the double judgment an affirmation is made the basis (*subjicitur*) and the matter of this underlying affirmation is the *subject*. The subject-concept and the predicate-concept can therefore not switch their positions. In the case of a judgment with double-affirmative quality there is another psychical reality corresponding to the reversal, but the one of these judgments can at least be considered as the equivalent of the other. If, however, the double judgment is affirmative-negative in its quality, an equivalence is not even archieved by its reversal. For if a P is denied of an affirmed S, this can also therefore be done because there is no P at all. In this case, however, the reversal that would deny an S of an affirmed P is false.

If in such cases the position of the terms is of the utmost logical significance, it follows from this immediately that for these very cases the division of syllogisms according to the four figures has its indisputable justification. But these are not the syllogisms which we have developed earlier and which must be made the basis for all others in which double judgments come into play.

Note. As is well known, a division into subject and predicate is also adopted in the case of simple judgments. Such judgments are not to be distinguished from the double judgments in their form. This is why the *grammarian* still speaks of subject and predicate in both cases. It is however clear from the foregoing discussion that those aspects which reveal in the *double judgment* one part of the matter as subject, another part as predicate, are not at all applicable any longer to the *simple* judgment, even if it is expressed in categorical form. For the psychologist and for the logician, the terms "subject" and "predicate" have application only in the *double judgment*. And if he – following the grammarian – applies these terms also to the parts of the matter of a *simple* judgment, let him bear in mind that he can do this only equivocally.

Bibliography

1 Brentano's Published Writings

Brentano, Franz 1862. *Von der mannigfachen Bedeutung des Seienden nach Aristoteles.* Freiburg i. Br.: Herder.
Brentano, Franz 1867. *Die Psychologie des Aristoteles, insbesondere seine Lehre vom ΝΟΥΣ ΠΟΙΗΤΙΚΟΣ.* Mainz: Franz Kirchheim.
Brentano, Franz 1874. *Psychologie vom empirischen Standpunkte*, vol. I. Leibzig: Duncker & Humblot.
Brentano, Franz 1877. Letter to Stumpf (5 May), in Kaiser-el-Safti 2014, 184–185.
Brentano, Franz 1889. *Vom Ursprung sittlicher Erkenntnis.* Leibzig: Duncker & Humblot.
Brentano, Franz 1892a. *Das Genie.* Leibzig: Duncker & Humblot.
Brentano, Franz 1892b. *Das Schlechte als Gegenstand dichterischer Darstellung.* Duncker & Humblot.
Brentano, Franz 1895. *Meine letzten Wünsche für Oesterrich.* Stuttgart: Cotta.
Brentano, Franz 1911a. *Von der Klassifikation der psychischen Phänomene.* Leipzig: Duncker & Humblot.
Brentano, Franz 1911b. *Aristoteles und seine Weltanschauung.* Leipzig: Quelle & Meyer.

2 Posthumously Published Editions of Brentano's Writings

Brentano, Franz, (eds.) Baumgartner, Wilhelm and Chisholm, Roderick 1982. *Deskriptive Psychologie.* Hamburg: Felix Meiner.
Brentano, Franz, (ed.) Kastil, Alfred 1929a. *Vom Dasein Gottes.* Leipzig: Felix Meiner.
Brentano, Franz, (ed.) Kraus, Oskar 1929b. *Über die Zukunft der Philosophie.* Leipzig: Felix Meiner.
Brentano, Franz, (ed.) Kastil, Alfred and Mayer-Hillebrand, Franziska 1970. *Versuch über die Erkenntnis.* Hamburg: Felix Meiner. 2nd edition.
Brentano, Franz, (eds.) Körner, Stephan and Chisholm, Roderick 1976. *Philosophische Untersuchungen zu Raum, Zeit und Kontinuum.* Hamburg: Felix Meiner.
Brentano, Franz, (ed.) Kraus, Oskar 1926. *Die vier Phasen der Philosophie und ihr augenblicklicher Stand nebst Abhandlungen über Plotinus, Thomas von Aquin, Kant, Schopenhauer und Auguste Comte.* Leipzig: Felix Meiner.
Brentano, Franz, (ed.) Kraus, Oskar 1930. *Wahrheit und Evidenz.* Leibzig: Felix Meiner.
Brentano, Franz, (eds.) Kraus, Oskar and Mayer-Hillebrand, Franziska 1968. *Psychologie vom empirischen Standpunkt. Dritter Band: Vom sinnlichen und noetischen Bewusstsein.* Hamburg: Felix Meiner.

Brentano, Franz, (eds.) Mayer-Hillebrand, Franziska 1952. *Grundlegung und Aufbau der Ethik*. Bern: Francke.

Brentano, Franz, (ed.) Mayer-Hillebrand, Franziska 1956. *Die Lehre vom richtigen Urteil*. Bern: Francke.

Brentano, Franz, (ed.) Mayer-Hillebrand, Franziska 1959. *Grundzüge der Ästhetik*. Bern: Francke.

Brentano, Franz, (ed.) Mayer-Hillebrand, Franziska 1966. *Die Abkehr vom Nichtrealen*. Bern: Francke.

Brentano, Franz, (eds.) Chisholm, R.M. and Marek, Johannes 1988. *Über Ernst Machs "Erkenntnis und Irrtum."* Amsterdam / Atlanta: Rodopi.

Brentano, Franz, (ed.) Rollinger, Robin 2010. *Logik* (notes edited from Brentano [EL 80]). (http://gams.uni-graz.at/context:bag-nachlass)

Brentano, Franz, (ed.) Fisette, D. 2013a "Moderne Irrthümer über die Erkenntnis über die Erkenntnis der Gesetze des Schließens", in Fisette and Fréchette 2013, 513–524.

Brentano, Franz, (trans.) Baltzer-Jaray, K. and Rollinger, R.D. 2013b "Modern Errors concerning the Knowledge of the the Laws of Inference", in Fisette and Fréchette 2013, 501–512.

Brentano, Franz, (ed. and trans.) Rollinger, Robin D. 2020, forthcoming. "Ontologische Fragen / Ontological Questions," in Fisette, Fréchette, Janousek (2020, forthcoming).

3 Archival Materials

Brentano, Franz 1871a. Letter to Anton Marty, dated 1 February. Houghton Library, Harvard.

Brentano, Franz 1871b. Letter to Anton Marty, dated 3 March. Houghton Library, Harvard.

Brentano, Franz 1871c. Letter to Anton Marty, dated 14 May. Houghton Library, Harvard.

Brentano, Franz Ps 53. *Fortsetzung der "Psychologie vom empirischen Standpunkte" bis zum dritten Buch*. MS from c. 1874. Houghton Library, Harvard.

Brentano, Franz Ps 62. *Plan für ein Psychologiekolleg*. MS from 1872/73. Houghton Library, Harvard.

Brentano, Franz Ps 78. *Ausgewählte Fragen aus Psychologie und Ästhetik*. MS from 1885/86. Houghton Library, Harvard. Partly published in Brentano, (ed.) Mayer-Hillebrand (1959).

Brentano, Franz EL 64. *Disputierungen*. Unpublished manuscript from 1876. Houghton Library, Harvard.

Brentano, Franz EL 72. *Die elementare Logik und die in ihr nötigen Reformen*. MS from 1878 and 1884/85. Houghton Library, Harvard.

Brentano, Franz EL 73. *Plan für die Logik*. Unpublished MS from 1869 or earlier. Havard, Houghton Library.

Brentano, Franz EL 74. *Psychognosie*. MS from 1890/91. Havard, Houghton Library. (Partly published in Brentano, [eds.] Chisholm and Baumgartner [1982]).

Brentano, Franz EL 75. *Zur Logik*. Unpublished MS from the late 1860s. Houghton Library, Harvard.

Brentano, Franz EL 77. *Plan für eine Logikvorlesung*. MS from 18 April 1875. Houghton Library, Harvard.

Brentano, Franz EL 81. *Framente über die Logik*. Early MSS on logic. Houghton Library, Harvard.

Brentano, Franz EL 82. *Von den Sophismen und ihrer Anwendung auf politischem Gebiet*. MS from 1876. Houghton Library, Harvard.

Brentano, Franz Th 22. *Theologie*. MS from 1870/71. Houghton Library, Harvard.

Brentano, Franz Th 31. *Vom Dasein Gottes. Erster Teil*. MS from c. 1871–c. 1892. Houghton Library, Harvard. Partly published in Brentano, (ed.) Kastil 1929a.

Brentano, Franz Th 32. *Vom Dasein Gottes. Zweiter Teil*. Houghton Library, Harvard. Partly published in Brentano, (ed.) Kastil 1929a. MS from c. 1871–c. 1892.

Brentano, Franz M 96. *Metaphysik*. Lectures from 1868/69 with later revisions. Houghton Library, Harvard.

Brentano, Franz LS 20. *Zeitbewegende philosophische Fragen*. MS from 1893/94. Houghton Library, Harvard.

Brentano, Franz LS 22. *Unsterblichkeit*. Lecture notes from 1875. Houghton Library, Harvard.

Brentano, Franz LS 23. *Über die Unsterblichkeit der Seele*. Lecture notes from 1869. Houghton Library, Harvard.

Brentano, Franz FrSchr 41. Lecture notes from Clemens, *Logik* (1859/60). Houghton Library, Harvard.

Brentano, Franz FrSchr 42. Summary of lecture notes from Clemens, *Logik* (1859/60). Houghton Library, Harvard.

Höfler, Alois E 2.1–2. *Die elementare Logik in die in ihr nötigen Reformen*. Notes from Brentano's lectures, 1884/85. Graz: Forschungsstelle und Dokomentationszentrum.

Hillebrand, Franz (no signature). *Die elementare Logik in die in ihr nötigen Reformen*. Notes from Brentano's lectures, 1884/85. Graz: Forschungsstelle und Dokomentationszentrum.

Husserl, Edmund Q 9. *Ausgewählte psychologische Fragen (die Raum-Theorien). Vorlesungen von Dr. Franz Brentano*. Copy from Franz Hillebrand's lecture notes, 1883. Leuven: Husserl Archives.

Husserl, Edmund Q 14. *Logik und Enzyklopädie der Philosophie von C. Stumpf*. Lecture notes from Halle, 1887. Leuven: Husserl Archives.

Leisching, Eduard Y 2 and Y 3. *Die elementare Logik in die in ihr nötigen Reformen*. Notes from Brentano's lectures (1884/85). Houghton Library, Harvard.

Leisching, Eduard Y 4. *Praktische Philosophie*. Notes from Brentano's lectures (1884/85). Houghton Library, Harvard.

Marty, Anton B 7. *Kollegien nach Brentano zur Logik*. Manuscript partly copied from Stumpf, c. 1869–c. 1871. Forschungstelle und Dokumentationszentrum für österreichische Philosophie: Graz.

Masaryk, Thomas (no signature). *Logik nach Prof. Brentano*. Notes from 1875. Forschungstelle und Dokumentationszentrum für österreichische Philosophie: Graz.

4   Other Writings

Albertazzi, Liliana 2006. *Immanent Realism: An Introduction to Brentano*. Dordrecht: Springer.

Antonelli, Mauro 2000. "Franz Brentano und die Wiederentdeckung der Intentionalität: Richtigstellung herkommlicher Missverstandnisse und Missdeutungen," *Grazer Philosophische Studien*, 58–59, 2000, pp. 93–117.

Antonelli, Mauro 2012. "Franz Brentano's Intentionality Thesis," in Salice, Alessendaro (ed.) (2012): *Intentionality* (2012), pp. 109–144.

Antonelli, Mauro and Frederico, Boccaccini (eds.) 2019. *Franz Brentano: Critical Assessments of Leading Philosophers*, vols. I–IV. London: Routledge.

Aristotle, (ed.) Barnes, Jonathan 1984. *The Complete Works of Aristotle*, vols. I–II. Princeton, NJ: Princeton University Press.

Arnauld, Antoine and Nicole, Pierre, (trans.) Buroker, Jill Vance (1996): *Logic or the Art of Thinking*. Cambridge: Cambridge University Press.

Bain, Alexander 1870. *Logic: Deductive and Inductive*, vols. I–II. New York / Cincinnati / Chicago: American Book Company.

Balmes, D. Jaime, (ed.) Esmoro, C. 1847. *Curso de Filosofía Elemental*. Paris: Garnièr Hermanos.

Balmes, Jakob, (trans.) Lorinser, F. 1852. *Lehrbuch der Elemente der Philosophie. Erste Abteilung: Logik*. Regensburg: Georg Joseph Manz.

Balmes, J., (trans.) Spellissy, J.M. 1873. *Elements of Logic*. New York City: O'Shea & Company.

Baumgartner, Wilhelm 2003. "Franz Brentano: 'Großvater der Phänomenologie'," in Tănăsescu and Popescu 2003, 15–60.

Beneke, Friedrich Eduard 1832. *System der Logik als Kunstlehre des Denkens*, vols. I–II. Berlin.

Bergmann, Julius 1879. *Reine Logik*. Berlin: Ernst Siegfried Mittler und Sohn.

Berger, Alfred von 1886. *Raumanschauung und formale Logik*. Vienna: C. Konegen.

BIBLIOGRAPHY 379

Betti, Arianna 2013. "We Owe it to Sigwart! A New Look at the Content/Object Distinction in Early Phenomenological theories of Judgment from Brentano to Twardowski," Textor 2013: 74–96.
Bolzano, Bernard, ed. Příhonský, F. 1851. *Paradoxien des Unendlichen*. Leipzig: C.H. Reclam.
Bolzano, Bernard, (trans.) Russ, S. 2004. *The Mathematical Works of Bernard Bolzano*. Oxford: Oxford University Press.
Bonino, Guido et al. 2014. *Defending Realism: Ontological and Epistemological Investigations*. Boston / Berlin / Munich: de Gruyter.
Cantor, Georg 1883a. *Grundlagen einer allgemeinen Mannigfaltichkeitslehre* Leipzig: Teubner.
Cantor, Georg 1883b. "Über unendliche lineare Punktmannichfaltigkeiten," (5th article), *Mathematische Annalen* 23: 545–586.
Cantor, Georg, (ed.) Zermelo, E. 1932. *Gesammelte Abhandlungen mathematischen und philosophischen Inhalts*. Berlin: Springer-Verlag.
Chrudzimski, Arkadiusz 2001. *Intentionalitätstheorie beim frühen Brentano*. Dordrecht / Boston / London: Kluwer.
Chrudzimski, Arkadiusz 2004. *Die Ontologie Franz Brentanos*. Dordrecht / Boston / London: Kluwer.
Clemens, Franz Jakob 1847. *Giordano Bruno und Nicholas von Cusa. Eine philosophische Abhandlung*. Bonn: J. Wittmann.
Clemens, Franz Jakob 1860. *Die Wahrheit in dem Streite über Philosophie und Theologie*. Münster: Theissing.
Cottingham, John 1984: "Translator's Preface [to *Meditations on First Philosophy*]", in Descartes 1984: 1.
Descartes, (trans.) Cottingham, J. et al 1984. *The Philosophical Writings of Descartes*, vol. II. Cambridge: Cambridge University Press.
De Morgan, August 1847. *Formal Logic, or the Calculus of Inference, Necessary and Probable*. London: Taylor & Walton.
de Spinoza, Benedict, (ed. and trans.) Curley, Edwin 1994. *The Spinoza Reader: The Ethics and Other Works*. Princeton, NJ: Princeton University Press.
Drobisch, Moritz 1863. *Neue Darstellung der Logik nach ihren einfachsten Verhältnissen*. Leipzig: Leopold Voss.
Exner, Sigmund 1889. "Über allgemeine Denkfehler," *Deutsche Rundschau* 4: 54–67.
Evra, James van 2008. "Richard Whately and Logical Theory," in Gabbay and Woods (2008), 75–91.
Enoch, W. 1893. "Franz Brentanos Reform der Logik," *Philosophische Monatshefte* 29: 433–458.
Fisette, Denis and Fréchette, Guillaume (eds.) 2013. *Themes from Brentano*. Brill / Rodopi: Leiden.

Fisette, Denis and Martinelli, Riccardo 2015. *Philosophy from Empirical Standpoint: Essays on Carl Stumpf*. Leiden: Brill / Rodopi.

Flint, R. 1876. Review ("critical notice") of Brentano 1874, *Mind* 1: 116–122.

Fréchette, Guillaume 2014. "Austrian Logical Realism? Brentano on States of Affairs," in Bonino et al. 2014, 379–400.

Frege, Gottlob 1879. *Begriffschrift, eine der arithmetischen Formelsprache des reinen Denkens*. Halle a. S.: Neibert.

Frege, Gottlob 1892. "Sinn und Bedeutung," *Zeitschrift für Philosophie und philosophische Kritik* 10: 25–50.

Gabbay, Dov M. and John Woods (eds.) 2004. *Handbook of the History of Logic*, vol. III: *The Rise of Modern Logic: From Leibniz to Frege*. Amsterdam / Elzevier.

Gabbay, Dov M. and John Woods (eds.) 2008. *Handbook of the History of Logic*, vol. IV: *British Logic in the Nineteenth Century*. Amsterdam / Elzevier.

Haack, Susan 1978. *Philosophy of Logics*. Cambridge: Cambridge University Press.

Hamilton, William, (eds. Mansel, H.L. and Veitch, John) 1860. *Lectures on Metaphysics and Logic*. Edinburg / London: William Blackwood and Sons.

Herbart, Johann Friedrich 1837. *Lehrbuch zur Einleitung in die Philosophie*. Königsberg: August Wilhelm Unzer.

Hillebrand, Franz 1891. *Die neuen Theorien der kategorialen Schlüsse*. Vienna: Alfred Hölder.

Höfler, Alois, in collaboration with Meinong, Alexius 1890. *Logik*. Prague / Vienna: Tempsky. Leipzig: Freytag.

Höfler, Alois 1921. "Die Philosophie des Alois Höfler," in Schmidt 1921, 117–160.

Hume, David, (ed.) Selby-Bigge, with text revised and variant readings 1978. *A Treatise of Human Nature*. Oxford: Clarendon Press.

Husserl, Edmund 1891. *Philosophie der Arithmetik. Psychologische und logische Untersuchungen*. Halle: Pfeffer.

Husserl, Edmund 1900. *Logische Untersuchungen*, vol. I: *Prolegomena zur reinen Logik*. Halle a. S.: Max Niemeyer.

Husserl, Edmund 1901. *Logische Untersuchungen*, vol. II: *Untersuchungen zur Phänomenologie und Theorie der Erkenntnis*. Halle a. S.: Max Niemeyer.

Husserl, Edmund 1903. "Bericht über deutsche Schriften für Logik 1895–1899," Archiv für systematische Philosophie 9, 113–132, 257–259, 393–408, 503–543.

Husserl, Edmund 1913. *Ideen zu einer reinen Phänomenologie und phänomenologischen Philosophie*. Halle a.S.: Max Niemeyer.

Husserl, Edmund 1929. *Formale und transzendentale Logik. Versuch einer Kritik der logischen Vernunft*. Halle a. S.: Max Niemeyer.

Husserl, Edmund, (ed.) Biemel, W. 1950. *Die Idee der Phänomenologie*. The Hague: Martinus Nijhoff.

Husserl, Edmund, (ed.) Rang, B. 1979. *Aufsätze und Rezensionen (1890–1910)*. The Hague: Martinus Nijhoff.

Husserl, Edmund, (ed.) Schuhmann, E. *Logik. Vorlesung 1896*. (*Husserliana-Materialien*, vol. I). Dordrecht: Springer.

Husserl, Edmund, (ed.) Rollinger, R.D. 2009. *Untersuchungen zur Urteilstheorie*. (*Husserliana*, vol. XL). Dordrecht: Springer.

Ierna, Carlo 2012. "Brentano and the Theory of Signs," *Paradigmi. Rivista di Critica Filosofica* 2: 11–22.

Jacquette, Dale (ed.) 2004. *The Cambridge Companion to Brentano*. Cambridge: Cambridge University Press.

Jerusalem, Wilhelm 1895. *Die Urteilsfunction. Eine psychologische und erkenntnistheoretische Untersuchung*. Leipzig / Vienna: Wilhelm Braumüller.

Jevons, William Stanley 1869. *Substitution of Similars*. London: Macmillan.

Jevons, William Stanley 1883. *The Principles of Science: A Treatise on Logic and Scientific Method*. London: Macmillan. 2nd edition.

Kaiser-El-Safti, Margaret (in co-operation with Binder, T.) (ed.) 2015. *Franz Brentano-Carl Stumpf: Briefwechsel 1867–1917*. Frankfurt a. M.: Peter Lang.

Kant, Immanuel, (ed.) Hartenstein, G. 1838. *Schriften zur Philosophie im Allgemeinen und zur Logik*. Leipzig: Modes und Baumann.

Kant, Immanuel (ed.) Weischeidel, Wilhelm 1974. *Kritik der reinen Vernunft*. Frankfurt a. M.: Suhrkamp. Texts A (1781) and B (1787).

Kant, Immanuel, (trans.) Smith, Norman Kemp 1929. *Critique of Pure Reason*. London: Macmillan and Co.

Kant, Immanuel, (trans.) Young, Michael, J. 1992. *Lectures on Logic*.

Kastil, Aflred, (ed.) Mayer-Hillebrand 1951. *Die Philosophhie Franz Brentanos. Eine Einführung in seine Lehre*. Salzburg: Das Bergland-Buch.

Kraus, Oscar 1919. *Franz Brentano. Zur Kenntnis seines Lebens*. Munich: Oskar Beck.

Kreibig, Josef 1909. *Die intellektuellen Funktionen. Untersuchungen über Grenzfragen der Logik, Psychologie und Erkenntnistheorie*. Vienna / Leipzig: Alfred Hölder.

Kriegel, Uriah (ed.) 2017. *The Routledge Handbook of Franz Brentano and the Brentano School*. London: Routledge.

Kriegel, Uriah 2018. *Brentano's Philosophical System: Mind, Being, and Value*. Oxford University Press.

Land, J.P.N. 1876a. "On a Supposed Improvement in Formal Logic," *Abhandlungen der könglichen niederländischen Akademie der Wissenschaften*: 1–15.

Land, J.P.N. 1876b. "Brentano's Logical Innovations," *Mind* 1: 289–292.

Lange, Friedrich Albert 1877. *Logische Studien. Ein Beitrag zur Neubegründung der formalen Logik und der Erkenntnistheorie*. Iserlohn: J. Baedeker.

Lapointe, Sandra (ed.) 2019. *Philosophy of Mind in the Nineteenth Century*. London: Routledge.

Lenzen, Wolfgang 2004. "Leibniz's Logic," in Gabbay and Wood 2004, 1–84.

Liebmann, Otto 1865. *Kant und die Epigonen. Eine kritische Abhandlung*. Stuttgart: Carl Schober.

Locke, John, (ed.) Nidditch, P.H. 1975. *An Essay concerning Human Understanding.* Oxford: Clarendon Press.

Marty, Anton IIIa/19. *Die Lehre des hl. Thomas über die Abstraction der übersinnlichen Ideen aus den sinnlichen Bildern.* Unpublished seminar thesis from 1867. Thomas Masaryk Archives, Prague.

Marty, Anton 1875. *Über den Ursprung der Sprache.* Würzburg: A. Stuber.

Marty, Anton Log 20/58. *Deduktive und induktive Logik.* Typed unpublished lecture notes (no date, c. 1900). Prague: Charles University Library.

Marty, Anton 1884. "Über subjectlose Sätze und das Verhältnis der Grammatik zu Logik und Psychologie", 1st, 2nd, and 3rd articles, *Vierteljahrsschrift für wissenschaftliche Philosophie* 8: 56–94, 161–192, 292–340.

Marty, Anton 1888. "Entgegnung," reply to Sigwart 1888, *Vierteljahrschrift für wissenschaftliche Philosophie* 12: 241–251.

Marty, Anton 1894. "Über subjectlose Sätze und das Verhältnis der Grammatik zu Logik und Psychologie", 4th and 5th articles, *Vierteljahrsschrift für wissenschaftliche Philosophie* 18: 320–356, 421–471.

Marty, Anton 1895. "Über subjectlose Sätze und das Verhältnis der Grammatik zu Logik und Psychologie", 6th and 7th articles, *Vierteljahrsschrift für wissenschaftliche Philosophie* 19: 19–87, 263–334.

Marty, Anton 1908. *Untersuchungen zur Grundlegung der allgemeinen Grammatik und Sprachphilosophie.* Halle a. S.: Max Niemeyer.

Mayer-Hillebrand 1956. "Vorwort der Herausgeberin," in Brentano 1956, v–xiv.

Meinong, Alexius 1886. "Zur erkenntnistheoretischen Würdigung des Gedächtnisses," *Vierteljahrsschrift für wissenschaftliche Philosophie* 10: 7–33.

Meinong, Alexius 1892. Review of Hillebrand 1892, *Göttingische gelehrte Anzeigen* 443–446.

Miklosich, Franz 1883. *Subjectlose Sätze.* Vienna: Wilhelm Braumüller.

Mill, John Stuart 1879. *A System of Logic: Ratiocinative and Inductive, being a Connected View of the Principles of Evidence and the Methods of Scientific Investigation,* 2 vols. London: Longmans, Green, and Co. (10th edition; 1st edition published in 1843).

Mill, John Stuart, (trans.) Schiel, J. 1877. *System der deductiven und inductiven Logik. Eine Darstellung der Principien wissenschaftlicher Forschung, insbesondere der Naturforschung.* Braunschweig: Friedrich Vieweg und Sohn.

Morscher, Edgar 1986. "Propositions and States of Affairs before Wittgenstein," in Nyíri 1986, 75–85.

Nyíri, J.C. (ed.) 1986. *Von Bolzano zu Wittgenstein. Zur Tradition der österreichischen Philosophie.* Vienna: Hölder.

Newman, Henry 1870. *An Essay in Aid of a Grammar of Assent.* London: Burns, Oates, & Co.

Oppy, Graham 2019. "Ontological Arguments," *Stanford Encyclopedia of Philosophy*. https://plato.stanford.edu/entries/ontological-arguments/

Pakaluk, Michael 1989. "Quine's 1946 Lectures on Hume," *Journal of the History of Philosophy* 27: 445–459.

Prantl, Carl 1855. *Geschichte der Logik*, vol. I. Leipzig: S. Hirzel.

Quine, Willard van Orman 1950. *Methods of Logic*. New York: Holt, Rinehart, and Winston. (2nd edition: 1959.)

Rancurello, Anton C. 1968. *A Study of Franz Brentano: His Standpoint and his Significance in the History of Psychology*. New York: Academic Press.

Rollinger, Robin D. 1999. *Husserl's Position in the School of Brentano*. Dordrecht / Boston / London: Kluwer.

Rollinger, Robin D. 2008a. *Austrian Phenomenology: Brentano, Husserl, Meinong, and Others on Mind and Object*. Heusenstamm: Ontos Verlag.

Rollinger, Robin D. 2008b. "Brentano's Psychology and Logic and the Basis of Twardowski's Theory of Presentations," Baltic International Yearbook of Cognition, Logic, and Communication 4: 1–23.

Rollinger, Robin D. 2010. *Philosophy of Language in the Work of Anton Marty: Analysis and Translations*. Amsterdam /New York: Rodopi.

Rollinger, Robin D. 2012. "Brentano's Psychology from an Empirical Standpoint: Its Background and Conception," in Tănăsescu 2012, 261–309.

Rollinger, Robin D. 2015. "Practical Epistemology: Stumpf's Halle Logic (1887)," in Fisette and Martinelli 2015, 75–100.

Rollinger, Robin D. 2019. "Brentano's Early Philosophy of Mind," in Lapointe 2019, 168–185.

Rollinger, Robin D. 202- (forthcoming). *Consciousness as Intentionality in Austrian Phenomenology: Analysis and Materials*. Dordrecht: Springer.

Russo, Antonio 2014. *Franz Brentano e Heinrich Denifle: Un carteggio inedito*. Rome: Edizioni Studium.

Russell, Bertrand 1918. *Mysticism and Logic and Other Essays*. London: Longmans, Green & Co.

Scholz, Heinrich, (trans.) Leidecker, Kurt. 1981. *A Concise History of Logic*. New York: Philosophical Library.

Sigwart, Christoph 1881. "Logische Fragen" (2nd article), *Vierteljahrsschrift für wissenschaftliche Philosophie* 5: 97–121.

Sigwart, Christoph 1888. *Die Impersonalien. Eine logische Untersuchung*. Freiburg i. B.: J.C.B. Mohr.

Sigwart, Christoph 1889. *Logik. Erster Band: Die Lehre vom Urtheil, vom Begriff und vom Schluss*. Freiburg i. B.: J.C.B. Mohr.

Simons, Peter 1987. "Brentano's Reform of Logic," *Topoi* 6: 25–38.

Simons, Peter 1992. *Philosophy and Logic in Central Europe: From Bolzano to Tarski*. Dordrecht: Kluwer.

Simons, Peter 2004. "Judging Correctly: Brentano and the Reform of Elementary Logic," in Jacquette 2004: 45–65.
Smith, Barry 1994. Austrian Philosophy: The Legacy of Franz Brentano. Chicago / LaSalle: Open Court.
Steinthal, Heymann 1888. Review of Sigwart 1888. *Zeitschrift für Völkerpsychologie* 18: 170–180.
Stumpf, Carl 1872. Letter to Brentano, 21 May in Kaiser-El-Safti 2015, 74–75.
Stumpf, Carl 1873. *Über den psychologischen Ursprung der Raumvorstellung*. Leipzig: S. Hirzel.
Stumpf, Carl 1883. *Tonpsychologie*, vol. I. Leipzig: S. Hirzel.
Stumpf, Carl 1890. *Tonpsychologie*, vol. II. Leipzig: S. Hirzel.
Stumpf, Carl 1919. "Erinnerungen an Franz Brentano," in Kraus 1919, 85–149.
Stumpf, Carl 1924. Self-portrait in Schmidt 1924, 205–265.
Stumpf, Carl, (trans.) Rollinger, R.D. 2019. *Tone Psychology*, vol. I. London: Routledge.
Tănăsescu, Ion (ed.) 2012. *Franz Brentano's Metaphysics and Psychology*. Bucharest: Zeta Books.
Textor, Mark (ed.) 2013. *Judgment and Truth in Early Analytic Philosophy and Phenomenology*. London: Pelgrave Macmillan.
Textor, Mark 2017. *Brentano's Mind*. Oxford: Oxford University Press.
Trendelenburg, Friedrich Adolf 1840. *Logische Untersuchungen*. 2 vols. Berlin: Gustav Berthge. 1st edition.
Trendelenburg, Friedrich Adolf 1846. *Historische Beiträge der Philosophie. Erster Band. Geschichte der Kategorienlehre*. Berlin: Gustav Berthge.
Trendelenburg, Friedrich Adolf 1862. *Logische Untersuchungen*. 2 vols. Leipzig: S. Hirzel. 2nd edition.
Trendelenburg, Friedrich Adolf 1868. *Elementa Logices Aristoteleae*. Berlin: Sumptibus Gustavi Berthge.
Trendelenburg, Friedrich Adolf 1870. *Logische Untersuchungen*. 2 vols. Leibzig: S. Hirzel. 3rd edition.
Trendelenburg, Friedrich Adolf (ed.), (trans.) Broughton, R. 1898. *Outlines of Logic: An English Translation of Trendelenburg's Elementa Logices Aristoteleae*. Oxford: Thos. Shrimpton & Son.
Twesten, August 1834. *Grundriß der analytischen Logik*.
Twardowski, Kasimir 1894. *Zur Lehre vom Inhalt und Gegenstand der Vorstellungen. Eine psychologische Studie*. Vienna: Hölder.
Twardowski, Kasimir, (eds.) Betti, A. and Raspa, V. 2016. *Logik. Wienerkolleg 1894/95*. Berlin: Walter de Gruyter.
Ueberweg, Friedrich, (trans.) Lindsay, Thomas M. 1871. *System of Logic and History of Logical Doctrines*. London: Longmans, Green, and Co.
Ueberweg, Friedrich, (ed.) Meyer, J.B. 1882. *System der Logik und Geschichte der logischen Lehren*. Bonn: Adolph Marcus. 5th edition.

Ueberweg, Friedrich, (ed.) Heinze, Max 1902. *Grundriss der Geschichte der Philosophie. Vierter Theil: Das neunzehnte Jahrhundert*. Berlin: Ernst Siegfried Mittler und Sohn.

Ulrici, Hermann 1852. *System der Logik*. Leipzig: T.O. Weigel.

Varga, Peter Andras 2016. "The Impersonalien Controversy in Early Phenomenology: Sigwart and the School of Brentano," in *Brentano Studien* 14, 229–280.

Wahle, Richard 1884. *Gehirn und Bewusstsein. Physiologisch-psychologische Studie*. Vienna: Alfred Hölder.

Whately, Richard 1855. *Elements of Logic*. Boston and Cambridge: James Monroe and Company.

Windelband, Wilhelm 1884. "Beiträge zur Lehre vom negativen Urtheil," in Zeller 1884, 167–195.

Windelband, Wilhelm, (trans.) Rollinger, R.D. 2019. "Contributions to the Theory of Negative Judgment," in Antonelli, Mauro and Frederico, Boccaccini 2019, vol. III, 131–148.

Wundt, Wilhelm 1877. "Über das kosmologische Problem," *Vierteljahrsschrift für wissenschaftliche Philosophie* 1: 80–186.

Wundt, Wilhelm 1880. *Logik. Eine Untersuchung der Principien der Erkenntnis und der Methoden wissenschaftlicher Forschung*, vol. I. Stuttgart: Ferdinand Enke.

Young, Micheal J. 1992. "Translator's Introduction," in Kant 1992: xv–xxxii.

Zeller, Eduard (ed.) 1884. *Strassburger Abhandlungen zur Philosophie*. Freiburg i. B.: Akademische Verlagsbuchhandlung.

Index of Names

Albertazzi, L.   5n9, 20n52, 24n
Anselm of Canterbury   19n51, 52f., 150, 222
Antonelli, A.   78n6
Aquinas (von Aquin), T.   12, 20, 44n14, 99, 148, 221
Aristotle (Aristoteles)   5n9, 7–10, 12, 20, 23, 25, 26n4, 35, 39, 45, 52, 58, 61, 64f., 72, 81f., 99f., 121, 147f., 150f., 154, 157, 167, 172, 175–179, 186, 197, 201, 211, 219, 221–224, 226, 230, 239, 243–250, 255f., 265, 268, 277, 282, 292, 332, 339, 370
Arnauld, A.   44n14, 148
Aron, O.   215, 280

Bacon (Baco), F.   25, 150f., 223
Bain, A.   62, 63n56, 147, 153, 159f., 220, 226, 231f., 300f., 316n57, 318n63, 322n72, 333, 356, 358n112
Balmes, J.   26n4
Bauer, A.   215, 280
Bekker, A.I.   7
Beneke, F.E.   300
Berger   215, 280
Berger, A.v.   360n114
Beethoven, L.v.   145n6, 218n7
Bergmann, J.   305, 306n40, 311n51, 316n57
Betti, A.   82n17
Bolzano, B.   21n56, 142, 180, 184, 189–192, 251, 253, 258ff.
Boole, G.   64, 66, 143, 155, 227, 283, 358n110, 359, 365
Bois-Reymond, du, E.   9

Cantor, G.   142, 180–185, 187, 189–192, 251ff., 256, 258ff.
Chrudzimski, A.   22n60, 78n4
Clemens, F.J.   6, 25–36, 10, 135
Comte, A.   12n31, 148, 221
Cottingham, J.   16n

De Morgan, A.   283, 292n, 318, 322, 358, 365n
Descartes, R.   7, 15f., 19n31, 45, 53, 64n58, 74, 97, 150f., 222f.
Donders, F.C.   206, 273
Drobisch, M.   327

Eder, A.   215, 280
Enoch, W.   86n32, 114n15
Epicurus   146, 219
Euler, L.   360
Evra, J.v.   3n1
Exner, S.   288f.

Fechner, G.   15, 163, 200, 235, 268
Feuchtwang, D.   215, 280
Fichte, J.G.   12
Flint, R.   65n61
Fréchette, G.   138n58
Frege, G.   4n5, 4n6, 79f.
Freud, S.   8
Fuchs   215, 280
Fulda, G.   215, 280

Gaunilo   54, 150, 222
Gauß, C.F.   165, 179f., 185, 237, 255
Goethe, J.W.v.   162, 164, 234f.

Haack, S.   4n5
Hamilton, G.   143, 282, 321, 322n71, 327, 365n118
Hanin   215, 280
Hartmann, E.v.   156, 229
Hedwig, K.   12n33
Hegel, G.W.F.   12, 40ff., 45, 144, 146, 217, 219, 284, 293f.
Helmholtz, H.   9n21, 163f., 235, 288f.
Herbart, J.F.   10, 53, 147, 150, 165, 170, 220, 223, 237, 241, 292n, 300f., 327
Herzog   215, 280
Hillebrand, F.   VII, 21, 79n9, 96, 106, 110, 114n14, 133, 141ff., 280
Hobbes, T.   322n71, 362
Höfler, A.   8n20, 9n21, 56f., 141f., 172n, 184n
Hume, D.   3f., 5n9, 9n21, 42, 46, 56, 75, 94, 150, 223, 301
Husserl, E.   80n11, 80n12, 84, 91f., 95, 123, 129, 137, 141f., 166n24, 215, 238n., 280

Ierna, C.   6n12

Jacquette, D.   5n9
Jerusalem, W.   114n15

INDEX OF NAMES

Jevons, W.   66, 143, 147, 155 f., 159 f., 220, 227 f., 231 f., 283, 316, 322, 334, 338, 344, 358, 365–368

Kant, I.   5n10, 8 f., 46, 53 f., 94, 106 ff., 112 ff., 117, 120–124, 130, 132n53, 137, 147, 150, 162, 186, 212, 220, 223, 234, 255, 255 f.n42, 278, 282, 316n57, 320, 326 f., 364
Kastil, A.   133
Kraus, O.   6n11, 12n32, 13n34
Kreibig, J.   106, 215, 281
Kriegel, U.   5n9

Lagrange, J.-L.   187, 256
Lambert, J.H.   155, 227
Land, J.P.N.   111n9, 156, 228
Lange, F.A.   64, 147 f., 152 f., 220, 225, 227, 282, 292n, 318, 330 f., 337, 356, 360
Laplace, P.-S.   93 f., 320
Lassaulx, E.v.   6
Leibniz, G.W.   4n4, 25, 64, 66, 151, 154, 165, 223, 227, 237
Leisching, E.   141 f., 145n3–6, 156n, 157n, 159n17, 160n19, 164n, 170n29, 174n34, 175n37–38, 179n44, 181n, 185n50, 186n52–53, 188n, 192n60, 195n67, 198n72–73, 201n76, 203n77, 204n78, 205n79, 215, 218n4–7, 228n15, 229n16, 231n18, 236n, 241n, 245n29, 246n31, 249n46, 251n38, 254n, 255n, 257n, 260n, 263n51–52, 265n58–59, 268n, 270n66–67, 271n69, 280
Lemberger, E.   215, 280
Lenzen, W.   4n8
Liebmann, O.   12n31
Locke, J.   7, 17, 25, 61, 82, 84, 86 f., 91, 152, 166, 225, 238
Lott, F.K.   170, 241
Lotze, H.   65, 200n, 267, 294 f., 322, 330n86, 334, 364

Marty, A.   7, 11, 19n, 20, 26, 42, 55, 65 f., 71, 106, 110 f., 116 f., 123, 152, 165, 225, 236, 298n20, 301n32, 304 f., 309
Masaryk, T.   8, 20, 83n
Mayer-Hillebrand, F.   79n9

Meinong, A.   8, 20, 42, 55 f., 95, 123, 129
Miklosich, F.   65n63, 336n
Mill, J. St.   12n31, 15, 17, 38, 41n9, 42, 45n16, 46n20, 49 f., 60 f., 63n56, 64, 71n72, 100n76, 109, 130 ff., 147, 149, 152, 160 f., 176, 215, 220, 222, 225, 232 f., 247, 285n, 294 f., 300 f., 316n57, 322n71, 328, 361, 363, 368
Morscher, E.   137n58
Müller, J.   162, 234

Newman, H.   44n14

Oppy, G.   54n29

Pakaluk, W.   4n7
Pascal, B.   103, 104, 146 ff., 220, 151, 221, 223
Peirce, C.S.   45n17, 137
Peano, G.   4n4
Pfann   216, 280
Plato (Platon)   52, 150, 222
Prantl, C.   362
Pseudo-Aristotle (Pseudo-Aristoteles)   198, 266

Quine, W.v.O.   4, 5n9

Rancurello, A.C.   24n
Rollinger, R.D.   12n29, 14n39, 18n47, 20n54, 42n11, 55n37, 71n69, 85n27, 92n42, 96n62, 98n68, 136n, 225n
Russell, B.   3, 4n4, 137
Russo, A.   25n3

Schelling, F.W.J.   12
Scholz, H.   5n9
Schleimacher, F.   12
Schmidkunz, H.   216, 280
Schröder, E.   4n4, 137
Sigwart C.   65, 82n17, 114n14, 129n47, 143, 288n9, 295–301, 303, 306 f., 310–317, 319 ff.
Simons, P.   5n9, 24n, 133n, 134n
Smith, B.   78
Spinoza, B.d.   11, 74, 145, 218
Steinthal, H.   311n51
Stumpf, C.   71n70, 72, 74, 84, 96, 114, 122 f., 137, 206n81, 207, 237n, 273

Trendelenburg, A.   6f., 12n33, 25, 66, 155n, 170, 186, 227n, 241, 255n, 256n42, 292n, 293, 318, 330f.
Twesten, A.   300
Twardowski, K.   8, 20, 55, 56n40, 82, 84, 95

Ueberweg, F.   7n17, 45n16, 128n, 132, 146, 219, 227n, 295–298, 300, 303, 316n57, 327, 333, 341
Ulrici, H.   300

Varga, P.A.   65n62

Wahle, R.   157, 229
Weise, C.   360
Whately, R.   46, 146, 219
Whitehead, A.N.   4n4
Windelband, W.   38, 114, 143, 283n3, 305–310
Wittgenstein, L.   4n4

Young, M.   5n10

Printed in the United States
By Bookmasters